THE NEW
EUROPE
AN ENCYCLOPEDIC ATLAS

THE NEW EUROPE

AN ENCYCLOPEDIC ATLAS

FOREWORD BY

THE RT HON SIR EDWARD HEATH KG MBE MP

MITCHELL BEAZLEY

Edited and designed by
Mitchell Beazley International Ltd
Michelin House, 81 Fulham Road, London SW3 6RB
and Bertelsmann Lexikon Verlag GmbH, Gütersloh/München, Germany

Project editors:	James Hughes, Monika Unger
Project designer:	Ted McCausland
Senior editor:	Alfred LeMaitre
Editors:	Ursula Blombach-Schäfer, Annabel Else, John Morton, Reela Veit
Map editor:	Julia Gorton
Editorial assistant:	Ulrike Becker-Buchner
Statistical research:	Elke Christoph, Regina Sinemus
Senior designer:	Hans Verkroost
Cartographic editor:	Andrew Thompson BA, MSc, DIC
Picture research:	Jan Croot, Ursula Nöll-Kaske
Production:	Günter Hauptmann, Sarah Schuman
Project management:	Wolf-Eckhard Gudemann, Peter Gutmann

Typeset by Litho Link, Wales
Reproduction by Scantrans Pte Ltd, Singapore
Printed and bound by Butler and Tanner Ltd

Foreword

When he was launching his theme of a united Europe more than 40 years ago, Sir Winston Churchill described Europe as "a rubble heap, a charnel house, a breeding ground of pestilence and hate." Now, 40 years on, the European Community is one of the few areas of unity and stability within an increasingly troubled and ever-changing world.

We have thus witnessed a remarkable historical success – its progress emphasized by recent revolutionary events in Eastern Europe. I am convinced that this progression has not yet been completed.

Throughout the 1990s we will see the forging of further and stronger financial, cultural and social links between the nations of Europe as differences are thrown aside in a lasting commitment to a future of peace and prosperity.

Thus in Britain, future generations will be party to an increasing sense of European unity as the nations of the Community, the non-affiliated states and the nations of the post-Communist Eastern bloc are increasingly drawn together to promote stability, trade and understanding.

In addition, a stable and united Europe will be better able to answer the challenges posed by conflict and disunity throughout the rest of the world. Europe itself will serve as a catalyst for an even wider global unity. By combining our strengths we have been able to minimize our weaknesses and, in the process, we have created a model fit to be emulated in all other continents.

It is for these reasons that I am delighted to be invited to write a Foreword for this book. If Britain is to take its place at the heart of Europe it is essential that the British have a greater understanding of the peoples and interests of other nations of Europe. This book helps to provide this information and I am happy to be associated with it.

Contents

The following abbreviations are found in the text:

CSCE Conference on Security and Cooperation in
      Europe
EC   European Community
EFTA European Free Trade Association
GDP   Gross Domestic Product (sum of all output
      produced by economic activity within that
      country)
GNP   Gross National Product (value of all goods
      and services produced by a country)

Europe: Land

THE CONTINENTS OF EUROPE AND ASIA form a single landmass often known as Eurasia. Europe occupies the western part of this landmass; the remaining 80 per cent is covered by Asia.

Europe's eastern frontier lacks a clearly defined physical boundary but runs down the Ural mountains and river to the Caspian Sea; in the west and north it is bounded by the Atlantic and Arctic Oceans, and the Mediterranean Sea marks its southern frontier. The continent's land area covers 4,066,000 square miles (10,532,000 square kilometres), making it the smallest of the continents after Australia. The British Isles, consisting of Great Britain and Ireland, are the continent's largest group of islands. They lie on the extreme edge of Europe, separated from the mainland by only 26 miles (42 kilometres) of sea.

The close association of land and sea in Europe, the presence of large natural waterways such as the River Rhine, and the comparative lack of major land obstacles, have all helped to encourage ease of movement for European peoples. The low-lying areas of the Netherlands and the North German Plain give way in the south to the European central upland region, including the central German uplands and the Ardennes Mountains. Few of these rolling uplands have peaks higher than 3,300 feet (1,000 metres), and many regions are still thickly forested.

Towering over this landscape stands Europe's largest mountain range, the snowclad Alps, which extend almost 750 miles (1,200 kilometres) from the Mediterranean coast to the Danube River at Vienna. With many peaks rising to heights of 10,000-14,000 feet (about 3,000-4,250 metres), the Alps form a climate barrier between Central Europe and the south of the continent, which benefits from the heat of Africa. Europe's highest point is not in the Alps but in the Caucasus range. This peak, Mount Elbrus, stands 18,481 feet (5,633 metres) above sea leavel. However, many geographers include both the Caucasus and the Alps in the so-called Alpine Mountain System, which runs across southern Europe from Spain to the Caspian Sea.

Climate

Most West European countries have a mild maritime climate, with prevailing west winds carrying the moist oceanic air masses inland. Central Europe, by contrast, experiences interaction between maritime air masses and those from the interior of the continent. This leads to colder winters and warmer summers, with much snowfall in the mountains. In eastern Europe, a continental climate brings hot summers, cold winters, and light rainfall.

The continent of Europe (*right*) shares one fifth of the world's largest landmass with Asia, and includes many islands, notably the British Isles. Western Europe has a long, uneven coastline, varied landscapes and few mountain barriers. In south central Europe, by contrast, the Alps rise to heights above 14,000 ft (4,265 metres).

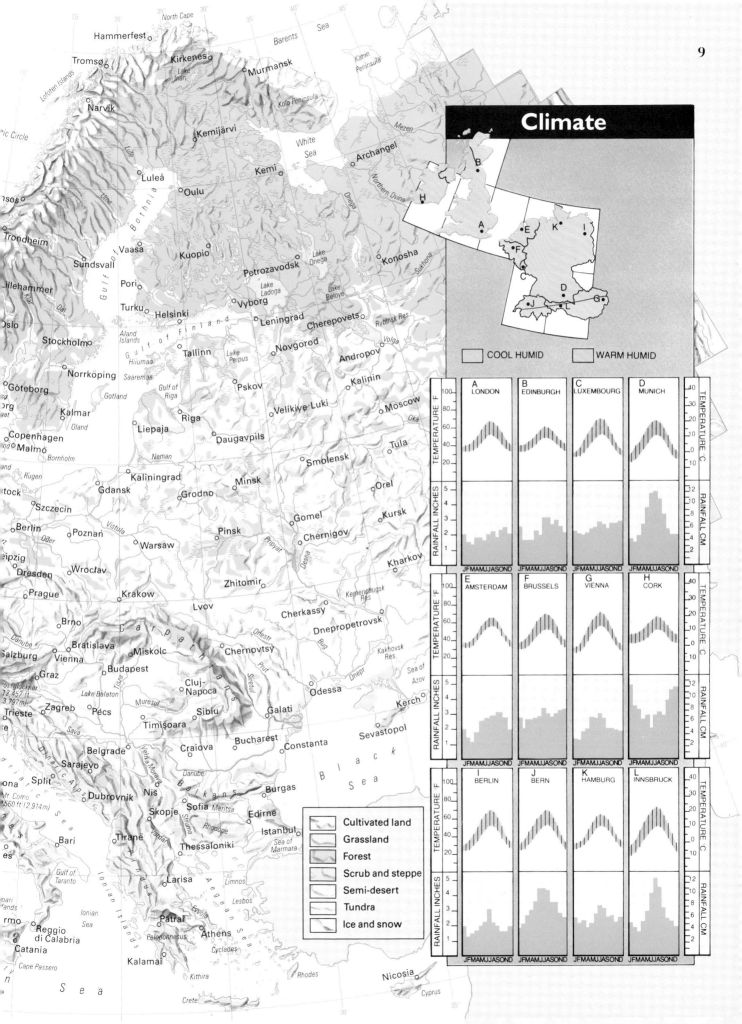

Europe: People

COMPARATIVELY SMALL IN SIZE BUT large in population, the continent of Europe contains almost 700 million people, and extends from the Atlantic to the Urals. But Europe's geographical boundaries have less significance than its political divisions, which have scarred the continent for hundreds of years. For despite its massive contribution to world history and culture, Europe has constantly suffered from disastrous conflicts, culminating in the catastrophe of World War II.

After this terrible war, in which as many as 50 million people may have died, the continent was split into two ideologically hostile blocs. The eastern section, dominated by the former Soviet Union, was virtually closed to the West for almost half a century until, in 1989, a wave of revolutions swept through Soviet-controlled countries. This led in 1991 to the collapse of Communism and the disintegration of the Soviet Union itself, to be succeeded by the so-called Commonwealth of Independent States.

However, the democratization of Eastern Europe brought its own intractable problems as the former Communist-dominated countries struggled to set up market-based economies in place of the old centralized systems. Outdated technology and severe pollution have compounded the difficulties, and since 1989 these nations have been going through an anxious period, with massive unemployment, inflation, and the need for assistance from Western democracies. Even worse, the new freedom has sometimes revived long-standing nationalist and ethnic disputes, from the smouldering conflict between Armenia and Azerbaijan to the tragic civil war in former Yugoslavia.

Towards a united Europe

A more positive legacy of World War II was the determination of some far-sighted statesmen to minimize further conflict by welding firm economic links between formerly combatant countries. This initiative led eventually to the emergence of today's European Community, an association of states which, despite numerous problems, has evolved into one of the world's most important socio-economic groupings.

But the European Community is about political as well as economic union. In 1992, the year of the so-called "Single Market", a reform programme was initiated to expand the EC's decision-making powers, enabling the member states to act as one in many political and social as well as financial areas. Some observers believe that this apparent centralization of powers will nevertheless allow more independence to the regions within EC countries. Others fear that it may diminish the national sovereignty of member states.

European Community: Origins

The EC flag (*above*) first flew in 1983 at the World Economic Summit at Williamsburg in the United States.

THE DREAM OF A UNITED EUROPE IS NOT new. It can be traced back almost a millennium to the late 1200s when the French thinker Pierre Dubois first advanced the outlines of such a concept. Later, in 1693, William Penn proposed the establishment of a European parliament as a means of ensuring peace. In the mid 1800s the Scotsman Charles MacKay suggested the formation of a "United States of Europe". Finally, Winston Churchill developed this idea in a famous speech at Zurich in 1946.

The practical reality of this dream of unity began to evolve after World War II. In 1948, Belgium, the Netherlands and Luxembourg formed an economic union known as Benelux. In 1950, Robert Schuman, the French Foreign Minister, called for a gradual process of integration of European states; at the same time, the French economist Jean Monnet worked out a plan for cooperation in the area of coal and steel, which would allow Germany to become an equal partner again. On April 18, 1951, the treaty founding the European Coal and Steel Community (ECSC) was signed. In this treaty, France, the Federal Republic of Germany, Italy, the Netherlands, Belgium and Luxembourg declared that they were prepared to subordinate their sovereignty in certain issues to the decisions of a common European government.

Using this industrial "community" as a beginning, plans for greater integration began to emerge. There was a growing body of feeling that the economic integration achieved so far should not remain restricted to heavy industry. In March 1957,

The EC map (*left*) shows how European unity stretches across the territory of 12 very different countries. In 1965, the European economic unions ECSC, EEC and Euratom were linked together. Although they have never formed a single unit, they do share common purposes and since 1967 come under the name of the European Community.

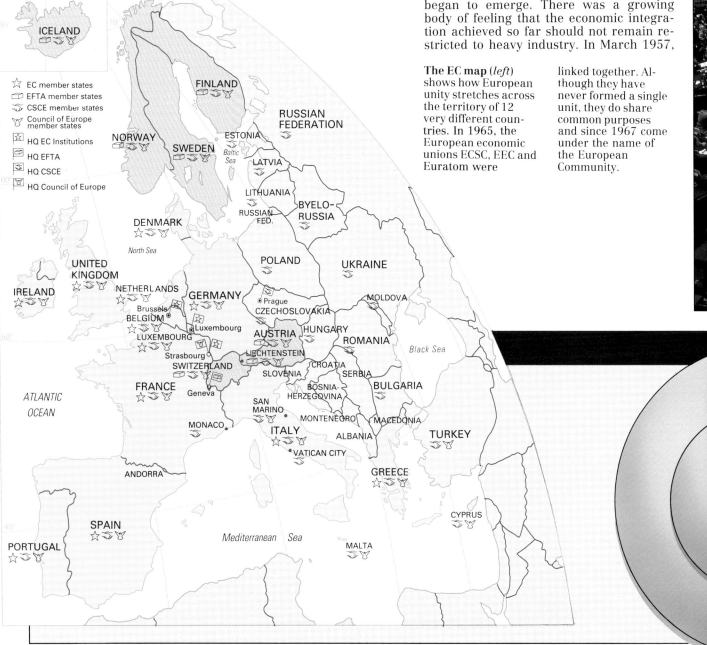

In 1950, **Robert Schuman** (*left*), the French Foreign Minister, launched his proposal for a European Coal and Steel Community. Schuman's plan is seen as the first real step in the creation of today's European Community.

The European Parliament (*below*) meets at the Palais de l'Europe in Strasbourg. MEPs tend to sit in multinational groups, and communicate with each other by simultaneous translation of speeches through headphones.

the supreme representatives of the ECSC member states signed the Treaty of Rome, the aim of which was to ensure the economic progress of the "European Economic Community" (EEC) by removing the tariff barriers which divided Europe. At the same time the European Atomic Energy Commission (Euratom) was founded for the development of the peaceful use of atomic energy. In 1967, the ECSC, EEC and Euratom were linked to form the European Community.

The expanding Community

Britain, Denmark and Ireland applied to join the six countries of the EEC in 1961, and again in 1966; they finally became members in 1973, turning The Six into The Nine. Greece became the tenth member in 1981, and Spain and Portugal joined in 1986. Since then, the EC's evident economic success has induced an increasing number of countries to apply for membership, including Turkey, Austria, Malta, Cyprus and Sweden, with Finland and Norway poised to follow. Meanwhile, the unification of Germany in October 1990 increased the size and population of the EC by some five per cent, raising it to more than 320 million. By 1992, almost all the nations of Europe were seeking some form of association with the 12 "core" countries of the EC, notably the formerly Communist countries of East Europe.

In addition to its economic success, the EC has also established itself as an important voice in political issues. Brussels is the European capital, but many of the 20,000 EC officials work in Luxembourg (seat of the Court of Justice and the Investment Bank) and Strasbourg (seat of the European Parliament). In Brussels, the Council of Ministers represents the governments of the 12 member states, while the European Commission acts as the EC's executive organ. In 1985 the EC countries signed an agreement designed to lead to closer economic, political and social integration by 1992.

In December 1991, the 12 EC member state leaders met at Maastricht, Netherlands, to sign a treaty to create a more united Europe, including various common social policies and Economic and Monetary Union (EMU). EMU included establishing a common European currency and a central European bank by 1999. But agreement only came after bitter argument, some wanting closer union, others being reluctant to lose control of their own affairs. The new treaty had to be ratified by every member state, either by parliamentary vote or by referendum. Maastricht problems resurfaced when Denmark rejected the treaty's terms in a referendum in June 1992, questioning the EC's future form.

Community Trade

52.7%	Federal Republic of Germany
56.9%	France
51.2%	United Kingdom
56.3%	Italy
69.7%	Netherlands
73.4%	Belgium and Luxembourg
58.4%	Spain
50.2%	Denmark
70.0%	Ireland
66.6%	Portugal
64%	Greece

The size of each circle reflects each country's volume of trade. In overall terms, the Federal Republic of Germany ranks as the E.C.'s biggest trader, with Greece ranking as the smallest.

European Community Trade (1988)

E.C.   World

The Community Today

ON JULY 1, 1987, THE SINGLE EUROPEAN Act was ratified by the European Community's 12 member states. This envisaged the creation of a single Community market by the end of 1992, an area "without internal frontiers, in which the free movement of goods, persons, services and capital is ensured." In December 1991, an EC summit meeting at Maastricht, Netherlands, achieved broad agreement on economic and political union. In June 1992, a Danish referendum rejected the terms of the treaty, checking the momentum of closer union between the EC states.

A common currency
The introduction of a single European currency unit (the ECU) had sound financial arguments in its favour, but also indicated the member states' strong desire for a collective identity. In 1992, silver and gold ECU coins had been minted, but not issued, and decisions on a common European currency must wait until 1997. Meanwhile, the ECU is used for many transactions. Backed by a large reserve fund, its value is reviewed every five years, and is determined by a weighted "basket" of currencies.

The central purpose of the ECU is to provide a common currency for the vast sums of money passing through the EC every year. At present, the national currency of each member state has a value against the ECU which can be realigned within the system of the Exchange Rate Mechanism (ERM). By these means, the economies of the EC states have attempted to converge, and inflation rates have come down. Many observers believe that the European Monetary System (EMS), adopted in 1979, will form a stable monetary zone uniting exchange rates and leading eventually to the adoption of a single currency.

Income for the European Community is drawn from several sources, including a proportion of the European valued-added tax (VAT), from customs duties imposed on goods imported from non-member states, and from member states' contributions based on their share of the Community's gross national product (GNP). In 1992, most of this money went to support agriculture in the form of farm price guarantees, but it was also used to fund projects in poorer regions and recession-hit areas of the EC.

Structure of the EC
The declared policy of the EC member states – to remove internal barriers and implement the Single Market programme – has provided a heavy workload for the EC's main institutions. These consist of the Council of Ministers, the European Commission, the European Parliament and the Court of Justice. To this should be added the

E.C. trade

Most EC countries depend on world trade and exports (*right*), so the Community has to keep a careful watch over external trade policies and customs tariffs. The European Commission in Brussels organizes EC trade agreements on a global scale. The Community also has its own policy towards the developing nations The Lomé Convention covers trade and aid with 65 countries in Africa, the Caribbean and the Pacific. Separate agreements have been signed with members of the Association of South-East Asian Nations (ASEAN), and North African States.

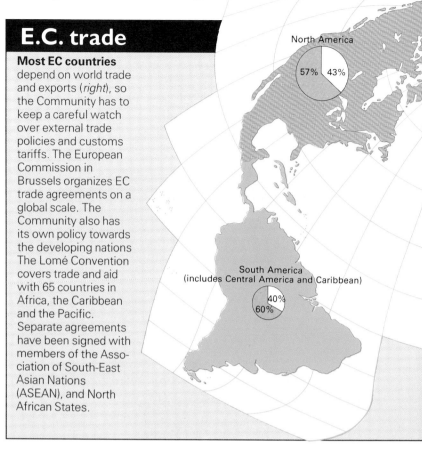

North America
57% 43%

South America
(includes Central America and Caribbean)
40%
60%

Alsace shepherds (*right*) bring their sheep to the forecourt of Strasbourg's Palais de l'Europe as a protest against certain EC agricultural policies.

The Ariane rocket (*below*) successfully demonstrated that in the field of satellite technology, the EC is able to hold its own with other powers.

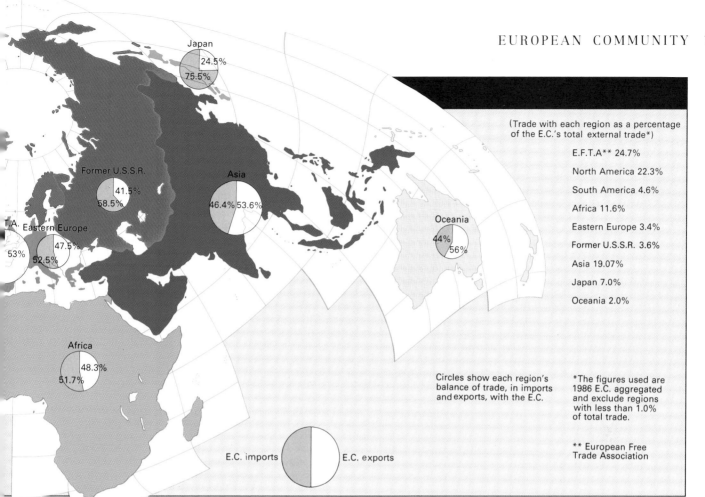

Japan
24.5%
75.5%

Former U.S.S.R.
41.5%
58.5%

Asia
46.4% 53.6%

F.T.A.
Eastern Europe
53%
47.5%
52.5%

Oceania
44% 56%

Africa
48.3%
51.7%

(Trade with each region as a percentage
of the E.C.'s total external trade*)

E.F.T.A** 24.7%

North America 22.3%

South America 4.6%

Africa 11.6%

Eastern Europe 3.4%

Former U.S.S.R. 3.6%

Asia 19.07%

Japan 7.0%

Oceania 2.0%

Circles show each region's
balance of trade, in imports
and exports, with the E.C.

*The figures used are
1986 E.C. aggregated
and exclude regions
with less than 1.0%
of total trade.

** European Free
Trade Association

E.C. imports   E.C. exports

European Council, comprising the political leaders of the EC states and their foreign ministers, together with the president of the European Commission. This body meets three or four times a year, and is beginning to replace the European Commission as the driving force of the Community.

The European Commission consists of 17 members (two from the five largest EC states, one from the rest) elected for a four-year term and appointed by the Council of Ministers from nominees of the member governments. Under the president (in 1992 France's Jacques Delors), this body puts proposals before the Council of Ministers and implements its decisions, as well as drafting the EC's budget. The Council of Ministers, composed of representatives from the member states, acts as the legislative arm of the Community, drafting laws proposed by the Commission after consultation with the European Parliament. It is regarded as the centre of political control of the EC.

The European Parliament consists of 518 members, directly elected for a five-year term by their own nations in numbers roughly proportional to the country's size (Britain has 81 members). The Parliament's role in legislative and budgetary decisions is at present restricted, but is likely to increase as an important measure of demo-

cratic control. The European Court adjudicates on Community law.

External relations

The European Commission – the EC's "government" in Brussels – has its own department of foreign affairs, maintaining diplomatic relations with many countries and groups of states. Economic and trade agreements have been signed with the European Free Trade Association (EFTA), the ASEAN states of Southeast Asia, and nearly 70 countries in Africa, the Caribbean and the Pacific (the Lomé Conventions). In 1991, negotiations began on agreements with the new democracies of central and eastern Europe, many of whom are seeking active participation in the Community.

The Danish rejection in 1992 of the Maastricht proposals raised fundamental questions on the Community's future role: a powerful central government with weak national governments, or a central authority with little power over national parliaments. The application of many EFTA members, Turkey, and former Communist countries, pointed to a much enlarged future Community. With far greater differences of culture and wealth between its member states, common purpose would be harder to achieve and could reduce the role of a central government.

GERMANY

Germany lies in the centre of Europe, between Atlantic western Europe and continental eastern Europe. The countries of Scandinavia lie to the north and the Alpine lands lie to the south. Germany's boundaries have changed dramatically over the centuries, and it was until recently divided into a western and an eastern state. However, it has always retained a central geographical and political position in Europe. For more than 2,000 years, different peoples with different lifestyles have mingled here, making the country a breeding ground for the interchange of social, intellectual and economic ideas. For the same reasons, perhaps, it has also suffered from a long history of political conflicts, disunity and confrontation.

At the end of World War II, Germany was partitioned by the victorious Allies. By 1949, a heavily guarded border divided the Federal Republic of Germany (FRG), or West Germany, from the socialist German Democratic Republic (GDR), or East Germany. World War II had devastated industrial centres and transportation networks, but an "economic miracle" put West Germany back on its feet by the mid-1950s. The country became the leading economic power of Western Europe, and has played an important part in the work of the European Community to bring together the democratic countries of Europe. The GDR, meanwhile, became a satellite of the Soviet Union, joining the Warsaw Pact military alliance and COMECON (Council for Mutal Economic Assistance). Its economy suffered due to Communist mismanagement, resulting in inefficient industries, relatively low living standards and severe ecological damage. Only in 1990 did Germany become united once again. The country now includes 16 federal states, or *Länder*, including the official capital, Berlin.

Germany's land area of 137,773 square miles (356,829 square kilometres) contains a population of some 79 million people. The cities of the heavily industrialized Ruhr contain around 11 million people, while Berlin is home to over three million. Other major cities include Cologne, Dresden, Frankfurt, Hamburg, Hanover, Leipzig, Munich and Stuttgart.

Visitors travelling through the German countryside are often surprised by the beautiful and ever-changing scenery to be found in this highly industrialized country, which also reveals such architectural treats as **Neuschwanstein Castle** (*left*) in Bavaria. Germany's varied landscape includes high mountain ranges, picturesque lakes, rivers fringed with vineyards and a coast lined with rolling sand dunes.

Germany Today

THE FEDERAL REPUBLIC OF GERMANY is a democratic federal republic consisting of 16 autonomous states, or *Länder*. Following the assimilation of the five states of the former German Democratic Republic (GDR) in October 1990, the states are: Baden-Württemberg, Bavaria, Berlin, Brandenburg, Bremen, Hamburg, Hesse, Mecklenburg-Western Pomerania, Lower Saxony, North Rhine-Westphalia, Rhineland-Palatinate, Saar, Saxony, Saxony-Anhalt, Schleswig-Holstein and Thuringia. Bavaria boasts the greatest land area and North Rhine-Westphalia the most inhabitants. Bremen ranks as the smallest in both respects.

Germany's constitution, known as the "Basic Law", forbids the abolition of these state divisions. Each state has its own constitution, and in certain legislative and administrative areas, notably education and culture, each state enjoys complete independence. Each elects a legislature, whose members serve four-year terms. With the exception of Bremen and Hamburg, the state legislature elects a minister president to head the state government.

The Basic Law came into force on May 24, 1949, at a time when it seemed that the division of Germany might not be shortlived. The Federal Republic chose this Basic Law, designed to "impose a new order on state life for a traditional period", instead of a constitution, to indicate that it was intended to be a temporary measure. Article 23 of the Basic Law gave other parts of Germany the opportunity of joining those areas already governed by it. On October 3, 1990, the states of the former GDR were assimilated under Article 23, and the Basic Law become a pan-German constitution.

The federal government
The head of the German state is the federal president, whose role is more symbolic than executive. He is elected to a five-year term by the Federal Convention, which consists of members of the 662-member parliament (*Bundestag*, or Federal Diet) together with an equal number of members elected by the states. In 1991 the president had offices in Berlin, the capital, and Bonn. In that year, it was decided to move the two houses of parliament to Berlin.

Votes are given value according to a system of proportional representation, whereby the size of a political party reflects its proportion of the total number of votes cast. In 1990, the Bundestag contained six political parties: the Christian Democratic Union (CDU), the Christian Social Union (CSU) and the Free Democratic Party (FDP) together form the government. The others are the Alliance 90/Green Party, the Democratic Socialist Party and the Social Democratic Party of Germany. The government consists of the federal chancellor, who is proposed by the president and elected by parliament, and the cabinet. The states play an important role in the Federal Republic legislation through the upper house (*Bundesrat*, or Federal Council).

Unification has brought problems as well as pride to the German people. In 1992, stringent measures to repair the disabled economy of the former GDR tested the resources of Germany to the limit, as well as causing considerable hardship and unemployment in the east.

FACT BOX

THE COUNTRY
Official name: Federal Republic of Germany
Capital: Berlin
Seat of Government: Bonn
Land regions: From north to south: North German Plain, Central Highlands, South German Hills, Black Forest in southwest, Bavarian Alps
Land area: 137,773 sq mi (356,829 km²)
Climate: Oceanic in northwest (mild summers and winters). Increasingly continental toward south and east (warmer summers and colder, snowy winters)
Main rivers: Rhine, Elbe, Danube, Main, Saale, Neckar, Oder
Highest elevation: Zugspitze 9,721 ft (2,963 m)
Lowest elevation: Sea level along the coast

THE GOVERNMENT
Form of Government: Parliamentary democracy
Head of State: Federal president
Head of Government: Federal chancellor
Administrative areas: 16 federal states
Legislature: Parliament: Bundestag (Federal Diet): 662 members, elected by the people for 4 years; Bundesrat (Federal Council): 68 members (3-5 representatives appointed by each federal state, depending on size of population)

Judiciary: Federal and state courts. Highest court: Federal Constitutional Court. Superior federal courts. Local courts and courts of appeal in each state
Armed forces: Total strength: 486,000. Men must serve 12 months from age 18

THE PEOPLE
Population (1990): 79,070,000
Language: German
Religion: Protestant (44%), Roman Catholic (36%)

THE ECONOMY
Currency: Deutsche mark
Gross Domestic Product per person (1990): US$ 18,878

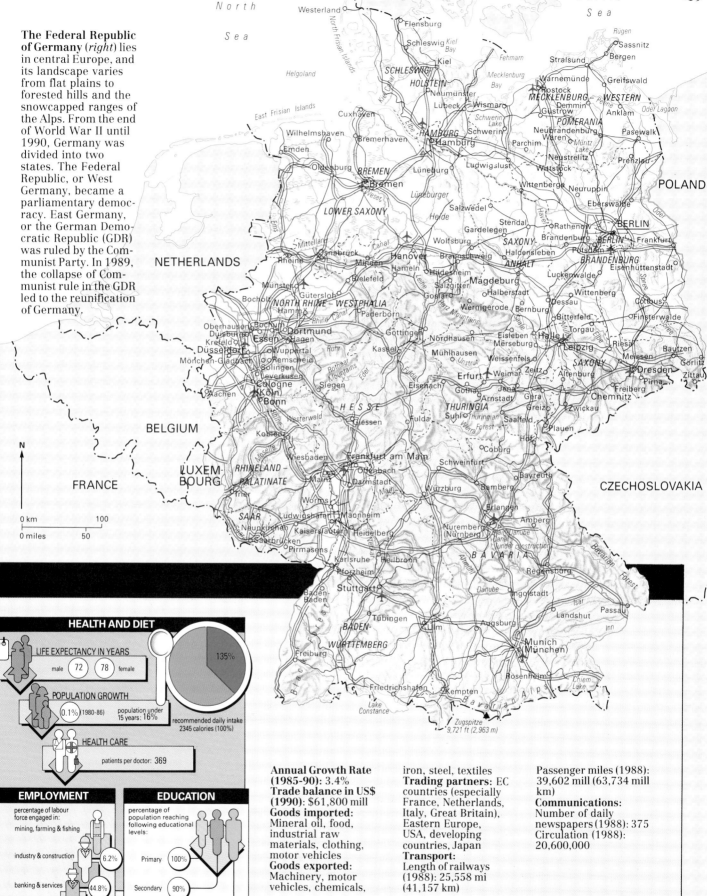

The Federal Republic of Germany (*right*) lies in central Europe, and its landscape varies from flat plains to forested hills and the snowcapped ranges of the Alps. From the end of World War II until 1990, Germany was divided into two states. The Federal Republic, or West Germany, became a parliamentary democracy. East Germany, or the German Democratic Republic (GDR) was ruled by the Communist Party. In 1989, the collapse of Communist rule in the GDR led to the reunification of Germany.

HEALTH AND DIET

LIFE EXPECTANCY IN YEARS

male 72   78 female

POPULATION GROWTH

0.1% (1980-86)   population under 15 years: 16%

135%

recommended daily intake 2345 calories (100%)

HEALTH CARE

patients per doctor: 369

EMPLOYMENT

percentage of labour force engaged in:

mining, farming & fishing

industry & construction   6.2%

banking & services   44.8%

48%

EDUCATION

percentage of population reaching following educational levels:

Primary   100%

Secondary   90%

Further   30.5%

Annual Growth Rate (1985-90): 3.4%
Trade balance in US$ (1990): $61,800 mill
Goods imported: Mineral oil, food, industrial raw materials, clothing, motor vehicles
Goods exported: Machinery, motor vehicles, chemicals, iron, steel, textiles
Trading partners: EC countries (especially France, Netherlands, Italy, Great Britain), Eastern Europe, USA, developing countries, Japan
Transport: Length of railways (1988): 25,558 mi (41,157 km)

Passenger miles (1988): 39,602 mill (63,734 mill km)
Communications: Number of daily newspapers (1988): 375
Circulation (1988): 20,600,000

GERMANY'S LANDSCAPE OFFERS TRE-
mendous variety, and ranges from low-
lying plains to forested hills and towering
snowcapped peaks. The country's major
landscape regions consist of the North German Plain, the Central Highlands and the
South German Hills. The Black Forest and
the Bavarian Alps form smaller but distinct
land regions. Proximity to the sea gives the
country a generally mild climate, although
southern regions experience more extreme
weather conditions.

The North German Plain slopes down towards the flat coastal areas along the North
Sea and the Baltic Sea. Covering much of
the country, it is the largest land region in
Germany. It is drained by broad slow-flowing rivers such as the Elbe, Ems, Oder,
Rhine and Weser.

Along the North Sea coast is an area of
shallows called the Wattenmeer. Just
offshore, the Frisian Islands, two strings of
low sandy islands, rise out of the shallows.
The cliffs of the rocky island of Helgoland,
31 miles (50 kilometres) offshore, tower
over the waters of the North Sea.

The region between the North Sea and
the Baltic is generally low and flat. It includes the southern part of the Jutland
peninsula. The sandy Baltic coastline usually enjoys calm seas and is pierced by a
number of long narrow wooded inlets and
peninsulas, especially on Rügen, Germany's
largest island.

The North German Plain itself is covered
with deep deposits of sand and gravel left
behind after the last Ice Age. The landscape
is mostly level, but glacial lakes and gentle
hills interrupt the prevailing flatness, notably the Wilseder Berg, which rises above
the heather and bush-clad stretches of
Lüneburger Heide. Broad and fertile river
basins, such as the Fulda and Werra, edge
southwards into the northern fringes of the
Central Highlands.

Central and Southern Germany

The Central Highlands extend from the Eifel
region west of the Rhine all the way to the
Erzgebirge (Ore Mountains) along Germany's border with Czechoslovakia. This
region consists of a series of jumbled
plateaus made up of ancient slates, sand-
stones and volcanic rocks. The landscape
ranges from almost flat land, through
gently rounded hills to dramatic mountain
areas. The Rhine, Germany's greatest natural traffic artery, squeezes through a
famous gorge that cuts through the Rhine
Massif (a high, plateau-like region) between
Bingen and Bonn. The mountainous stretch
of country formed by the Taunus, Wester-
wald and Eifel uplands is thickly forested.
The sheltered valleys that hug the banks of
the Rhine are extremely fertile.

The Oker River
(*above*) has its source
in the Harz Moun-
tains, on the northern
edge of Germany's
Central Highlands.
Some of the peaks in
the region reach
heights of more than
3,000 feet (910
metres).

**The mountainous
Black Forest** region
(*left*) takes its name
from the thick forests
which cloak its granite
and sandstone hills.
Lying in southwest
Germany, the Black
Forest is well known
for its many mineral
springs.

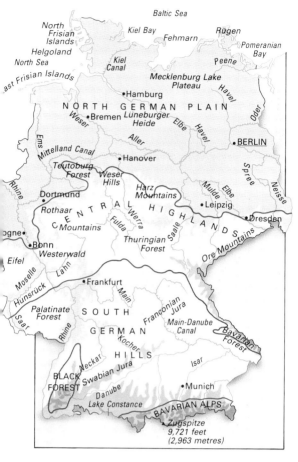

The landscape of Germany (*left*) embraces the sweeping flatlands of the North German Plain, the plateaus and mountains of the Central Highlands and the forested South German Hills. In the South, the Bavarian Alps form part of Europe's largest mountain system. The Alps contain the Zugspitze, Germany's highest point, which attains a height of 9,721 feet (2,963 metres). The North German Plain covers the largest area of the country. Most of the plain lies less than 300 feet (90 metres) above sea level. Major rivers include the Elbe, Ems, Oder, Rhine and Weser. The mighty Danube River flows eastward from its source in the Black Forest. Germany enjoys a generally mild climate due to the influence of the sea.

Lüneburger Heide (*below left*), on the North German Plain, forms one of the largest areas of heathland in Germany. Largely infertile, it supports mainly sheep and forestry. In 1921, it became Germany's first nature reserve.

The steep Stubbenkammer chalk cliffs (*above*) on the island of Rügen rise to a height of 594 feet (181 metres). Located in the Baltic, the island is a popular resort. Sand-bars and numerous islands characterize the Baltic coast.

The heavily wooded low mountains of Hesse rise between the Rhineland and Thuringia, marking the start of the South German Hills. Ancient trade routes skirt the extinct volcanoes of the Vogelsberg and the Rhön, and carve a path into the North German Plain. Drainage of this region is carried out by rivers such as the Rhine, Main, Saale and Neckar which flow generally northward. Only the Danube, which drains the South German Hills, flows eastward.

The Black Forest, a high rugged region in the southwest of the country, lies to the east of the upper reaches of the Rhine. Characterized by clumps of dark spruce and fir, the region is rich in mineral springs. The highest peak in the Black Forest is the Feldberg, rising to an impressive 4,898 feet (1,493 metres) in height.

The terraced landscape of the South German Hills is laid out like the steps of a staircase. Fertile, heavily-populated basins are overshadowed by the bleak plateaus of the Swabian and Franconian Jura – a chain of mountains whose face rears steeply up to 1,300 feet (400 metres).

As well as these upland regions, the South German Hills include the foothills of the Alps. In the south, the majestic snow-capped Bavarian Alps sweep up to the highest peak in Germany, the 9,721-foot (2,963-metre) Zugspitze.

A Rhine Cruise

THE RHINE RIVER IS NOT ONLY EUROPE'S most important waterway; it also possesses some of the continent's finest scenery. This can be seen at its best from the deck of a boat, and the white fleet of the Cologne-Düsseldorf steamer company exists to provide this unmissable opportunity for visitors to enjoy a trip through the historic heartland of Germany.

Father Rhine, as the Germans affectionately call their river, is at its historic best between the ancient cities of Cologne and Mainz, which lie about 116 miles (185 kilometres) apart. For 2,000 years, these cities have vied with each other in beauty, wealth and importance. Both began as Roman fortresses, both became Christian bishoprics in the 300s, and then archbishoprics in the 700s. Today, both are justifiably proud of their cathedrals and churches, their universities and museums, their bridges and, not least, their colourful and historic carnivals.

The Lower Rhine Basin shapes the landscape on both banks of the river upstream from Cologne and beyond. Around the city of Bonn, the scenery becomes pleasantly hilly. On the left bank the Siebengebirge, a chain of extinct volcanoes, provide a spectacular panorama. Then the Drachenfels (Dragon Rock), rising steeply up from the river's right bank, forms one half of the famous "Gateway to the Rhine Paradise", sharing the honour with Bad Godesberg on the left bank.

Koblenz

In the 1800s, Koblenz was described as one of the strongest fortresses on the Rhine. However, the citizens of Koblenz did not share this warlike reputation. "The people are sociable, friendly and cheerful", wrote an observer in the last century. "The women are mostly pretty, even beautiful. The wine and bread are splendid; the air, as a result of the many rivers that come together there and the mountains that shelter it, is pure and mild. And the countryside! What hills, what valleys and fields and meadows, old castles, villages, lakes and rivers; what variety and harmony!" Any modern visitor would happily agree with this opinion.

The rivers Moselle and Lahn flow into the Rhine near Koblenz, which marks the beginning of that wildly romantic stretch of river that most travellers dream about when they mention the Rhine. Between Koblenz and Bingen, writers have noted a darkly demonic element, a fascinating melancholy. Even modern technology, from tugs with their convoys of barges to the express trains that whisk along both banks of the Rhine like snakes, has not managed to dispel the brooding, sombre atmosphere.

A heavily laden barge (*above*) passes historic landmarks at Kaub. This stretch of the Rhine flows between steep banks, offering romantic vistas to tourists. But the force of the current still presents navigational problems.

Rüdesheim's cobbled streets (*right*) invite visitors to sample the atmosphere of the ancient town.

Grapes from the steep slopes of the Rhine (*below*) yield fine wines prized by connoisseurs.

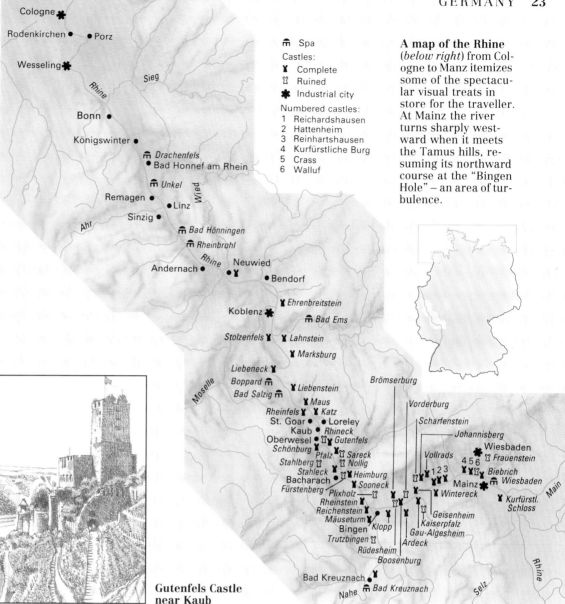

A map of the Rhine (*below right*) from Cologne to Manz itemizes some of the spectacular visual treats in store for the traveller. At Mainz the river turns sharply westward when it meets the Tamus hills, resuming its northward course at the "Bingen Hole" – an area of turbulence.

Spa

Castles:
- Complete
- Ruined
- Industrial city

Numbered castles:
1 Reichardshausen
2 Hattenheim
3 Reinhartshausen
4 Kurfürstliche Burg
5 Crass
6 Walluf

Gutenfels Castle near Kaub

More than 60 picturesque Rhine castles stand between Cologne and Mainz in the so-called Narrow Valley, where the river cuts through the slate mountains. These castles were originally erected to protect trade routes or to serve as customs posts. In their day, they were often seen as "the worst sort of nuisance and highway robbery". Surviving castles include Burg Stolzenfels and Katz, Marksburg, the so-called "Enemy Brothers" Sterrenberg and Liebenstein, and the Pfalz, built by Ludwig the Bavarian on a rocky island in the Rhine near Kaub. Near Bingen, the strategically placed Mäuseturm stood on a little island in the raging current, where its customs officers kept a close check on vessels using the river.

The famous "Rhine melancholy" is at its strongest at the Lorelei, an echoing rock near St. Goarshausen. Here legend has it that a maiden threw herself into the Rhine after being rejected by a faithless lover. She became a siren who lured fishermen to their destruction. The legend has inspired German authors and poets from Brentano to Heinrich Heine.

The Rheingau

Between Bingen and Mainz, the Taunus and Rheingau hills force the river westward from its normal northward flow. This has created a region between Rüdesheim and Eltville which is protected from biting north winds and caressed by the midday sun. The Romans planted vineyards here almost 2,000 years ago, and to this day it still produces the sweetest grapes, yielding the finest German white wines. The Rheingau, which the poet Goethe called "a blessed region, evoking a feeling of well-being and contentment", hints nostalgically at a paradise long lost on the banks of the Rhine.

Berlin

BERLIN IS BY FAR THE LARGEST CITY IN Germany, but it has only been capital of Germany for a relatively short period. Located on the North German Plain, at the junction of the Spree and Havel rivers, the city was first the capital of Brandenburg-Prussia. From the foundation of the German empire in 1871 until the disintegration of Hitler's Third Reich in 1945, Berlin was capital of a unified Germany. After World War II, the city was divided by the Allied powers, and its eastern half later became the capital of the German Democratic Republic (GDR). From 1961 until 1989, a high wall physically separated the city's eastern and western halves. During this period, divided Berlin often became the centre of international political interest.

History

Human settlement in the glacial valley of the Spree River began around the time of the birth of Christ, with the settlements of the Germanic Semnones, the Burgundians and the Slavs. By the 1200s, two small towns – Koelln and Berlin – stood on either bank of the Spree. The two towns formed an alliance to ward off marauders, and were intermittently members of the Hanseatic League. In the 1400s, Koelln became the residence of the Electors of Brandenburg, members of the Hohenzollern family, and Berlin strengthened its position as a trading town. The Thirty Years' War brought misery to Berlin, but it recovered during the rule of the Great Elector, Frederick William of Hohenzollern (1620-88).

Together with three neighbouring communities, the two towns became officially unified in 1709, under the former Elector Frederick III (1657-1713), who had become King Frederick I of Prussia in 1701. Some of the city's most significant buildings date from this period, including the *Zeughaus* (Arsenal), and Charlottenburg Palace, begun in 1695. The Brandenburg Gate, a large stone monument completed in 1791, still serves as a symbol of Berlin. From the Brandenburg Gate runs *Unter den Linden*, once the grandest of Berlin's avenues.

A melting-pot

As Berlin grew, its population swelled with an influx of southern Germans, Dutch, Flemings, French Huguenots (Protestants), Bohemians, Silesians, Pomeranians, East Prussians, Poles and Jews. These new immigrants gave the city a cosmopolitan flavour. However, the city's enormous rate of growth also created enormous social problems. The works of Heinrich Zille (1858-1929) and Gerhart Hauptmann (1862-1946) portrayed life in Berlin's crowded tenement slums.

Just as Berlin became Germany's leading industrial city, so it also became a leading city of science and culture, and the political focus of the nation. It reached its zenith shortly before World War I, and again in the time of the Weimar Republic. During this period, the Charlottenburg area of the city became its second centre. Because of its location next to the navigable waters of the Spree, it became the location not only of major industrial enterprises such as Siemens and Borsig, but also of many scientific and cultural establishments, such as the Technical University, the Berlin Opera and the Schiller Theatre. At this time, the Kurfürstendamm became a major commercial centre. This two-mile (3.2-kilometre) avenue sweeps through the heart of the city, and is still a paradise for shoppers and pleasure-seekers alike. At its eastern end rises the bomb-scarred tower of the Kaiser Wilhelm Memorial Church. Badly damaged in World War II, the building is a stark reminder of the futility of war.

A city divided and reunited

Berlin was devastated by Allied bombing during World War II. On May 2, 1945, the city surrendered to the Soviet Red Army, bringing Adolf Hitler's Third Reich to an end. The victorious Allies divided the city into four sectors, controlled respectively by France, Great Britain, the Soviet Union and the United States. Although Berlin lay deep within the Soviet zone of occupied Germany, it remained under four-power administration. In 1948-49, the Berlin Airlift enabled the Western Allies to overcome a Soviet blockade of rail, road and water routes, and keep the city supplied. In 1949, the Soviet Union made East Berlin – the Soviet zone of occupation – capital of the new German Democratic Republic (GDR). East and West Berlin became separate cities, each with its own administration, police and public utilities.

In 1961, the government of the GDR decided to close its frontiers. It ordered police and soldiers to build a massive wall, splitting Berlin in two. Backed by armed guards, barbed wire and minefields, the Berlin Wall ran for a length of 26 miles (42 kilometres). However, in November 1989, internal political upheavals forced the GDR to open its borders. Destruction of the Wall began, and with the reunification of Germany in 1990, Berlin once again became a united city with a single administration. The city was also officially reappointed capital of Germany. On October 3, 1990, Berlin's restored *Reichstag* (parliament building) was the setting for the formal ceremonies marking German reunification. In 1991, the federal parliament voted to move both government and parliament to Berlin from their former home in Bonn.

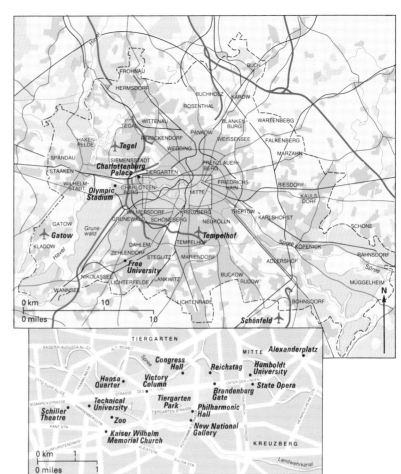

Cafes on the Kurfürstendamm (*above*), one of Berlin's busiest avenues, provide a resting place for shoppers. In the background stands the ruined Kaiser Wilhelm Memorial Church, flanked by its modern successor.

The Berlin Wall (*left*), a forbidding barrier of concrete slabs, minefields and barbed wire, once split the city in two. Built in 1961 by the East German government, the Berlin Wall symbolized Germany's forty-year division.

Old Berlin (*below*) once occupied only the right bank of the Spree River. It later united with its neighbour, Koelln (or Cölln). It was not until 1709 that the townships merged with other outlying settlements to form modern Berlin.

Berlin (*above*) constitutes one of Germany's 16 federal states, and is also the official capital of the country. Located at the junction of the Spree and Havel rivers, the city contains many historical and cultural landmarks.

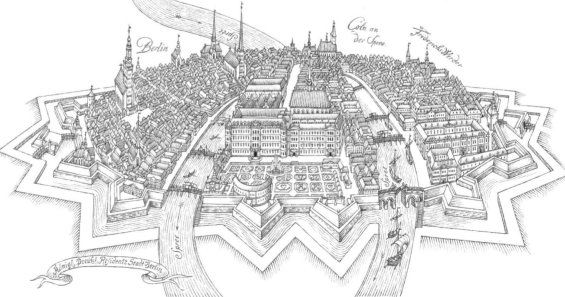

Roots & Traditions

1 Ore Mountains
2 Munich
3 Landshut
4 Bad Hersfeld
5 Thuringia
6 Hameln

LONG BEFORE "GERMANS" AS SUCH existed, certain Germanic tribes spread out far beyond the frontiers of today's German nation. And even now, each "tribe" stubbornly hangs on to its own particular language, culture and, to a certain extent, political convictions.

What, then, is a "German"? It is necessary to go back all the way to Charlemagne (AD 742-814) to find out. His dominions embraced not only his ancestral Frankish empire but also northern Italy and the Germanic homelands as far as the Elbe and the Saale. Contemporary Latin documents mention a *lingua theodisca* or *theudis*. The German word *theuda* meant "the common people". Hence the *lingua theodisca* was the language spoken by the common people. The *lingua Romana*, on the other hand, was the language of Rome. This was the language of government, Christianity, and the law. But the emperor wanted his people to learn about justice, the law, and religion in their own tongue. As a result, an all-embracing German language evolved in order to provide a means of communication free from the splintering effects of regional dialects.

The Old High German spoken by the Carolingians (c.750-1050) at first developed into Middle High German during the reign of the Hohenstaufen emperors (1138-1254). Later, New High German emerged when Martin Luther (1483-1546) made a translation of the Bible. But "standard German" over the centuries was above all a written language. For daily conversation, the people used their own individual dialects.

Today's rapid, up-to-date channels of communication ensure that most Germans use standard German or *Hochdeutsch* (High German). However, regional dialects still survive; in some parts of the country these are looked on mainly as historical curiosities, but elsewhere they are still the everyday "language". A considerable variation exists between dialects, and it sometimes happens that a German visiting another region may have difficulty in following an ordinary conversation. However, Germany's regions differ in other ways, too. In recent years, regional cultural associations dedicated to the preservation of local costumes, dances and traditions have increased in popularity.

Folk festivals

Much German folklore, hoary with age, barely survives today. Traditions and customs that once formed the warp and weft of a peasant's daily round – seedtime and harvest, animal husbandry, and rural community life – have all but died out. The traditions and skills of various craftsmen have fallen to the levelling hand of wholesale in-

May Day celebrations reveal their pagan origins in the maypole (*above*). In Bavaria, every village takes pride in its own "May Tree", decked out in the Bavarian colours of blue and white, and often decorated with wooden carvings. A group of Bavarian women (*right*) suggests a more Christian mood. In this region many people still wear traditional costumes on feast days.

dustrialization. Many guilds, too, based on the principle of mutual assistance, disappeared forever when today's anonymous insurance systems took over. However, in the Erzgebirge (Ore Mountains) and the Vogtland, the inhabitants keep alive the ancient history of this region, with its strong mining character, in the form of processions, traditional costumes and songs.

But traditional folk festivals and days of remembrance, often ignoring regional boundaries, still flourish. They include the Munich Oktoberfest, the Prince's Wedding in Landshut, and the Lullus Festival in Bad Hersfeld. The mountain festivals in the south and the shooting festivals in the north have also survived.

Shrovetide customs have remained very much alive, even away from the main carnival centres such as Cologne, Mainz, and Munich. They are particularly strong in southwestern Germany. Lively children's festivals welcome summer at Whitsuntide and challenge winter at the turn of the year. In the predominantly Catholic south of the country, traditional festivals are leavened with religious processions, pilgrimages, and ceremonies. In Thuringia, the *Thüringer Kirmes* (Thuringian Fair) is still celebrated in the old style. Among the Sorbs of eastern Saxony, traditional marriage rituals remain in use to the present day.

A wedding procession (*bottom*) provides an occasion for Sorbs to display their rich costumes. This ethnic minority live along the Spree River in Upper and Lower Lusatia, and keep their own language and traditions very much alive.

Shrovetide festivals like the Alemannic festival in southwest Germany (*below*) sometimes feature pagan masks to "frighten away" the winter. These examples are worn by two members of the local "Fools Guild".

The "Pied Piper" of Hameln (*left*) leads a procession of children out of the Lower Saxony town in an annual summer commemoration of the famous ratcatcher legend. The alleged departure of the children in 1284 is often linked with the historic German colonization of the east. Other authorities connect the event with Nicholas of Cologne, who in 1212 led thousands of German children on the ill-fated Children's Crusade.

Festivals

THE FEDERAL REPUBLIC OF GERMANY has a wealth of festivals of all kinds – concerts, operas, plays, and dance. Large and small towns alike put on their festival for a few days or weeks, some in established theatres such as the Bayreuth Festival or the Ruhr Festival, others using open-air stages like the Karl-May Plays in the town of Bad Segeberg.

Festivals, ancient and modern

Passion Plays have been performed in Oberammergau since 1634, and this event ranks as the oldest festival in Germany. It dates back to a decision made by the inhabitants after the great plague epidemic of 1633, which killed one in ten of the townsfolk. When the epidemic had passed, those who survived promised, as a sign of their gratitude, to perform the story of Christ's Passion every 10 years. About half a million people stream into Oberammergau to attend the performances, which last some five hours and involve the participation of 1,400 residents of the town.

In Berlin there are festivals almost all the year round. This festival scene was initiated in 1951 with the International Film Festival, a competition involving the most recent films from all over the world. In 1964, the Berlin Jazz Festival was set up, and has grown until it is now one of the most important international jazz events. The focus of this entire festival industry, however, is the Berlin Festival itself, lasting about five weeks and offering concerts, opera and ballet.

But it is not only the cities which mount festivals; many small towns do so, too. Drama productions take place every summer in the ruins of the Bad Hersfeld convent; the Ruhr Festival in Recklinghausen offers both classical and modern plays, concerts and art exhibitions.

The majority of festivals in Germany feature musical events, for example the opera festival in Munich, the music festival in Kassel and the summer music festival in Hitzacker. Some concentrate on a single composer: thus Mozart is celebrated in Würzburg, Schumann in Zwickau, Beethoven in Bonn, and in Munich they honour the great son of that city – Richard Strauss.

A fanfare of festivals

Early music, performed with quaint, old-fashioned instruments, forms the core of the Herne festival. At Donaueschingen, by contrast, the music festival offers contemporary compositions. Just one instrument, the organ, is honoured at the Nuremberg international organ festival. But the most famous event in international terms is undoubtedly the Richard Wagner festival in Bayreuth. This was inaugurated in 1876 by

Festival calendar

A map of sites (*right*) shows some of the many festivals that can be enjoyed throughout Germany.

Ansbach:
Bach Festival (*July-August*)

Augsburg:
Mozart Festival (*May*)

Bad Hersfeld:
Theatre Festival (*July-August*)

Bad Segeberg:
Karl-May Plays (*July*)

Bayreuth:
Wagner Festival (*July-August*)

Berlin:
International Film Festival (*February-March*)
Drama Festival (*May*)
Berlin Festival (*September-October*)
Jazz Festival (*November*)

Bonn:
International Beethoven Festival (*September*)

Donaueschingen:
Festival of Contemporary Music (*October*)

Hanover:
Music and Drama at Herrenhausen (*May-September*)

Hitzacker:
Summer Musical Festival (*July-August*)

Herne:
Early Music Festival (*December*)

Kassel:
Music Festival (*September-October*)

Leipzig:
International Bach Festival (*every 4 years*)

Munich:
Drama Festival (*May*)

Opera Festival (*July-August*)

Nuremburg:
Organ Festival (*June-July*)

Oberammergau:
Passion Play (*every 10 years, during summer months*)

Recklinghausen:
Ruhr Festival (*May-June*)

Schleswig-Holstein:
Music Festival (*June-August*)

Schwetzingen:
Festival (*May*)

Witten:
Festival for Modern Chamber Music (*April*)

Würzburg:
Mozart Festival (*June*)

Zwickau:
Schumann Festival (*every 4 years, June*)

Wagner himself with a performance of the great four-opera cycle, *The Ring of the Nibelung*. Since then, Wagner fans have come to Bayreuth every year.

A very recently instituted event is the Schleswig-Holstein music festival, which offers internationally renowned musicians the chance to meet every year. Initiated in 1986 by the pianist Justus Frantz, it lasts two months, with concerts in castles, churches, barns, or in the open air.

The International Bach Festival in Leipzig can look back on a much longer tradition. The famous *Thomanerchor* (Thomas Choir) keeps the legacy of Johann Sebastian Bach (1685-1750) very much alive, with performances of the composer's major oratorios, as well as motets composed for the choir. Born in Eisenach, the great composer worked from 1723 to 1750 as a cantor in St. Thomas' Church.

The Wagner Festival House (*right*) in Bayreuth becomes a meeting place for the rich and famous during July and August, when the Richard Wagner Festival takes place. Wagner lived and composed several operas in Bayreuth. He is buried here and his house is now a museum. A dominant force in Western culture, Wagner changed the balance of operatic works so that the music and the drama combined to produce a single artistic unity.

A religious fresco on an Oberammergau house (*above*) reflects the vow the population made in 1633 to perform a Passion Play every 10 years out of gratitude for the eventual passing of a devastating outbreak of plague.

The Berlin Philharmonic Orchestra (*below*), seen here under the direction of Claudio Abbado in the city's Philharmonic Hall, represents one of the pinnacles of German musical life. Berlin's musical calendar is a full one, and the city's "Festival Week", held every year for five weeks in September-October, presents a wide range of musical events, including opera and ballet. Berlin is also the home of major international jazz, film and theatre festivals.

SWITZERLAND

The **Matterhorn** (*left*) is the most celebrated of all the mountains of the Swiss Alps, and its famous silhouette is used as a symbol of many Swiss goods sold all over the world. Every year hundreds of mountaineers attempt to climb it, while winter sports enthusiasts come to ski on the surrounding slopes.

The people of Switzerland have three official languages (German, French and Italian), but have developed a remarkably resilient and unique national identity. The common history of Switzerland goes back to the 1200s and is symbolized in the stories of the legendary hero William Tell and his battles against tyranny and oppression. Nowadays the democratic principle of individual freedom has extended into many aspects of life in Switzerland. The country has maintained political neutrality throughout this troubled century, and although it is an important international meeting-place, Switzerland is not a member of the United Nations (UN).

It is extraordinary that in a land of such great diversity of language, culture and religion, the people have been able to maintain a unified identity. Perhaps this is helped by the fact that the 23 cantons (states) have preserved their historical separateness and political autonomy, while still being united under the principles of the federal republic. A measure of the internal stability of the country as a whole is the fact that although frequent referendums are held at local or national levels on specific subjects, there has always been a unified outcome, and there has been no change of government for several decades. If financial prosperity is also a sign of inner stability, then Switzerland must be one of the world's most stable countries. The banks which crowd the streets of Zurich might be modest in appearance, but they house immense wealth.

Switzerland is famous for many of its high-quality manufactured products. These include pharmaceutical goods, precision instruments and machines, chocolates and fine cheeses. But the country also has a lively and colourful culture. On the traditional side, there are the peasant farmers and shepherds, the horn-blowers and yodellers, who are still proud of their costumes and their ancient customs.

A number of celebrated artists and writers have been of Swiss parentage. They include the painter Paul Klee and the novelist and playwright Max Frisch. Other famous Swiss include Paracelsus (the founder of modern medical science), the architect Le Corbusier, the philosopher Jean-Jacques Rousseau, and the psychiatrist Carl Gustav Jung.

Switzerland Today

THE PRESENT-DAY GOVERNMENT OF Switzerland stems from the constitution of 1848 which divided political powers between the central government and the state government of the cantons. This system has created a unique example of direct democracy within a federal republic, uniting the country as a whole while at the same time respecting the varied needs of the different regions. As a result the Swiss have been able to maintain their local differences in language, custom and tradition, while still having an overall national identity. The spirit of fierce independence which always characterized the cantons has not been dimmed, in spite of the uniformities of our modern age, and differences are still to be seen from region to region.

Switzerland's remarkably successful political system has its roots in the cooperative tradition of the peasant communities of the Middle Ages. They realized that they must help each other in order to resist the pressure of foreign domination. The three original cantons of Uri, Schwyz (which later gave its name to the country) and Unterwalden, were first unified in the Confederacy of 1291. Their struggle against the domination of the Austrian Habsburgs came to be symbolized in the legendary story of William Tell, the champion of the Swiss ideal of the triumphant independent spirit.

Swiss legislation today is dealt with by the two houses of the Federal Assembly: the National Council and the Council of States. The 200 members of the National Council are elected to four-year terms from election districts based on the distribution of population. The Council of States is composed of

A traffic policeman (*below*) keeps watch on the busy streets of Bern, the Swiss capital. The centre of the city lies in a loop of the river Aare and is dominated by the tall spire of the Minster, a large Gothic cathedral. The city was founded in 1191, and joined the Swiss Confederation in 1353. It is now the capital of the *canton* (state) of Bern, the second largest in Switzerland. Bern's heraldic emblem is the brown bear, which features on its coat of arms.

FACT BOX

THE COUNTRY
Official name: Swiss Confederation
Capital: Bern
Land regions: From NW-SE: Jura Mountains, Swiss Plateau, Swiss Alps
Land area: 15,943 sq mi (41,293 km²)
Main rivers: Rhine, Rhône, Inn, Ticino
Climate: Varying greatly depending on relief and altitude. Generally warm summers with high rainfall; cold winters
Highest elevation: Dufourspitze of Monte Rosa 15,203 ft (4,634 m)
Lowest elevation: Shore of Lake Maggiore 633 ft (193 m) above sea level

THE GOVERNMENT
Form of Government: Federal republic
Head of State: President
Head of Government: President of Council of States
Administrative areas: 23 cantons (3 of which are divided into half cantons)
Legislature: Federal Assembly: National Council (200 members, elected to 4-year terms from election districts in proportion to population), Council of States (46 members, 2 from each canton, 1 from each half canton)
Judiciary: Highest Court: Federal Tribunal. Lower courts in cantons

Armed Forces: Militia (citizens' army). Men must take part in series of military training periods between ages 20-50

THE PEOPLE
Population (1990): 6,710,000
Languages: German, French, Italian (official), Romansh. Schwyzerdütsch spoken in German areas
Religion: Roman Catholic (48%), Protestant (44%)

THE ECONOMY
Currency: Swiss franc
Gross Domestic Product per person (1990): US$ 33,995
Annual Growth Rate (1985-90): 2.9%

Switzerland (*right*), is sandwiched between Germany, Austria, France and Italy. The Jura mountains run along its northern edge while the Mittelland forms a lowland corridor along the east-west axis of the country.

two members from each of the cantons and one from the three half-cantons. Their terms of office range from one to four years. The seven cabinet members of the Federal Council are elected by the Federal Assembly and serve a four-year term. Every year a member of the council is chosen to act as President, but he is seen as a chairman and not a head of state. The council is obliged to include two members from each of three political parties (Christian, Radical and Social Democrat) and one member from the smaller Swiss People's Party. However, there are few political differences between these parties, and they are able to cooperate easily on most issues. In spite of their democratic principles, the Swiss have been surprisingly slow in granting equal rights to women, and it was not until 1971 that women won voting rights in national elections. Elisabeth Kopp was the first woman to be elected to the Federal Assembly in 1981.

Citizens' rights

A vivid example of the particularly Swiss notion of direct democracy is the annual citizen's assembly which is still held in one canton, as well as in the three half-cantons. At an open-air gathering, or *Landsgemeinde*, the people vote on important issues of government and constitution by a show of hands. The universal rights of *referendum* and *initiative* provide a crucial interaction between the citizens and the state laws which govern them. Any legislative decision, apart from the budget, can be put to the vote, so long as there are 50,000 citizens or eight cantons in support of the petition. Any changes in the constitution must be passed through the referendum system, and a petition of 100,000 or more can force a change in government or an amendment to the constitution. In a referendum held in March 1986, three-fourths of the country's voters expressed opposition to joining the United Nations, and their wishes had to be obeyed. However, in 1992 broad agreement was reached on the question of EC membership, with a majority of the population favouring association with the Community.

Although Switzerland is a neutral country, a factor which allowed it to remain relatively unscathed during both world wars, it does not neglect its safety. A large portion of the annual budget is spent on defence, and its citizens can be called on at any moment to obey the call to defend the country. There is no standing army, but all men must complete a period of national service.

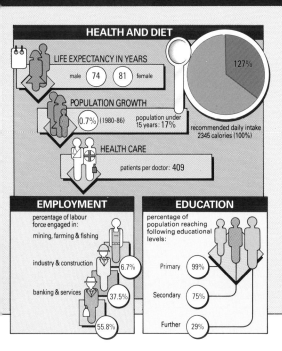

Trade Balance in US$ (1989): $1,429 mill
Goods imported: Machinery, precious metals, vehicles, raw materials
Goods exported: Metals, industrial machinery pharmaceuticals, chemicals, watches
Trading partners: EC countries, EFTA countries, USA, Japan
Transport: Length of railways (1988): 3,127 mi (5,034 km)
Passenger miles (1988): 7,699 mill mi (9,204 mill km)
Communications: Number of daily newspapers (1988): 98
Circulation (1988): 3,280,000

People

THE SWISS PEOPLE ARE PROUD OF THEIR national independence, and also of their long tradition of freedom. These two factors have been crucial in making it possible for several different linguistic, religious and national groups to live side by side in a state of remarkable harmony.

A confederation of tongues

The division of Switzerland into four distinct linguistic communities is the most striking sign of the diversity of its population. More than two-thirds of the population speak a German dialect called *Schwyzerdütsch* (Swiss German), while the remainder are distributed among three of the Latin-based languages: French is spoken in western Switzerland, Italian in Ticino and the southern part of Grisons, while about one per cent of the total population speak a Latin dialect known as *Romansh*. Many official publications appear in all four languages.

Everyone in Switzerland needs to master several languages, which may be one reason why the country has become home to many international organizations. Even the German-speaking majority has learned to live with variants of their language. The German dialects differ greatly. A German-speaker from Bern sounds quite different from his fellow countryman from Zurich. In most everyday situations they talk to each other in Schwyzerdütsch, but in written forms and in schools the very different form of High German predominates. However, in keeping with the independent spirit of the Swiss, the use of Schwyzerdütsch is encouraged, particularly in the fields of radio and television. In contrast, the Swiss versions of French and Italian vary little from the standard forms.

Compared with other countries with minority languages, the linguistic variety in Switzerland has aroused little serious conflict. In the 1970s the French-speaking minority in Bern campaigned for a canton of their own. This resulted in the formation of Jura in 1979. Religious differences have also been happily tolerated. About half the population are Roman Catholics and about 44 per cent are Lutheran or Calvinist Protestants. All denominations are distributed throughout the various linguistic regions, and this has meant that, rather than emphasizing differences, religion has played a positive role in neutralizing them.

Settlement patterns

Since so much of the country stretches across high Alpine regions, with large-scale settlements only in the valleys, the bulk of the population is concentrated in the Swiss Plateau area that extends between the Alps and the Jura Mountains. In numerical terms then, the typical Swiss is a lowlander – not an inhabitant of the mountains. Although Bern is the capital of Switzerland, three Swiss towns have more inhabitants – Zurich, Basel and Geneva. Even so, no Swiss city has more than half a million inhabitants.

A sanctuary for all

Over the centuries Switzerland has served as a sanctuary for the victims of political and religious oppression. The Huguenots (French Protestants) came in the 1600s, and more recently the Russian revolutionaries Bakunin and Lenin spent long years of exile here. Thomas Mann and other giants of German literature sought refuge in Switzerland while the Nazis were in power in their homeland. During the two world wars, Switzerland took a position of political neutrality, and gave shelter to thousands of refugees from a number of countries. Even today some 30,000 recognized political refugees have made this country their home.

More than a million foreigners live in Switzerland, and about half of them come from Italy and Spain. These represent almost one-sixth of the total population, and a further 250,000 foreigners commute across the border to work in Switzerland even though they are not residents. This influx of foreign labour is especially prevalent in the vast and highly profitable hotel business. Since the 1960s, Switzerland has introduced much stricter immigration rules, and this means that anyone who wishes to become a Swiss citizen for private rather than political reasons has a difficult bureaucratic path to follow. An application for citizenship can only be submitted after 12 years of legitimate residence. Successful candidates also need to have integrated themselves into Swiss society.

Language Areas

□ German □ French ▨ Romansh ▨ Italian

The language divisions of Switzerland (*above*) reflect the diverse origins of its people. Around 70% speak German and 19% speak French. The Italian-speakers are about a tenth, while only one per cent speak Romansh.

The Alpine Swiss (*left*) are descended from Germanic people who colonized the country centuries ago. The largest linguistic group, the German-speakers, dominate the central, northern and eastern regions of Switzerland.

The French-speaking parts of Switzerland enjoy a warm, sunny climate suitable for the production of fruit and vegetables (*below*). Sheltered by the Savoy and Valais Alps, the area is commonly known as the Swiss Riviera.

The Lavaux vine-yards (*left*) produce a dry white wine, generally regarded as Switzerland's finest. In common with their neighbours to the west, the French-speaking Swiss are masters of the cultiva-tion of the vine.

Many of the Italian-speaking Swiss (*above*) resemble the Italians in both their looks and their love of good food. Located in southern Switzerland, the Italian-speaking cantons enjoy a shel-tered position with a mild climate.

OF ALL SWITZERLAND'S FOLK FESTIVALS, that of the city of Basel is perhaps the most colourful and exciting. Basel's Shrovetide Carnival spills far beyond the confines of the city itself. In the week following Ash Wednesday, at a time when other carnivals have already ended, Basel bustles with masked revellers in fancy dress. Part of this tradition extends back to the early Middle Ages. But the famous *Morgenstreich* (Morning Pranks) is little more than 150 years old. It begins at four o'clock on the Monday morning and marks the start of three days of revelry.

The procession through the streets

Masked drummers, pipers, and others carrying lanterns stream into the market place in Basel. They form so-called Shrovetide clans and have often spent months preparing for just this event. On the stroke of four, they leave their meeting place and march through Basel in almost menacing fashion. Their lanterns splash golden light along the dark streets of the old city. This eerie atmosphere recalls an earlier age when Shrovetide was a time for spreading terror rather than an occasion for merriment. It was meant to drive out the demons of winter and at the same time serve as a release of pent-up tensions.

Individual revellers wear a variety of masks and fancy dress according to choice, but the clans are decked out in uniform costume for the afternoon processions. These costumes are specially designed to represent the particular theme for the current year, and vary annually. The main theme is emphasized by the numerous brightly coloured lanterns. These are each carried by four to six men and are decorated with verses and mottoes. The marchers also hand out so-called *Zeedel* (leaflet) verses to spectators along the route.

Among the standard masks that appear regularly in Basel are those of Harlequin, Pierrot and Waggis. Waggis has chunky cheeks, a huge nose, and wears a blue check smock. Speaking in Alsace slang he makes fun of the peasant farmers who in earlier days used to make a pilgrimage to the "big city" (Basel) to sell their wares.

Other kinds of masks and fancy dress worn either by individuals or organized groups enhance the colourful scene. They include masks with enormous beaks or pigs' heads, and costumes representing skeletons, foetuses, and aliens from outer space. Such weird and imaginative costumes seem to extend back to those wild, demon-like figures that once appeared in Little Basel on the opposite bank of the Rhine, as heralds of Shrovetide. There, the Honourable Companies of Little Basel, which evolved from the medieval corpor-

The Basler *Fasnacht* celebrations (*above*) go on for three days and nights, starting on the Monday after Ash Wednesday. Revellers gather in "cliques" or "clans" before parading through the town.

The annual cheese festival (*right*) at Hasliberg is held in September. The cheese produced during the summer is divided among the villagers. This traditional *Chästeilet* takes place in rural communities all over the country.

An Alpine herdsman (*above*) attends the Appenzell cattle market in eastern Switzerland. Both men and women wear costumes emblazoned with traditional embroidered flowers. This man has a milking pail on his back.

The yodelling festival in Burgdorf (*top*) includes the Alphorn, developed as a means of communicating between Alpine pastures. Fashioned from a hollowed-out pine tree, the Alphorn produces a low, penetrating note.

ations, hold their annual *Gryffemähli* (Gryphon Feast) on the 13th, 20th, or 27th of January. The celebrations begin with one distinguished member, known as the Wild Man, floating down the Rhine to a salute of guns. He is met on the Little Basel shore by two masked figures – *Vogel Grief* (the Gryphon) and *Leu* (the Lion). The three of them then go on to the Middle Rhine Bridge, which links Little Basel with Greater Basel. Each dances to a drum beat in honour of Little Basel, keeping his back turned on Greater Basel. The three figures have an escort of four *Uelis* (owls) who collect money for charity along the route.

Other festivals

Similar festivals, stemming from old guild traditions, take place in other Swiss towns. The *Zürcher Knabenschiessen* (Zurich Boys' Shooting Festival) is staged during the second weekend in September. The *Sechseläuten* (Six O'Clock Ceremony) provides impressive parades each spring, performed by a wide range of traditional groups. Festivals celebrating the passing seasons flourish particularly in rural areas of Switzerland. They include colourful and noisy mid-winter charity processions such as the *Umgang der Silvesterkläuse* (Procession Round St. Silvester's Shrines) in the Appenzell hinterland, the *Klausjagen* (St. Nicholas Chase) in Oberägeri in December, and the *Räbenkilbi* (Beet Fair) at Richterswil on the Lake of Zurich. The *Maibärenfest* (May Bear Festival) at Bad Ragaz features (along with some other communities in the Geneva area) a green-clad demon of the woods. In the autumn, harvest festivals take place, as well as those celebrating the return of cattle from their upland pastures.

Once in every 25 years, a famous winegrowers' festival is held in Vevey, on Lake Geneva. This honours the most successful growers in the entire region. The traditional *Chästeilet* takes place at the end of September in the Justis Valley, which forms part of the Bernese Oberland overlooking Lake Thun. All the way from the Appenzell to the Valais Alps the people can find good reasons for a festival of some kind. They celebrate in particular events relating to seasonal movements of cattle.

Midsummer festivals are always accompanied by much horn-blowing and flag-waving. They include cow fights to select the leaders of the herds. The people also stage *Schwingen* contests. These tests of strength between two rival Alpine herdsmen consist of a wrestling match in which the participants try to throw their opponent to the ground. Shooting festivals, held each year on the Wednesday before the 11th November in many Swiss cantons, attract the country's finest marksmen.

Liechtenstein

TUCKED BETWEEN SWITZERLAND AND Austria, and measuring only 16 miles (26 kilometres) by 3.7 miles (6 kilometres), the principality of Liechtenstein is one of the world's smallest countries. Yet this tiny Alpine state is full of scenic delights. From the lush valley of the Rhine River, the scenery changes to a landscape of steep rocky slopes, leading into the Rätikon mountains where the snow-capped Vorder-Grauspitz climbs to 8,527 feet (2,599 metres).

In the flat Rhine valley, a mild climate encourages the cultivation of wheat, maize and tobacco. But this occupies only a quarter of the country's total area of 62 square miles (160.5 square kilometres): the rest of Liechtenstein is devoted to the traditional pursuits of cattle-raising and forestry.

The principality signed a commercial and customs treaty with Switzerland in 1924, and uses Swiss currency. Switzerland also runs its communications and represents its diplomatic and commercial interests.

From agriculture to industry

Agriculture dominated Liechtenstein's economy until quite recently, but the rapid expansion of industry, trade and communications, combined with a decline in farming, has brought great changes in working conditions. Today only about four per cent of the 13,000-strong workforce is employed in agriculture and forestry. In just a few decades, the principality has undergone an economic miracle, evolving from a poor and underdeveloped country to one of the richest in the world.

Industry in Liechtenstein concentrates on the production of specialized high-value products, from pharmaceuticals and precision instruments to false teeth. Liechten-

Tiny Liechtenstein lies along the Rhine River (*right*), but includes lofty mountains and Alpine meadows, as well as rich agricultural land. The Prince of Liechtenstein's art collection (*upper right*) in the royal castle in the capital of Vaduz, is one of the finest private collections in the world. Most of the principality's population of 28,000 attend a yearly celebration (*lower right*) marking the state's independence (1866).

FACT BOX

THE COUNTRY
Official name: Principality of Liechtenstein
Capital: Vaduz
Land regions: Rhine Valley in west, mountainous in east and south
Land area: 62 sq mi (160.5 km²)
Climate: Mild for its alpine location. Warm summers, relatively mild winters
Main rivers: Rhine (is western border); Samina, Valorschbach
Highest elevation: Vorder-Grauspitz 8,527 ft (2,599 m)
Lowest elevation: Ruggeller Riet 1,411 ft (430 m)

THE GOVERNMENT
Form of Government: Constitutional monarchy
Head of State: Prince
Head of Government: Collegial Board (Council of 5 senior civil servants)
Administrative areas: 11 communes
Legislature: State Parliament (Landtag): 25 members, elected by the people for 4 years
Judiciary: Supreme Court, Superior Court, county court
Armed forces: None

THE PEOPLE
Population (1990): 28,000

Language: German (official)
Religion: Roman Catholic (87%), Protestant (8%)

THE ECONOMY
Currency: Swiss franc
Gross Domestic Product per person: n.a.
Annual Growth Rate: n.a.
Trade Balance: Sfr 737.6 mill
Goods imported: Raw materials, machinery, metal and chemical products, minerals
Goods exported: Agricultural products, cotton textiles, heating appliances, precision instruments.

N

0 km 5
0 miles 5

stein also offers tax benefits to foreign companies, and is therefore popular as a "tax haven". Many foreign firms have set up their headquarters in Liechtenstein, which benefits from the tax revenues these provide. Liechtenstein's postage stamps have long been a top-selling item, but today stamp sales contribute only about 10 per cent of the national budget, as opposed to 50 per cent in the past.

History

The year 1719 saw the creation of the principality of Liechtenstein within the Austrian empire. However, the House of Liechtenstein can trace its history back to the 1100s, when it was resident in Lower Austria. Its name derives from the Liechtenstein fortress at Mödling outside the gates of Vienna. It was not until 1938 that Vaduz Castle became the permanent residence of this ancient family. This palace now houses one of the finest private art collections in the world.

Liechtenstein has enjoyed neutral, independent status since 1866, but it was not until after World War I that it broke its strong ties with Austria in favour of a loose union with Switzerland. In 1921, the constitution was changed to make the absolute monarchy a constitutional monarchy.

Men over 20 are legally required to vote, but women have only had the right to vote since 1984. As in Switzerland, the political system includes the use of the *referendum* (when a proposed law is submitted to the electorate for approval) and the *initiative* (which allows voters to propose laws).

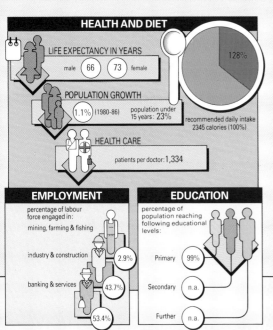

HEALTH AND DIET

LIFE EXPECTANCY IN YEARS

male (66) (73) female

128%

POPULATION GROWTH

(1.1%) (1980-86) population under 15 years: 23%

recommended daily intake 2345 calories (100%)

HEALTH CARE

patients per doctor: 1,334

Trading partners: Switzerland, EC, EFTA
Transport: Length of railways (1989): 11.5 mi (18.5 km)
Communications: Number of daily newspapers (1988): 2 Circulation (1988): 15,600

EMPLOYMENT

percentage of labour force engaged in:

mining, farming & fishing

industry & construction 2.9%

banking & services 43.7%

53.4%

EDUCATION

percentage of population reaching following educational levels:

Primary (99%)

Secondary (n.a.)

Further (n.a.)

Austria's magnificent architecture hints at its former grandeur perhaps more graphically than anything else could. The historic imperial castle at **Schönbrunn** (*left*) and the Vienna Hofburg bear witness to the once great stature of the Habsburg monarchy, whose empire stretched out over the greater part of the Danube basin. The Austrians abolished the monarchy in 1918, but in numerous traditions the remnants stay alive, not least in descriptions of food dishes such as *Kaiserschmarrn* (Emperor's flan), one of the sweet dishes for which the Austrians are famous.

One indication of the importance of the old Austro-Hungarian empire is the size of the capital city, Vienna, which contains one-fifth of the country's population. Vienna was, and still is, more than a political capital: it is a cultural centre which has provided leading figures in the modern world, even after World War I. Celebrated artists, philosophers and scientists, from Arnold Schönberg to Sigmund Freud, established the importance of Vienna for our age. Some impression of the atmosphere of those days is to be found in the few remaining old Viennese coffee-houses, the meeting-places for intellectuals and citizens. Politically, the city still remains the gateway to the Balkans from central Europe; and Austria's neutrality has made it a suitable meeting place for East-West negotiations.

The larger of the provincial towns form a significant cultural and economic counterweight to Vienna: Salzburg, Mozart's town; Graz, the centre for modern literature; and Bregenz, with its festival on a stage on the lake. As well as being known for its "high" art, in the form of festivals, and for its concert halls, Austria has become the country whose artists and cabaret performers are famous for their fertile imagination and for their black humour. Folk music with fiddles, zithers, and accordions accompanies happy hours of celebrations and dancing. Austrian cooking has had the benefit of being influenced by a variety of other cuisines: particularly famous are its pastries and sweet dishes, from the light, small semolina dumplings of Salzburg to a wide variety of other puddings.

Even if Austria is, in cultural terms, a very rich and varied country, the majority of visitors come because of the landscape – the mountains and lakes. The mountains have long since been made accessible for those touring by car. On the Grossglockner Alpine Highway, built in 1935, one can drive right up to the foot of the Grossglockner glacier and admire the highest mountain in the country from the sun terrace of a mountain tavern.

Austria Today

AUSTRIA IS A DEMOCRATIC STATE WITH a firmly established place in the international community. It joined the United Nations in 1955 and the Council of Europe in 1956. Membership of the European Community, with which it has a free trade agreement, was proposed in 1989. With the construction of the Vienna International Centre, known as UNO (United Nations Organization) City, the capital of Austria became the UN's third home, after New York and Geneva.

The country's current political system was created at the end of World War II, and in its making the Austrians continued the traditions of the 1920 constitution, which was elaborated after the collapse of the imperial and royal monarchy. The country comprises a democratic federal state with a two-chamber parliamentary system: this consists of a National Council or *Nationalrat* and the Federal Council or *Bundesrat*. Each of the nine provinces elects its own provincial assembly (*Landtag*). The head of each one is the *Landeshauptmann*. In Vienna this position is occupied by the city's mayor.

The members of the National Council are elected by proportional representation (where the number of seats held by a party reflects the total number of votes it has received). Voters must be 19 or more years of age on January 1 of the election year. There are nine constituencies, corresponding to the number of provinces. The Federal Council represents the interests of the provinces, and its members are delegates from the provincial assemblies. It may veto decisions of the National Council but the latter has the power to lift the veto.

The National and Federal Councils together form the Federal Assembly, whose duty it is to inaugurate the Federal President. The President, directly elected by the people for a period of six years, is the head of state. He nominates and has power of dismissal over the Federal Chancellor or *Bundeskanzler*, and through him has the same power over the ministers. The Federal President has the right to dissolve the National Council, and is commander-in-chief of the army.

The political scene

From the later 1940s until the 1980s, Austria's political scene was characterized by continuity and stability. The government was formed by members of the two largest parties in the National Council, the Austrian Socialist Party (ASP) and Austrian People's Party (APP). In 1983 the ASP-APP coalition ended for a time, when electoral gains by the Austrian Freedom Party (AFP) enabled it to form a coalition government with the ASP. In 1986, the ASP-APP coalition returned to power when votes swung towards the conservative right (although 1986 also saw the alternative United Green Party achieve parliamentary representation for the first time). The 1990 election resulted in another victory for the ASP-APP coalition.

Austria enjoys a close relationship between politics and economics, linking powerful business interests with professional organizations and trades unions. The Economic Association of the APP controls the Chambers of Commerce. In the same way, the APP's Farmers' Union controls the Chambers of Agriculture.

FACT BOX

THE COUNTRY
Official name: Republic of Austria
Capital: Vienna
Land regions: Granite Plateau in north, Eastern Forelands (incl. Vienna Basin), Alpine Forelands, Northern Limestone Alps, Central Alps, Southern Limestone Alps
Land area: 32,377 sq mi (83,855 km²)
Climate: Central European continental. Warm summers, cold snowy winters. Alpine climate in higher mountain ranges
Main rivers: Danube, Inn, Enns, Drava, Mur
Highest elevation: Grossglockner 12,457 ft (3,797 m)

Lowest elevation: Neusiedler Lake 377 ft (115 m) above sea level

THE GOVERNMENT
Form of Government: Federal republic
Head of State: President
Head of Government: Chancellor
Administrative areas: 9 provinces
Legislature: National Council (Nationalrat): 183 members, elected by the people for 4 years); Federal Council (Bundesrat): 63 members, elected by provincial governments
Judiciary: Supreme Court, higher provincial courts, provincial and district courts; various special courts

Armed Forces: Total strength: about 55,700. Men must serve a minimum 6 months

THE PEOPLE
Population (1990): 7,710,000
Language: German (official). Serbo-Croatian, Magyar and Slovene spoken by minorities
Religion: Roman Catholic (about 89%), Protestant (6%), Jewish

THE ECONOMY
Currency: Schilling
Gross Domestic Product per person (1990): US$ 20,647
Annual Growth Rate (1980–89): 1.9%
Trade Balance in US$ (1989): –$6,444 mill

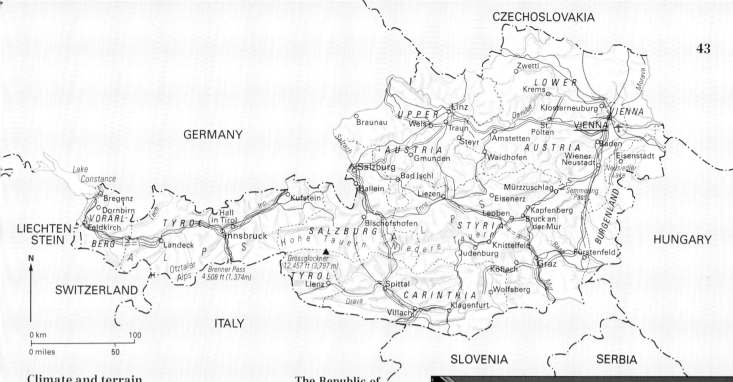

Map labels:
CZECHOSLOVAKIA
GERMANY
LIECHTEN-STEIN
SWITZERLAND
ITALY
SLOVENIA
SERBIA
HUNGARY

Zwettl, Krems, LOWER, Linz, Klosterneuburg, VIENNA, Braunau, Wels, Traun, St. Pölten, VIENNA, Steyr, Amstetten, AUSTRIA, Baden, Salzburg, Gmunden, AUSTRIA, Waidhofen, Wiener Neustadt, Eisenstadt, Bad Ischl, Liezen, Mürzzuschlag, Neusiedler Lake, Hallein, Eisenerz, Semmering Pass, Kufstein, BURGENLAND, Hall in Tirol, Bischofshofen, STYRIA, Kapfenberg, Leoben, Bruck an der Mur, Bregenz, Dornbirn, VORARL-BERG, Feldkirch, TYROL, Innsbruck, SALZBURG, Hohe Tauern, Niedere Tauern, Knittelfeld, Fürstenfeld, Landeck, Judenburg, Ötztaler Alps, Brenner Pass 4,508 ft (1,374m), Grossglockner 12,457 ft (3,797 m), Köflach, Graz, TYROL, Lienz, Spittal, CARINTHIA, Wolfsberg, Villach, Klagenfurt

Lake Constance

N

0 km 100
0 miles 50

Climate and terrain

The Austrian climate has four sharply defined seasons. Warm moist winds from the west bring snow and rainfall, while those from the east are drier. Altitude and local winds produce enormous variation in temperature from place to place.

The Austrian landscape ranges from high mountains to lowland plains. The Eastern Alps cover two-thirds of the country, the remainder being made up of gentle rolling hills and broad flat areas. Only about one-quarter of the country lends itself well to human settlement. Consequently, the population density of the country as a whole is low. Population growth has been negligible for a number of years.

The Republic of Austria (*above*) lies in central Europe, and borders some seven nations. The Alps occupy about two-thirds of the country's territory. A separate mountainous area, the Granite Plateau, occupies northern Austria. The valley of the Danube River and the gentle plains of the southeast contain major population centres such as Graz and the capital, Vienna.

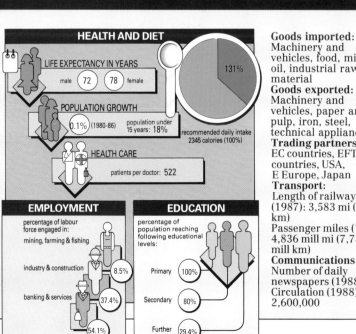

HEALTH AND DIET

LIFE EXPECTANCY IN YEARS
male 72   78 female

131%

POPULATION GROWTH
0.1% (1980-86)   population under 15 years: 18%

recommended daily intake 2345 calories (100%)

HEALTH CARE
patients per doctor: 522

EMPLOYMENT
percentage of labour force engaged in:
mining, farming & fishing
industry & construction   8.5%
banking & services   37.4%
54.1%

EDUCATION
percentage of population reaching following educational levels:
Primary   100%
Secondary   80%
Further   29.4%

Goods imported:
Machinery and vehicles, food, mineral oil, industrial raw material
Goods exported:
Machinery and vehicles, paper and pulp, iron, steel, technical appliances
Trading partners:
EC countries, EFTA countries, USA, E Europe, Japan
Transport:
Length of railways (1987): 3,583 mi (5,767 km)
Passenger miles (1988): 4,836 mill mi (7,783 mill km)
Communications:
Number of daily newspapers (1988): 32
Circulation (1988): 2,600,000

Austria's Parliament Building (*above*), fronted by a 13-foot (4-metre) statue of the Greek goddess Athena, stands in the centre of Vienna, on the city's broad Ringstrasse. The building was completed in 1883, and its Greek classical style reflects the ancient origins of modern political democracy. Meetings of both houses of Austria's legislature have taken place here since 1918. In the background rises Vienna's *Rathaus* (town hall).

Vienna

VIENNA, ONCE THE HEART OF THE mighty Habsburg empire, is today the least spoiled of all the great old European cities. A treasurehouse of art and culture, this city of parks and palaces, of coffee-houses and cake shops, seems too grand for the small, mountainous country of which it is the capital. As a Viennese citizen has noted, it was a city with everything needed for the cultural life of a great power, but the country had become impoverished.

Vienna stands on the slopes of the Vienna Woods (Wienerwald) on the south bank of the Danube, and traces its origin back more than 2,000 years. Situated on the crossroads of the Danube and the trade route between the Baltic and the Mediterranean, it was ideally placed to develop into the focus of a large trading region. From 1273, it was the residence of the Habsburg rulers.

When Empress Maria Theresa came to the throne in 1740, Vienna became the social and political centre of the monarchy, as well as a magnet for European art and culture. No other city has been home to so many great composers, including Gluck, Haydn, Mozart, Beethoven, Schubert, Bruckner, Brahms and the "King of the Waltz", Johann Strauss Jr. Today Vienna retains its status as a cultural centre. Its Burgtheater, State Opera, Theater in der Josefstadt, Vienna Symphony Orchestra, and Vienna Boys' Choir all enjoy a worldwide reputation. As well as the University, founded in 1365, the Academy of Fine Arts, and many other institutes of learning, Vienna possesses world-famous art collections, archives and museums.

The Inner City
The symbol of Vienna is the great south tower of St. Stephen's Cathedral, at 446 feet (136 metres) one of the world's highest church towers and Austria's most important Gothic monument. From the top, the visitor can look down on the Inner City, a confusion of narrow cobbled streets, courtyards, churches and palaces. Notable buildings include the city's oldest church, St. Ruprecht's, with its "Black Madonna" whose aid was invoked against plague in the Middle Ages. In contrast, the nearby Church of St. Peter (modelled upon St. Peter's in Rome) dates in its present form only to the 1700s, although it is said to occupy the site of a church founded by Charlemagne in 792.

At the heart of the city lies the Hofburg, the Imperial Castle. For more than 600 years this was the seat of Austrian rulers, nearly all of whom added extensions, until today this "city within a city" of palaces, squares and gardens contains no less than 2,600 rooms and occupies some 47 acres (19 hectares). The Hofburg is the official seat of the Austrian Head of State. It also houses the Congress Centre, several museums, the State Apartments and Treasury and, perhaps most famous, the Spanish Riding School. Here, the renowned Lippizaner "silver stallions" are stabled in a palace and perform their elegant displays in the Winter Riding School, built in 1729-35.

Vienna has many splendid examples of the Baroque style of architecture, a highly ornamental style of the 1600s and 1700s. These include the Imperial Palace of Schönbrunn, the Belvedere Palaces (now housing art collections) and St. Charles Church with its spectacular frescoes. But it is the unassuming Capuchin Church which houses the Imperial Vault, since 1633 the last resting place for members of the Habsburg dynasty.

Between 1858 and 1865, Vienna's old fortifications were razed and replaced by the Ringstrassen, a band of roads round the Inner City. Rapid industrial expansion encouraged the construction of grandiose buildings along the 2.5 miles (4 kilometres) of the Ringstrassen, including the Court Theatre, New University, Opera House, Parliament and City Hall.

An international centre
A city of trade fairs and congresses, Vienna is Austria's most important trade and ser-

At the Spanish Riding School (*below*), riders in historical costume display the famous "silver stallions". The school dates back to the 1500s, when Emperor Maximilian II introduced the breeding of Spanish horses in Austria.

St Stephen's Cathedral (*right*) forms the central point of Vienna's Inner City. Its south tower, Vienna's chief landmark, offers a superb view of the city from the "watch room", which stands at the top of a flight of 312 stairs.

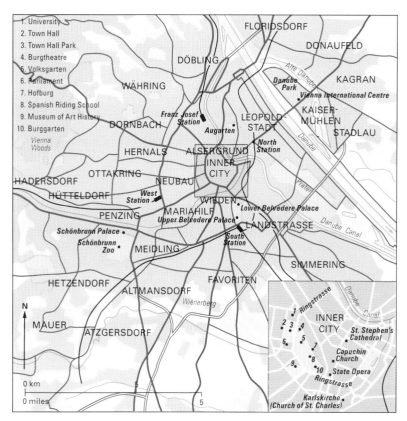

1. University
2. Town Hall
3. Town Hall Park
4. Burgtheatre
5. Volksgarten
6. Parliament
7. Hofburg
8. Spanish Riding School
9. Museum of Art History
10. Burggarten

Vienna (*above*), one of the world's great tourist cities, lies on the banks of the Danube in the north-easterly foothills of the Alps. Despite the diminished size of the territory of which it is the capital, Vienna retains an international style and flair. At its heart lies the Inner City, which contains many of Vienna's finest museums and historic buildings, as well as its best shops. It also contains the capital's two most attractive parks, the Volksgarten with its rose trees, and the Burggarten.

Cakes and pastries (*left*) are very popular with the Viennese, who particularly like to eat them as an afternoon snack with coffee, preferably at an open-air cafe. The Viennese cafe society tradition goes back centuries.

vices centre, as well as the nation's key industrial region. The main industries are electronics and foodstuffs, chemicals and engineering, fashion and handicrafts, as well as tourism. But perhaps the most significant aspect of Vienna today is represented by the towering concave facade of the office blocks of UNO City, the Vienna International Centre, for the city on the Danube is now the official seat of numerous United Nations bodies such as the International Atomic Energy Authority (IAEA) and the High Commission for Refugees.

As the former capital of a multi-ethnic empire, Vienna has a long history as the focus for immigrants from all corners of the Habsburg realms, a refuge for religious and ethnic minorities, and a meeting place for a vast variety of national cultures. In 1814-15 the city hosted the Congress of Vienna, which was to re-draw the political map of Europe after the defeat of Napoleon I. Today Vienna is the centre for international conferences such as those of the Organization of Petroleum-Exporting Countries (OPEC) and the Conference on Security and Cooperation in Europe (CSCE). It was in Vienna that the leaders of the United States and the Soviet Union met for the first time in 1961, and the city continued to be important as a meeting place and a bridge between East and West.

People

AUSTRIA'S LONG AND COMPLEX HISTORY has given its people a more mixed ancestry than the populations of neighbouring countries. In fact, neighbouring peoples have contributed greatly to that same population, so that it is true to say that there is really no such thing as a typical Austrian. Although some 98 per cent of the people speak the official language, German – sometimes with distinctive accents, especially in and around Vienna – regional variations, or dialects, are equally widespread and varied.

Particularly individual are the dialects of the southern and western provinces of Carinthia, Tyrol and Vorarlberg; in the higher Alps, the local manner of speaking varies from one valley to the next. In some areas there remain linguistic minorities who have not been totally assimilated. For example, in Burgenland – the eastern province that borders Hungary – there is a small Hungarian-speaking community and a much larger group of Croats who have been there since the 1600s. In the north-eastern province of Lower Austria (which borders Czechoslovakia) there are a few Czech speakers; in the southern Tyrol (bordering Italy), a few communities speak Italian; and in southern Carinthia (bordering Slovenia) and to a lesser extent in the neighbouring province of Styria, there are quite a number of Slovenes. During the 1970s, the Slovene community was the focus of some civil unrest through non-assimilation. The remaining provinces of Salzburg and Upper Austria are dominated by Bavarian culture.

In such a mountainous country, geography has naturally influenced where people live. Mountain ranges cover some three-quarters of Austria's total land surface. The eastern Alps occupy virtually all of the west, south and centre of the country. A separate area of highlands known as the Granite Plateau occupies much of the north. The result is that most people have tended to congregate in the lowland areas. The districts around Vienna, particularly to the south of the Danube, are home to about 20 per cent of the Austria's entire population of roughly 7.5 million. An additional 30 per cent of the population live in other urban centres such as Salzburg, Innsbruck, Linz and Graz.

The people of Austria enjoy an extremely high standard of living. Most Austrians make their homes in modern, well-appointed apartment buildings. The cities combine historic and contemporary architecture with efficient public transportation and other services, and good facilities for recreation and cultural activities. Austria is world-renowned for its excellent cuisine, particularly meat dishes (with

dumplings, potatoes or pasta), cakes and pastries. The leading areas of economic activity in the cities are high-quality machine-building and metal-working.

Standards of living are high in Austria: unemployment is low; welfare benefits are exceptionally good; medical care and education are free; and the maximum working hours and minimum days of holiday are regulated by the government at generous and health-oriented levels.

The timeless countryside

In spite of its impressive urban centres, half of Austria's people still live in rural areas, most in single-family homes built to designs that are traditional to their province and area. Only 20 per cent of the land can be used for growing crops – yet the efficiency of the privately-owned farming communities is such that they are able to supply 75 per cent of the country's cereal and vegetable requirements, and 100 per cent of the meat, milk and eggs required. It is also out in the countryside that the grapes and grain are cultivated that are used to make Austria's famous wines and beers. Forests cover about 40 per cent of the country. On the mountain slopes, large stands of spruce and other coniferous trees support Austria's timber and paper industries.

All Austrians are fond of outdoor life, and even city-dwellers tend to spend weekends or days off in the countryside, summer and winter, where they can camp, jog, boat, fish, hike, climb, ski or skate. Team and indoor sports are also popular, notably football (soccer), ice hockey and curling.

Almost all Austrians have a strong feel for the traditions of their own province or area. Traditional costumes – which differ mostly in pattern or decoration but are otherwise

Women from the Traunsee region (*above left*) in the Salzkammergut area of Upper Austria wear their traditional costumes for a *Corpus Christi* procession. These traditions of local dress are kept alive by regional associations and clubs. In Upper and Lower Austria, village women still wear silk clothing and gold-embroidered bonnets for festivals and holidays.

For the Corpus Christi procession (*above*) at Lake Hallstatt, which is enclosed by high mountains, the Holy Sacrement must be carried by water.

Many Austrian farmers operate small dairies (*right*), in which they turn milk from their herds into cheese.

A waitress in Vienna's Grinzing area (*top right*) carries a tray of its famous wines.

A masked procession in the Tyrol (*right*) keeps alive a centuries-old Shrovetide custom.

to a largely standard design – are worn frequently for civic occasions and festivals. Music at such occasions tends to be played by brass bands, who play folk tunes rather than the works of Austria's most famous composers. However, compositions by the Strauss family may well be included.

Religion and customs

Much of the inspiration behind Austria's musical heritage comes from the religious faith of its people. Austrians are free to worship as they please, but the Roman Catholic Church receives an official state subsidy and claims the adherence of about 90 per cent of the population. A further 6 per cent are Protestant. Before the Nazi Holocaust during World War II, Austria had a large and distinguished Jewish population. Today only around 12,000 Jews still live in Austria, mostly in and around Vienna.

The Alps

Edelweiss

Alpine lily

Trumpet gentian

EUROPE'S LARGEST MOUNTAIN SYSTEM, the Alps, extend for about 750 miles (1,200 kilometres) through south-central Europe, from southern France to eastern Austria. In addition to snow-capped peaks, the Alps contain many diverse landscapes, with rolling hills and wide valleys, lakes and rivers, forests and pastures.

Mont Blanc is the most famous Alpine peak, and at 15,771 feet (4,807 metres) it is also the highest. Mont Rosa is a close second at 15,203 feet (4,634 metres), and the Matterhorn, the most dramatic in the Alps, reaches 14,691 feet (4,478 metres).

Formation of the Alps

It is said that a great sea, the Tethys, once covered what is now the Alpine region. About 130 million years ago the sea bottom was gradually folded and buckled to form ridges and valleys of limestone sediment. In some areas huge masses of rock were raised up on top of others. This whole process occurred in stages, sometimes fast and sometimes slow, as can be seen from the alternations between steep mountain walls and flat plateaus. The chief ranges of the Alps were established about 15 million years ago. But the process is not yet finished. At Brig in Switzerland the land is still rising at a rate of ¹⁄₁₆ inch (1.7 mm) per year.

At the same time as the upward thrusting movement, the process of erosion was also taking place. Most of the debris that was eroded away collected on the northern edge of the Alps in flat basins which at times held water. The remainder was lifted up along with the rocks and sediment.

The Alps owe their present appearance to the effects of the Pleistocene Ice Age, which began about two million years ago, and ended some 10,000 years ago. Much cooler temperatures meant that the Alps were largely covered by ice. The glaciers edged downhill, transforming the landscape by the grinding and gouging force of their great weight. Valleys were changed from V-shaped grooves to U-shaped troughs. The glaciers carried rock fragments, boulders and gravel fields along with them, and these piled up at the edge of the ice. When the ice melted, the deposits formed dams across the valleys, and these eventually filled up with water to create beautiful lakes such as Constance, Lucerne and Como. Today there are an estimated 1,300 glaciers, covering two per cent of the Alps, most of which lie in the western regions.

Plant and animal life

Inevitably, altitude is a crucial factor affecting both plant and animal life in the Alps. The land can be cultivated up to about 2,000 feet (600 metres) although the zone of permanent settlement can reach 6,600 feet (2,000 metres). At this height the natural vegetation consists of deciduous (leaf-shedding) forests of oak and beech. Evergreen forests including pine, spruce and fir dominate the zone from 5,000-6,000 feet (1,500-1,800 metres). Only hardy species such as stone pines and alders grow at above 6,000 feet (1,800 metres). Alpine mountain pastures stretch upwards from about 6,000 feet (1,800 metres). Although snow-bound in winter, the meadows are rich in characteristic vegetation in the summer months, with gentians, globe-flowers, sunroses, aconites and stemless thistles. These small plants have large, brightly coloured flowers. Up to the snowline the vegetation becomes patchy, and above the snowline only primitive plants such as lichens and the glacier buttercup can grow.

The Lammergeier or lamb vulture (*above*) is now a rare sight in the Alps. It nests on high ledges and feeds on dead animals.

Because they are remote and inaccessible, the Alps form a natural sanctuary for wild life. Deer, martens, hares, ravens and splendid Alpine butterflies inhabit the coniferous forests. In and above the Alpine zone, chamoix, roe deer, red deer, ibex and marmot are to be found. The Alps are also the home of a variety of bird species including choughs, curlews, doves, jackdaws and grouse. Birds of prey are becoming rarer but there are still significant numbers of eagles, falcons and owls.

A number of national nature parks have been set up to try to protect the Alpine plants and wildlife. These include the Swiss National Park with an area of 65 square miles (169 square kilometres), the Gran Paradiso National Park and the Hohe Tauern Nature Park. However, the modern phenomenon of mass tourism is a real threat, even to these nature reserves.

Alpine flowers (*top*) adapt to upland conditions with their small size, bright colours and short stems.

Towering peaks (*right*) of the Swiss Alps include the Eiger, on the left, and the Jungfrau, right. Separated by a huge glacier, both mountains top 13,000 feet (3,962m). The north face of the Eiger is a challenge to mountaineers.

BEF

Jung 13,642 ft (4,

L. Geneva

• Geneva

Annecy •   Chamonix •   Matte 14,692 ft (4,4
L. Annecy

Mt. Blanc
15,771 ft (4,807 m) P

Gran Para 13,323 ft (4,

Grenoble •   Isère

Les Ecrins ▲
13,461 ft (4,103 m)

Western   Alps

• Gap   Mt. Viso
12,602 ft (3,841 r

• Barcelonnette

Mt. Pelat ▲
10,016 ft (3,053 m)   Maritime

Digne •   Cima di Argentera ▲
10,817 ft (3,297 m)

San

MONACO
Nice •

Cannes •

Stemless thistle

Mountain avens

Linz

Danube

VIENNA

L. Constance

Bregenz

Bavarian Alps

Inn

Enns

Dachstein
9,826 ft (2,995 m)

Zurich

St. Gall
(St. Gallen)

Hochkönig ▲
9,639 ft (2,938 m)

Graz

L. Zurich

Rhine

Eastern Alps

Innsbruck

Hohe Tauern

ucerne

VADUZ

Grossvenediger ▲
12,008 ft (3,660 m)

Grossglockner
12,457 ft (3,797 m)

Hochalmspitze
11,023 ft (3,360 m)

Brenner Pass

Klagenfurt

Todi ▲
11,877 ft (3,620 m)

▲ Piz Buin
11,086 ft (3,312 m)

Collalto
11,270 ft (3,435 m)

aken

Davos

Wildspitze
▲ 12,382 ft (3,774 m)

Eiger
13,025 ft (3,970 m)

Central Alps

Piz Kesch
11,214 ft (3,418 m)

Finsteraarhorn
14,022 ft (4,274 m)

St. Moritz

Ortles
12,812 ft (3,905 m)

Bolzano

Triglav ▲
9,393 ft (2,863 m)

Rheinwaldhorn
11,161 ft (3,402 m)

Dolomites

Marmolada
10,964 ft (3,342 m)

Aletschhorn
'63 ft (4,195 m)

Piz Bernina ▲
13,284 ft (4,049 m)

Presanella ▲
11,656 ft (3,556 m)

Ljubljana

att

L. Maggiore

Adamello
11,660 ft (3,554 m)

Trento

urspitze
3 ft (4,634 m)

L. Lugano

L. Como

Bergamo

Brescia

L. Garda

an Alps

A L P S

The Alps (*above*)
stretch from the
Mediterranean Sea to
Vienna, forming part
of France, Switzer-
land, Germany,
Austria, Slovenia
and Italy. Geog-
raphers divide them
into west, central and
eastern parts: the
Western Alps include
the system's tallest

peak, Mont Blanc,
but the mountains of
the Central Alps are
generally higher; the
Eastern Alps begin
east of Lake Con-
stance. Alpine climate
varies with height,
temperatures de-
creasing by an aver-
age 2°F (1°C) for each
650-foot (200-metre)
rise in altitude.

CZECHOSLOVAKIA

Czechoslovakia is a landlocked nation lying in the heart of Europe. The country borders Poland, Germany, Austria, Hungary and Ukraine, and occupies a total area of 49,373 square miles (127,876 square kilometres). Rugged mountains and rolling hills cover much of the landscape. The country's three main regions are Bohemia, Moravia and Slovakia. Located in the western half of the country, Bohemia and Moravia are heavily industrialized, while Slovakia in the east is mainly agricultural. Major rivers include the Elbe (known as Labe in Czech), whose source lies in the Sudetes Mountains, and the Morava, a tributary of the Danube. The Danube forms part of Czechoslovakia's southern border.

Czechoslovakia's population trace their descent from the Slavs, a tribal people who settled in the region in the AD 500s. The population consists of two closely related Slavic peoples, the Czechs and Slovaks. The country's two official languages, Czech and Slovak, share many characteristics with other Slavic languages. However, both use the Roman alphabet rather than the Cyrillic alphabet developed in the AD 900s by Greek monks. Most Czechs live in Bohemia and Moravia rather than in Slovakia.

Heritage

Bohemia and Moravia at one time enjoyed great cultural prominence in central Europe, and this eminence lasted for more than 1,000 years. The city of Prague *(Praha in Czech and Slovak)*, one of Europe's loveliest capitals, lies on both banks of the Vltava River in western Czechoslovakia. The famous statue of St Wenceslas, in Prague's **Wenceslas Square** *(right)*, commemorates the pious prince-duke of Bohemia who helped to spread Christianity through the region during the 900s. Murdered in 929, Wenceslas soon became the patron saint of Bohemia. In the late 1300s, Prague became the capital of the Holy Roman Empire under Charles IV, King of Germany and Bohemia. This period saw the foundation, in 1348, of Prague's Charles University, which ranks as one of the five oldest universities in Europe.

One of Europe's first revolutions took place on Bohemian soil in 1419. It occurred when followers of the Bohemian religious reformer John Hus (c.1372-1415) clashed violently with the Church in Rome after Hus had been burnt at the stake. The rebellion of the Hussites led to a period of civil war.

The "Second Bohemian Revolution" began as a civil war between Catholics and Protestants in Prague, in 1618. Within a few years, the Habsburg emperor and almost all of Europe's great powers had entered the conflict, which ravaged much of Central

Europe and came to be known as the Thirty Years' War.

Czech and Slovak art and culture flourished in imperial times and spread as far afield as Germany, France, and Italy. Today, the romantic works of Bedřich Smetana (1824-84) form a regular part of international concert and operatic programmes, as does the music of Antonín Dvořák (1841-1904).

Czechoslovakia's strong literary tradition owes much to writers such as Karel Čapek (1890-1938), and Jaroslav Hašek (1883-1923), and above all to Franz Kafka (1883-1924), whose powerful novels portray man's reaction to a nightmarish world. Contemporary writers include Pavel Kohout (b. 1928), Milan Kundera (b. 1929), and Václav Havel (b. 1936), who became president of the country in December 1989. Czech writers traditionally express a strong sense of national freedom, often hidden by satire or fantasy.

National development

From 1526, Bohemia and Moravia formed part of the huge multinational empire ruled by the Habsburg emperors. The Slovaks, by contrast, formed part of the kingdom of Hungary since as far back as the AD 1000s. As a result, the Slovaks found it more difficult to establish and maintain a national identity. A written Slovak language did not emerge until the 1800s. One of the greatest Slovak writers, Alexander Petrovics (1823-49), was known to the literary world as Sándor Petöfi, and died fighting for Hungary's freedom.

Until 1918, Bohemia, Moravia, and Slovakia formed part of the Austro-Hungarian empire. Even before the collapse of the dual monarchy at the end of World War I, the Czechs and the Slovaks agreed to form a common state. They received the backing of the victorious Allies. The new state became a parliamentary democracy, but Czechoslovakia's first taste of independence lasted only until 1938.

This new republic was home to many minorities. The three million *Sudeten* Germans, living mainly in Sudetenland, in the north and northwest of the country, formed a ready excuse for Adolf Hitler's annexation of the Sudetenland in 1938. Hitler occupied the whole of the country six months later.

After World War II, Czechoslovakia regained its pre-1938 borders, minus a small area ceded to the Soviet Union. In 1948, the country became a Communist People's Republic. In 1968, a brief period of liberal reform, known as the "Prague Spring", ended when Soviet and Warsaw Pact troops invaded Czechoslovakia. But in 1989, the Communist regime collapsed, and a new era dawned for Czechoslovakia.

AFTER WORLD WAR II, CZECHOSLOVAKIA set up an all-party government. However, Communist pressure led in 1948 to the formation of a government dominated by the Communist Party. Czechoslovakia became a satellite of the Soviet Union. In 1968, a brief flowering of reform, known as the Prague Spring, ended with a Soviet-led invasion. At this time, the unified Czechoslovakian Socialist Republic became a federal state made up of Czech and Slovak Socialist Republics. In June 1992, almost three years after the end of Communist domination, the process of separation went much further, and the two republics initiated a formal end to their 74-year existence as a single national unit.

During the 1970s and 1980s, the Communist Party exercised tight control over the economy and opposition political activity. In spite of persecution, which included banning people from professions and long-term prison sentences for dissidents, a courageous civil rights movement grew up during the 1970s. This movement, called "Charter 77", invoked international human rights agreements, such as the Helsinki Agreement of 1975, and demanded that the government observe them.

The Velvet Revolution
The year 1989 marked a period of momentous change in Eastern Europe. The Soviet government indicated that its satellites must now decide their future for themselves. In Czechoslovakia, strikes and mass demonstrations took place. At the end of that year, the Communist regime collapsed. On December 28, 1989, Alexander Dubček,

The health resort of Mariánské Lázně (*above*) in western Bohemia enjoyed great renown in the days of the Austro-Hungarian empire, when it was known as Marienbad. Today, many Czechs visit its more than 40 mineral springs, which became popular in the early 1800s. The town lies in the heavily populated Bohemian Mountains.

FACT BOX

THE COUNTRY
Official name: Czech and Slovak Federative Republic
Capital: Prague
Land regions: Bohemian Mtns., Sudetes Mtns., Bohemian Basin, Bohemian-Moravian Highlands, Moravian Lowlands, Danubian Lowlands, Western Carpathians
Land area: 49,373 sq mi (127,876 km²)
Climate: Continental, with warm summers and cold winters. Lowlands warmer and drier than mountains
Main rivers: Vltava, Morava, Elbe
Highest elevation: Gerlachovský Štít 8,711 ft (2,655 m)

Lowest elevation: 308 ft (94 m), near Hungarian border

THE GOVERNMENT
Form of Government: Parliamentary democracy
Head of State: President
Head of Government: Prime Minister
Administrative areas: 10 regions, 2 city areas
Legislature: Federal Assembly: House of Nations (150 members) and House of the People (200 members)
Judiciary: Supreme Court, regional and district courts
Armed forces: Total strength: about 200,000. Conscription after age 18

THE PEOPLE
Population (1991): 15,568,000
Language: Czech and Slovak (both official). Minorities speak own language
Religion: Roman Catholic (about 65%), Protestant (about 8%), Jewish, Orthodox minorities

THE ECONOMY
Currency: Koruna
Gross Domestic Product per person (1990): US$2,839
Annual Growth Rate (1985-90): 0.9%
Trade balance in US$ (1990): $695 mill
Goods imported: Iron and other ores, mineral oil, machinery, industrial gas

The Czech and Slovak Federative Republic (*right*), commonly known as Czechoslovakia, lies in the heart of Europe. Mountains and hills cover much of its area.

who led the Prague Spring 20 years earlier, was elected Chairman of the Federal Assembly. The following day, he installed the writer Václav Havel as State President.

During this "Velvet Revolution", the word "Socialist" was removed from the nation's official name. The long-felt wish of the Slovaks to have their independent existence publicly documented was also granted. As a result, Czechoslovakia officially became The Czech and Slovak Federative Republic. However, some observers predicted that nationalist forces in Slovakia would prove to be a danger for the unity of the fledgling democracy.

June 1990 saw the first free parliamentary elections for more than 40 years. President Havel won re-election to a two-year transitional period. Civic Forum, the opposition group which spearheaded the 1989 revolution, together with its Slovak ally, the Public Against Violence, won a substantial majority in both chambers of Czechoslovakia's federal parliament.

Parliament was elected to serve only a two-year term, when the members were entrusted with the responsibility of drafting a new constitution. The Federal Assembly, Czechoslovakia's parliament, consists of the House of Nations, 75 Czech and 75 Slovak delegates, and the 200-member House of the People.

In July 1990, Václav Havel formally took office as President of the Republic. Shortly afterwards, the Soviet Union withdrew its troops from Czechoslovakia. The country began the difficult process of shedding Communism in favour of democratic government, and the transition to a market economy.

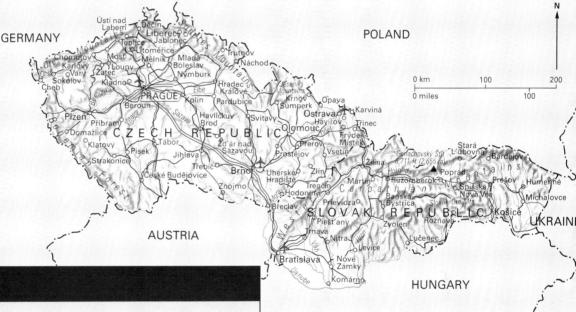

People

Czechs outnumber Slovaks by about two to one. Czech and Slovak, both official languages, are sufficiently similar for a speaker of one to understand a speaker of the other. But many Slovaks resent Czech dominance in the government and the economy. Slovak nationalism has grown during the post-Communist recession. In June 1992, the left-wing nationalist party, Movement for a Democratic Slovakia, led by Vladimir Meciar won almost half the seats in the Slovak parliament. This electoral victory greatly accelerated the drive for Slovak independence.

Today, 600,000 Hungarians form the largest minority in the country. Other minority groups include some 60,000 Germans, along with Poles, Ukrainians, and Russians. These minorities all enjoy equal political rights and full religious freedom.

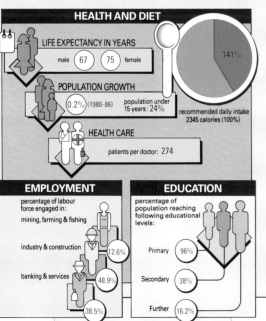

HEALTH AND DIET

LIFE EXPECTANCY IN YEARS

male 67   75 female

POPULATION GROWTH

0.2% (1980–86)   population under 15 years: 24%

141%

recommended daily intake 2345 calories (100%)

HEALTH CARE

patients per doctor: 274

EMPLOYMENT

percentage of labour force engaged in:

mining, farming & fishing   12.6%

industry & construction   48.9%

banking & services   38.5%

EDUCATION

percentage of population reaching following educational levels:

Primary   96%

Secondary   38%

Further   16.2%

Goods exported: Coal, iron and steel, machinery, vehicles, glass, textiles, agricultural products
Trading partners: USSR successor states, Germany, Poland, Switzerland, Austria, successor states to Yugoslavia, Egypt
Transport: Length of railways (1986): 8,149 mi (13,116 km) Passenger miles (1986): 12,387 mill (19,935 mill km)
Communications: Number of daily newspapers (1988): 30 Circulation (1988): 5,139,000

Prague

PRAGUE, THE CAPITAL AND LARGEST city of Czechoslovakia, is often referred to as the "Golden City". This name evokes the city's exceptional beauty, which could almost be the setting of a fairy tale. Miraculously, Prague's old centre has been well preserved. It largely escaped bombing in World War II and today boasts a concentration of historic buildings virtually unrivalled in Europe. Located on both banks of the Vltava River, the city contains a population of 1,215,000. As well as being a major cultural centre, the city ranks as one of Czechoslovakia's chief industrial centres.

Beginnings

According to legend, Prague was founded in around AD 800 by Princess Libuse, who had a vision of a glorious city while standing on a rocky outcrop above the right bank of the Vltava River. At this very spot, the Royal Palace of Vysehrad was built in the 1000s. However, the original settlement of Prague took place on the opposite bank of the river. At the end of the 800s, the first Czech kings founded the massive hilltop citadel on *Hradčany* (Castle Hill), which dominates the city's silhouette.

As late as 1784, Prague officially consisted of four separate townships. Across the river from Hradčany, at the intersection of important trade routes, the commercial district of *Stare Mesto* (Old Town) grew up. Its population grew from the 1200s onwards through the influx of German colonists. Within this district also lived a large and flourishing Jewish community, confined after the 1200s inside their own walled ghetto. The walls were only pulled down in the 1800s, but one of the original synagogues has survived, and is the oldest in Europe.

Between Hradčany and the river, within the outer wall of the citadel, King Otakar II founded the Lesser Town of Prague in 1257, later to be known as the *Malá Strana*, or Lesser Quarter. Finally, in 1348 Charles IV created the *Nove Mesto* or New Town, extending south of the *Stare Mesto* and down to Vysehrad. Today, the *Nove Mesto* is Prague's business quarter, and contains Wenceslas Square, a wide boulevard lined with hotels and shops.

The golden age

Under Charles IV, King of Bohemia and later Holy Roman Emperor, Prague emerged as a truly great city. It became a formidable political and economic power and a cultural centre of international renown. In 1348, Charles founded Charles University, which ranks today as the oldest university in central Europe. He attracted to his court such luminaries as the Italian poet Petrarch (1304-74). The German architect

Waltzing couples in a Prague park (*below*) convey the graceful atmosphere of Czechoslovakia's historic capital city. Probably founded in the AD 800s, the city formerly served as the capital of the kingdom of Bohemia.

High above the Charles Bridge, the spires of St. Vitus' Cathedral crown Prague's *Hradčany* (*right*), or Castle Hill. The Hradčany is also the site of Prague Castle, once the residence of the kings of Bohemia.

Peter Parler transformed the cathedral of St. Vitus, on Hradčany, into a work of dazzling scale and engineering brilliance. Parler also linked the district of *Malá Strana* and *Stare Mesto* with one of the most famous bridges in Europe, a structure known as the Charles Bridge.

Prague retained its position right up to the beginning of the 1600s. In the late 1500s, the Habsburg Emperor Rudolf II turned Prague into a centre of astronomy and the occult, bringing together leading astronomers such as Johannes Kepler (1571-1630) and Tycho Brahe (1546-1601). Magic has played an important role in the history of Prague. The leader of Prague's Jewish community in Rudolf's time, the Rabbi Lowe, is reputed to have created here an artificial human being known as the *Golem*. It was at Prague, too, that the legendary Doctor Faustus sold his soul to the devil, and where Mozart later wrote his opera, *The Magic Flute*.

Religious wars and conflict between the Habsburgs and the Czech nobility wrought havoc on the city in the early 1600s. In 1618, a confrontation in Prague between Bohemian nobles and the representatives of the Habsburg emperor led to the devastating Thirty Years' War. The subsequent triumph of both the Habsburgs and the Roman Catholic Church led to an intensive

rebuilding campaign in the late 1600s, which gave the city its present appearance.

Modern times

Whereas neighbouring Vienna and Budapest acquired wide boulevards and imposing apartment blocks in the late 1800s and early 1900s, the old centre of Prague remained unchanged. During this period, Prague experienced a lively cultural revival. In a tiny rented house high up on Hradčany, the novelist Franz Kafka drew inspiration for his great imaginative novel, *The Castle.*

The great events of modern Czech history also took place on Prague's streets. In 1968, Soviet tanks rolled through the city, snuffing out the brief Prague Spring. However, in 1989, crowds thronged Wenceslas Square as the Communist regime gave up power, and Czechoslovakia returned to democracy.

Traders in a street market (*above*), supply Prague residents with fresh vegetables. The city today contains a population of more than one million.

Although Prague's houses (*below left*) recall Bohemia's golden age, the streets of the *Malá Strana* (Lesser Quarter) show neglect. The Communists built new suburbs, but there is still a housing shortage.

Prague (*below*) lies on the Vltava River in western Czechoslovakia. Largely untouched by war, this beautiful city presents many unique artistic and architectural treasures. The *Stare Mesto* (Old Town),

Prague's historic centre, contains the Old Town Hall, with its famous mechanical clock. Wenceslas Square links the Stare Mesto with the *Nove Mesto* (New Town), which dates from the 1800s.

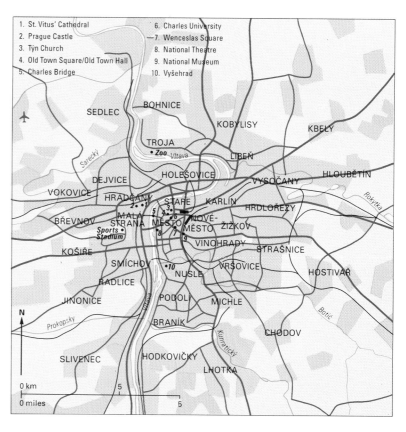

1. St. Vitus' Cathedral
2. Prague Castle
3. Týn Church
4. Old Town Square/Old Town Hall
5. Charles Bridge
6. Charles University
7. Wenceslas Square
8. National Theatre
9. National Museum
10. Vyšehrad

Land and Economy

CZECHOSLOVAKIA LIES IN THE HEART OF Europe. The Elbe, Oder, and Danube rivers link the country to three seas: the North Sea, the Baltic, and the Black Sea. In general, the landscape is mountainous, but varies spectacularly from west to east. Forests cover more than one-third of the country.

The Morava River which flows from north to south through the central lowlands of the country, divides the Czech regions of Bohemia and West Moravia in the west from East Moravia and Slovakia. The Bohemian Mountains rise in the extreme west of the country, and include the Erzgebirge (Ore Mountains) with their mineral springs. More than 50 still survive in the region, and include world famous Karlovy Vary (Karlsbad) with its hissing geyser, and the health resort of Mariánské Lázně (Marienbad). Sadly, air pollution has affected much of the surrounding woodland.

Farther south lies the Bohemian Forest, where forested hills containing abundant coal and uranium rise to a height of 4,590 feet (1,400 metres). Tourists today wander along forest paths that were once the haunt of bold robbers.

The higher and steeper Sudetes Mountains rise in north-central Czechoslovakia and define the country's border with Poland. The region is heavily populated and includes industrial towns, resorts, and farms in the valleys. Plains and rolling hills cover north-central Bohemia, a region known as the Bohemian Basin. Many streams and rivers rise in the surrounding hills, and water this fertile farming region. They include the Vltava River, which flows northward towards Prague from its source in the Bohemian Forest.

Southern Bohemia consists largely of the Bohemian-Moravian Highlands – a region of low hills and plateaus. This predominantly farming area, dotted with small towns and villages, extends into southwestern Moravia. The breweries of Plzeň produce world-renowned beers.

The centre of the country consists of the fertile, densely populated Moravian Lowlands, which cover the valley of the Morava River. Important industrial centres include Ostrava and Brno, Czechoslovakia's third city after Prague and Bratislava.

Southwestern Slovakia, separated from Hungary by the River Danube, forms the Danubian Lowlands. The city of Bratislava ranks as the region's industrial centre. However, as in the Moravian Lowlands to the northwest, farming is the main occupation of the population. In spite of marshy conditions in the south, farmers produce maize, wheat, and pigs.

Most of the remainder of Slovakia presents a rugged landscape of forested mountains known as the Western Carpathians.

The city of Plzeň (*right*), in western Bohemia, ranks as one of Czechoslovakia's major industrial centres. Its factories produce transport equipment, as well as the famous Bohemian beers.

A craftsman in Karlovy Vary inscribes a floral design (*above*) onto a glass bowl. Bohemia's glass industry dates from the 1600s.

The picturesque town of Mikulov (*left*) lies on the edge of the rolling Moravian Lowlands of central Czechoslovakia. This densely populated region forms a division between the highland regions of Bohemia and the Western Carpathians.

These two traders in Bratislava's market (*below*) wear the headscarves that are still characteristic of rural women in Slovakia. Located on the Danube River, Bratislava is the capital of Slovakia.

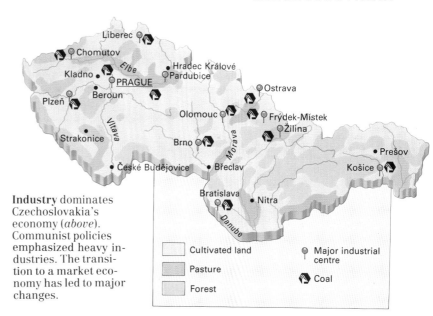

Industry dominates Czechoslovakia's economy (*above*). Communist policies emphasized heavy industries. The transition to a market economy has led to major changes.

Cultivated land

Pasture

Forest

Major industrial centre

Coal

The Carpathians form part of central Europe's great mountain system, which includes the Alps. Generally lower than the Alps, the Czechoslovakian portion of the Carpathians includes the High Tatras, which fringe northern Slovakia, the Low Tatras, and the Slovak Ore Mountains. Czechoslovakia's highest mountain, Gerlachovský Štít in the High Tatras, rises to a height of 8,711 feet (2,655 metres). The "good robber" Jurai Janosik, a hero of traditional Slovak folk song, made these mountains and forests his domain. The forests support the country's lumber and paper industries. Embedded among the peaks of the High Tatras are the so-called "eyes of the sea" – small, crystal-clear lakes enclosed by sheer cliffs. At the southern edge of the Carpathian foothills lies the Slovakian plain. Its maize fields make it the principal food source of Slovakia.

The economy

Czechoslovakia's industrial development began in the late 1700s, and Bohemia and Moravia were major manufacturing areas by the mid-1800s. Industry expanded between the two world wars, making Czechoslovakia one of Europe's most industrialized countries. Industry dominates the economy today, and Prague, Plzeň, Brno, and Ostrava rank as the main manufacturing centres. Heavy industries include steel, transport equipment and other machinery. Light industry includes food processing, and the manufacture of ceramics, paper, shoes and textiles. Bohemia's glass industry still attracts renown, as do the products of the country's brewers.

From 1945, socialist rule transformed the economy. State authorities took over manufacturing, services, retailing, and private industry. They concentrated on the expansion of heavy industry. By 1960, however, economic development had faltered.

Although farmland covers about 55 per cent of the country's land area, farming employs only about eight per cent of the workforce. Under socialist rule, state farms and cooperatives supplied almost all the country's agricultural produce. In terms of output, they lagged far behind that of Western farmers. However, small private farms and businesses alleviated the shortfall.

Until 1989, Czechoslovakia relied heavily on trade with the Soviet Union and other members of COMECON. With the end of socialist control, the ailing Czech economy embarked on badly needed economic reforms. The government is rapidly privatizing many businesses and industries, and hopes to attract large-scale foreign investment. The country has also begun to tackle the serious problem of industrial pollution caused by outdated and inefficient plants.

POLAND

Poland lies in central Europe, and its troubled history reflects its geography. Except in the south, Poland has no natural frontiers. In the west, the Oder and Neisse rivers mark its border with Germany. To the east lies Byelorussia and Ukraine, while to the northeast Poland adjoins a small enclave of the Russian Federation. South of the Carpathian and Sudetes Mountains lies Czechoslovakia. The landscape of Poland consists mainly of flat plains or low hills, interspersed with lakes. Long sandy beaches fringe Poland's Baltic coastline. The historic port of Gdańsk lies on the Baltic near the mouth of the Vistula River.

In the 1500s, the kingdom of Poland was the leading political and military power in Eastern Europe. The Wawel fortress in **Kraków** (*right*) was the residence of the Polish kings in those days. However, it went into a long period of decline during the 1600s and 1700s. Its existence as a state ended in 1795, when Russia, Prussia and Austria finally divided what was left of Poland amongst themselves. However, the Polish people never lost touch with their traditions, culture, language and their Roman Catholic faith.

"Poland is not yet lost. . ." runs a Polish song from 1796, later to become the national anthem. The people of Poland stubbornly rejected foreign domination. The 1800s saw a number of nationalist rebellions, all of which ended in tragic defeat. Poland came into existence again after World War I, but its independence lasted barely 20 years. In 1939, Hitler and Stalin signed a non-aggression treaty, which contained a secret agreement to partition Poland. Hitler's armies swept into Poland in September 1939, an event which signalled the start of World War II. At the same time, the Soviet Union seized its portion of Poland. In 1941, Hitler invaded the Soviet Union, and Poland became a German colony. Poland suffered terribly under occupation. The Poles put up bitter resistance, and many fought abroad with the Allies.

After Germany's defeat a new Polish state was born, but it was independent only in name. From 1948, its society and economy were entirely controlled by a Communist government until 1988, when large-scale protests led to elections in the following year, triggering the disintegration of the Communist Eastern bloc.

Religion and culture

The Poles preserved their sense of national identity in part through their adherence to the Roman Catholic Church. The Poles adopted Christianity in AD 966, and have remained loyal to Roman Catholicism ever since. Today, more than 90 per cent of Poles are Roman Catholics. For centuries, they saw themselves as the bastion of the Christian

West. In 1656, the famous Black Madonna of Częstochowa was elevated by royal decree to the status of "Queen of the Crown of Poland" after Poland won an important victory over Sweden. In 1683, the Polish King John III Sobieski (1624-96) saved Vienna from capture by the Ottoman Turks.

During the years 1795-1918, when the Polish state did not exist, most Poles were under pressure to become either Germanized or Russianized. The Germans were Protestant, the Russians Orthodox. Their Roman Catholic faith distinguished the Poles from both, and so their church became the focus for their stubborn nationalism.

The church's stature grew during the years of occupation and Communist rule. During the German occupation, the clergy shared the people's suffering and many died in prisons and concentration camps. After the war, the Communist government tried to break the influence of the church, and imprisoned Stefan Cardinal Wysziński (1901-81), head of the Polish church, from 1948 to 1956. During this period, going to church became a sign of resistance and of faith in Poland's eventual resurrection. In 1978, the election of the Archbishop of Kraków, Karol Cardinal Wojtyla (b. 1920), as Pope John Paul II, greatly reinforced this belief. Even after the imposition of martial law in 1981, when the newly formed free trade union Solidarity was banned, many Poles wore the image of the Black Madonna as a defiant substitute for their Solidarity badges. The advent of non-Communist government in the late 1980s signalled the victory of Polish defiance.

The Polish language also enabled the Poles to preserve their national identity. During the 1800s, neither the Prussian nor the Russian authorities permitted the use of the Polish language in any institution of education from primary school to university. The language survived as the means of communication amongst Poles, as well as in songs, prayerbooks and literary works.

In the 1500s Mikołaj Rej and Jan Kochanowski were the first to write poetry in Polish. Since that time, the Poles have made major contributions to world literature and the arts. Leading Polish writers of the 1800s included the poet Adam Mickiewicz, the playwright Wyspiański and the novelist Sienkiewicz, author of *Quo Vadis?*, who won the Nobel Prize for Literature in 1905. The poet Czeslaw Milosz won the Nobel Prize in 1980. The *Polonaise* and the *Mazurka* were originally Polish country dances which the composer Frédéric Chopin (1810-49) refined and gave to the world. Polish film directors, such as Andrzej Wajda, Krzystof Kieslowski and Polish-born Roman Polanski have produced many compelling works. Today, Polish culture is gaining strength from Poland's return to democratic government.

Poland Today

POLAND WAS THE FIRST EAST EUROPEAN country to move from foreign domination to national independence, from a one-party state to multi-party democracy, and from socialism to a free market economy. Until 1989, the Communist Party controlled the government of Poland. Known as the Polish United Workers Party (PUWP), the Communists governed with the support of the small United Peasant Party and the Democratic Party. However, in the 1980s, Poland was politically transformed.

The birth of Solidarity
In 1980, protests and rioting greeted the government's announcement of increased food prices. This uprising also resulted in the humiliation of the government of Edward Gierek. Workers went on strike at the giant Lenin shipyard in Gdańsk, and demanded the right to form an independent trade union. Led by the electrician Lech Walesa and advised by intellectuals such as Jacek Kuron and the newly founded Committee for Social Self-Defence (CSSD), the workers occupied the shipyard, forcing the government to negotiate. When Gierek resigned, the Central Committee of the PUWP elected Stanislaw Kania to replace him. In November, the strikers won recognition for Solidarity, the new non-Communist organization of free trade unions.

The new union rapidly gained members. Early in 1981, it demanded a plebiscite on the government's credibility. At the end of 1981, the military intervened and declared martial law. A Military Council of National Salvation, headed by General Wojciech Jaruzelski, assumed the responsibilities of government. Jaruzelski's use of martial law probably averted the risk of Soviet invasion, but led to the arrest and imprisonment of most leading members of Solidarity. Although banned, the organization continued to exist under a Provisional National Coordinating Committee. Valuable moral support came from outside the country in 1983, when Walesa was awarded the Nobel Peace Prize. In the mid-1980s, waves of arrests alternated with periodic amnesties. In 1984, secret police officers kidnapped and later murdered the outspoken pro-Solidarity priest, Father Jerzy Popieluszko. The murder led to a new wave of unrest. However, by late 1986, most political prisoners had been freed.

In the late 1980s, the tide in Poland turned toward liberalization. The new Soviet leader, Mikhail Gorbachev, made clear that the USSR would no longer enforce its will on its East European satellites. The government used the Roman Catholic Church to negotiate with the still-banned Solidarity. The visits of Polish-born Pope John Paul II in 1979, 1983 and 1987 reinforced the church's influence with the people.

In 1988, renewed inflation sparked new strikes and Solidarity again emerged within factories and in public. The government proposed "round-table" discussions with the People's Committees which supported Solidarity and were now invited to share in planning reforms leading to a free market economy. The government announced elections and allowed non-Communist groups to organize and put forward candidates.

In the next year, the people voted strongly for Solidarity-backed candidates, and a coalition government emerged. In the new

FACT BOX

THE COUNTRY
Official name: Republic of Poland
Capital: Warsaw
Land regions: Coastal Lowlands, Baltic Lakes Region, Central Plains, Uplands, Carpathian Forelands, Western Carpathian Mountains, Sudetes Mountains
Land area: 120,728 sq mi (312,683 km²)
Climate: West and coastal area: temperate. Inland and east: continental with short summers and cold, snowy winters
Main rivers: Vistula, Warta, Oder
Highest elevation: Rysy 8,199 ft (2,499 m)
Lowest elevation: Sea level along the coast

THE GOVERNMENT
Form of Government: Parliamentary democracy
Head of State: President
Head of Government: Prime Minister
Administrative areas: 49 voivodships (provinces)
Legislature: National Assembly: Lower chamber (Sejm) (460 members) and upper chamber (Senate) (100 members)
Judiciary: Supreme Court, Supreme Administrative Court, province and county courts
Armed forces: Total strength: about 400,000. Men must serve after age 19

THE PEOPLE
Population (1990): 38,183,200
Language: Polish
Religion: Roman Catholic (about 90%). Protestant, Jewish, Eastern Orthodox minorities

THE ECONOMY
Currency: Zloty
Gross Domestic Product per person (1988): US$1,860
Annual Growth Rate (1985-90): −0.3%
Trade balance in US$ (1990): $1,410 mill
Goods imported: Machinery, vehicles, mineral oil, oil products, chemical products, food products, grain, wool, cotton, iron ore

Map labels

DENMARK

Baltic Sea

RUSSIAN FED.

LITHUANIA

Ustka · Gdynia · Sopot · Gulf of Gdańsk · Vistula Lagoon

Kołobrzeg · Słupsk · Gdańsk · Tczew · Elbląg · Bartoszyce · Suwałki

Świnoujście · Koszalin · Starogard Gdański · Malbork · Lake Mamry · Ełk · Augustów

Stettin Lagoon · Szczecinek · Chojnice · Olsztyn · Lake Śniardwy

Szczecin · Stargard Szczeciński · Piła · Bydgoszcz · Grudziądz · Ostróda · Szczytno

Oder · Gorzów Wielkopolski · Inowrocław · Toruń · Działdowo · Łomża · Białystok

Zielona Góra · Gnieznno · Włocławek · Ciechanów · Narew · Ostrołęka

Nowa Sól · Poznań · Warta · Kutno · Płock · WARSAW · Bug · BYELO-RUSSIA

Głogów · Leszno · Konin · Pruszków · Siedlce

Lubin · Rawicz · Kalisz · Łódź · Skierniewice · Otwock · Biała Podlaska

Bolesławiec · Ostrów Wielkopolski · Pabianice · Tomaszów Mazowiecki · Piotrków Trybunalski · Puławy

Legnica · Wrocław · Radomsko · Skarżysko-Kamienna · Radom · Lublin

Jelenia Góra · Świdnica · Brzeg · Kielce · Starachowice · Chełm

Wałbrzych · Bielawa · Opole · Częstochowa · Ostrowiec Świętokrzyski · Zamość

Kłodzko · Nysa · Bytom · Chorzów · Tarnobrzeg · Stalowa Wola

Zabrze · Gliwice · Sosnowiec · Mielec · Rzeszów

Rybnik · Katowice · Tychy · Tarnów · Dębica · Przemyśl

Racibórz · Jastrzębie-Zdrój · Kraków · Nowy Sącz · Krosno · Sanok

Cieszyn · Bielsko-Biała · *Western Carpathian Mountains* · UKRAINE

Rysy 8,199 ft (2,499 m)

CZECHOSLOVAKIA

N

0 km — 100 — 200
0 miles — 100

Poland (*above*) occupies a large area in east-central Europe. Extensive plains stretch across the country, but mountains define its southern borders. The country only assumed its present frontiers in 1945. In 1948, Polish Communists took control. In the 1980s, the rise of Solidarity, a free trade union organization, led to major political changes. By 1990, Poland had achieved full democracy.

A Roman Catholic priest hears confession (*right*) in Częstochowa, home of the revered icon of the Black Madonna. Most Poles are Roman Catholics, and the church has played a key role in politics.

100-member Senate, Solidarity supporters took every seat but one. In the lower house, the 460-member Sejm, 65 per cent of the seats had been reserved for the PUWP and its allied parties. However, these parties deserted the Communists, giving Solidarity's supporters a majority in the lower house as well. Tadeusz Mazowiecki became Poland's first non-Communist prime minister since World War II. In 1990, Walesa became president, and the government introduced stringent austerity measures to tackle the country's deepening economic crisis, caused by its huge foreign debt burden and inefficient industries. These reforms led to rising unemployment and a demand for policies more geared to social needs.

Administration and education

Two houses, the Senate and the Sejm, make up the National Assembly, Poland's parliament. The National Assembly passes laws, supervises the branches of government, and elects the president. The Sejm elects a cabinet, known as the Council of Ministers, composed of the prime minister and other ministers. Poland's president acts as head of state, and his wide responsibilities include foreign policy and the dissolution of the National Assembly. Poland consists of 49 provinces, known as *voivodships*, each divided into urban and rural communities. An elected People's Council, headed by a Presidium, governs each province.

Education is free in Poland, and children must attend school from age 7 to 15. Poland first established a ministry of education in 1773, and today the government still runs the school system. To attend one of Poland's 10 universities or its many technical institutes, secondary school students must pass examinations. Poland's oldest university, at Kraków, dates from 1364.

HEALTH AND DIET

LIFE EXPECTANCY IN YEARS
male (67)   (75) female

POPULATION GROWTH
(0.8%) (1980–86)   population under 15 years: 26%

123%
recommended daily intake 2345 calories (100%)

HEALTH CARE
patients per doctor: 487

EMPLOYMENT

percentage of labour force engaged in:

mining, farming & fishing

industry & construction — 30.2%

banking & services — 38.1%

31.7%

EDUCATION

percentage of population reaching following educational levels:

Primary (100%)

Secondary (80%)

Further (17.8%)

Goods exported: Machinery, coal, food products, ships, electro-engineering products, transport products, chemicals, iron, steel, textiles, timber

Trading partners: Successor states of Soviet Union, Germany, Czechoslovakia, Great Britain

Transport: Length of railways (1987): 14,687 mi (23,637 km) Passenger miles (1987): 30,012 mill (48,300 mill km)

Communications: Number of daily newspapers (1986): 45 Circulation (1986): 7,480,000

POLAND LIES IN EASTERN CENTRAL Europe and covers an area of some 120,728 square miles (312,683 square kilometres). The country appears on the map roughly as a square, whose sides run north-south and east-west. The Baltic Sea influences the climate of the north of the country. For the most part, Poland's landscape is flat and rolling, forming part of the great plains of northern Europe. However, southern Poland contains impressive mountain scenery.

Along the Baltic coast the shore consists of long stretches of sandy beach, broken by the deltas of the Oder and Vistula rivers. The Oder constitutes Poland's border with Germany, and near its mouth lies the port of Szczecin. At the mouth of the Vistula, on the Gulf of Gdańsk, lie the great ports of Gdańsk and Gdynia. These three cities are the only major urban centres on Poland's Coastal Lowlands.

Moving inland from the narrow coastal region, the ground rises to the Baltic Lakes Region, a hilly area dotted with small lakes among its hills and forests. Peat bog covers much of the area, making it unsuitable for farming. Economically, the region produces little but timber. However, its scenic beauty makes it a popular holiday area for Poles, who come to camp, trek and fish. In this remote region, wild swans flap through the silent night and vast, untidy storks' nests sit atop spires and chimneys.

South of the lakes, and covering the country from west to east, lie the great Central Plains. Occupying almost half of Poland, the Central Plains constitute the country's chief agricultural area. In spite of poor, sandy soils, farmers here produce potatoes, rye, sugar beets and other crops. In this area too lie some of the country's most important cities including Bydgoszcz, Poznań, Wrocław and the capital, Warsaw. East of the Vistula lie areas of vast untouched forest, full of ancient trees. In the nature reserve of Puszcza Kampinoska near Warsaw, elk, wolves and wild boar live a protected existence. However, wildlife enjoy no protection from the pollution carried down on the Vistula from the industrial areas of southern Poland, where environmental pollution is the worst in Eastern Europe.

South and east of the Central Plains rise the Polish Uplands, an area rich in resources for both agriculture and industry. The soil is fertile and the area around Katowice represents one of the world's largest coal fields. The region also contains deposits of copper, lead and zinc.

South of the Polish Uplands, the ground rises again to the Carpathian Forelands lying between the Vistula and the San rivers. This is one of the most densely populated areas in Poland, with its richest soils and important iron and steel industries

around the historic city of Kraków.

Along Poland's southwestern border stand the Sudetes Mountains whose topmost ridge forms part of Poland's frontier with Czechoslovakia. At the western end stands the Karkonosze range, whose highest peak, Sniezka, rises to 5,256 feet (1,602 metres). To the west, the range loses altitude towards the Neisse and the taller peaks give way to rounded mountains covered with forest, most rising to an altitude of less than 5,000 feet (1,500 metres). Here, mouflons (mountain sheep) and other rare animals survive in nature reserves. The broad lower valleys between the mountains support crops and pasture, and contain textile-producing centres.

In Poland's jutting southeastern corner the Carpathian Forelands rise to the Western Carpathian Mountains, consisting of the Beskid and Tatra chains. Dense forests cover the gentle domes of the Beskids. Only a few peaks rise above the tree line, but Babia Góra to the west in the High Beskids stands at an altitude of some 5,660 feet (1,725 metres). In days gone by, the mountain was the fabled gathering place for great witches' sabbaths. In the Low Beskids, in the southeastern corner of Poland, the virgin forests are still the home of bears, wolves, European bison and lynx.

Beyond the Beskids rise the Tatra Moun-

The town of Elk (*left*) lies in northeastern Poland, a forested region containing numerous lakes and swamps. The landscape owes its appearance to the action of glaciers. The region is a popular vacation area.

Sandy beaches (*below*) fringe Poland's Baltic coastline. Major cities in the coastal region include Gdańsk. The Baltic moderates the climate of northern Poland. South of the Coastal Lowlands lies a belt of forest.

tains, a panorama of ancient craggy peaks, deep broad valleys and numerous cascading waterfalls. The scenery of the Tatras includes crystal-clear lakes, dark forests of pine and larch, brilliant green meadows studded with rowan trees and above all, the great peaks themselves. Rysy peak, on the Czech border, ranks as Poland's highest mountain, and attains an altitude of 8,199 feet (2,499 metres).

Climate

Poland occupies a position between the moist Atlantic-influenced climate of central Europe and the more extreme continental climate of eastern Europe. Except for the extreme southern rim of the country, Poland presents no natural barriers to the movement of air-masses, causing sharp changes of weather from place to place. Although Poland measures only about 375 miles (600 kilometres) from north to south and from east to west, its climate varies greatly from one part of the country to another. In general, the north enjoys a milder climate, while cooler conditions prevail in mountainous zones. Polish winters are either warm and wet or dry and very cold. Winter temperatures average 26°F (−3°C), but can vary widely. In summer, temperatures average 73°F (23°C) in July, but often exceed 86°F (30°C).

The high peaks of the Tatras (*left*), near Zakopane, represent part of the Western Carpathian Mountains. The range defines Poland's southern borders. The forests of this region contain abundant wildlife.

Small farming communities (*above*) dot Poland's Central Plains. Extending across the entire country, the Central Plains form Poland's main farming area. Major cities include Łódź Poznań, Wrocław and Warsaw.

Warsaw

THE SLASKO-DABROWSKI BRIDGE SPANS the Vistula, the broad river that divides Warsaw, Poland's capital. But it is more than a link between the city's eastern and western sectors. It is a bridge between the sometimes troubled realities of Warsaw's present and the glories of its past.

Visible from the bridge, in the Praga district east of the Vistula, rise huge blocks of workers' apartments. Poland's Communist rulers built these after World War II to ease a chronic housing shortage. To the west rises the pink, onion-domed central tower of the Royal Castle (*Zamek Krolewski*), dominating the "Old Town" (*Stare Miasto*). On the western side of the bridge, the visitor steps back in time.

The "Old Town"

Although the present building is in the Baroque style of the 1600s-1700s, the castle has been a royal residence since the late 1200s, when Warsaw was the capital of the dukedom of Mazovia. It now houses a magnificent collection of tapestries and paintings, including views of Warsaw painted in 1767-80 by the Venetian artist Bernardo Bellotto (1720-80).

Outside the Royal Castle, the Column of King Sigismund III, erected in 1644 to commemorate the monarch who moved Poland's capital from Kraków to Warsaw in 1596, forms the centrepiece of Zamkowy Square. Nearby is the so-called "Tin-Roofed Palace" (*Pod Blacha*), noted for the decorative panelling of its steep attic storey. Similar attics, called "Warsaw lanterns", crown many of the four- or five-storey buildings that flank the Market Square (*Rynek*). The walls of these shops and houses are bright with coloured plasterwork, and ancient wrought iron signs proclaim the goods for sale. Banks of flowers shade cafes where Varsovians (the citizens of Warsaw) relax with friends. The Rynek is one of the most beautiful town squares in Europe. However, like many monuments of old Warsaw, its medieval splendour actually dates back no more than 40 years.

The Historical Museum of Warsaw, on the northern side of the Rynek, provides an answer to this mystery. The museum demonstrates how the city's history more than justifies its Latin motto, *Contemnit procellas*, which means "defier of the storms". Three times in its 1000-year existence, invaders have sought totally to destroy Warsaw. A Swedish army devastated it in 1656, and in 1794 Varsovian resistance to Prussian occupation left much of the city in ruins. By far the worst destruction took place during World War II. Savagely bombed and shelled during the German invasion of 1939, Warsaw suffered further damage during the Jewish uprising of 1943,

when the ghetto quarter in eastern Warsaw was levelled. In 1944, the Polish Home Army rose against the Germans in Warsaw. After three months' fighting the rebellion was suppressed. The vengeful German forces then attempted to level the entire city before the arrival of Soviet troops.

Rebuilding the city

During World War II, when their country became a German province, some 85 per cent of Varsovians died or were driven from their city. In 1945, when Warsaw achieved at least limited freedom as the capital of the Soviet-dominated Polish People's Republic, returning exiles set to work to rebuild their city. Massive high-rise apartment blocks, large factories and oppressive official buildings soon dominated the skyline. The Palace of Culture and Science was a gift to the city from the Soviet dictator Stalin in 1954.

But old Warsaw, like historic Poland, still lived in the hearts of its citizens. In a remarkable labour of love, they set about rebuilding the "Old Town" in its former beauty. The remaining fragments of ancient buildings and monuments were incorporated into careful reconstructions, based on surviving house and street plans, old photographs and the paintings and sketches made by Bellotto and other artists. The task did not end until completion of the recon-

The Palace of Culture and Science (*above*), a gift from the Soviet Union, dwarfs the apartment blocks of modern Warsaw. Almost destroyed in World War II, Poland's capital today displays both old and new faces.

The Column of King Sigismund III (*right*) stands in Zamkowy Square before Warsaw's Royal Castle. Erected in 1644, the monument honours the Polish king who moved the nation's capital from Kraków to Warsaw.

Historic Warsaw (*far right*), capital of Poland, lies on both banks of the Vistula River in east-central Poland. With a population of more than 1,659,400, the city ranks as the largest in Poland, and is a major industrial centre

Warsaw's Old Market Square (*above*), or Rynek, contains some of the city's loveliest buildings, and houses elegant cafes and shops. Rebuilt after war damage, the alleys of the "Old Town" (*right*) display an old-world charm.

struction of the Royal Castle in 1981.

Today, Warsaw ranks as a great cultural centre, as well as a focus of industry and trade. As Poland's economy sheds the influence of Communism, Western consumer goods flow in increasing quantities into the stores of Marszałkowska Street. However, many citizens prefer to walk south down the broad avenue, towards the lovely gardens surrounding the restored Lazienki Palace, a Polish monarch's summer resort built on a lake island in the 1700s. Among the many monuments in the Lazienki Park is that of the composer Frédéric Chopin (1810-49), born near Warsaw. In his honour, the city hosts an international piano competition every five years.

A figure of the warrior goddess Syrena, the city's patron, commemorating the heroes of World War II, stands in front of the Wielki Theatre, one of numerous playhouses and concert halls. Songs of praise fill the rebuilt Cathedral of St. John, chief of the city's many Roman Catholic churches, which houses the tomb of Poland's great patriotic novelist Henryk Sienkiewicz (1846-1916). King Sigismund III once more stands proudly on his column at the heart of the "Old Town", protected by the rebuilt city walls and the fortress known as the *Barbican*, the symbol of Poland's unconquerable spirit.

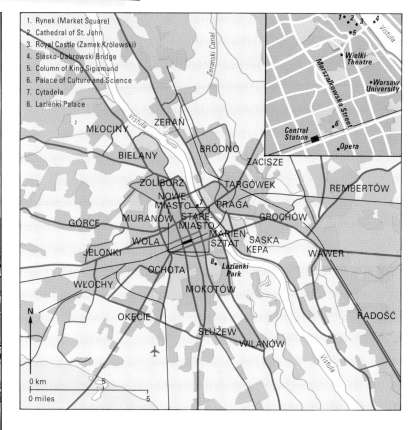

1. Rynek (Market Square)
2. Cathedral of St. John
3. Royal Castle (Zamek Królewski)
4. Slasko-Dabrowski Bridge
5. Column of King Sigismund
6. Palace of Culture and Science
7. Cytadela
8. Lazienki Palace

WASTELANDS OF SOLIDIFIED MOLTEN rock, forced from deep beneath the Earth's crust, combine with tracts of perpetual snow and ice to form Iceland's strange landscapes. The snow and ice indicate the island's location just to the south of the Arctic Circle, while the molten rock betrays the fact that Iceland straddles a break in the Earth's surface. This fault line is known as the Mid-Atlantic Ridge. It marks the point on the Earth's crust where the American continent split away from Europe and Africa. The chain of volcanoes running down the centre of the ocean provides further evidence of the geological instability which has shaped Iceland's dramatic landscape. Thus Iceland is one of the most active volcanic regions in the world, and yet can boast a glacier, Vatnajökull, which has an area equal to that of all the glaciers of Europe combined.

Formation and composition

Iceland was formed in geologically recent times, some 65 million years ago, when undersea lava flowing from a ridge on the seabed reached the surface of the sea. As recently as 1963, a new Icelandic island, Surtsey, emerged in just this way when a submarine volcano erupted off the southwest coast. Iceland's own geological foundations have still not come to rest, for the upper levels of the island are pushing past one another at varying speeds, causing frequent earthquakes.

The island contains about 200 volcanoes, the most famous of which is Mount Hekla. Viking seafarers of the Middle Ages believed that this was the mouth of hell itself. Its last major eruption took place in 1948, but it is still far from extinct, and other volcanoes continue to threaten the lives and property of Icelanders. In 1973, a volcano on the island of Heimaey showered burning embers and ash over the island's main town, forcing its evacuation.

Accompanying features of this volcanic activity are the bubbling mud-holes and the sulphur-rich, boiling water which bursts out of the ground in many springs and geysers – gushers of steam and hot water. *Geysir*, Iceland's most spectacular hot-water spouter, has given its name to all such springs, and at regular intervals sprays hot water almost 200 feet (60 metres) into the air.

Iceland's many volcanoes have formed a barren tableland, the inland plateau, that covers most of the island. This averages a height of 1,640 feet (500 metres) above sea level, with its highest point climbing to 6,592 feet (2,119 metres) at Mount Hvannadalshnúkur. Here the land surface is composed of basalt (hard volcanic rock) and lumps of volcanic lava, unearthly land-

Green fields surround a small farm (*below*) on the coastal lowlands of Iceland. Most farmers raise sheep and cattle as well as fodder for the animals in winter. Root crops, especially potatoes and turnips, are also grown.

High pastures fringe the icefield (*right*) on the edge of the inland plateau. Only about one per cent of Iceland's surface can be used for agriculture. A lava flow in the foreground gives evidence of the island's volcanic origin.

scapes that match descriptions from the tales of Viking settlers 1,000 years ago.

Elsewhere, the Ice Age has stamped Iceland's landscape with its strange markings. Vanished glaciers have carved trenches around the coasts to create the deep, narrow inlets called *fiords*. Others have gouged out holes in the land, forming numerous lakes. Glaciers still cover about 12 per cent of Iceland's area, sometimes reaching thicknesses of almost 4,000 feet (1,220 metres).

Countless rivulets of meltwater run out from the edge of the glaciers, coloured a dirty yellow by quantities of mud. Heavy rainfall or warm summer weather quickly causes rivers to become swollen on their way to the sea. Dense, massive basalt rocks form steps up to 200 feet (60 metres) in height, creating magnificent waterfalls. Iceland's rivers provide energy for several hydroelectric plants on the island.

Climate and wildlife

The warm North Atlantic Current reaches Iceland from the south, warming the coastal lowlands throughout the year and keeping the harbours free of ice. Thus Iceland enjoys a comparatively mild climate with frequent rainfall, patchy sunlight and medium-force winds. Yet its northern location makes it one of the so-called "lands of

the midnight sun". In mid-June the day lasts almost 24 hours. In December, of course, it is dark for a similar length of time.

Little vegetation can take root in the unquiet landscapes that make up most of Iceland's interior. The porous volcanic surface of the inland plateau does not encourage plant growth. Only hardy species such as lichen, moss, heather and various grasses manage to form a meagre covering. The coastal areas, by contrast, are relatively fertile, and some farmers can raise more than one crop of hay from their land, providing food for hardy Icelandic ponies, as well as for herds of cattle and sheep. Lamb plays a large part in most Icelanders' diet, and a special Icelandic delicacy is boiled sheep's head.

The only animal native to Iceland is the Arctic fox, but the island is home to some 240 species of migrant birds, including swallows, whooper swans and puffins, attracted by its lush coastal meadows and plankton-rich waters. Fish species include cod, haddock, halibut, flounder and herring. Several varieties of whale and seal benefit from this abundance. Inland, the lakes and rivers contain plentiful stocks of trout and salmon, but this fisherman's paradise is marred to some extent by huge colonies of midges, particularly on Lake Mývatn, the "lake of midges".

Black ash (*left*) from a volcano on Heimaey blots out the island's only town in an eruption of 1989. After a silence of more than 5,000 years, the volcano first erupted in 1973, driving away the town's inhabitants with a lava flow that enlarged the island by almost one square mile (2.6 square kilometres), and altered the harbour's shape. About 5,000 people were evacuated, only for the process to be repeated 16 years later with another volcanic eruption.

Svartsengi geothermal power station (*below left*) taps energy from deep inside the Earth's crust. The waters of its swimming pool contain dissolved minerals thought to have health-giving properties.

Fish are processed at a factory near Reykjavik (*below*). Fishing plays a central role in Iceland's economy. About a fifth of the workforce are involved in the industry, either catching, salting or freezing fish for export.

Iceland Today

AN ISLAND IN THE FAR NORTH ATLANTIC, on the edge of the Arctic Circle, Iceland lies between Greenland to the west and Norway to the east. A break in the Earth's crust (an extension of the Mid-Atlantic Ridge) runs through the island, making it vulnerable to earthquakes and volcanoes. Iceland has been called "The Land of Frost and Fire" because of its strange landscape, where ice fields and glaciers share space with active volcanoes, hot mineral-laden springs and spouting geysers. Its people trace their origin to the fierce Scandinavian seafarers known as Vikings, but can claim to have set up the world's first democratic assembly, the *Althing*, in AD 930.

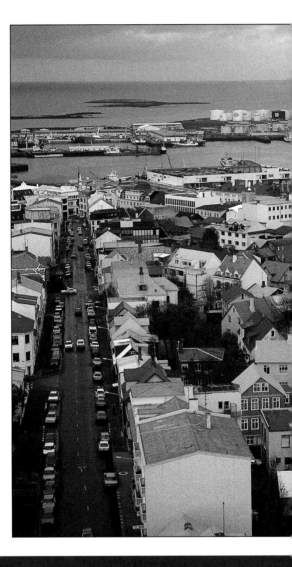

The people

Despite their ancestry, modern Icelanders have the reputation of being a peace-loving and friendly people. Their language, Icelandic, is closely related to the Viking tongue of Old Norse, and has hardly changed for centuries. Iceland's great age of literature, when the poet Snorri Sturluson wrote down Icelandic family histories and tales of gods and heroes, dates back to the 1200s. Yet Icelanders today can read the ancient sagas and *eddas* (poems) with ease. In terms of science, technology and living standards, Icelanders are firmly in the present; but they retain traces of an earlier world. For instance, they have no fixed surnames or family names, but take on a second name simply by adding *-son* (son) or *-dóttir* (daughter) to their father's first name.

Apart from earlier communities of Irish monks, Iceland's first settlers arrived with the Norwegian adventurer Ingólfur Arna-

FACT BOX

THE COUNTRY
Official name: Republic of Iceland
Capital: Reykjavík
Land regions: Inland plateau with volcanoes; lowlands on coasts
Land area: 39,800 sq mi (103,000 km²)
Climate: Cool temperate oceanic; influenced by Gulf Stream. Mild summers, cool winters
Main rivers: Thjórsá, Jökulsá á Fjöllum, Skjálfandafljót, Hvitá
Highest elevation: Hvannadalshnúkur 6,952 ft (2,119 m)
Lowest elevation: Sea level along the coast

THE GOVERNMENT
Form of Government: Parliamentary republic

Head of State: President
Head of Government: Prime Minister
Administrative areas: Provinces, districts and municipalities
Legislature: Parliament (Althing): upper chamber (21 members) and lower chamber (42 members). 4-year terms
Judiciary: Supreme Court, Urban and rural district courts
Armed forces: No forces of its own

THE PEOPLE
Population (1990): 255,000
Language: Icelandic
Religion: Protestant (Evangelical Lutheran): 97%

THE ECONOMY
Currency: Krona
Gross Domestic Product per person (1990): US$22,595
Annual Growth Rate (1985-90): 2.4%
Trade balance in US$ (1989): US$12 mill
Goods imported: Mineral oil, machinery, vehicles, fruit and vegetables, raw materials
Goods exported: Fish, fish products
Trading partners: USA, Germany, former Soviet Union,
Communications: Number of daily newspapers (1987): 6 Circulation (1987): 100,000

son in about 870. But the country lost its independence to Norway in 1262, and came under Danish control in 1380, when Denmark united with Norway. Icelanders suffered neglect and repression at the hands of their Danish rulers, especially during period of famine in the late 1700s. They also suffered from severe natural disasters, including volcanic eruptions in the 1700s that destroyed huge areas of farmland.

In the 1800s, Iceland began to gain some independence from Denmark. The Althing was reopened in 1843, and by 1874 Iceland controlled its own economy. It was recognized as a self-governing unit in 1918, although it remained within the kingdom of Denmark. During World War II, Denmark was occupied by Germany, while the Allies kept control of Iceland. The modern Republic of Iceland was proclaimed on June 17, 1944, at the historic site of Thingvellir, where the Althing had been established just over 1,000 years before.

Since independence, power has usually been shared between different political parties forming coalition governments. Iceland has a president as head of state, but the prime minister runs the government. In June 1980, Vigdís Finnbogadóttir was elected president, thus becoming the first woman to be elected head of state.

Population and economy

Iceland is the most sparsely populated country in Europe, with less than six persons per square mile (two per square kilometre). About 90 per cent of the people live close to the coast, which the North Atlantic Current keeps comparatively warm, and nearly 40 per cent live in or near the capital, Reykjavík. Most Icelanders enjoy a high standard of living, but life on this faraway island is expensive, and a huge range of products needs to be imported from Europe and the USA.

Fishing and fish-processing are by far the most important of Iceland's industries, providing employment for 13 per cent of the population, and accounting for some 70 per cent of its exports. But in the late 1980s, catches of fish fell, and a worldwide ban on the hunting of endangered whale species damaged Iceland's economy. The country has tried to expand its range of manufactured products, and a clever use of natural hot springs to heat greenhouses has reduced imports of fresh fruit and vegetables. But Iceland's reliance on fish threatens its high standard of living. Tourism could have great potential; in 1990 more than 130,000 tourists visited the island, fascinated by its contrasts of ice and fire. It may turn out that Iceland's greatest asset will be found in its geology. There are also plans to export an abundance of geothermally generated electricity, though laying power cables will be extremely expensive.

Iceland's capital, Reykjavík (*left*), ranks as the nation's largest city and its trading centre. Its facilities include two theatres, a university and a symphony orchestra. About one-third of all Icelandic people live in the capital.

Iceland (*below*), an island of volcanic origin, lies in the North Atlantic Ocean just south of the Arctic Circle. A number of large ice sheets cover some of the surface of the interior, while almost all of the settlements cling to the coasts.

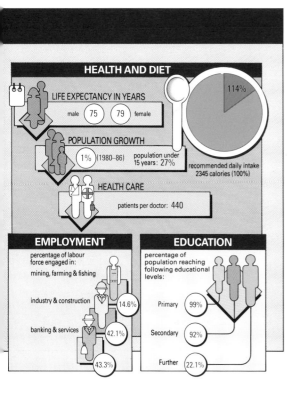

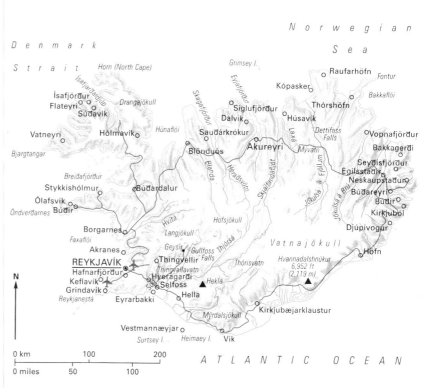

FINLAND

Finland, called *Suomi* in the Finnish language, extends northwards from the Baltic Sea into the Arctic Circle. It is a country noted for the beauty of its **lakes, islands and forests** (*right*). Scattered over its land area are some 60,000 lakes, in which lie more than 30,000 islands. Many more thousands of islands lie in the Gulf of Bothnia and Gulf of Finland, off in the country's rocky western and southern Baltic coasts. Dense forests of pine, spruce and birch cover nearly two-thirds of the land.

About one-third of the country, including part of the great wilderness of Lapland, lies within the Arctic Circle, where the short summer season consists of some 70 days of almost continual daylight. On winter nights, by contrast, it is the *aurora borealis* ("northern lights") that colour the skies in eerie pastel shades.

The Finnish people differ from the other peoples of northern and eastern Europe, the Scandinavians and Slavs, in both language and culture. For many centuries, Finland was dominated by its powerful neighbours, Sweden to the west and Russia to the east, but the Finns have always proudly preserved their national identity. Their contribution to the world's culture ranges from the poetry of the *Kalevala* ("land of heroes"), the Finnish national epic, to the music of the composer Jean Sibelius (1865-1957). Today the Finns are especially noted for the skills of Finnish designers and architects, among whom the architects Eliel Saarinen (1873-1950) and Alvar Aalto (1898-1976) are particularly well known. The Finns also invented the sauna bath, an enjoyable dry-heat bath that cleanses and relaxes, and is often followed by a cold plunge.

People from the east

The Lapps, who now constitute a small minority of the population, are Finland's earliest known inhabitants. The Finnish people, who probably came from an area between the Volga River and the Ural Mountains in Russia, began to settle in the Baltic region before 1000 BC. By the early Christian era they had forced the nomadic Lapps to retreat to the far north.

From around AD 1000, both Sweden and Russia tried to bring Finland under their rule. By around 1200, Sweden was the dominant power, although Finns retained equal rights with the many Swedish settlers. Swedish became the official language and Catholicism the official religion. In the 1500s, when Finland was a Swedish duchy, the country followed Sweden in adopting the Lutheran (Protestant) religion.

Russia, fearing Swedish expansion, sought to dominate the strategically important territory on its western border. In the

1500s-1700s it fought a series of wars with Sweden for possession of Finland. In the Great Northern War (1700-21), and later during the 1700s, Russia occupied all Finland but failed to hold it. In 1809, however, Russia invaded and conquered the country, and Tsar Alexander I (1777-1825) was proclaimed ruler of the autonomous (self-governing) Grand Duchy of Finland.

An independent nation

Finnish nationalism, which had survived centuries of Swedish domination, was made even stronger by Tsarist attempts to "Russianize" the country. In 1905, a nationwide protest, when all Finns refused to work for six days, forced Tsar Nicholas II (reigned 1894-1917) to abandon his policy of destroying Finnish independence. When the Bolshevik (Communist) revolution of 1917 deposed the Tsar, Finland declared its independence, which was recognized by the Bolsheviks. However, a Finnish civil war followed between the socialist Red Guard, aided by the new Russian regime, and the antisocialist White Guard, assisted by German troops. The White Guard triumphed and its leader, Carl Gustaf Mannerheim (1867-1951), briefly ruled as Regent, retiring when a republican constitution was adopted in 1919.

In 1921, a quarrel between Finland and Sweden over possession of the Åland Islands was settled in Finland's favour by the League of Nations. But Russia maintained its claim to the eastern Finnish region of Karelia. In November 1939, Soviet troops invaded Finland. After heroic resistance, led by Mannerheim, the Finns were forced to admit defeat in the 15-week long "Winter War". A peace treaty, in March 1940, ceded southern Karelia (about 10 per cent of Finland's total land area) to the Soviet Union. In 1941, hoping to regain the territory, Finland assisted Germany's attack on the USSR. Karelia was briefly retaken, but in 1944 a Soviet counteroffensive drove out the Finns and Germans, who laid waste much of the territory as they withdrew.

Finland's losses in World War II were heavy. Some 150,000 Finns were killed or badly wounded; southern Karelia was permanently lost; and Finland had to make heavy reparations (payment for war damage) to the USSR. The postwar period, however, saw the improvement of relations with the USSR, which now had the territory it desired. By avoiding conflict with Soviet interests, Finland was able to ensure that its independence was no longer threatened by its powerful neighbour. At the same time, it was able to strengthen its social and economic links with the Scandinavian countries and the nations of the European Community.

Finland Today

THE REPUBLIC OF FINLAND PROCLAIMED its independence from Russia in July 1917. In July 1919, after a period of civil war, it adopted a democratic constitution, which remains largely unchanged. This gives supreme executive power to the president, who acts as the head of state and is elected for a six-year term by the direct vote of all citizens over the age of 18. Until 1988 the president was chosen by the members of an Electoral College. The Electoral College may still be convened if no presidential candidate gains an overall majority.

A democratic country, where all citizens enjoy freedom of speech and equal rights, Finland has a constitution that allows the president unusually wide powers. Subject to the law of the land, he may issue any orders he believes to be necessary. He is the supreme authority on foreign relations and the armed forces, and has the power to veto (reject) decisions made by the parliament. But the president's veto may be overruled if parliament again votes for the decision.

The great powers of the presidency stem from Finland's need for a strong spokesman in its dealings with the Soviet Union, dating back to the foundation of the republic. This was particularly important immediately after World War II, during which Finland twice fought the Soviet Union. In 1948, Juho Paasikivi (1870-1956), president from 1946 to 1956, was able to conclude the Finno-Soviet Pact of Friendship, Cooperation and Mutual Assistance (renewed in 1955, 1970 and 1983). This firmly established Finland's neutral but friendly relationship with its powerful eastern neighbour. Paasikivi's neutralist policies were continued by Urho

Kekkonen (1900-86), president during the period 1956-81, and Mauno Koivisto (b.1923), president since 1982.

Government

Finland's single house of parliament, the *Eduskunta*, has 200 members, elected by the votes of all citizens, but the president may dissolve the Eduskunta and call for new elections at any time. The head of government, the prime minister, is chosen by the president, who must also approve the prime minister's choice of cabinet members to head government departments.

Parliamentary elections are based on a system of proportional representation (PR). This means that the number of seats a political party gains in the Eduskunta depends upon its share of the total votes cast. In Finland, as in other countries where the PR system is used, it is often difficult for any single party to establish an overall majority. Thus Finland has almost always been governed by a coalition, in which a number of parties join together to form a government. Although this means that many different political points of view are represented in the legislature, it leads also to frequent political crises and new elections when the coalition parties cannot agree.

Finland is divided into 12 provinces for the purposes of local administration. For each province the president appoints a governor who exercises his powers through local officials. The provinces are further subdivided into some 500 sub-units, covering cities, towns and country districts. The citizens of each sub-unit elect a local council to govern their area. The councils may

FACT BOX

THE COUNTRY
Official name: Republic of Finland
Capital: Helsinki (Swedish: Helsingfors)
Land regions: Coastal Lowlands, Lake District in centre, Upland District in north; Coastal Islands
Land area: 130,559 sq mi (338,145 km²)
Climate: Short, warm summers, cold winters (lasting about 6 months in north, but less harsh in S/SW). Little rainfall; most rain during summer months
Main rivers: Kemijoki, Ounasjoki, Muonio
Highest elevation: Mount Haltia 4,344 ft (1,324 m)
Lowest elevation: Sea level along the coast

THE GOVERNMENT
Form of Government: Parliamentary republic
Head of State: President
Head of Government: Prime Minister
Administrative areas: 12 provinces, divided into communes. Åland Islands (special status)
Legislature: Parliament (Eduskunta) with 200 members, elected to 4-year terms
Judiciary: Supreme Court, Supreme Administrative Court, regional appeals courts, district courts
Armed forces: Total strength: 31,000. Men must serve between 8-11 months after age 17

THE PEOPLE
Population (1990): 4,975,000
Language: Finnish, Swedish (both official); Lapps speak own language
Religion: Protestant (Evangelical Lutheran): about 95%; Orthodox

THE ECONOMY
Currency: Markka
Gross Domestic Product per person (1990): US$27,586
Annual Growth Rate (1985-90): 3.5%
Trade balance in US$ (1990): $308 mill
Goods imported: Mineral oil, fuel, machinery, chemical products, fruits, vegetables, industrial raw materials,

A statue (*left*) of Finnish soldier and statesman Marshal Mannerheim (1867-1951) stands guard before Helsinki's elegant Parliament Building. Mannerheim defended Finland during World War II, serving as president 1944-6.

Finland (*below*), the "land of 1,000 lakes", lies within two arms of the Baltic Sea. Most Finns live in the southern part of the country, where the climate is relatively mild. Northernmost Finland lies within the Arctic Circle.

collect their own taxes to maintain public services and carry out local projects.

Minorities

The Åland Islands, off the southwest coast, are mainly inhabited by people of Swedish descent, and came under Finnish rule in 1921. They are partly self-governing, with a parliament thay may pass laws on all matters concerning the islands' internal affairs. Swedish is recognized as an official language, along with Finnish, although only about five per cent of Finland's population is of Swedish ancestry.

In addition to its Swedish minority, Finland includes a number of Lapps in the north and about 6,000 Gypsies.

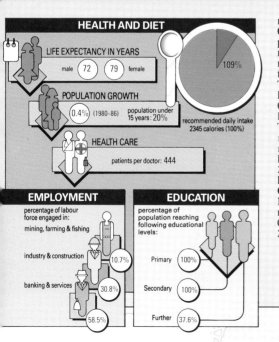

manufactured goods
Goods exported: Paper, pulp, wood products, metal products, machinery, ships, textiles
Trading partners: Russia, Sweden, Germany, Great Britain, France, USA
Transport: Length of railways (1985): 5,551 mi (8,934 km)
Passenger miles (1985): 2,003 mill (3,224 mill km)
Communications: Number of daily newspapers (1988): 66
Circulation (1988): 2,665,000

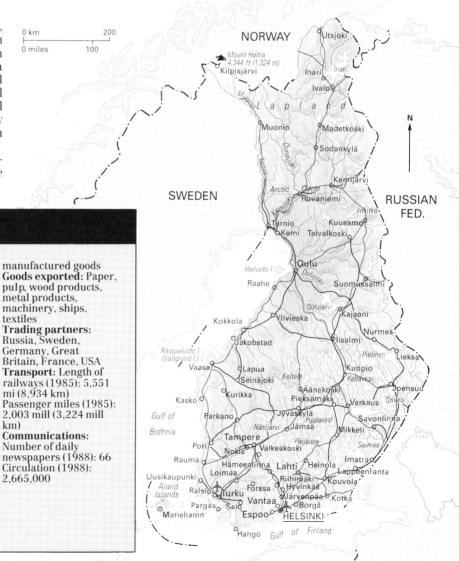

A BEAUTIFUL AND LARGELY UNSPOILT country, Finland has landscapes characterized by huge tracts of forest and countless lakes. The country extends some 640 miles (1,030 kilometres) from deep within the Arctic Circle in the north, to the Baltic Sea in the south. Much of Finland consists of a low-lying plateau, with an average height above sea level of only 400-600 feet (120-180 metres). It includes a large number of islands, some lying offshore and others within many of its numerous lakes.

Finland's landscapes were formed by the effects of glaciation, or ice action. For more than one million years, a thick layer of ice covered the land. As the glaciers advanced, they ground down the rocks, digging out what are now shallow lake basins and pushing up great mounds of debris. The melting of the ice layer, completed less than 10,000 years ago, left these ridges of debris, called terminal moraines, to mark its gradual retreat.

Major land regions

The country's coastline runs for 1,462 miles (2,353 kilometres) along two arms of the Baltic, the Gulf of Bothnia to the west and the Gulf of Finland to the south. The coasts are generally rocky and low-lying and are broken by many small bays. For much of the winter the coastal waters are frozen, and ice-breaking ships must be deployed to keep open harbours. Several thousand islands lie off the coasts. The most important of these is the Åland group, which lie off the southwest coast and are home to a predominantly Swedish-speaking population, assigned to Finland by the League of Nations in 1921. Åland and some other islands are popular holiday resorts; others are the homes of communities of fisherfolk; many more remain barren and uninhabited.

The Coastal Lowlands of southern Finland rank as the country's most densely settled area. Most town-dwelling Finns, who make up some 68 per cent of the population, live in the cities of the south, notably Helsinki (the capital), Tampere, Turku, Lahti and Pori. The best farmland is also found in this region, where the deepest, richest soil occurs in shallow, glacially-formed depressions known as kettleholes.

Two parallel ridges of the great terminal moraine, called Salpausselka, run in a southwest-northeast curve from the Hango peninsula across the country to the north of Lahti. These form the southern boundary of the Lake District. About half of this beautiful region is covered by water. Thousands of lakes lie among dense forests, where the brown bear, wolf and lynx are among the species protected in nature reserves. Many of the lakes are divided by *eskers*, long ridges of glacially deposited gravel. The

A lake near Kuopio (*right*) captures the magical quality of central Finland's landscape, with its interplay of lakes, islands, inlets and natural coniferous forest. Water covers almost half of the Lake District region.

A Lapp from northern Finland (*above*) takes her child on an outing in a purpose-built baby buggy with sled runners for wheels.

The Åland Islands (*right*) only became part of Finland in 1921. Most islanders speak Swedish, enjoy full self-government, and object to being called Finns. Most work as fisherfolk, but tourism is becoming important.

Low hills rise above the forests of Finland's Upland District (*top right*), gradually yielding to the treeless tundra of the north. The region is home to many animals not seen in the wild elsewhere, especially elks.

A trapper's hut (*bottom right*) bears the marks of modern technology with its motorized sled. Few people live in the inhospitable north of Finland, the majority inhabiting the warmer Coastal Lowlands of the south.

largest body of water, Lake Saimaa, measures 680 square miles (1,760 square kilometres). Frequent steamers ply routes between the towns lying along the Saimaa Lake System, which stretches for 185 miles (298 kilometres). A network of channels and canals links one lake to another and leads at last (through territory belonging to the Russian Federation) to the Gulf of Finland and to St Petersburg.

Marsh and mountain

North of the Lake District lie the hills and marshlands of the Upland District. The marshes are the habitat of Finland's largest animal, the elk. These magnificent animals have been reduced in number in the past by hunting and forestry, but today they are carefully protected, and may number as many as 120,000. In the far north, marsh and woodland give way to the barren plain of the Arctic tundra, where Lapp herdsmen tend semi-domesticated reindeer.

Finland's only mountains are found in the extreme northwest, on the Norwegian border, where Haltia rises to 4,344 feet (1,324 metres). Finland's longest river, Kemijoki, on which there are important hydroelectric projects and rich salmon fisheries, rises near the Russian border and flows generally southwest for some 340 miles (547 kilometres) through the Upland District to the Gulf of Bothnia.

Climate

Despite its northerly position, Finland as a whole enjoys a surprisingly mild climate. This is largely due to the warm Gulf Stream current that reaches as far as the west coast of Norway. Winters are long, of course, and often harsh, with icebreakers working continuously to keep the ports open for commercial and passenger traffic. But most Finns welcome the arrival of the snow, for it gives them a chance to indulge their favourite recreations of ice-skating, ski-jumping and cross-country skiing. Northern Finland lies within the Arctic Circle, and therefore experiences periods of continuous daylight during the summer. In the far north of the country, this period last up to two months, with an equivalent period of complete darkness during the winter.

The Finnish sauna

The dry-heat bath known as the sauna (pronounced *sow-na*) has become a familiar, if expensive, item in many Western households. But in Finland, where it originated more than 1,000 years ago, it is a national institution. Bathers absorb the fierce warmth from oven-heated stones, made even hotter when water is thrown on them. They also slap their bodies with birch twigs (*vihta*) to increase circulation. The traditional climax involves a roll in the snow outside.

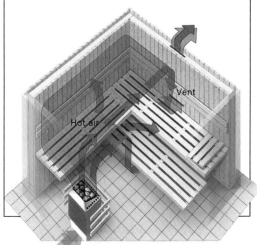

Vent

Hot air

Cold air

SWEDEN

One of the largest countries in Europe – only Russia, France, and Spain are larger – Sweden is also one of the most thinly populated. More than half of the country is covered by forests, and about 14 per cent lies inside the Arctic Circle. Sweden's northern wilderness is mainly populated by a nomadic people called Lapps, with a language and lifestyle very different from that of the Swedes.

Sweden occupies more than half of the Scandinavian peninsula, with a long coastline, numerous beautiful lakes such as **Lake Kallsjön** (*right*), and thousands of islands. The Swedish people speak a language similar to that of their Scandinavian relatives, the Norwegians and the Danes. In the Middle Ages, Scandinavian seafaring people, known as Vikings, travelled far and wide. Those from modern Norway and Denmark ventured west and southwest, settling in the British Isles, northern France, Iceland and the Faeroes. Swedish Vikings sailed eastwards across the Baltic, reaching the Black Sea by way of the Volga and Dnepr rivers, and founding the city of Kiev in AD 900. Tall, blond and blue-eyed, many Swedes still display the physical characteristics of their adventurous ancestors. Yet modern Sweden is a prosperous, liberal and peace-loving country that contrasts strongly with its warlike and piratical past.

The standard of living enjoyed by most Swedes is one of the world's highest. This is partly due to the relatively small population and partly to the skill with which they have developed their natural resources. A broad welfare system offers free education, handsome pensions, and housing assistance, providing security and well-being for all. However, a centre-right government elected in 1991 is reducing benefits, and the high taxes needed to pay for them.

History

Sweden's name derives from the Svear people, who were known to the Romans 2,000 years ago. The Svear conquered the North German tribe of the Gauts, who lived around Lake Vänern in the southern part of the peninsula, and seized the islands of Gotland and Öland. In the 800s their descendants began to range southeast across the Baltic, and in the next centuries penetrated as far as the Volga and Dnepr rivers. Living partly by trade and partly by looting, these Viking warriors sailed their terrifying longships far to the south, crossing the Black Sea to Constantinople, the capital of the Byzantine empire, where they provided men for the Byzantine emperor's hand-picked bodyguard (the Varangian Guard).

By the 1000s, the Swedes controlled much of what is now Sweden. Christianity,

which had been introduced two centuries earlier by Saint Anskar, became established under King Olof Skotkonung, and strongly influenced the development of society. The clergy abolished slavery, founded schools, encouraged the arts, and set up a legal system. Missionaries went out to Finland, to be followed by soldiers, and Finland became Swedish territory in 1249.

During the late Middle Ages, Sweden's economy was dependent on the group of powerful commercial cities of north Europe called the Hanseatic League. In 1388, however, wishing to shake off the power of the League, a group of nobles chose Margrete, queen of Norway and Denmark, to be their queen as well. This union of Scandinavian countries lasted for more than a century.

Despite the union, however, relations were often strained between the three Scandinavian countries, and in 1523 the Swedish nobleman Gustavus Vasa defeated the Danes and took Sweden out of the union. As King Gustavus I, he centralized the country's government, developed trade and industry, modernized the armed forces, and encouraged the Lutheran form of Christianity among his people. Many historians consider that Gustavus I laid the foundations of the present-day Swedish state.

The modern period

Over the next two centuries, Sweden gained territories in many areas of north Europe, but defeat came in 1709, when Russian troops under Peter the Great defeated Swedish forces at Poltava. In 1720, the Swedish parliament took over many of the monarch's powers, and for 50 years the country enjoyed a period of parliamentary government known as the Age of Liberty. In the early 1800s, Sweden was caught up in the war against the French leader Napoleon I and his allies, gaining Norway from Denmark, but losing Finland to Russia. This marked an end to Sweden's involvement in military affairs, and the country has been neutral ever since. An new constitution was established in 1809, and the new king, Bernadotte, a former general in Napoleon's army, was elected in 1818. Sweden's present royal family descends from him.

The 1800s brought economic growth and also social problems; nearly half a million people emigrated between 1867-86, most to the United States. But manufacturing and forestry industries expanded, and by 1900 Sweden was regarded as an important industrial nation. After Norway achieved independence in 1905, Sweden began to develop the concern for social welfare that has been such a feature of the country for so long, and the 1930s saw the introduction of important social measures that were later expanded and refined.

Sweden Today

FOR MANY YEARS SWEDEN APPEARED not only as one of the most prosperous but also as one of the most progressive societies in the world. First proposed by a Social Democratic government in 1932, the Swedish economic system known as the "middle way" did not discourage private enterprise, but sought to direct its profits towards the creation of a society where equality was the main object. After World War II, this policy led to many reforms to "level out social advantage and disadvantage". As a result, high taxes paid for an extensive welfare system that included housing, education, medical care and old-age provision. Events in the 1980s suggested that the burden of taxation was proving too heavy for some people. Change came in 1991, with the election of a centre-right coalition, set to reduce taxes and cut government spending.

Government

Sweden has a democratic parliamentary system, with a constitutional monarch to represent the country at home and abroad. Parliament, called the *Riksdag*, rules the country, with executive power in the hands of the majority party or group of parties, led by a prime minister and his or her cabinet. A system of proportional representation, whereby the number of seats held by each party reflects the number of votes it has gained, ensures that minorities have some say in decision-making.

Sweden's concern for fairness is seen in the office of the ombudsman, an official appointed to investigate complaints by private citizens against governmental or even military decisions. This office has existed in Sweden since 1809, and the system has been adopted in a modified form by many other countries.

In foreign affairs, Sweden has followed a policy of non-involvement for more than 150 years (although in 1991 it applied for entry to the European Community). Sweden's traditional non-aligned position is supported by a strong and independent national defence system based on a modern arms industry and 10 months' military service for males over 18 (although conscientious objectors may be assigned to community rather than military activities). But Sweden's neutrality does not prevent it from taking a firm line on many issues, and Swedish statesmen have played an important part in influencing world opinion. Sweden traditionally extends its concern for its own citizens to include disadvantaged people elsewhere. The country provides considerable development aid to the Third World, and also acts as a sanctuary for refugees from many parts of the world.

Education in Sweden is free and compulsory from ages 7-16. There are six universities, the oldest of which, Uppsala, was founded in 1477. Standards of education are high, with literature, history and the arts playing an important part in many Swedes' adult interests. Students often exchange visits with their contemporaries in Europe and the United States, and many Swedes speak English or German fluently.

About 85 per cent of Swedes live in cities, where the majority enjoy a lifestyle that would be considered luxurious in other parts of the world. Most families own at least one car, and many also possess a

FACT BOX

THE COUNTRY
Official name:
Kingdom of Sweden
Capital:
Stockholm
Land regions: Kölen Mountain Range (in north), Inner Northland, Swedish Lowland in centre/south, South Swedish Highland. Islands off the coast
Land area: 173,649 sq mi (449,750 km²)
Climate: Generally mild summers. Winters are mild in south and long and cold in north
Main rivers: Torne, Lule, Vindel, Ume, Dal
Highest elevation: Mount Kebnekaise 6,926 ft (2,111 m)
Lowest elevation: Sea level along the coast

THE GOVERNMENT
Form of Government: Constitutional monarchy
Head of State: King
Head of Government: Prime Minister
Administrative areas: 24 counties
Legislature: Parliament (Riksdag) with 349 members, elected to 3-year terms
Judiciary: Supreme Court, Courts of Appeal, regional and district courts
Armed forces: Total strength: 59,350 men. Men must serve between 7-15 months after age 18

THE PEOPLE
Population (1990): 8,590,000

Language: Swedish. Finnish and Lapp minorities speak own language
Religion: Protestant (Evangelical Lutheran): 95%

THE ECONOMY
Currency: Krona
Gross Domestic Product per person (1990): US$ 26,356
Annual Growth Rate (1985-90): 2.1%
Trade balance in US$ (1989): $2,719 mill
Goods imported: Mineral oil, coal, vehicles, food, cattle
Good exported: Machinery, cars, chemicals, wood pulp, paper and other wood products, iron ore and steel

cabin in the country or by the sea which they visit at weekends. Both the road and the railway networks are good, and road transport vehicles carry almost as many goods as do the railways.

There are excellent facilities for skiing, ice hockey, skating and track athletics, while the popularity of tennis is evidenced by Sweden's success on the international stage. Cross-country skiing and sailing in small boats are enjoyed by most Swedes, and festivals are celebrated enthusiastically, particularly at mid-summer. About 95 per cent of the population belong to the state Evangelical Lutheran church, but church-going tends to be widespread only on special occasions.

HEALTH AND DIET

LIFE EXPECTANCY IN YEARS

male 74   80 female

112%

recommended daily intake 2345 calories (100%)

POPULATION GROWTH

0.2% (1980–86)   population under 15 years: 18%

HEALTH CARE

patients per doctor: 387

EMPLOYMENT

percentage of labour force engaged in:

mining, farming & fishing   4.1%

industry & construction   29.2%

banking & services   66.7%

EDUCATION

percentage of population reaching following educational levels:

Primary   100%

Secondary   91%

Further   31.2%

Trading partners: Germany, Great Britain, Norway, Denmark, USA, Finland, France, Benelux countries, OPEC countries
Transport: Length of railways (1986): 7,279 mi (11,715 km) Passenger miles (1986): 3.95 bill (6.36 bill km)
Communications: Number of daily newspapers (1988): 107 Circulation (1988): 4,387,000

Riddarholmen (Nobles' Island) (*above left*), in the foreground of this picture of Stockholm, contains ancient buildings that reflect Sweden's historic past, especially the square of the High Court (Svea Hovrätt).

Sweden (*above*) ranks as one of the largest and least crowded countries in Europe. Skilful use of natural resources has brought wealth, equitably distributed to raise living standards for all levels of the population.

A PARADISE FOR NATURE-LOVERS, Sweden is renowned for the spectacular beauty of its glistening lakes, its snow-capped mountains, its rushing rivers and its rocky offshore islands. The Swedish people greatly enjoy outdoor activities, and take advantage of these features to camp on islands or by lakes, or to go cross-country skiing. The quantities of wildlife, including moose, lynx, deer and fox, have traditionally encouraged hunting as a recreation, while an abundance of salmon, trout and pike in the rivers provides anglers with a chance to exercise their skills.

North and central Sweden

The last Ice Age was largely responsible for the landscapes of this beautiful country, which some geographers divide into four land regions. In the northwest, bordering Norway, the Mountain Range land region marks the remains of ancient rocks that have been worn away by ice action. Here the Kölen Mountains reach a height of some 6,600 feet (2,000 metres), and are covered in snow and ice for much of the year. This area includes many glaciers and the large Sulitelma icefield. Much of the region lies above the Arctic Circle, where cold conditions prevent tree growth at heights above 1,600 feet (488 metres). The Mountain Range lies in the western part of Sweden's largest district, Lapland, home to an ethnically distinct people called the Lapps, or *Sami*. The Lapps are popularly known as the nomadic people who follow their domesticated herds of reindeer. However, by the early 1990s there were only about 2,700 Lapps actively involved with reindeer in Swedish Lapland, out of a total of about 17,000. Most Lapps today live by fishing or farming, or work in cities.

East and south of the Mountain Range lies the Inner Northland region, which slopes gently eastward towards the Gulf of Bothnia. The northern part of this area, within the Arctic Circle, consists mainly of high heathland and treeless tundra, a landscape that would seem to be monotonous yet has a strange magic of its own. The region is thinly populated, but attracts many tourists. Bear, lynx and wolverine are found in some places, especially in the Muddus National Park. Endless forests of fir and spruce cover the Inner Northland region, crossed by numerous fast-flowing rivers, which provide energy for hydroelectric schemes. Evidence of Sweden's iron-working industry can be seen in many places.

The evergreen forests give way to leaf-shedding hardwoods in the more southerly district of Dalarna, centred on Lake Siljan. In this area some of Sweden's most colourful midsummer celebrations take place, giving the area its nickname of the "Folklore District". Within the lake, the island of Sollerön marks a place where the so-called "church boats", oared vessels that ferry villagers to lakeside churches, are still built from local wood. These boats are of great interest to archaeologists, for their construction closely follows that of the Viking vessels which carried their warlike crews over vast distances in the Middle Ages.

Southern Sweden

Most of Sweden's population is found in the Swedish Lowland, which occupies the southern third of the country. The region includes the major cities of Stockholm, Göteborg and Malmö, and contains most of the country's fertile land. Sweden's extensive forests ensure that only about seven per cent of the total land area is cultivated, but about 40 per cent of the Swedish Lowland consists of farms.

Many lakes lie in this area, relics of the Ice Age, including Lake Vänern, the largest in western Europe. Another big lake, Mälaren, was a bay open to the sea until as recently as AD 1200, when it was enclosed by land still rising as a result of the melting of ice masses. The Göta Canal, one of the engineering wonders of the world when it was built in the early 1800s, links Göteborg in the west to Stockholm in the east by way of the lakes. The three-day boat trip between

The craggy shoreline of Gotland (*left*), with its free-standing limestone pillars (*raukar*) brings to mind its historic past as a stronghold for Viking seafarers. Gotland ranks as the largest of Sweden's many islands.

More than 1,312ft	More than 400m
656-1,312ft	200-400m
Less than 656ft	Less than 200m

Bohuslän (*right*), the most westerly of Sweden's provinces, stretches from Göteborg north to the Norwegian border. Its coastline of granite rocks has been worn smooth over thousands of years by wind and water.

Lake Siljan (*left*), lies at the centre of Dalarna province in Central Sweden. A storehouse of old Swedish folk traditions, the region's forested uplands and lush valleys attract many tourists in the summer.

Birch forests (*below*) provide a beautiful setting for a country cottage (*stugor*) near Uppsala, northwest of Stockholm. Nearly 20% of Swedish households own a *stugor* where they can enjoy unspoilt countryside.

Sweden's land area (*left*) includes a long coastline with many offshore islands. Treeless tundra and dense forests dominate the cold northern regions, homeland of the Lapp people. Most Swedes live in the warmer south.

Fertile plains characterize the so-called Swedish Lowland (*above*) in the more southerly part of the country. The region includes many lakes, and also contains Sweden's major cities and the bulk of its population.

the two cities counts as one of the high points in any visit to Sweden.

The Götaland Plateau, also known as the South Swedish Highland, lies inland in the southern tip of the country. It has poor soil, a small population, numerous swamps and lakes, and extensive forests.

Climate and wildlife

Sweden's climate varies greatly between the Arctic north of the country and the temperate south. Warm summers and mild winters are frequent in the south, with prevailing winds from the Atlantic Ocean. Further north, summers remain pleasant but winters become much colder. In the far north of the country, eastern winds may sharply lower the daytime temperature, and snow may cover the ground for six months of the year. Above the Arctic Circle, the "midnight sun" remains continuously above the horizon for a full 24-hour period. In winter, of course, it does not rise above the horizon for an equivalent period.

Mountain hares, foxes, red squirrels, weasels and elks are found in many parts of Sweden. Red deer are common in the south, and waterfowl haunt the huge lakes. There are many birds of prey, as well as owls, ptarmigans, grouse and woodcock. Reptiles, by contrast, are comparatively rare, and the only poisonous snake is the viper.

Stockholm

SWEDEN'S CAPITAL CITY OF STOCKHOLM has been called "the city that floats on water", for it occupies a series of islands and peninsulas connecting Lake Mälaren and the Baltic Sea. To the east of the city, an estimated 25,000 islands encourage the Swedish love affair with the sea, for almost every Stockholm household either owns a small boat or wishes passionately to do so. It is estimated that one in five Stockholm families owns a yacht.

Numerous bridges, old and new, span the 14 islands on which Stockholm is built. About 1,480,000 people live in the city, making it by far the largest urban area in this thinly populated country. Today's city lies partly on Lake Mälaren and partly on Saltsjon, leading towards the islands and the Baltic Sea. Stockholm's setting of wooded hills and sea vistas, enhanced by fine old buildings and elegant modern architecture, make it one of the world's most attractive capitals.

The Old Town

At the heart of the city lies the Old Town *(Gamla Stan)* on the islands of Staden, Helgeandsholmen and Riddarholmen. Its medieval plan is still partly visible, with narrow streets and ancient buildings, archways, courtyards and small squares. It was here, in 1252, that the Regent of Sweden, Birger Jarl, fortified a settlement to protect it from attack from the sea. At about the same time, Stockholm was granted a charter giving it the status of a town and guaranteeing royal protection and exemption from taxes to its Hanseatic (north German) merchant citizens. The German connection survives in the names of some of the streets and buildings of Gamla Stan, notably the *Tyska Kyrka* (German church). To the west of this building lies the old *Riksbank* (1670), probably the oldest bank building in the world.

The main part of the Old Town, on the island of Staden, contains the Royal Palace, built in the early 1700s. Beyond it stands Stockholm's cathedral, the *Storkyrka* (great church), consecrated in 1306 but rebuilt in the Baroque style from 1736-43. Here too is the parliament building (*Riksdaghuset*, and the Riddarholm Church where Swedish royalty has worshipped and been buried since the 1500s, when Stockholm became the country's capital city.

An expanding city

As Swedish influence expanded in the world during the 1600s, Stockholm grew with it. In 1635 Norrmalm, a community north of the Old Town centred on two ancient monasteries, was incorporated into the city. Norrmalm is now the commercial centre of Stockholm, its busy streets lined with offices and shops. Much of it was rebuilt in the 1950s and 1960s, with areas restricted for pedestrians' use – a scheme that marked a pioneering Swedish innovation in town planning. This district contains the city's largest department stores, *Nordiska Kompaniet* and *PUB*. It also includes Stockholm's central railway station, main post office, Opera House, Concert Hall and National Museum. The *Klara Kyrka*, near the station, dates from the 1500s, and its tall spire overlooks a pleasant churchyard containing the graves of several celebrated Swedish poets.

East of Norrmalm, the district of Östermalm contains the Royal Library in Stockholm's largest inner-city park, the Humlegården. To the west of Norrmalm, the island of Kungsholmen possesses the Law Courts and the main police station. The City Hall (*Stadshuset*), with its tower 348 feet (106 metres) in height, looks out over the shore of Lake Mälaren and across to Riddarholmen. The suburb also has many hospitals and schools, and the Royal Mint.

Stockholm's expansion continued in the late 1600s to cover the large island of Södermalm, which is reached by means of a double bridge from the Old Town. The district contains a residential area and several impressive churches, as well as the harbours of Stadgården and Hammarby.

Sergelstortet (*above*) with its towering obelisk and array of fountains, marks the centre of modern Stockholm. Its architecture contrasts sharply with the buildings of the city's old quarter.

Strandvägen (*right*), one of Stockholm's finest streets, can be viewed across the inlet of Nybroviken; Stockholm's numerous waterways allow its citizens to indulge their passion for sailboats.

Gamla Stan (*left*), Stockholm's historic old quarter, lies at the heart of the modern city. Its narrow lanes and quaint architecture faithfully reflect Stockholm's origins as a Baltic trading city during the Middle Ages.

The "floating city" of Stockholm (*below*) spreads over several islands, and combines ancient and modern buildings. Sights include the Royal Palace, the Cathedral (*Storkyrka*), the Knights' House (*Riddarhuset*), and Riddarholm Church. Across the water, the Town Hall (*Stadshuset*) with its square tower acts as a universal landmark, while the National Museum, on the peninsula of Blasieholmen, contains Sweden's finest art collection.

Industry first arrived in Stockholm during the 1700s, but the city's skyline is not marred by the presence of factories, foundries and engineering works, as is the case in some other Swedish towns.

Between Södermalm and Östermalm lies the large island called Djurgården, where there is an enormous park and open-air museum known as Skansen. In addition to a zoo and restaurants there is a fun fair and, on the shore, the warship *Wasa*, which sank nearby on its maiden voyage in 1628. Recovered in 1961, the ship has been magnificently restored, and today presents a complete picture of naval life more than three centuries ago. Also on the island are the Nordic Museum and the Royal Armoury, together with many notable art museums and galleries.

Stockholm today

Stockholm's expansion continued in the 1950s and 1960s, when an efficient underground system was constructed. Today the city gives an impression of space, airiness and modernity, despite the fact that it accounts for over 20 per cent of Sweden's total production, with more than 20,000 companies. Trees, waterways and occasion outcrops of living rock all combine to create a natural background to a flourishing and comfortable modern city.

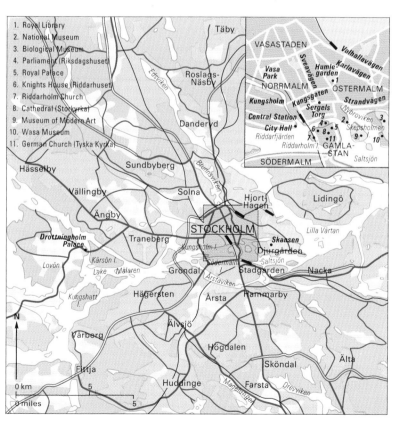

1. Royal Library
2. National Museum
3. Biological Museum
4. Parliament (Riksdagshuset)
5. Royal Palace
6. Knights House (Riddarhuset)
7. Riddarholm Church
8. Cathedral (Storkyrka)
9. Museum of Modern Art
10. Wasa Museum
11. German Church (Tyska Kyrka)

NORWAY

Along, narrow country in the far north-west of Europe, Norway lies on the western side of the Scandinavian peninsula. Its extensive coastline includes numerous narrow, steep-sided inlets, called fiords, formed by ice action millions of years ago. Many of these make excellent harbours, and have helped to develop Norway's ancient seafaring tradition. The region has bred a nation of bold mariners from the earliest times, as seen in rock carvings dating from 2000 BC. In the Middle Ages, Norwegian, or Norse, seafarers, known as Vikings, sailed far and wide in search of plunder and land. More than 400 years before Columbus "discovered" the New World in 1492, the Norse adventurer Leif Ericson and his crew had reached the North American coast, sailing from Greenland.

Eastern Norway shares a boundary with Sweden, while in the far north, beyond the Arctic Circle, the country curves eastward to border Finland and Russia. Much of Norway is mountainous, but two lowland areas surround the cities of Trondheim and Oslo, the capital. Most Norwegians live on or near the coast, mostly in small settlements grouped around a **harbour** (*right*), partly because of the nation's reliance on the sea, but also because the mountainous inland areas are colder.

People

The people of Norway have much in common with their Scandinavian relatives, the Swedes and the Danes. Many are tall, with fair hair and blue eyes. A different people, the Lapps, live in the far north, above the Arctic Circle. The region called Lapland includes parts of Norway, Sweden, Finland and Russia. It consists for the most part of a treeless zone, called tundra, with permanently frozen subsoil. Lapland contains about 1,500,000 people, but only about 45,000 of these are Lapps. About 20,000 of them live in Norway.

Norway has a small population, numbering little more than four million. Norwegians enjoy a high standard of living, and their educational and welfare services rank among the highest in the world. About two-thirds of the population live in cities, but few of these contain more than 50,000 people. Most Norwegians love outdoor sports, especially skiing – which was developed in Norway.

History

People were living in coastal Norway even before the end of the last Ice Age, about 11,000 years ago, but by 2000 BC a different group of people began to move in. These were Germanic tribes, who settled in Norway and have constituted the majority ever

since. At first the tribes formed small communities, led by local chiefs. From about AD 800, Norse Viking buccaneers began their 250-year reign of terror, raiding neighbouring regions such as the Baltic States, the British Isles, northern France and Ireland. During this period they also formed settlements in many of these places, as well as reaching Iceland, Greenland, the Faeroe Islands, and even North America.

In AD 872 the first king of Norway, Harald I (Fairhair), subdued many local chiefs, and imposed his leadership over much of the country. However, full unification did not come until the early 1000s under King Olav II. The king also forced his subjects to become Christians, by threatening to kill them, and his religious zeal was recognized in 1031, when he became the country's patron saint. But a pagan element lingered beneath the surface; many of Norway's wooden "stave" churches are still decorated with carvings that suggest non-Christian themes.

Trade expanded and the church grew more powerful after the end of the Viking age, but civil wars broke out between 1130 and 1380. During this period, the north German merchants of the Hanseatic League became economically dominant in Norway. In the mid-1300s, bubonic plague destroyed about half of the country's population, weakening Norway's power still further.

The Scandinavian countries of Norway and Denmark merged in 1380 under Queen Margrete, daughter of the king of Denmark. For a time Sweden, the third Scandinavian country, was part of this union, but in 1523 it broke away. Norway, however, remained a part of Denmark until 1814, when Denmark ceded the country to Sweden. Norway was by this time an important shipbuilding country, due to its supplies of timber, and by the end of the 1800s owned a large merchant fleet. But it was not until 1905 that it achieved independence from Sweden. In the decades before independence, as many as 600,000 Norwegians emigrated to the United States, and the connection between these two countries remains strong.

World War II and after

During World War II Norway was occupied by German forces, but King Haakon VII escaped and formed a government in exile in London. Meanwhile, Norwegians carried on a brave resistance to the occupation forces. After the war, in spite of considerable losses, Norway rebuilt its fleet and industries with help from the USA, and by the mid-1950s was thriving. The discovery of oil and natural gas deposits in the North Sea during the 1970s renewed the strength of the country's economy.

NORWAY'S KING, AS CONSTITUTIONAL monarch, is held in great respect (and affection) by virtually all his people, although his political power is very limited. He presides over state occasions, and appoints or receives the resignations of state officials. He is also head of the official Evangelical Lutheran Church, to which about 88 per cent of Norwegians belong.

Government and politics

The actual government of the land is in the hands firstly of the prime minister – who is the leader of the most numerous party in the parliament – and of the 17 other members of the Cabinet (Council of State) whom he or she chooses to act as ministers of the various government departments, but who are not themselves members of parliament.

The parliament of Norway is called the *Storting* ("Great Assembly"). It has a single chamber consisting of 157 members elected by the vote of all citizens aged 18 or more. But 39 of the members are elected by the assembly to act as a second chamber, the *Lagting*, to discuss and pass or reject new laws once the remaining 118 (the *Odelsting*, or "Freeholders' Assembly") have passed them. A bill that is not agreed on by the two sections of the Storting separately may still be passed by a two-thirds vote of the Storting as a whole.

There are six major political parties. The largest of them is the Social-Democratic Labour Party although, through coalitions of the remaining parties, they have not always been in power. In elections, voting takes place on the basis of proportional representation from the 19 counties that make up Norway. This is essential in a country in which the population density in areas of the south may be up to 80 times that of northern districts.

For local administration, 18 of the 19 counties (the exception is the city of Oslo) have a governor, nominated by the Cabinet. Further administration is in the hands of city, town or district councils. Norway's judicial system provides for a Supreme Court, five High Courts, and county and town courts. There are also local arbitration tribunals.

Norway's armed forces comprise a total of about 34,000 personnel, including men between the ages of 19 and 44 who are undergoing the compulsory 12 to 15 months' training in the services. In addition there are around 85,000 reservists. Norway also provides training facilities for troops from NATO countries, especially training in Arctic conditions.

Education and social welfare

Educational standards are extremely high. Education is free and compulsory for children between the ages of 7 and 16. Opportunities for further academic or vocational study are available to all. There are four universities and many regional colleges and technical institutions.

As in most of Scandinavia, welfare services are provided in abundance. Large families are encouraged – the population is officially considered to be too small – with tax concessions and state grants. State aid also contributes towards free medical and hospital care for all, towards benefits for the elderly, the handicapped, and the

A market trader (*above*) prepares a bouquet for sale in Bergen. Most Norwegians have much in common with the other Scandinavian countries, Sweden and Denmark.

FACT BOX

THE COUNTRY
Official name: Kingdom of Norway
Capital: Oslo
Land regions: Mountainous Plateau, SE and Trondheim Lowlands; about 150,000 islands. Jan Mayen and Svalbard
Land area: 149,405 sq mi (386,958 km²), incl. Svalbard and Jan Mayen
Climate: Temperate on west coast (Gulf Stream), colder inland. Rainfall declines from west to east
Main rivers: Glåma, Lågen, Otra
Highest elevation: Galdhøppigen 8,100 ft (2,469 m)
Lowest elevation: Sea level along the coast

THE GOVERNMENT
Form of Government: Constitutional monarchy
Head of State: King
Head of Government: Prime Minister
Administrative areas: 19 counties, including Oslo. Territories: Svalbard, Jan Mayen
Legislature: Parliament (Storting): 157 members, 4-year terms; divides into Lagting (39 members) and Odelsting (118 members)
Judiciary: Supreme Court of Justice, Superior Courts, county and town courts
Armed forces: Total strength: 34,100. Men after age 19 must serve 12-15 months

THE PEOPLE
Population (1990): 4,212,000
Language: Norwegian (Bokmål and Nyrnorsk); Lapps speak own language
Religion: Protestant (mainly Evangelical Lutheran – about 95%)

ECONOMY
Currency: Krone
Gross Domestic Product per person (1990): US$24,960
Annual Growth Rate (1985-90): 1.6%
Trade balance in US$ (1989): $3,385 mill
Goods imported: foods, minerals, manufactured goods, chemicals, vehicles, iron, steel

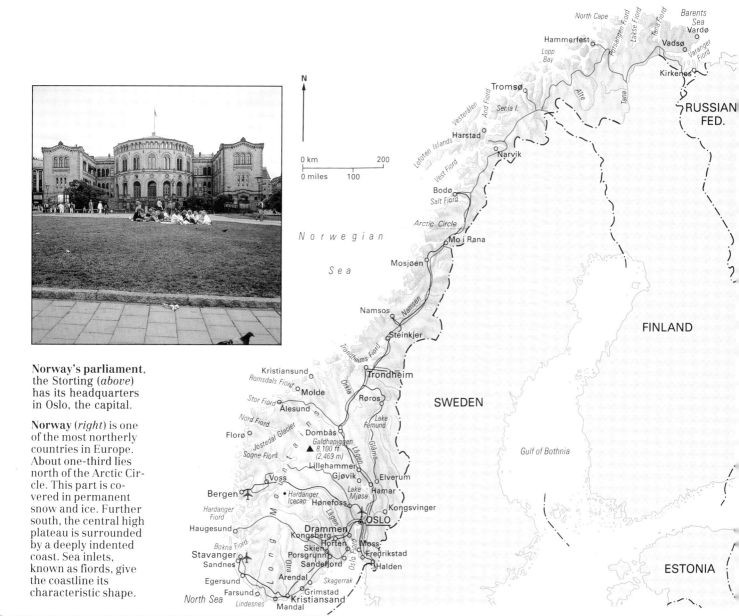

Norway's parliament, the Storting (*above*) has its headquarters in Oslo, the capital.

Norway (*right*) is one of the most northerly countries in Europe. About one-third lies north of the Arctic Circle. This part is covered in permanent snow and ice. Further south, the central high plateau is surrounded by a deeply indented coast. Sea inlets, known as fiords, give the coastline its characteristic shape.

bereaved, and towards a guaranteed four weeks' holiday for all the country's employees. These conditions apply to all Norwegian citizens, including of course the 20,000 or so Lapps (or Sami) of the far north, and the 10,000 people of Finnish descent who live in the far north of Norway.

Physical activity is important to Norwegians, and sports facilities are excellent and available to all. Winter sports, such as skiing, ski-jumping, ice-hockey and ice-skating, enjoy great popularity. The main summer sports are soccer, athletics, fishing and rowing. Many families spend weekends at log cabins in the country.

Norway is also celebrated for its contribution to the arts. Among the best-known are Henrik Ibsen's plays, Edvard Grieg's music, Gustav Vigeland's sculptures and Edvard Munch's paintings. Major themes in the arts are the stories of the Old Norse gods, traditional to the majority Norwegian-speaking population. The Lapps and Finns have their own traditions, some of which involve individual styles of music and costume.

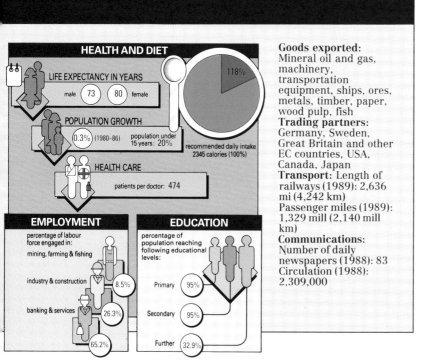

HEALTH AND DIET

LIFE EXPECTANCY IN YEARS

male 73   80 female

POPULATION GROWTH

(0.3%) (1980–86)   population under 15 years: 20%

118%

recommended daily intake 2345 calories (100%)

HEALTH CARE

patients per doctor: 474

EMPLOYMENT

percentage of labour force engaged in:

mining, farming & fishing

industry & construction   8.5%

banking & services   26.3%

65.2%

EDUCATION

percentage of population reaching following educational levels:

Primary 95%

Secondary 95%

Further 32.9%

Goods exported: Mineral oil and gas, machinery, transportation equipment, ships, ores, metals, timber, paper, wood pulp, fish

Trading partners: Germany, Sweden, Great Britain and other EC countries, USA, Canada, Japan

Transport: Length of railways (1989): 2,636 mi (4,242 km) Passenger miles (1989): 1,329 mill (2,140 mill km)

Communications: Number of daily newspapers (1988): 83 Circulation (1988): 2,309,000

NORWAY CONTAINS SOME OF THE MOST spectacular scenery in the world. It owes much of its beauty to the North Atlantic Current (part of the Gulf Stream). Without the current's warming effect Norway might be as desolate as Greenland or Siberia, which lie at roughly the same latitude but support little animal or plant life. In Norway, sheep graze on the northernmost rocky outcrops even in winter. The coast generally remains ice-free throughout the year. The North Atlantic Current also brings a good deal of rain annually, transforming the country to a vivid green in summer. Even as far north as the Lofoten Islands, 150 miles (240 kilometres) north of the Arctic Circle, January temperature can be 45°F (25°C) higher than the average for that latitude.

There are, however barren and inhospitable areas in Norway. Many lie inland, within the Arctic Circle, where the warming effect of the North Atlantic Current is blocked off by coastal mountain ranges. Similar areas are found in Norway's northern island territories in the Arctic Ocean. These are Svalbard, Jan Mayen Island and the tiny Bear Island. Most of these barren areas are mountainous, their rocks scored and smoothed by the glaciers of the Ice Age, and some are covered in snow and ice all the year round. One such is the Jostedal Glacier in the southwest of the country, which is Europe's largest ice field outside Iceland. The Hardanger Plateau, farther southwest still, is the largest highland plain in Europe, covering 4,500 square miles (11,700 square kilometres). It is broken by many lakes and deep valleys created by glaciers. Rivers form spectacular waterfalls when they plunge over the edge of the plateau.

Mountains and lowlands

The major mountain range of northern Norway is the Kjølen Mountains, lying along the border with Sweden. Farther south the Dovre Mountains run across the country from east to west. The Long Mountains, which rise in the south of the country, include a chain of peaks and glaciers famous in Norse mythology. This is Jotunheim ("home of the giants"). It contains the highest peak in Norway, Galdhøpiggen, which rises to 8,100 feet (2,469 metres).

The country's major lowland areas lie in the southeast. The most important areas are the Southeastern Lowlands around the Glåma River system and the Trondheim Lowlands. Both have long been important areas of human settlement. The Trondheim Lowlands surround a former capital of Norway, Trondheim. The Southeastern Lowlands lie around Oslo, the present capital.

The Southeastern Lowlands comprise the middle and lower valleys of several large

A tranquil scene (*below*) in the Southeastern Lowlands is typical of the landscape around Oslo. This gently rolling area is the most suitable for farming. It contains the major centres of settlement in the country.

Sunset bathes a classic Norwegian fiord (*right*) in pink light. The almost vertical sides of the fiord were carved by a mighty glacier during the last Ice Age. Beautiful, deep fiords are a major feature of Norway's western coast.

rivers, notably the Glåma which extends 372 miles (598 kilometres). Water is a predominant feature of the countryside. The rivers provide highways along which timber from the hillside plantations and natural woodlands is easily and cheaply transported to sawmills and paper works. The waterfalls in their steep valleys have been harnessed to provide hydroelectric power. Lake Mjøsa is one of a number of narrow lakes that lie in the area. Although the lowlands are by no means flat, slopes here are less steep than elsewhere in Norway. Much of the nation's total land area devoted to agriculture (about three per cent) lies here. It is also the warmest part of Norway during the summer. Oslo, Norway's capital and main manufacturing centre, lies at the heart of the lowlands.

The Trondheim Lowlands are, if anything, flatter, for they embrace the ends of several wide valleys. Located farther to the north, where Norway changes shape from relatively broad to comparatively narrow, these valleys constitute the country's rare natural routes where railways can traverse the country and cross into Sweden. Elsewhere, the rugged terrain limits railway development. The total length of track in Norway is only around 2,636 miles (4,242 kilometres), in comparison with 54,000 miles (86,840 kilometres) of roads.

1

A wooden "stave" church (*above*) built in the 1100s, nestles among the forested slopes of central Norway.

The white waters of the Stigfoss waterfall (*left*) crash down the steep sides of a valley in the Mountainous Plateau region. Norway's combination of high mountains, glaciers and water provides a wealth of dramatic scenery.

Norway's deep fiords (*below*) were formed during the last Ice Age. Before glaciation (1) the coastline consisted of gently rolling highlands which reached down to the sea. During glaciation (2) the valleys were deepened and widened by the scouring action of the ice. As the ice moved along the valley, soil and rocks were plucked from the valley walls and floor. This debris was deposited offshore, sometimes in the form of small islands (skerries). The highest parts of the land were carved into sharp points (known as *nunataks*). After glaciation (3) the sea level rose, "drowning" the reshaped valley.

Coasts and islands

The Norwegian coastline is one of the most indented in the world. It is broken by hundreds of fiords and peninsulas and fringed by some 150,000 islands and skerries (rocky islands). If all its inlets and peninsulas are measured, the Norwegian coastline's full length is around 13,260 miles (21,351 kilometres), or about half the distance around the Equator. The coastal waters are rich in cod and other valuable food fish. Between two of the outer Lofoten Islands flows the tidal current famous as the Maelstrom, a huge whirlpool.

One further geographical feature distinguishes Norway from most other European nations: its northerliness. Kjøllefjord, on the peninsula of Nordkinn, is probably the most northerly village in mainland Europe. North Cape, or Nordkapp, to which many tourists travel, is farther north but is on an island. Kjøllefjord lies 312 miles (500 kilometres) directly north of the Arctic Circle. Here the winter sun does not rise above the horizon, and in summer does not set below it. At Tromsø, the sun remains above the horizon for three months (May-July). This period of so-called "white nights" characterizes the "lands of the midnight sun", a title that northern Norway shares with the Arctic regions of Sweden, Finland and the Russian Federation.

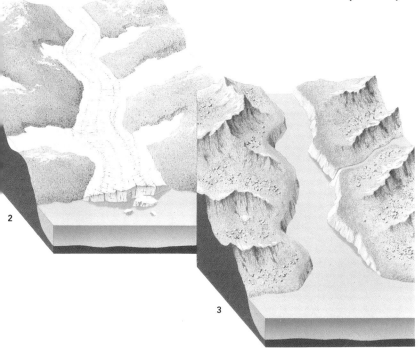

2

3

DENMARK

THE DANISH LANDSCAPE OWES MOST OF its features and its character to the Ice Age, when vast ice-sheets advanced several times southwards from Scandinavia. Inside and ahead of them, the ice-sheets brought masses of rocks and boulders, many crushed almost to powder. Where the ice stopped, this debris piled up in banks and ridges, called moraines. Glacial deposits of this kind almost completely cover the flat layers of limestone that form the underlying rock of the Jutland peninsula and the islands. Only in very few places is the bedrock visible, for example in Lim Fiord, and the islands of Møn and Bornholm.

The smooth curves of Denmark's Western Dune Coast are made up of banks of sand left behind when the Ice Age ended. Inland, the Western Sand Plains are flat areas which include numerous fiords that were once connected to the sea. The East-Central hills (including the islands of Denmark) and the Northern Flat Plains were once underneath the ice sheets. Their deep, fertile soils make them the country's most agriculturally productive region.

In the west, the winds off the Atlantic provide a harsher (though still mild) climate than to the east and on the islands, where in general the climate is more continental. Over the whole country, the prevailing winds are from the west, ensuring a relatively high average annual rainfall of around 24 inches (61 centimetres). The undulating terrain is nowhere high or rugged enough to prevent winds, rain or sea mists from spreading right across the country. The highest point in Denmark, Yding Skovhøj, halfway up the eastern side of the peninsula, rises to only 568 feet (173 metres). Winter conditions tend to be cold, especially if the wind changes to easterly, and temperatures often remain below freezing point for one month at a time.

The peninsula of Jutland (Jylland) occupies around 70 per cent of Denmark's land area. However, more people live on the islands, particularly Sjælland, Fyn, Møn and Lolland although only about 100 of Denmark's islands are inhabited.

The economy

The geography and the climate of Denmark permit around 75 per cent of the country's land area to be used for agriculture. Most farms are small, averaging 37 acres (15 hectares) in area. Isolated, whitewashed farm buildings surrounded by fertile fields represent a typical view of the Danish countryside. Stock raising – pigs, beef and cattle – is now the major farming activity. Many grains (especially barley) and vegetables are grown, primarily for animal feed, but with some surplus for export. About 60 per cent of all agricultural produce is exported, and Danish cheeses, butter and bacon are world-famous.

Only about 10 per cent of Denmark is forested, and these woodlands supply only half the nation's annual timber requirement. However, the coastal waters are rich in such fish as cod, herring, whiting and sprats, and the fishing industry is both modern and economically important. The major fishing port is Esbjerg, an artificially created harbour on the North Sea coast.

Denmark has few other natural resources. North Sea wells produce some oil and natural gas, but almost half of the country's energy needs must be imported. The only other minerals mined are chalk and industrial clays. Even the rivers are too slow-flowing across the flattish land to be used for hydroelectric power.

Industry and tourism

Modern and specialized manufacturing industries now employ three times more people in Denmark than agriculture, forestry, fishing and mining combined. Most of these industries process agricultural produce; others use imported raw materials. Products range from foodstuffs and beer to textiles, diesel engines, furniture, steel, porcelain, chemicals, machinery, electronic equipment and silverware. Coastal yards repair or fit out ships. The government has made great efforts to encourage the modernization and expansion of all industry.

Since the 1970s tourism has also earned Denmark considerable revenue. Copenhagen, the largest city in northern Europe, has many attractions. Self-catering and camping holidays in the countryside have become popular for visitors from surrounding countries, many of whom arrive by sea aboard modern Danish ferries.

Denmark's major trading partners include the other nations of the European Community (EC), notably Germany and Britain, and the Nordic Council countries, especially Sweden. Although Denmark's economy is strong, there remain one or two less favourable economic factors. During the early 1990s the government came under strong pressure to reform taxation rates. It was pressed to reduce the size of the national debt to foreign financial institutions, interest on which was by then approaching some 19 per cent of the country's annual budgetary expenditure.

Inflation in Denmark may be lower than in other EC members, but by 1991 unemployment was some 10.5 per cent of the workforce. For all that, Denmark's Gross National Product (the total value of all goods and services produced within the country per year) continues to be one of the highest, in terms of its population, of the world's industrialized countries.

The Danish economy (*right*) is based on food-processing and manufacturing industries, mostly located near the city of Copenhagen. Products include electrical equipment, engines, ships and farm produce.

Fishing boats are pulled up for the night onto dune-lined beaches characteristic of eastern Jutland (*left*). The fishing industry (*below*) exploits the resources of the nearby North Sea. Much of the catch is exported.

Skagerrak
Skagen
Hirtshals
Frederikshavn
Læsø
North Sea
Ålborg
Langerak
Lim Fiord
Kattegat
Lemvig
Randers
Struer
Grenå
Jutland
Guden
Århus
Silkeborg
Ringkøbing
Helsingør
Vejle
COPENHAGEN
Fredericia
Esbjerg
Odense
Sjælland
Kolding
Fyn
Baltic Sea
Svendborg
Als
Nakskov
Møn
Sønderborg
Falster
Bornholm
Lolland
Rønne

Cultivated land

Heath and coastal dunes

Forest

Fish

Main industrial centres

Esbjerg (*below*), Denmark's most important fishing port, has a huge harbour on the North Sea coast. Its facilities include factories for processing the catch. The port is also the centre for Danish North Sea oil exploration.

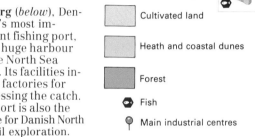

Sheer cliffs (*far left*) carved by the sea from creamy-coloured chalk are a famous landmark on the island of Møn. The cliffs rise to over 400 feet (122 metres) above a beach which can only be reached by steep steps.

A whitewashed farmhouse (*left*) stands in lush green fields on the island of Aero. The famous fertile soil of Denmark derives from deposits of sands and fine clays left behind at the end of the last Ice Age.

Denmark Today

THE KINGDOM OF DENMARK IS A SMALL nation in northern Europe. It includes the Jutland peninsula, which projects northward from Germany and divides the North Sea from the Skagerrak and Kattegat channels to the Baltic Sea, and 482 islands. Most of the islands, of which only about 100 are inhabited, lie very close to the peninsula or to each other.

Although it is one of the smallest countries in Europe, both in terms of area and population, Denmark today is among the most prosperous states in the world. In former centuries it held considerable power over neighbouring lands, and had some colonial possessions in the Caribbean, West Africa and India. The huge island of Greenland and the much smaller Faeroe Islands (in Danish, Føroyar) in the North Atlantic are Danish territory, although they are for the most part self-governing.

Denmark's terrain is largely low-lying and excellent for agriculture. However, since Denmark entered the European Community in January 1973 the country's industrial production has almost doubled, leading to a movement of people from the land. The capital, Copenhagen, is the country's major economic centre and its metropolitan area houses more than one-fourth of the nation's people. It is sited predominantly on Sjælland, the country's largest island. A smaller part of the city lies on the adjacent island of Amager.

National and local government
The Danish sovereign, Queen Margrethe II, came to the throne in 1972. Although her duties are largely ceremonial, she enjoys great popularity with her people, and is highly respected. The government is headed by the prime minister, the leader of the party with most seats in parliament, who nominates a Council of State (cabinet). The single house of parliament, the *Folketing*, has 179 members. Of this number, 135 are elected by the votes of all Danes aged 18 or over; as are two members from Greenland and two from the Faeroes. The remaining 40 members come from the various political parties, on the basis of their share of the total vote in the elections. Most postwar governments have been coalitions of centre-left or centre-right parties. The final decision on many proposed laws is by custom presented to the people in the form of a national vote or referendum.

For the purposes of local administration, Denmark is divided into 14 countries and two large municipalities: Copenhagen and Frederiksberg (a suburban extension of Copenhagen). The countries are subdivided into municipalities, each of which has an elected municipal council which is headed by a mayor.

The people
The Danish people have much in common with their neighbours in Sweden and Norway to the north. The similar languages and common Nordic heritage unifies them culturally and historically. Indeed, for 130 years the three nations were all part of the Union of Kalmar, until Sweden broke away in 1523.

As in most of Scandinavia, the government's welfare programme is extensive. Many state-funded benefits are available to

FACT BOX

THE COUNTRY
Official name: Kingdom of Denmark
Capital: Copenhagen
Land regions: Country consisting of Jutland Peninsula and islands. Jutland: Dune Coast and Sand Plain in west, Flat Plains in north. East Jutland and islands covered by hills. Bornholm Island off Swedish coast. Territorial possession: Greenland
Land area: 16,632 sq mi (43,077 km²)
Climate: Temperate. Western areas are mildest and receive most rain. Mild summers; winters can be cold in east
Main rivers: Guden, Skjern

Highest elevation: Yding Skovhøj 568 ft (173 m)
Lowest elevation: Sea level along the coast

THE GOVERNMENT
Form of Government: Constitutional monarchy
Head of State: King or queen
Head of Government: Prime Minister
Administrative areas: 14 counties with further divisions, plus 2 municipalities
Legislature: Parliament (Folketing) with 179 members, including 2 members each from Greenland and the Faeroe Islands; all members elected to 4-year terms

Judiciary: Supreme Court, 2 High Courts, lower courts, special courts
Armed forces: Total strength: about 76,200. Conscription: men must serve 9-12 months

THE PEOPLE
Population (1990): 5,120,000
Language: Danish
Religion: Protestant (Evangelical Lutheran): about 98%

THE ECONOMY
Currency: Krone
Gross Domestic Product per person (1990): US$24,458
Annual Growth Rate (1985-90): 2.3%
Trade balance in US$ (1989): $1,417 mill

Denmark (*right*) consists of the Jutland Peninsula and a number of islands to the east. The peninsula projects north from mainland Europe. The islands lie between the Kattegat, a narrow extension of the North Sea, and the Baltic Sea. Greenland, a large island in the Atlantic, is a province of Denmark, whilst the Faroe Islands are a self-governing part of the Danish kingdom.

A soldier of the Royal Guard (*left*) parades outside the Amalienborg Palace in Copenhagen. The ceremonial changing of the guard takes place at noon every day of the week.

anyone living in the country. Taxes are necessarily high in order to pay the cost of such benefits, but so is the general standard of living.

Education is free and compulsory between the ages of 7 and 16. There are three universities, of which the University of Copenhagen, founded in 1479, is the oldest and largest. Men between the ages of 20 and 25 are liable to conscription into the armed services for nine months.

Denmark is noted for its art, music and literature. Much cultural activity centres on ancient Nordic legend. Another important cultural influence is the Evangelical Lutheran Church, to which about 97 per cent of Danes belong. Although the Danish parliament controls the church, it does not interfere with religious worship.

Denmark's only significant minority is a group of about 30,000 people who have German ancestry. They live in the south of the country, close to the border with Germany. Denmark once ruled the north German region of Schleswig-Holstein, but lost its sovereignty in 1864. Along with significant numbers of Swedes and Norwegians, many Danes have emigrated to other parts of the world. Between 1870 and 1920, around 350,000 Danish people migrated to the United States alone, and have taken their love of good food, especially sweet Danish pastries and the traditional open sandwiches, with them.

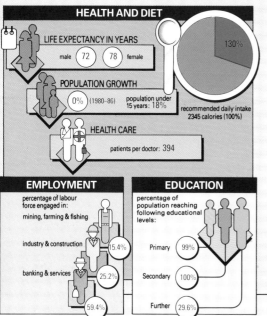

HEALTH AND DIET

LIFE EXPECTANCY IN YEARS
male 72 78 female

POPULATION GROWTH
0% (1980-86) population under 15 years: 18%

130% recommended daily intake 2345 calories (100%)

HEALTH CARE
patients per doctor: 394

EMPLOYMENT

percentage of labour force engaged in:

mining, farming & fishing

industry & construction 15.4%

banking & services 25.2%

59.4%

EDUCATION

percentage of population reaching following educational levels:

Primary 99%

Secondary 100%

Further 29.6%

Goods imported: Machinery, mineral oil, oil products, chemical products, vehicles, iron, steel, yarns, textiles, paper
Goods exported: Meat and dairy products, machinery, textiles, medicine, fish
Trading partners: Germany, Great Britain and other EC countries, Sweden, Norway, Finland, USA
Transport: Length of railways (1985): 1,535 mi (2,471 km) Passenger miles (1985): 2,801 mill (4,508 mill km)
Communications: Number of daily newspapers (1988): 46 Circulation: (1988): 1,842,000

Copenhagen

COPENHAGEN, DENMARK'S CAPITAL AND largest city, began as a small fishing village in the mid-1000s. Its fine harbour, ideally sited as a ferry station for the short sea voyage across the Oresund to Sweden, led to the settlement's steady growth as a trade centre. This attracted pirates, but in 1167 Archbishop Absalon of Roskilde built a castle to protect its harbour, and from then on the seaport's development was assured. It soon earned the name of København ("traders' centre"), and in 1254 was granted a town charter.

The town continued to grow in size and importance, attracting the jealous wrath of the predominantly German Hanseatic merchants, who razed the castle to the ground in 1369. Nonetheless, the rebuilt settlement became the residence of Denmark's monarchs in 1416, and in 1443 replaced Roskilde as Denmark's capital city.

In the 1600s, Copenhagen was attacked and pillaged by Swedish forces. The 1700s saw the outbreak of epidemics and fires that killed many of its citizens. In the early 1800s, during the Napoleonic Wars, British ships blockaded and bombarded the city, resulting in widespread destruction by fire. It was not until the 1850s that more prosperous times enabled the city to grow. Most of the defensive ramparts were removed, although they are commemorated in the names of the suburbs *Nørrebro*, *Vesterbro* and *Osterbro* (after the north, west and east rampart bridges respectively). This period saw the city's expansion to the north and west, and also its economic growth, with the development of industries including shipbuilding, hardware manufacturing and brewing.

Modern Copenhagen

Today, Copenhagen remains Denmark's chief commercial centre and port, and houses a high proportion of the country's people. The total population of the city centre is almost 473,000, but nearly twice as many again live in the metropolitan area, including the municipality of Frederiksburg, and its suburbs. Copenhagen has also overflowed from its original island Sjælland onto the neighbouring island of Amager (where Copenhagen's airport, Kastrup, is situated), taking in the once separate suburb of Christianshavn.

It was King Christian IV (1580-1648) who gave Copenhagen several of its most beautiful buildings. Especially notable is the stock exchange, said to be the oldest of its kind still in use for its original purpose, and remarkable for its spire adorned with entwined dragons' tails. The moated church of Holmens Kirke is also credited to Christian IV, as is Rosenborg Palace, once the sovereign's spring and autumn residence

Town Hall Square (*right*) lies close to the centre of Copenhagen. It acts as a focal point of the city and is surrounded by open-air cafes and impressive buildings. These include the Town Hall itself, with its high tower, built in the late 1800s. The beautiful Dragon Fountain, in the centre of the square, is dedicated to Hans Christian Andersen (1805-75), the famous Danish writer of fairy tales.

The "Little Mermaid" (*top*), a bronze statue of one of Andersen's best-loved characters, watches over Copenhagen's harbour. Close by, the cruise ships belonging to the Danish royal family are anchored.

The Tivoli Gardens amusement park (*above*) is a popular landmark. The Chinese pagoda, which is picked out at night by hundreds of tiny lights, is one of the park's many attractions.

but now a historical museum. Its exhibits include the Danish crown jewels. The palace stands in the King's Park (*Kongens Have*), the oldest park in Copenhagen.

Another park, of a rather different kind, is the world-famous Tivoli Gardens, one of the world's earliest and most famous amusement parks. Tivoli was built in 1843 and modelled upon London's now-vanished Vauxhall Gardens. Today up to 4.5 million visitors a year between May and September come to enjoy its numerous shows, games and rides, its 22 restaurants, its museums, concert hall and puppet theatre, its vast flower gardens, and its novelty events and entertainments.

To the east of Tivoli stands Christiansborg Palace, the imposing seat of the Danish parliament (*Folketing*) since 1918. The same building houses the supreme court and the audience chambers where the queen meets her ministers in the council of state and receives guests. Completed in 1928, the palace stands on the site of the castle of Archbishop Absalon, the ruins of which may be viewed beneath the present building.

The Royal Palace

A little farther east still, just the other side of what used to be the picturesque *Nyhavn* (the "New Harbour", once a scenic canal linking the King's Square with the sea) is Amalienborg Palace. The palace, actually a square of four mansions in the rococo style, has been a royal residence since 1794. When Queen Margrethe and her family are present, the Danish royal standard flies above Amalienborg, and each day at noon the sentries perform the colourful ritual of the changing of the guard, a popular tourist attraction.

As well as historic buildings, Copenhagen has a wealth of museums. Amongst these the City Museum is devoted to Copenhagen's history, while the National Museum specializes in Danish history from prehistoric times, with fine collections including Stone Age tools, Bronze Age musical instruments and Viking rune stones. The city has many churches, some with exquisite statuary or paintings, ranging in style from the severe neoclassical cathedral to the onion-domed Russian church. Winding canals add to the historic atmosphere and also remain active waterways. On the Nyhavn Canal, an 1853 lightship (now a floating museum) is moored near the embarkation point for the hydrofoil to Sweden. On the harbourside promenade, the statue of the Little Mermaid (a character from one of Hans Christian Andersen's most popular fairy tales) provides a fitting emblem for this maritime city.

Brightly-coloured gabled houses line Nyhavn (*left*). They reflect the prosperity of Danish commerce in the 1700s and 1800s. Nyhavn's many restaurants attract tourists; the harbour is a terminal for the ferry to Sweden.

The city of Copenhagen (*right*) lies to the east of the country, close to Sweden. It covers part of the islands of Sjælland and Amager. About 25% of Denmark's people live in or close to the city. Copenhagen is the industrial and commercial centre of Denmark. However, the busy capital also houses a number of major tourist attractions, notably the famous Tivoli Gardens and the renowned National Museum. Other attractions include the Amalienborg Palace and the Royal Danish Ballet.

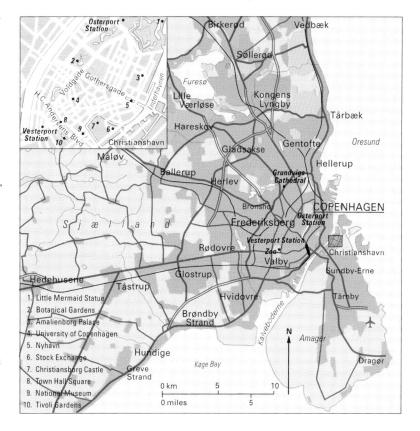

1. Little Mermaid Statue
2. Botanical Gardens
3. Amalienborg Palace
4. University of Copenhagen
5. Nyhavn
6. Stock Exchange
7. Christiansborg Castle
8. Town Hall Square
9. National Museum
10. Tivoli Gardens

Lithuania

THE REPUBLIC OF LITHUANIA IS THE largest and most southerly of the three Baltic republics of the former Soviet Union. Like Estonia and Latvia, Lithuania regained its independence in 1991.

Lithuania lies between Latvia to the north, Byelorussia to the east and Poland to the south. To the southwest lies the small Russian enclave of Kaliningrad. Part of its Baltic coastline comprises a long, wide sandspit that cuts off the Kursiu Marios Lagoon. Into this lagoon empties the Nemunas, a major river that runs westwards from Byelorussia, and forms much of Lithuania's southern border. The capital, Vilnius, lies in the southeast.

The land

Lithuania's terrain is mainly low and rolling. There are many rivers and more than 2,800 lakes. Wolves still survive in areas where the original mixed forest cover remains. However, much has now been cleared for agriculture or industry. The climate varies between maritime and continental, and is cold in winter.

People

Around 80 per cent of the country's population are Lithuanians; the rest are Russians, Poles and Byelorussians. Almost all speak Lithuanian, an Indo-European language of ancient form, which is related to Latvian.

In 1386, Lithuania's ruling family was united with the rulers of Poland, founding a dynasty which lasted some 400 years. Union with Poland led to the country's conversion to Roman Catholicism, and most Lithuanians still adhere to the Roman Catholic faith. In 1795, Lithuania was conquered by Russia, which annexed it in 1815.

Germany occupied Lithuania in World War I. From 1918 the country was obliged to wage a war of independence against Poland. Lithuania won its independence in 1920 but was soon affected by its larger neighbours again.

The signing of the German-Soviet non-aggression treaty in August 1939 led directly to Soviet occupation in 1940. As a Soviet republic, Lithuania became heavily industrialized, with emphasis placed on heavy engineering, fuel refining, chemical synthesis, metal-working and machine-building, as well as the manufacture of bricks, plastics and textiles. Many workers were imported from Russia to work in the new industries. As a result, Lithuania's population enjoyed a relatively high standard of living.

In the later 1980s, nationalist feeling was encouraged by the policy of *perestroika* (restructuring) pursued by Soviet leader Mikhail Gorbachev. New political groups were formed. Chief among these was *Sajudis*, which at first sought only the improvement of civic rights. Under a democratically elected government headed by *Sajudis*, Lithuania unilaterally declared independence in March 1990. In reaction, the Soviet government halted the supply of vital raw materials. In January 1991, a display of Soviet military force in the capital left 14 dead and about 700 injured. The collapse of central authority in the Soviet Union led to formal recognition of Lithuanian independence in September 1991.

Government

The Lithuanian government is headed by a prime minister and a cabinet together responsible to a single-chamber Supreme Council under a chairman and a presidium. Local administration consists of municipal councils at city, town, and district levels. Courts of justice are presided over by elected judges and assessors.

Economy

Lithuania's economy is still dominated by heavy industry, and relies on imports of energy and raw materials. The government has embarked on reforms, to attract foreign investment, and to transfer state-owned enterprises into private hands. Much of the equipment in Lithuanian factories is outdated and inefficient, producing dangerously high levels of pollution.

Official name: Republic of Lithuania
Capital: Vilnius (Vilna, in Russian)
Land area: 25,170 sq mi (65,200 km^2)
Land regions: Mostly glacial lowlands; chains of hills in southeast and north, with plains and depressions between; coast flat and sandy with dunes
Climate: Temperate overall: maritime by coast; progressively continental inland
Highest elevation: Juozapine Hill in the Medininku Uplands: 965 feet (294 metres).
Lowest elevation: Sea level

Government: Single-chamber parliament (Supreme Council)
Head of state: Chairman of the Supreme Council
Population: 3,690,000 (1991)
Languages: Lithuanian (official), Russian
Religion: Predominantly Roman Catholic (Christian)
Currency: Rouble.
GDP per capita: 2,427 roubles (1988)

In Lithuanian, the name of the capital Vilnius (*left*) means "amber site". The city today has more than 590,000 residents (16% of the entire population of Lithuania), and is an important industrial centre.

The Republic of Lithuania (*above*) ranks as the largest of the three Baltic States. Its landscape is mainly rolling, with numerous lakes and small rivers. Ethnic Lithuanians make up more than three-quarters of the country's population.

Lithuania was annexed by Stalin in 1940. In the 1980s, a significant nationalist movement arose, and in 1990, Lithuania became the first of the Baltic States to declare its independence from the Soviet Union.

The *Sajudis* – the anti-Soviet Lithuanian liberation movement – adopted the red, gold and green flags of the country's previous days of independence under which to hold its rallies in Vilnius (*below*).

Lithuania still has some forested areas, and more than 2,800 lakes (*left*). The undulating countryside is given over mostly to large fields of crops or pastureland; sand-dunes line the coast.

A newly married couple (*above*) visits the "Hill of Crosses" at Siauliai, a monument to Lithuanian national pride and to the Roman Catholic faith of the majority of the population.

Latvia

ONE OF THE THREE FORMER BALTIC republics of the Soviet Union, the Republic of Latvia achieved formal independence in September 1991. The country lies between Estonia to the north, the Russian Federation and Byelorussia to the east and southeast, and Lithuania to the south. Its Baltic coastline, to the west and north, extends for more than 300 miles (500 kilometres). About half of the country's population of 2,680,000 lives in or near the capital, Riga.

The land

Latvia covers an area of some 24,900 square miles (64,600 square kilometres). The countryside is low and undulating, broken by numerous ridges formed at the retreat of the last Ice Age. Central Latvia is divided between the extensive Zemgale Plain in the southwest, and the Vidzeme Uplands, which include the highest point, Gaizinkalns, which stands at 1,024 feet (312 metres) above sea level. To the east lie the Latgale Uplands. There are more than 12,000 rivers, most of them short. The longest is the Daugava (Dvina), whose source is in Russia. There are also some 3,000 shallow lakes dotted over the country. Mixed forest covers about 20 per cent of Latvia's area, and there are large areas of peat bog and swampland. The climate is damp but temperate.

People and history

Latvia is unusual in that only 52 per cent of its people are native Latvians (Letts). Russians brought in by the Soviet policy of resettlement represent another 34 per cent, and the rest consist of Byelorussians, Ukrainians, Poles and Lithuanians. Only the Letts speak the national language, Latvian, an Indo-European language ancient in form but with many words borrowed from Russian and German.

The ancestors of the present-day Latvians inhabited the country well before AD 900. From the Middle Ages onward, parts of it – especially the area around Riga – were occupied by the Teutonic Knights, the Swedes, and after 1721, by Russians and by German overlords. Until the 19th century, the Letts continued to live as serfs on the large German-owned estates in the Baltic region. Social deprivation inflicted by estate-owners

FACT BOX

Official name: Republic of Latvia
Capital: Riga
Land area: 24,938 sq mi (64,500 sq km)
Land regions: Mostly glacial lowlands; chains of hills and plains in centre and east; some swamps and peat bogs; coast flat and sandy with dunes
Climate: Temperate; maritime by coast; progressively continental inland; subject to rapid changes of weather conditions
Highest elevation: Gaizinkalns in the Vidzeme Uplands: 1,024 feet (312 metres)

Lowest elevation: Sea level at coast
Government: Single-chamber parliament (Supreme Council)
Head of state: Chairman of the Supreme Council
Population: 2,680,000 (1991).
Languages: Latvian/Lettish (official), Russian
Religion: Mostly Evangelical Lutheran; some Russian Orthodox
Currency: Rouble
GDP per capita: 2,630 roubles (1988)

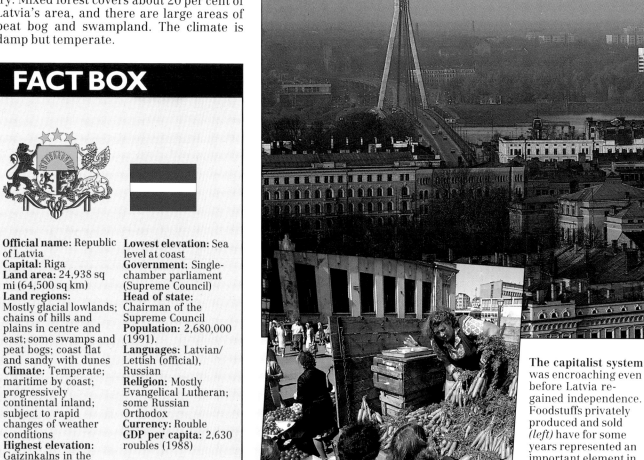

The capitalist system was encroaching even before Latvia regained independence. Foodstuffs privately produced and sold *(left)* have for some years represented an important element in the local economy and standard of living.

To older Latvians, an oilrig *(left)* still seems badly out of place in the rural landscape. Since World War II, the emphasis of the Latvian economy has shifted from agriculture to industrial production.

The tiny Republic of Latvia *(right)* lies on the Baltic coast. The country's landscape is mainly low-lying, with some uplands towards its eastern borders. After more than 50 years under Soviet domination – during which time it was known as the Latvian Soviet Socialist Republic – Latvia regained its independence in September 1991. The country has few natural resources but hopes that increasing contacts with Western Europe will boost its economy and attract investment.

A pine forest *(below)* fringes the beach near the Baltic resort of Jūrmala, not far from Riga. The beaches of this once-popular holiday centre have unfortunately now been polluted by effluent from a cellulose works nearby.

An elegant suspension bridge *(above)* spans the western branch of the River Daugava in Riga. The Latvian capital has been important since the 13th century, when it was a Hanseatic League port.

drove many Letts to join Russian revolutionary groups during the early 1900s. It was not until 1920, after the fall of the Russian monarchy in 1917, that Latvia first became an independent state. Independence lasted for less than 20 years. The onset of World War II, and specifically the German-Soviet non-aggression treaty of August 1939, saw the nation fall beneath the Soviet yoke.

As a Soviet republic, Latvia had huge numbers of its own citizens deported for resettlement elsewhere, and had to take in even greater numbers of Russian immigrants. Agriculture – once the basis of the economy – was neglected in favour of huge industrial complexes. As a result, Latvia's major industries today include machine-building and metalworking, petrochemical processing, the manufacture of building materials, electrical engineering, and timber and wood-pulp processing.

In the later 1980s, the policy of *perestroika* (restructuring) pursued by the Soviet government led to a resurgence of Latvian nationalism. The republic's government declared independence in May 1990. However, full independence was not officially recognized until September 1991, after the collapse of the military coup in the Soviet Union in August of that year.

Government and economy

Latvia's government is headed by a Supreme Council, with a Presidium led by a chairman. There is also a Council of Ministers. The constitution provides for democratic elections to elect members to a single-chamber parliament.

Latvia's economy is still dominated by heavy industry, and relies on raw materials imported from the former Soviet Union. Like the other Baltic States, the country is in urgent need of new investment.

Estonia

THE REPUBLIC OF ESTONIA, WHICH regained its independence in 1991, is the most northerly of the three former Baltic republics of the Soviet Union. The country lies on the Baltic Sea and the Gulf of Finland; to the south is Latvia, to the east of the Russian Federation. Estonia includes many islands, both large and small, to the north and west. The largest, Saaremaa, occupies an area of 1,032 square miles (2,673 square kilometres). The country's eastern border runs through two sizeable lakes, Peipsi and Pihkva. Estonia's capital city, Tallinn, is home to 30 per cent of the country's total population of 1,582,000.

Landscape

The terrain is low but undulating, averaging only about 165 feet (50 metres) above sea level. The highest point is Suur Munamägi in the far south, which stands at a height of 1,043 feet (318 metres) above sea level. Inland of the predominantly rocky coast, there are areas of low-lying marsh and bog. There are numerous rivers and streams: some northward-flowing rivers cascade down a steep bank into the Gulf of Finland. Of the 1,400 lakes, a few have been harnessed to generate hydroelectric power. Mixed coniferous and deciduous (leaf-shedding) forest covers about 40 per cent of Estonia's land surface. The forests support a

range of wildlife that includes wolves, elk, bears and wild boar.

The country's climate is cool and wet. Precipitation – either in the form of rain or snow – is high: up to 20 inches (50 centimetres) near the coast, and 28 inches (70 centimetres) in the interior. In exceptionally cold winters the coastal waters freeze over.

People

Around 62 per cent of the population are native Estonians, who make up no less than 87 per cent of the rural population. Another 30 per cent are Russians brought in by the Soviet policy of resettlement. In the cities, there are small minorities of Ukrainians, Byelorussians and Finns. Few non-Estonians speak the national language, Estonian, which closely resembles Finnish.

The Estonian people have lived in their country for more than 2,000 years, mostly under Danish, German or Russian rule. In the 1200s, Estonia fell into the hands of the Teutonic Knights, an order of German crusaders formed in the 1100s. German merchants and estate-owners formed an upper class for several centuries. Although they spoke a foreign language, the German rulers shared with the Estonian peasants a common adherence to Protestantism. In 1710, the Russian tsar Peter the Great (1672-1725) conquered Estonia which, like

FACT BOX

Official name: Republic of Estonia.
Capital: Tallinn
Land area: 17,457 sq mi (45,215 km²)
Land regions: Glacial lowlands; chains of morainic hills in south; some swamps and peat bogs; coast rocky with many islands, but banked steeply on Gulf of Finland
Climate: Temperate, but wet
Highest elevation: Suur Munamägi in the south-east: 1,043 feet (318 metres)
Lowest elevation: Sea level

Government: Single-chamber parliament (Supreme Council)
Head of State: Chairman of the Supreme Council
Population: 1,582,000 (1991)
Languages: Estonian (official), Russian
Religion: Mostly Evangelical Lutheran; some Russian Orthodox
Currency: Kroon
GDP per capita: 4,017 roubles (1989)

In Estonia's capital Tallinn, the flower-sellers (*above*) are as popular with the passing customers as are their counterparts in the Finnish capital Helsinki, only some 52 miles (85 kilometres) across the Gulf of Finland.

Estonia's renowned folk-song festival (*right*) is held every five years in Tallinn and draws large crowds, some from abroad. The Estonians have a strong musical – and especially choral – tradition.

the rest of the Baltic region, remained part of Russia until the end of World War I. The country enjoyed a brief period of independence from 1920 until 1939, when the German-Soviet non-aggression treaty doomed it to Soviet occupation in 1940. Some 60,000 Estonians were deported, and over the next three decades over half a million Russians settled in the country, as industrial enterprises were set up. The well-organized farming system was forcibly reorganized into large state-owned farms, known as collectives. However, the collective system was so inefficient that by the late 1970s, the authorities allowed the sale of produce grown on small private plots.

In the late 1980s, the policy of *perestroika* (restructuring) implemented by Soviet leader Mikhail Gorbachev raised the hope that Estonia might again achieve independence. Following the attempted coup in the Soviet Union in August 1991, the Soviet government recognized Estonian independence on September 4, 1991.

Government and economy

The Estonian government is headed by a prime minister and 21-minister cabinet. The government is responsible to the elected 105-member single-chamber Supreme Council, which is led by a chairman who also acts as head of state. Local affairs are run by councils at county (*maakond*), district and parish (*vald*) levels.

Estonia's economy includes a flourishing agricultural sector and an oil-extraction industry. However, the economy remains tied to light industry and machine-building, both of which require a constant supply of scarce and expensive raw materials. Although Estonia's diverse economy gave its people a relatively high standard of living, many of the country's factories are now badly outdated, and produce large amounts of pollutants. Estonia has urgently sought new investment from Western nations. A serious fuel oil shortage, once sold cheaply by the USSR, now hinders economic growth.

Rolling lowlands, with extensive forests and numerous lakes *(above)* are typical of the Estonian landscape. However, decades of reliance on oil-driven industry have resulted in widespread environmental damage.

The Republic of Estonia *(below)* is the most northerly of the three Baltic States. Since formal independence in 1991, Estonia has pursued closer economic links with Western countries, notably Finland.

ALMOST ENTIRELY SURROUNDED BY land, the Baltic seems more like an inland lake than a sea, and its waters are far less salty than those of most other seas. It lies between the Scandinavian peninsula and the northern coast of Europe, and is bordered by Sweden, Finland, Estonia, Latvia, Lithuania, Russia, Poland, Germany and Denmark. Narrow outlets link it with the North Sea to the west. In the Middle Ages it was the economic centre of a group of north European ports known as the Hanseatic League, and a meeting place of many peoples. Its economic importance has declined, but it still boasts major port cities such as Stockholm, Helsinki, St Petersburg, Riga, Gdańsk and Kiel.

Composition

The Baltic Sea resembles a finger some 950 miles (1,530 kilometres) in length and averaging 120 miles (190 kilometres) in width. The Gulf of Bothnia and the Gulf of Finland form two long extensions to the sea. The Baltic receives fresh water from rivers, snow and rain. The salt water that it receives from its narrow outlets to the North Sea is cold and high in salt content, making it very heavy. As a result, it hardly mixes with the surface water, which remains remarkably fresh.

As an environment for living organisms, however, the Baltic contains several unfavourable factors. With salt content and temperature gradually rising, the amount of life-giving oxygen in the waters of the Baltic is decreasing from natural causes. Meanwhile, human activity poses an even greater problem with the pollutants that are used in the surrounding countries. Destructive industrial wastes flow into the Baltic in large quantities, while nitrates and phosphates from fertilizers cause an over-rapid growth of the tiny organisms called plankton. When plankton dies, sinks to the bottom, and decomposes, it takes large amounts of oxygen from the water and also produces a life-restricting gas called hydrogen sulphide. As a result, parts of the Baltic have already become a "dead sea", despite the fact that Baltic countries have now agreed on close cooperation in conservation measures.

Human activity

Protected from the strong tides of the North Sea, the Baltic enables ships to move easily around the coasts, joining together the surrounding countries in a commercial network that goes back more than 1,000 years. The relatively fresh waters of the Baltic have preserved many wrecks from destruction by wood-eating marine organisms, so that archaeologists can reconstruct the story of the Baltic seafarers in

Gdańsk (*above*), an important Baltic port and shipbuilding centre in modern Poland, contains a number of handsome buildings. Many date from its period as a major medieval trading city.

The Baltic Sea (*right*) has only a narrow outlet to the North Sea, making it practically a lake. Peoples around its shores have used it for maritime trade and traffic from the earliest times, especially during the Middle Ages with the emergence of the powerful trading cities of the Hanseatic League. Today, about 18 million people, as well as much industry, crowd its shores. Metal-processing and chemical works, and pulp and paper mills, regularly discharge their wastes into its waters. Almost landlocked, the sea suffers serious pollution.

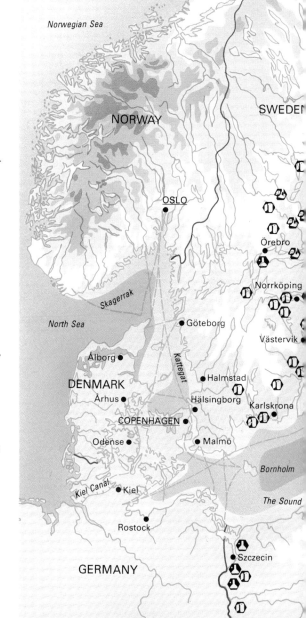

Chemical
Pulp and paper
Steel and metal
● Major town
-- Ferry route

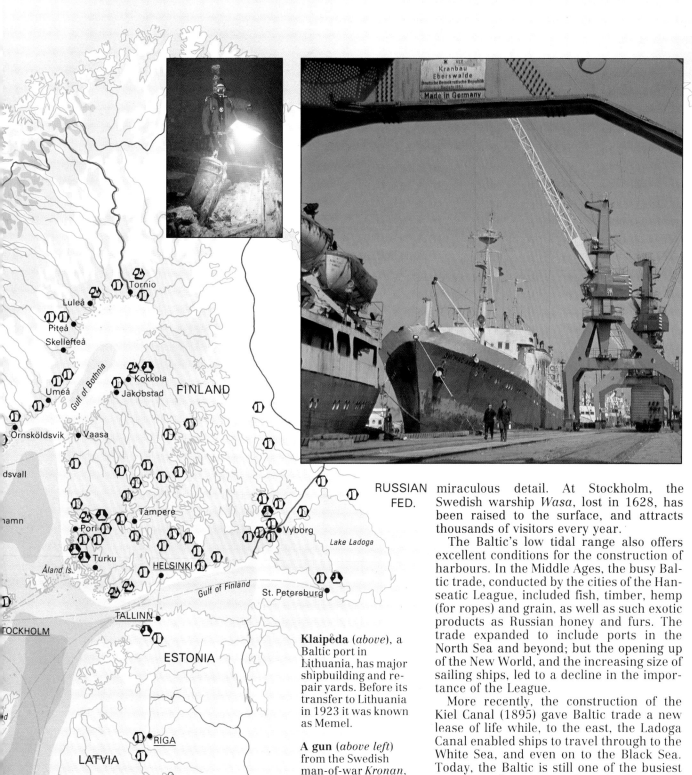

RUSSIAN FED.

Klaipéda (*above*), a Baltic port in Lithuania, has major shipbuilding and repair yards. Before its transfer to Lithuania in 1923 it was known as Memel.

A gun (*above left*) from the Swedish man-of-war *Kronan*, lost in 1676, lies on the seabed near Kalmar, Sweden. The Baltic's brackish waters make it a treasure trove for archaeologists, since wood-eating marine organisms are absent, allowing wrecks to survive like "time capsules" from the past.

miraculous detail. At Stockholm, the Swedish warship *Wasa*, lost in 1628, has been raised to the surface, and attracts thousands of visitors every year.

The Baltic's low tidal range also offers excellent conditions for the construction of harbours. In the Middle Ages, the busy Baltic trade, conducted by the cities of the Hanseatic League, included fish, timber, hemp (for ropes) and grain, as well as such exotic products as Russian honey and furs. The trade expanded to include ports in the North Sea and beyond; but the opening up of the New World, and the increasing size of sailing ships, led to a decline in the importance of the League.

More recently, the construction of the Kiel Canal (1895) gave Baltic trade a new lease of life while, to the east, the Ladoga Canal enabled ships to travel through to the White Sea, and even on to the Black Sea. Today, the Baltic is still one of the busiest stretches of water anywhere in the world. Timber and fish remain the main items of Baltic trade, but traditional shipping now shares space with commercial and passenger ferries connecting Denmark, Sweden and Finland with German Baltic ports. Ferry traffic has also grown along the south coast of the Baltic, where a railway ferry connects Mukran on Rügen Island with Klaipéda in Lithuania, and a car ferry joins Gdańsk and Travemünde in Germany.

Britain ranks low in size among the world's independent countries, though for more than 200 years its importance has been out of all proportion to its size. It was the first country to develop industry, and it once ruled the largest empire in history. Industrial might and imperial expansion made Britain not only the richest, but also the most powerful nation in the world.

Since 1945, Britain's power has been much reduced. Nearly all of its former colonies have become independent countries, though most of them have retained links with Britain and each other through the Commonwealth of Nations. This free association of countries from every continent shares a common tongue, English, the world's leading business language, and many parliamentary and other traditional British institutions. Britain's parliament is often called the "Mother of Parliaments", because so many countries have borrowed features from it.

The British love of tradition is seen in the red coats and "bearskins" of the **Brigade of Guards** *(left)*, but the country has changed enormously since 1945. The crippling costs of World War II, the end of its empire, the decline of older industries, and mounting competition from other industrial countries have created complex economic problems. By 1990, it stood sixth in terms of its total Gross National Product, behind the United States, Japan, Germany, France and Italy, while in terms of its Gross National Product per head of population it ranked only 20th in the world. Revenues from North Sea oil in recent years may have tended to conceal its economic weakness, despite an impressive increase in productivity. In addition, the nature of Britain's economy is also changing. Though trade with Commonwealth countries remains significant, Britain's most important trade is now with the other countries of the European Community.

Yet few Britons instinctively see themselves as Europeans. When questioned, most of them would not even call themselves Britons. Instead, they prefer to regard themselves as being English, Northern Irish, Scots, or Welsh. This is a reminder of the fact that Britain, or, officially, the United Kingdom of Great Britain and Northern Ireland, is really a union of four countries: England, Scotland, and Wales (which together form Great Britain), and Northern Ireland. Each of these countries has its own dialects, culture, history, and traditions. But when danger is perceived to threaten the country's interests, local nationalism and differences are temporarily forgotten, to be traditionally superseded by a staunch and determined patriotism.

Great Britain Today

BRITAIN IS A CONSTITUTIONAL MONarchy, whose constitution is not a written document. It consists instead partly of statute (laws passed by Parliament), partly of common law (based on customs and beliefs), and partly of convention. The supreme authority, Parliament, consists of the monarch, an elected, 650-member House of Commons, and a non-elected House of Lords. The House of Lords has about 1,170 members, including two archbishops and 24 bishops.

The British monarch is also head of the Commonwealth of Nations (an association of about 50 nations that grew out of the British Empire), and head of state in 17 Commonwealth countries. The Commonwealth is one international forum used by Britain to promote its policies, along with the European Community, and the North Atlantic Treaty Organization which includes Britain's traditional ally, the United States; it is also an active member of the United Nations.

The executive is headed by the government, consisting of the Cabinet, led by the prime minister (normally leader of the majority party in the House of Commons), and other ministers. The government departments responsible for national administration are run by civil servants, who remain in office whatever the party in power. England and Wales share a legal system, but Scotland and Northern Ireland each have their own separate legal systems.

Fifty-three counties make up their main local government units in England and Wales outside Greater London. Scotland is divided into nine regions and three island

Number 10 Downing St (*above*) is the official residence of the prime minister. The elegant house dates from the 1700s.

authority areas, and Northern Ireland has 26 district councils. Northern Ireland once had its own parliament, but internal troubles have forced the British parliament to rule it directly since 1972.

The people

Britain is densely populated, with 92 per cent of the people living in urban areas. English is the official language, but about 20 per cent of the people of Wales also speak Welsh, and 79,000 Scots speak a form of Gaelic. Some nationalists favour regional autonomy, or home rule, though the Welsh and Scots voted against it in 1979. In Northern Ireland, a mainly Roman Catholic minority favours unification with the Republic of Ireland, but the Protestant majority wants to remain a part of Britain.

The British are a mixture of peoples, whose ancestors include Celts, Romans, Angles, Saxons, Scandinavians, and Normans. Since the 1950s, people from Commonwealth countries, especially from South Asia and the West Indies, have settled in Britain. By the early 1990s, Great Britain contained about 2.4 million non-whites, more than two-fifths of whom were born in Britain. Most Britons have a high standard of living, though Britain's Gross National Product (the value of all goods and services produced yearly) is lower than that of several of the 12 EC nations.

About two-thirds of adult Britons belong in theory to a Christian church, but few attend regularly. The monarch heads the Church of England but not that of Scotland. There are also about five million Roman Catholics and about 1.75 million Muslims.

FACT BOX

THE COUNTRY
Official name: United Kingdom of Great Britain and Northern Ireland
Capital: London
Land regions: From N-S: Scottish Highlands, Central Lowlands, Southern Uplands, Pennines, Wales, Southwest Peninsula, English Lowlands, Northern Ireland
Land area: 94,248 sq mi (244,100 km²)
Climate: Mild oceanic (Gulf Stream), but variable. Temperate summers and winters. Highest rainfall in W
Main rivers: Thames, Severn, Wye, Tyne, Clyde, Humber, Ouse
Highest elevation: Ben Nevis 4,406 ft (1,343 m)

Lowest elevation: The Fens 15 ft (4.6 m) below sea level

THE GOVERNMENT
Form of Government: Constitutional monarchy
Head of State: King or Queen
Head of Government: Prime Minister
Administrative areas: England: 39 counties, 6 metropolitan counties; Wales: 8 counties; Scotland: 9 regions, 3 Island Areas; N Ireland: 26 districts
Legislature: House of Commons (650 members, elected by the people every 5 years); House of Lords (1,170 hereditary and life peers, bishops and

law lords)
Judiciary: Separate systems in England/Wales, Scotland, Northern Ireland. House of Lords is supreme court of appeal
Armed Forces: Standing army on voluntary basis. Total strength: 312,500 plus reserves

THE PEOPLE
Population (1991): 55,487,000
Language: English (official). Welsh and Gaelic spoken in parts of Scotland and Northern Ireland
Religion: Anglican (48%), Protestant (7%), Roman Catholic (10%), Muslim (3.2%), Jewish (n.a.)

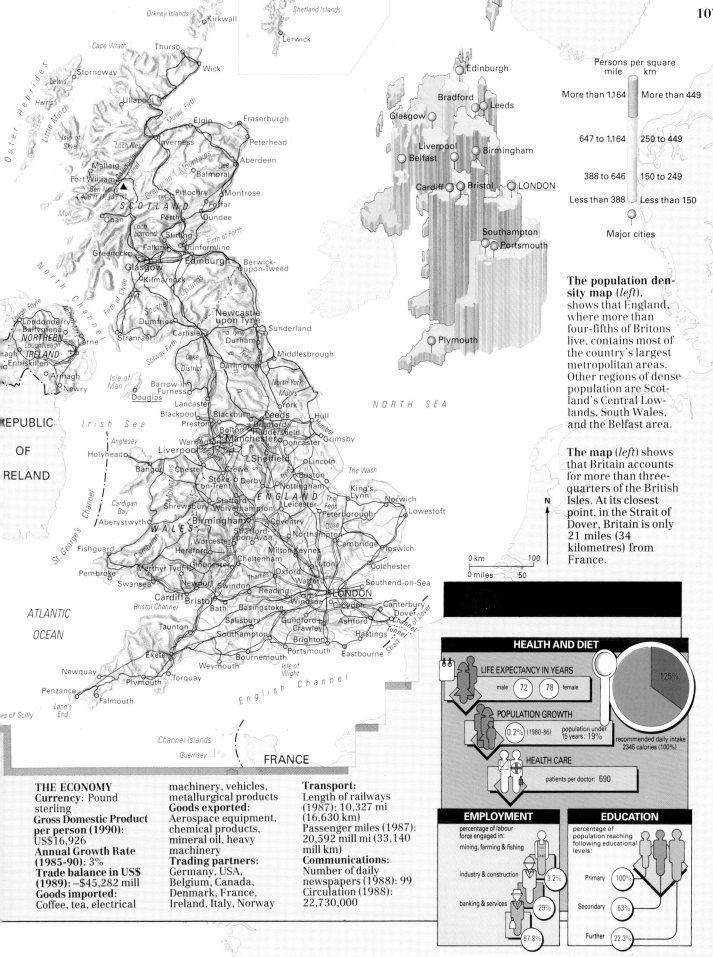

Orkney Islands — Kirkwall
Shetland Islands — Lerwick

Cape Wrath — Thurso — Wick
Stornoway — Ullapool
Lewis — Harris — Isle of Skye — Little Minch — Outer Hebrides — North Minch

Elgin — Fraserburgh — Peterhead
Inverness — Loch Ness — Grampian Mountains — Aberdeen
Mallaig — Fort William — Ben Nevis 4,406 ft (1,343 m) — Dee — Balmoral
Mull — Oban — SCOTLAND — Pitlochry — Forfar — Montrose
Loch Lomond — Perth — Dundee
Stirling — Firth of Forth
Greenock — Falkirk — Dunfermline — Berwick-upon-Tweed
Glasgow — Edinburgh
Kilmarnock — Southern Uplands

North Channel
Londonderry — Ballymena — Larne
NORTHERN IRELAND — Lough Neagh
Enniskillen — Armagh — Newry
Lough Foyle — Antrim Mts

REPUBLIC OF IRELAND

Dumfries
Stranraer — Carlisle — Newcastle upon Tyne — Sunderland
Tyne — Durham
Solway Firth — Tees — Middlesbrough
Lake District — Darlington
Isle of Man — Douglas — Barrow-in-Furness — North York Moors
Lancaster — York
Blackpool — Blackburn — Leeds — Hull
Preston — Bolton — Bradford — Huddersfield — Humber
Warrington — Manchester — Doncaster — Grimsby
Liverpool — Sheffield — Lincoln
Bangor — Chester — Crewe — Derby — Trent — Boston
Holyhead — Anglesey — Stoke-on-Trent — Nottingham — The Wash
Cambrian Mountains — Shrewsbury — Stafford — Wolverhampton — ENGLAND — Leicester — King's Lynn — Norwich
Cardigan Bay — Aberystwyth — Birmingham — Coventry — The Fens — Peterborough — Lowestoft
WALES — Worcester — Stratford-upon-Avon — Northampton — Ouse — Ipswich
Fishguard — Hereford — Milton Keynes — Cambridge — Colchester
Pembroke — Merthyr Tydfil — Gloucester — Cheltenham — Oxford — Luton
Swansea — Newport — Thames — Watford — Southend-on-Sea
Cardiff — Bristol — Swindon — Reading — LONDON — Croydon — Canterbury — Dover
Bristol Channel — Bath — Basingstoke — Windsor — Channel Tunnel
Taunton — Salisbury — Guildford — Ashford — Strait of Dover
Southampton — Crawley — Brighton — Hastings
Newquay — Exeter — Bournemouth — Portsmouth — Eastbourne
Penzance — Plymouth — Torquay — Weymouth — Isle of Wight
Land's End — Falmouth
Isles of Scilly

ATLANTIC OCEAN
Irish Sea
St. George's Channel
English Channel
NORTH SEA

Channel Islands — Guernsey — FRANCE

N
0 km 100
0 miles 50

Glasgow — Belfast — Edinburgh — Bradford — Leeds — Liverpool — Birmingham — Cardiff — Bristol — LONDON — Southampton — Portsmouth — Plymouth

Persons per square
mile   km

More than 1,164 — More than 449

647 to 1,164 — 250 to 449

388 to 646 — 150 to 249

Less than 388 — Less than 150

Major cities

The population density map (*left*), shows that England, where more than four-fifths of Britons live, contains most of the country's largest metropolitan areas. Other regions of dense population are Scotland's Central Lowlands, South Wales, and the Belfast area.

The map (*left*) shows that Britain accounts for more than three-quarters of the British Isles. At its closest point, in the Strait of Dover, Britain is only 21 miles (34 kilometres) from France.

THE ECONOMY
Currency: Pound sterling
Gross Domestic Product per person (1990): US$16,926
Annual Growth Rate (1985-90): 3%
Trade balance in US$ (1989): −$45,282 mill
Goods imported: Coffee, tea, electrical machinery, vehicles, metallurgical products
Goods exported: Aerospace equipment, chemical products, mineral oil, heavy machinery
Trading partners: Germany, USA, Belgium, Canada, Denmark, France, Ireland, Italy, Norway

Transport:
Length of railways (1987): 10,327 mi (16,630 km)
Passenger miles (1987): 20,592 mill mi (33,140 mill km)
Communications:
Number of daily newspapers (1988): 99
Circulation (1988): 22,730,000

HEALTH AND DIET
LIFE EXPECTANCY IN YEARS
male 72 — 78 female
POPULATION GROWTH
0.2% (1980-86) — population under 15 years: 19%
HEALTH CARE
patients per doctor: 690
125%
recommended daily intake 2345 calories (100%)

EMPLOYMENT
percentage of labour force engaged in:
mining, farming & fishing — 3.2%
industry & construction — 29%
banking & services — 67.8%

EDUCATION
percentage of population reaching following educational levels:
Primary — 100%
Secondary — 83%
Further — 22.3%

England

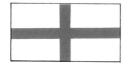

ENGLAND MAKES UP JUST OVER 53 PER cent of Britain, covering an area of 50,373 square miles (130,478 square kilometres). But it has 83 per cent of its population (46,161,000). It is an overcrowded country, especially in the southeast (which became even more densely populated in the 1980s). Yet despite its high population density, England retains rural areas of great charm, some magnificent scenery, and a wealth of historic buildings. Tradition and ceremony are other features of England that attract tourists to its shores. Tourism is now a major industry. An estimated 1.4 million people work in jobs supported directly or indirectly by tourist spending.

The land

England is a small country – no place is more than 75 miles (120 kilometres) from the sea – but it has a wide variety of landscapes. The chief uplands are in the north and west. They include the dome-shaped Cumbrian Mountains, which contain England's highest peak, Scafell Pike, lying 3,205 feet (977 metres) above sea level, and its largest lake, Windermere. To the east lies the Pennine range, the "backbone" of northern England, and the Yorkshire Moors. In the southwest are the moorlands of Exmoor and Dartmoor. Parts of these uplands are now protected as national parks.

But most of England is low-lying, with long ranges of hills, such as the limestone Cotswolds and the chalk Chilterns, separated by fertile valleys and basins, and drained by such rivers as the Thames (the longest river entirely in England), the Severn (which is longer but rises in Wales), and the Trent. The flattest area, the Fenlands around the Wash, contains much land which has been reclaimed from the sea. England also includes the Scilly Isles in the far southwest, and the Isle of Wight.

England's animal life has been depleted by the destruction of environments, though many rare species are now protected in nature reserves and sites of special scientific interest. Some animals, including foxes and kestrels, have shown an astonishing aptitude for life in crowded, built-up areas. Foxes in particular have become skilful scavengers in the outskirts of big cities.

Western England lies in the path of the prevailing southwesterly winds, which give the region a rainy climate, especially in upland areas, and generally mild temperatures. The east is drier and often subject in winter to northeasterly winds which rapidly lower temperatures. Above all, England's climate is changeable, which explains why it traditionally ranks as the most popular topic of conversation among English people.

The people

Until the late 1700s, England had an agricultural economy. But industrialization led to a great expansion of towns so that today more than 90 per cent of the population lives in urban areas. Areas of densest population are in London and the Thames estuary, West Yorkshire and the industrial cities of the northwest, the northeast, and the Midlands, around Birmingham. England contains eight of Britain's ten largest urban areas. These are, with 1991 population estimates, Greater London (6,377,900), Greater Manchester (2,582,400), Birmingham (934,900), Leeds (674,400), Sheffield (499,700), Liverpool (448,300), Bradford (449,100) and Bristol (370,300).

The move of population from rural to urban areas reflected a shift in the economy from agriculture to industry. Although no longer a major employer, farming is highly efficient, but the economy of England, the most developed part of Britain, is still based mainly on manufacturing and trade. In recent years, however, traditional industries have declined. Ageing machinery and foreign competition have caused the closure of many industries, including steel mills and shipbuilding yards. Even car production has had problems, though there has been a major expansion of less labour-intensive high technology industries.

The decline in manufacturing has also been accompanied by a rise in service industries, including government, finance and business services. For example, about 75 per cent of employees in London and the southeast now work in service industries.

One group of service industries is concerned with leisure activities. Most people have much more free time than earlier generations, and the proportion of older, retired people is steadily increasing. Leisure activities include many kinds of sport, especially soccer, and outdoor recreations. Many English people visit their local public house, where they can buy alcoholic and other drinks, and meet their friends.

The official church is the Church of England, or the Anglican Church. But church membership, at 13 per cent of the population, is lower than in the rest of Britain.

Changing economic conditions have led to regional differences in prosperity. In the last 20 years, the fastest developing areas have mostly been in southern England, and this has led to talk of "two nations", a prosperous south and a less prosperous north. An even more marked contrast is the relative economic status of England as compared with other parts of Britain. In 1988, the unemployment rate in England was well below that of Wales, Scotland and Northern Ireland. However, by 1992 rates had risen faster in England than elsewhere.

The Lake District (*above*) is the finest of England's national parks, celebrated for its beauty.

Tyne Bridge (*far left*) recalls Newcastle's period as a major European industrial centre.

Blackpool (*left*) has long been a holiday resort for England's northern industrial workers.

The Channel Tunnel (*below*), begun in 1988, has ended England's separation from the European continent.

Wales

WALES COVERS 8.5 PER CENT OF BRITAIN, a land area of 8,019 square miles (20,768 square kilometres), with a population of 2,805,000. Most Welsh people trace their ancestry to a Celtic race that lived in Britain before the Anglo-Saxon influx in the 400s AD. Nearly 20 per cent speak the ancient Celtic language of Welsh. Welsh and English are both official languages.

Most Welsh people treasure their language and ancient culture. Their literature is one of Europe's oldest, and Wales is famed for its music, especially choral singing. Festivals called *eisteddfodau* celebrate Welsh poetry, prose and music. The Royal National Eisteddfod, held every August, is conducted entirely in Welsh. The International Musical Eisteddfod is held at Llangollen in North Wales.

The nationalist Plaid Cymru party in Wales favours independence from Britain, while other people favour the establishment of a Welsh parliament which would take over executive powers from the central government. But Welsh voters rejected this proposal in a referendum in 1979. Instead, Wales elects 38 out of the 650 members in the British House of Commons, while the day-to-day administration of the country is handled by the Welsh Office in the country's capital, Cardiff. A member of the British Cabinet, the Secretary of State of Wales, is the head of the Welsh Office.

The land

The Cambrian Mountains cover about two-thirds of Wales. The highest peak, Snowdon (*Eyri* in Welsh), reaches 3,560 feet (1,085 metres) in the north. Sheep farming is the chief occupation on the higher moorlands.

The lower parts of Wales include mostly narrow coastal plains, which are bordered in places by some majestic scenery, and the lower sections of river valleys. The longest rivers are the Severn and Wye, both of which empty into the Bristol Channel in the southeast. The largest Welsh island is Anglesey, (or Mon in Welsh), which is separated from the northwestern mainland by the narrow Menai Strait. Off the northwest coast of Anglesey is Holy Island, which contains Holyhead, ferry port for Dublin.

Wales has three national parks: Snowdonia, the Brecon Beacons, and the Pembrokeshire Coast. These and other protected areas have offered sanctuary to animal species that are now rare in England.

The lowlands of Wales have a mild, moist climate. Spring comes so early in the southwest that the farmers there have an advantage over those to the east. The rainfall is heaviest on the uplands, which get more than 79 inches (200 centimetres) per year, while parts of Snowdonia have up to 197 inches (500 centimetres).

The people

The most densely populated regions are in the old mining valleys and industrial cities in the south. The largest urban areas (1988 population figures) are Cardiff (278,900), Swansea (187,400), and Newport (129,500). Wrexham Maelor (114,600) is the most densely populated district in North Wales. There are small coastal towns, but the uplands are sparsely populated.

About four-fifths of Wales is classed as farmland, but from the middle of the 1800s, rural areas became depopulated as people moved into the coal-mining and manufacturing towns. Wales has two main coalfields, one in South Wales and a smaller one in the north-east. But coal-mining, together with traditional tin plate and iron and steel industries, have declined in recent years, though Wales still produces one-third of Britain's steel and about nine per cent of its coal. At the same time, however, many new light industries have been established and Wales is becoming a centre of electronics industries, with investment from Japan and the United States.

Leisure activities in Wales are much the same as in other parts of Britain, but the Welsh national game is undoubtedly rugby football. The annual international matches against England, France, Ireland, and Scotland attract passionate interest.

Coal mining villages, such as Abercynon, (*left*), are found along the valleys of South Wales. In 1804, the inventor Richard Trevithick drove a steam engine from Merthyr to Abercynon, thus beginning the world's railway age.

Prince Charles received the title of Prince of Wales in 1969 at Caernarfon Castle (*below*). This custom began in 1301 with Edward I, who installed his infant son as Prince of Wales on the grounds that he spoke no English.

The Pass of Llanberis (*left*), lies southeast of Llanberis, the starting point for the rail ascent of Snowdon. The Snowdonia National Park covers 845 square miles (2,190 square kilometres) of superb, unspoilt scenery.

The Royal National Eisteddfod (*above*), a great festival of music and the arts, is held every year in August alternately in towns and cities in North and South Wales. This Welsh-speaking festival began more than 1,400 years ago.

London

LONDON IS BRITAIN'S CAPITAL AND chief tourist attraction. The Romans founded the original Londinium in AD 43. The City of London, which now stands on the former Roman settlement, is a small area that plays a major part in Britain's economy, because it is a world centre of banking, commerce and insurance. Greater London, which had a population of 6,377,900 in 1991, includes the City of London and 32 boroughs (local government areas). Among its population are about 1,000,000 immigrants. This has given London a cosmopolitan multi-ethnic character.

The Great Fire of 1666 nearly destroyed London. But from the ashes arose a new city crowned by Sir Christopher Wren's St Paul's Cathedral. St Paul's survived the bombing in World War II and continued to dominate London's skyline until the construction of tall offices and apartment blocks which began in the 1960s. This redevelopment has altered the character of London, but it is not to everyone's taste. In recent years, London has also suffered from unemployment, crime, and drug addiction, especially in the poor districts.

More welcome changes were the Clean Air Act of 1956, which eliminated the toxic London smogs, and the opening of a flood barrier at Woolwich in 1984 to prevent potentially disastrous tidal floods.

Central London is the main focus of tourism. The Tower of London, once a royal prison, now houses the Crown Jewels. Westminster boasts the Houses of Parliament, Westminster Abbey, the Roman Catholic Westminster Cathedral, and Buckingham Palace. Nearby are London's main shopping districts, parks, and cultural institutions. London has more than 40 major theatres, five full-time symphony orchestras, the Royal Opera House, and many great art galleries and museums. The South Bank on the Thames is a huge cultural complex, with concert halls, the National Theatre, and art galleries.

London has a comprehensive system of underground and surface railways. As the railways reached outwards, London absorbed many ancient settlements, such as Hampstead and Greenwich, and many of these still retain a "village" flavour. The rail network also enabled people who worked in London to live outside the city.

London is rich in traditional ceremonies, such as the Lord Mayor's Show and the State Opening of Parliament, but it is also a thriving city with an economy based on service industries and manufacturing. Central London, however, is no longer a major port. The old docks, located near the financial zone have been rebuilt as a fashionable residential and recreational area.

The City of London (*right*), the business heart of the capital, stands on the site of the old Roman settlement of Londinium. Since World War II, rebuilding has led to modern office blocks dwarfing older, elegant buildings.

Trafalgar Square (*left*) commemorates Lord Nelson's naval victory in 1805 and contains Nelson's Column. Bordering the square are the National Gallery and the church of St Martin-in-the-Fields, built in 1726.

Portobello Road street market (*right*) attracts a host of weekend buyers and stretches more than a mile down a quaint old road. It is best known for its silver, but includes all kinds of collectables.

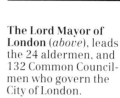

The Lord Mayor of London (*above*), leads the 24 aldermen, and 132 Common Councilmen who govern the City of London.

The Horse Guards Parade (*above*), is the scene of one of London's most spectacular ceremonies, the Trooping of the Colour, performed on the Queen's birthday. Nearby, the royal Household Cavalry holds a daily parade.

The map of London (*below*), shows Greater London, which sprawls across the Thames basin. From the central area (a map of which is inset), Greater London extends outwards. It is divided into the City of London and 32 local

government boroughs. Glittering royal and other ceremonies, historic buildings, elegant shops, and a wealth of cultural activities in central London help to make Britain's capital the country's leading tourist attraction.

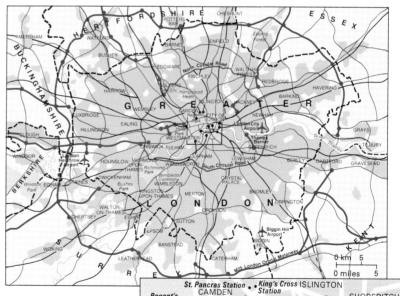

Public houses (*above*), where drinks and, usually, food are on sale, are popular meeting places where Londoners like to meet and relax.

1. Buckingham Palace
2. Westminster Abbey
3. Houses of Parliament
4. Big Ben
5. Trafalgar Square
6. Leicester Square
7. British Museum
8. Covent Garden
9. Royal Festival Hall
10. National Theatre
11. St. Paul's Cathedral
12. Tower of London

Scotland

SCOTLAND

● Edinburgh

SCOTLAND IS THE MOST THINLY populated part of Britain. With a land area of 29,794 square miles (77,167 square kilometres), it covers 32 per cent of the total but contains only 9 per cent of the population (4,957,000). Most sparsely populated are the Highlands and Islands, which cover about half of the country. Here live people who preserve traditions based on loyalty to their clans (families with a common ancestor and the same name).

A strong sense of identity and a resentment for what is seen to be a centralized, English-dominated parliament has led some Scots to advocate nationalism and the establishment of an elected parliament in the capital Edinburgh. The issue failed to win the necessary 40 per cent support of the electorate in a referendum held in 1979. Today, Scotland sends 72 members to the House of Commons. The day-to-day administration is handled by a member of the British Cabinet, the Secretary of State for Scotland.

The land

Scotland has three main land regions: the Northern Highlands and Islands, the Central Lowlands, and the Southern Uplands. The Highlands are divided into the Northwest Highlands and the Grampian Mountains by a deep valley, Glen More, which contains Loch Ness, supposed home of the famous "monster". Britain's highest peak, Ben Nevis at 4,406 feet (1,343 metres), lies in the Grampian Mountains. The Highlands are dotted with lochs (lakes), the largest of which is Loch Lomond, north of Glasgow. Glasgow itself is in the fertile Central Lowlands which are drained by the Clyde, Forth, and Tay rivers. The Southern Uplands is a region of moorland and pasture.

Scotland has three regional parks and 40 national scenic areas that cover 13 per cent of the land. These areas are the last refuge of the British subspecies of the wild cat, and the main home in Great Britain of the blue or mountain hare. Native red deer and roe deer graze in the Highlands.

Because of its northerly position, Scotland is generally colder than the rest of Britain, but the climate is still mild – a result of the warming influence of the Atlantic Gulf Stream. Rainfall is heaviest on the western mountains. Snowfall in the Grampian Mountains is often sufficient for skiing.

The people

As elsewhere in Britain, there has been a steady drift of people from the land, especially from the Highlands and Islands, to urban areas. About three out of every four Scots now live in the Central Lowlands, which contain the cities of Glasgow and

A Highland piper (*below*) in traditional costume performs at a gathering of the clans. The Scottish bagpipe is an instrument of great antiquity whose plaintive tones perfectly express Scotland's often tragic story.

Loch Awe (*right*), near Oban, is one of the many beautiful lakes of the Scottish Highlands. On its banks are ruins associated with past clan conflict, including Kilchurn Castle, built by Sir Colin Campbell in 1440.

Edinburgh. Other cities include the oil and fishing port of Aberdeen, and Dundee.

Coal-mining, steel and shipbuilding industries have declined, accelerating the rate of Scottish emigration to England and beyond. Emigration was slowed down in the 1970s by the development of the North Sea oilfields, which provided jobs and created new industries, including chemical works and financial and business services. But it did little to halt the industrial decline in the Central Lowlands, though new light engineering and electronics industries have been set up.

Not all Scots emigrate because of unemployment. For years, talented Scots have left their mark on many parts of the world as missionaries, doctors, business people, and, perhaps above all, as engineers. They were products of Scotland's strong and independent tradition of education. Scotland also has a distinctive legal system, which absorbed elements of European legal systems. Scotland's official church is the Presbyterian Church of Scotland.

Tourism is important and increasing. Attractions include the magnificent scenery, and events such as the Highland Games and the annual Edinburgh International Festival. Among major leisure activities are golf, which originated in Scotland, and soccer, the leading spectator sport.

The distilling of Scotch whisky, (*below*) began more than 500 years ago. This distillery at Tain on Dornoch Firth produces Glenmorangie Scotch, and is one of more than 100 distilleries in Scotland. The ancient industry of Scotch distilling remains a major export earner. About half of the exports go to the United States. Other traditional industries for which Scotland is noted include the manufacture of high-quality tweed and other textiles.

The annual Edinburgh International Festival (*left*), is held in late summer. It includes musical and dramatic performances, and a spectacular Tattoo on the Castle Esplanade. The Festival also features dance and cabaret.

Mallaig (*above*), on the northwest coast of Scotland, is an important herring port. Scottish ports account for more than three-quarters of the total fish landed in Britain. Other major ports include Aberdeen and Fraserburgh.

Northern Ireland

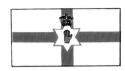

NORTHERN IRELAND

Belfast

NORTHERN IRELAND, A PROVINCE OF the United Kingdom, occupies the north-eastern section of Ireland. It was originally made up of six counties (Londonderry, Antrim, Tyrone, Fermanagh, Down, and Armagh), but in 1973 a reorganization of local government replaced those counties with 26 districts. The province is often informally called Ulster, one of the four historic regions of Ireland when the island was a single unit. In the 1500s and 1600s the English government systematically settled Protestant English and Scottish emigrants in the area, thus laying the seeds of a conflict that has endured to this day.

Northern Ireland occupies 5,452 square miles (14,121 square kilometres), about one-sixth of Ireland, with a population of 1,570,000. Two-thirds of the people are Protestants, the remainder being Roman Catholics. This sharp religious division has been largely responsible for the tragic events that have overshadowed the province ever since its creation in 1920. Conflict has continued between terrorist organizations and British security forces for much of the period. The present crisis has smouldered on, often erupting into acts of violence since 1969. But in 1985, an Anglo-Irish agreement raised hopes for an eventual solution, given time and tolerance.

In 1920, the British enacted a law separating Northern Ireland from the rest of Ireland, and granted home rule to the six Northern Irish counties. The remaining 26 Irish counties rejected the Act and in 1921 formed the Irish Free State, known today as the Republic of Ireland. Since that time, people in the Republic and the Roman Catholic minority in Northern Ireland have tried to make common cause.

From 1969 onwards, violence escalated in the province. A large peacekeeping force of British soldiers was stationed there, but in 1972 the worsening situation led to direct rule by the United Kingdom Parliament in London. The pro-Catholic IRA (Irish Republican Army) stepped up their violence, which resulted in predictable reaction from Protestant paramilitary groups.

The land

Northern Ireland's rocky coastline contains many inlets and sea loughs (lakes) of great beauty. A famous coastal landmark is the Giant's Causeway, a few miles northeast of Portrush. This is a headland made up of thousands of almost identical basaltic columns formed by a flow of lava into the sea.

Many loughs also occur inland, of course. Lough Neagh, near the centre of the province, covers 150 square miles (388 square kilometres) and is the largest lake in the British Isles.

Three mountain groups straddle the province. The largest of these are the Mountains of Antrim in the north-east. The River Bann separates this plateau from the Sperrin Mountains to the west. The romantic Mourne Mountains, in the south-east, contain the highest point in the province – Slieve Donard, which rises to 2,796 feet (853 metres). The land surface of the province slopes down to boggy regions in the centre. The longest rivers are the Bann and the Foyle.

The climate of Northern Ireland is mild and damp, with rainfall decreasing from west to east. The Atlantic Gulf Stream helps to warm the coast.

The people

Most of the people are of Scottish or English descent. About half live in farm regions, but there has been a steady drift from the countryside to the towns. The traditional

The Mourne Mountains (*left*) look down benevolently on a harvest scene in Co. Down, where a picnic meal of homemade soda bread and jam is being prepared. Many Northern Irish farms are small and lack mechanization.

The "Lusty Man" (*right*), the stone figure of a pagan god dating from about AD 500, greets visitors to the lovely and unspoilt lake of Lough Erne, Co. Fermanagh. The statue is carved with two heads to give all-round vision.

industries of shipbuilding, agriculture, and linen manufacture declined after the 1950s and many workers lost their jobs. By the 1980s, the face of industry had greatly changed. Engineering, chemicals, electronics, and man-made fibres absorbed many of the unemployed. But even these new industries were hampered by rampant terrorism. Nevertheless, tourism grew, and as a result, service industries benefited.

The mountains, moors and coasts of the province offer a wide variety of unspoilt scenery and recreation. Popular holiday resorts include Portrush and Bangor. Carrickfergus Castle and Castlecool, among many others, display a wealth of historical buildings. Belfast, the capital of the province, offers all the attractions of an important city and port. Many visitors also travel to Northern Ireland for the pleasures of water sports, golf and horse-racing.

Ulster Orangemen (*above*) prepare for the annual commemoration of the "Glorious Twelfth" – the July 12, 1690 victory of Protestant King William III over Catholic James II at the Boyne. The Orange Society is dedicated to maintaining Protestant political rule.

Short's of Belfast (*left*) is a major employer, engaged in a broad range of aerospace projects in collaboration with other international manufacturers.

Ireland, a large North Atlantic island nestling on the western edge of the British Isles, richly deserves its age-old nickname of the Emerald Isle. Five-sixths of the island make up the independent Republic of Ireland. The remaining northeastern sixth, called Northern Ireland but widely known as Ulster, has remained part of the United Kingdom of Great Britain and Northern Ireland.

Rich grazing slopes *(left)* in the east of the Republic contrast vividly with the heather-covered hills and mountain lakes of the west. In the centre, flat green fields and peat bogs (a major source of fuel) feature prominently. All round the rugged coast, a rim of broken mountains defies the often turbulent seas. The mild humid climate seems to change from day to day. But down in the south-west corner, in County Kerry, the warm Gulf Stream nurtures even subtropical plants into outdoor growth.

The easy-going Irish are great talkers, especially over glasses of the dark brown beer, or stout, called Guinness (after the name of the most famous brewery). A dazzling variety of authors, playwrights and poets has raised Irish literature to enviable heights. World-famous writers from this tiny country range from Sheridan, Wilde and Yeats to Shaw, Synge, O'Casey, Beckett and Joyce.

The Irish have a love affair with music. Skilled pipers and harpists have helped to spread their folk music all over the world. In the field of art, masterpieces like the illuminated *Book of Kells* bear glowing testimony to a skill going back to the 700s or 800s AD.

Most Irish people trace their roots back to Celtic ancestors. The magic of that period is still felt in half-forgotten tales of banshees, fairies, and pagan gods. But when St. Patrick converted the nation to Christianity in the 400s, Roman Catholicism kindled the people's faith with an undying flame. Today 95 per cent of the people are Roman Catholics. The clash with Northern Ireland's overwhelmingly Protestant culture has done much to stir up Ireland's stormy past and embattled present.

It is sometimes said that more Irishmen live abroad than in Ireland. And most of them, including many famous sons and daughters, express a nostalgic longing to revisit their homeland. Visitors flock in their millions to the Emerald Isle to savour the lush green magic of the countryside, the irresistible choice of sporting activities, from angling to horse-racing, the romance of the past, and the unrivalled warmth of Irish hospitality.

IRELAND IS A SOVEREIGN, INDEPENDENT democratic republic. The national parliament is made up of the president and two chambers. The president is the official head of state and is elected by direct vote of the people to a seven-year term. He or she is also eligible for not more than a second term. Presidential powers are limited to approving political appointments, signing laws, and summoning parliament.

The House of Deputies, called *Dáil Éireann*, consists of 166 members. The Senate, called *Seanad Éireann*, has 60 members. Both Houses meet in Leinster House in Dublin. The *Taoiseach* (prime minister), appointed by the president, is the real head of government. He serves a maximum of five years and is usually the leader of the majority party in the House of Deputies. He chooses the other members of parliament to serve in the Cabinet.

Ireland at the present time has four main political parties. They are the Labour Party, the Republican Party (*Fianna Fáil*), Gaelic People (*Fine Gael*), and the Progressive Democratic Party.

The judicial system consists of the Supreme Court, which is the nation's highest court, and below it, the High Court. There are also a number of lower courts. The president appoints judges for life.

Local government is administered by 26 counties (but Tipperary is divided in two for administrative purposes). The cities of Cork, Dublin, Galway, Limerick, and Waterford are county boroughs.

Ireland honours several international commitments. She is a member of the UN (United Nations), the OECD (Organization

Irish-language areas (*above*), where Irish Gaelic is the everyday language, are collectively known as the *Gaeltacht*. Elsewhere, English is spoken.

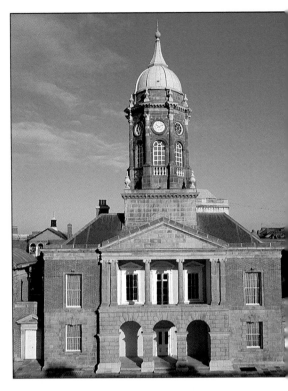

Dublin Castle (*above*), once the symbol of English rule in Ireland, now contains the Republic's State Paper Office. Since 1938, Irish presidents have been inaugurated in St. Patrick's Hall, in the castle's State Apartments.

The Republic of Ireland (*right*) is a scenically beautiful, mainly agricultural country occupying about five-sixths of the island of Ireland. The remainder consists of Northern Ireland (which remains a British possession).

FACT BOX

THE COUNTRY
Official name: Republic of Ireland (Gaelic Éire)
Capital: Dublin
Land regions:
Lowlands in centre. Mountain ranges along the coast (Donegal Mtns. in NW, Mtns. of Mayo and Connemara in W, Mtns. of Kerry in SW, Wicklow Mtns. in E). Rugged western coastline with islands
Land area: 27,136 sq mi (70,284 km²)
Climate: Oceanic, influenced by Gulf Stream. Mild, plenty of rainfall
Main rivers: Shannon, Liffey, Blackwater, Suir, Barrow
Highest elevation: Carrauntoohill 3,414 ft (1,041 m)

Lowest elevation: Sea level along the coast

THE GOVERNMENT
Form of Government: Parliamentary republic
Head of State: President
Head of Government: Prime Minister
Administrative areas: 4 provinces, 26 counties, 5 boroughs
Legislature: Parliament: House of Deputies (166 members, elected by the people for 5 years), Senate (60 appointed and chosen members),
Judiciary: Supreme Court, High Court, district courts
Armed Forces: Voluntary service. Total strength: 13,000

THE PEOPLE
Population (1990): 3,720,000
Language: Gaelic (official), English
Religion: Roman Catholic (about 95%), Protestant (5%)

THE ECONOMY
Currency: Irish pound
Gross Domestic Product per person (1990): US$11,952
Annual Growth Rate (1985-90): 3.5%
Trade balance in US$ (1989): $3,247 mill
Goods imported: Fruits, grains, machinery, vehicles, mineral oil, plastics
Goods exported: Beverages, chemicals, dairy products, meat, textiles

ATLANTIC

OCEAN

Malin Head

North Channel

Letterkenny

NORTHERN
IRELAND
(U.K.)

Mountains
of
Donegal Donegal

Donegal Bay

Erris Head

Sligo

Monaghan

Ballina

Iron
Mountains

Dundalk

Mountains
of Mayo

C O N N A C H T

U L S T E R

Westport

Longford

Boyne

Drogheda

Irish

Claremorris

Roscommon

Navan

Sea

Clifden

Tuam

Mullingar

Mountains
of
Connemara

Lough
Ree

Athlone

Royal Canal

DUBLIN

Ballinasloe

Galway

Grand Canal

Dun Laoghaire

Galway Bay

Gort

L E I N S T E R

Liffey

Bray

Aran Islands

Lough
Derg

Portlaoighise

Wicklow
Mountains

Wicklow

Ennis

Nenagh

Carlow

Arklow

Kilrush

Shannon

Limerick

Kilkenny

Barrow

M U N S T E R

Tipperary

Suir

Dingle

Clonmel

Wexford

Tralee

Mallow

Waterford

Rosslare

Killarney

Blackwater

Dungarvan

Carnsore
Point

Carrauntoohill
3,414 ft (1,041 m)

Cork

Youghal

St.

George's Channel

Macgillycuddy's
Reeks

Bandon

Kinsale

Bantry

Cape Clear

N

0 km   50   100

0 miles   50

for Economic Co-operation and Development), and the European Community (EC). Her armed forces are modest in size, all members being volunteers.

The people
About three-fifths of Ireland's 3.7 million people live in cities and large towns. The remainder live in small townships, villages, or on farms in rural areas. Only Dublin, the capital, and Cork, have more than 100,000 inhabitants. Irish (a Gaelic language) is the first official language and English the second. But everybody speaks English. The government requires that schools teach Irish in order to keep the language alive. The Irish-speaking areas of the country are collectively known as the *Gaeltacht*, and are mainly located in rural districts in the western parts of the country. These areas receive special treatment.

The standard of living varies from fairly prosperous in urban areas to depressed in some rural regions. Ireland ranks 60th in the world in terms of gross domestic product. About a quarter of this is contributed by manufacturing, mining, and utilities, and one-tenth by agriculture. Meat, dairy products, and livestock account for 15 per cent of all exports. Machinery, chemicals, textiles, and clothing are the main industries, with chemicals and electrical machinery making up 40 per cent of exports.

Education
All children between 6 and 15 years of age are required by law to go to school. Private organizations (mainly the Roman Catholic Church and the Church of Ireland) control almost all Irish schools. But the government does provide financial support and, as a result, most primary and secondary education is free.

Religion has played a fundamental role in the history of Ireland. About 95 per cent of the people are Roman Catholics. Their faith dominates some government policy, extending to censorship of some books and plays, and promulgating strict laws on divorce. The sharp contrast with Northern Ireland's mainly Protestant beliefs has contributed much to acts of terrorism across the border. The IRA (Irish Republican Army), banned by the Irish government, has taken particular advantage of these religious differences to attempt to bring about by force the unification of all Ireland.

It is often said the Church has majority support for its stand against abortion and divorce. The Church campaigned against the Treaty of Maastricht, fearing it would lead to enforcement of liberal EC abortion policies in Ireland. But strong public support for the treaty in a 1992 referendum showed reduced acceptance of Church policies.

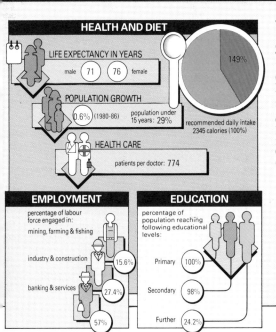

HEALTH AND DIET

LIFE EXPECTANCY IN YEARS

male 71   76 female

POPULATION GROWTH

0.6% (1980-86) population under 15 years: 29%

149%

recommended daily intake 2345 calories (100%)

HEALTH CARE

patients per doctor: 774

Trading partners:
Great Britain and EC countries, USA, Canada
Transport:
Length of railways (1987): 1,208 mi (1,944 km)
Passenger miles (1989): 743 mill (1,196 mill km)
Communications:
Number of daily newspapers (1989): 7
Circulation (1989): 690,648

EMPLOYMENT

percentage of labour force engaged in:

mining, farming & fishing

industry & construction 15.6%

banking & services 27.4%

57%

EDUCATION

percentage of population reaching following educational levels:

Primary 100%

Secondary 98%

Further 24.2%

IRELAND TODAY IS A PROSPEROUS agricultural country which has benefited from its membership of the European Community. The general appearance of the place, however, remains endearingly old-fashioned and run-down, thus gratifying the expectations of visitors. The Irish rightly complain about this view of their land, but are not above exploiting it: a popular series of postcards called "the Real Ireland" concentrates on the country's colourful, antiquated and sometimes bizarre shopfronts and bars. One even shows the famous Cork store which combines the functions of a grocer, a bar and a funeral parlour.

A way with words
Irish people are generally thought of as warm, friendly and talkative; and so they are, but many Irish enjoy playing up to their

Irish fascination with horses
(*above*) runs through the entire nation. This has brought prosperity as well as entertainment, with Irish-bred steeplechasers and hurdlers leading the field on today's British racecourses. Steeplechasing was invented in Ireland as long ago as 1752.

popular image, talking with great flights of fancy as though they have indeed kissed the fabled Blarney Stone (in County Cork), which confers the "gift of the gab". Irish jokes, which show them up in an unflattering light, were originally a form of racial abuse, but are today told with as much relish by the Irish themselves as they are by foreigners.

If the Irish of today seem to show little interest in visual matters, they make up for this with a verbal fluency and a poetic turn of phrase that are rarely found elsewhere. With their genius for expression, a day of constant rain becomes a "soft day", and a glass of the national drink of Guinness, topped with blackcurrant juice, is transformed into a "blood on the moon". Perhaps the brilliant gift for intricate decorative embellishment, shown by the medieval Irish artists and scribes in their illuminated

manuscripts, carvings and jewellery, has been passed on in the profuse, whimsical and endlessly involved quality of Irish conversation today.

Most Irish people are keen on sports. Their fondness for horses and horse-racing has produced some 30 race courses up and down the country. Famous events include the Irish Derby and the Irish Grand National, while the Dublin Horse Show attracts thousands of visitors from abroad each August. Other outdoor sports include soccer, Gaelic football, rugby, and hurling.

The Irish Revival
For much of the period of English domination, art and architecture in Ireland mirrored English tastes. Grand stately homes based on English models were erected in wild areas of the countryside, and are recognizable as Irish only by the state of decay which most of them have now reached, and by the notoriously eccentric Anglo-Irish families who run them. By the late 1800s, however, the growth of nationalism led to an outpouring of native talent in Ireland itself, a cultural rebirth known as the "Irish Revival".

All the major figures associated with this movement, such as the poet William Butler Yeats, his painter brother Jack, and the playwrights John Synge and Sean O'Casey, were actively involved in the cause of Irish freedom. Their number included remarkable women such as the portraitist Estella Solomons and the painter and politician Countess Markievicz (born Constance Gore-Booth), who in 1918 became the first woman member of the British Parliament (but refused to take her seat). Such forceful figures helped Ireland gain its freedom, and won Irish women the vote several years before the women in Great Britain.

Irish exiles
However, many of Ireland's greatest cultural figures have stayed obstinately away from their home country. Oscar Wilde (1854-1900), who perfected Irish wit, lived in London, as did the playwright George Bernard Shaw (1856-1950). The two most influential Irish writers of this century, James Joyce (1882-1941) and Samuel Beckett (1906-90), settled in Paris, joining a thriving Irish intellectual community.

At its most characteristic, Irish literature has much in common with music, the sounds of words and the rhythms of the prose being more important than precision of meaning. Ireland's contribution to music itself has been less important, and limited mainly to folk music. However, this remains a vital focus of Irish life with its harps, pipes and other traditional instruments from Ireland's Celtic past.

A wandering musician (*above left*) plies his trade at Whitegate Pony Races, Co. Clare. Folk music is alive and well in Ireland, a living tradition enjoyed everywhere. Young people have developed the old tunes with real enthusiasm.

Peat-cutting in Connemara (*above*) conjures up a traditional image of Ireland. The county forms part of Connacht, where 20,000 people still speak Irish Gaelic. Irish-speakers today number about 80,000.

A shopkeeper at Athlone (*left*) proudly displays his wares and a "typically Irish" shop window arrangement. Athlone numbers less than 9,000 people although it is the largest town in the county of Westmeath.

Netherlands means literally "the under-lands", an excellent description of a country where almost half the landmass has been wrested and recovered from the waters. More than 40 per cent of this small, highly developed and heavily populated country in northern Europe once consisted of sea, swamp or lake; but over the centuries new land has constantly been created by pumping out the water to form solid earth, the so-called *polders*. Today, these drained areas represent some of the richest and best organized farmland in the world.

Much of the Netherlands is below sea level, and this land is criss-crossed by a network of drainage ditches and canals which dissect the green of the polders. Often the only way to the next town is over one of the many drawbridges, which are raised to allow water traffic to pass through lush pastureland and fields full of vegetables. Characteristic of the Dutch countryside are the numerous **windmills** (*left*), which were originally built to transfer water from the drainage ditches into the larger canals.

In spring, large areas of the Netherlands are covered in a fragrant and colourful carpet of flowers. The fields of tulips, daffodils and hyacinths attract hundreds of thousands of tourists to the Netherlands at weekends. In summer, people flock to the seaside resorts on the North Sea coast, particularly Scheveningen, Noordwijk, Zandvoort and Egmond. For nature-lovers, the vast expanses of dunes in North Holland are a unique experience, while the IJssel-meer and the many lakes and canals offer recreation to water sports enthusiasts.

One of the favourite means of transport in this flat landscape is cycling. There are an estimated 11 million bicycles and 7,400 miles (11,000 kilometres) of cycle tracks in the Netherlands. The most popular sport, however, is ice-skating, which reaches its climax in the famous *Elfstedentocht* (Eleven-cities tour), skated on frozen canals through the province of Friesland.

The Netherlands have much to offer the tourist packed into a very small area. The peaceful and idyllic north is in sharp contrast to the urban agglomeration of the *Randstad Holland*. Nevertheless, even Amsterdam, the lively and modern capital of the Netherlands, appears a typically Dutch town, with its historic merchant's houses, miles of canals and countless bridges. There is folklore in abundance – processions, festivals, markets and fairs. The cheese market in Alkmaar, the flower auctions in Aalsmeer, and the villages where national costume is still worn express a long tradition.

THE NETHERLANDS IS SO DENSELY populated and the landscape for the most part is so flat, that the Dutch have needed to develop a special kind of tolerance towards their many neighbours. This goes some way towards explaining the Dutch love of order, and a quality of comfortable good fellowship known as *gezelligheid*. On a more subtle level, it has led to a particularly Dutch form of liberalism and tolerance, qualities that have deservedly earned the Netherlands today a reputation as one of the front-runners in Europe in the fight for human rights and environmental issues.

A traditional society

The Netherlands is open to change and innovation, but the state, and indeed the society as a whole, is still deeply rooted in tradition. The country is a constitutional monarchy, but the present monarch, Queen Beatrix, is not merely a figurehead; she is also involved in the process of forming a new government, and has powers to influence legislation through her Council of Ministers. The Queen's birthday (*Koninginnendaag*) on April 30 is celebrated with fairs, carnivals and markets.

Religion plays a less crucial role than in days past, and the old antagonism between Catholics and Protestants has virtually disappeared in everyday life. The country's political parties still reflect aspects of the old separatism, but the increase of prosperity and the generally high standard of living has created a middle class which is not so closely identified with politics or religious issues, but sees itself as a member of the wider European Community.

Politics and government

The Netherlands is a constitutional monarchy, with a democratic system of government based on the Constitution of 1814. The Dutch parliament, known as the States-General, meets in the Hague, the seat of the country's government. The States-General consists of two houses, the 75-member First Chamber, and the 150-member Second Chamber. Members are elected for six-year terms to the first, and for four-year terms to the second. Only the Second Chamber can propose or amend laws, and the monarch must sign all laws passed by the States-General. The monarch is head of state, and on the advice of the government, appoints many of the country's highest officials, including the 17 judges of the High Court of the Netherlands, the country's highest court. The prime minister, appointed by the monarch, acts as head of the government.

The country consists of 12 provinces, each headed by an appointed commissioner, and an elected council whose members serve four-year terms. In towns and cities, an appointed burgomaster acts as chief executive. The territory of the Netherlands also includes the island groups of the Netherlands Antilles, and the island of Aruba, located in the Caribbean Sea.

Town and country

Since the mid-1950s, the Netherlands has moved from being a relatively poor, agriculturally based society, to being a highly industrialized and technically advanced state. Its key position at the mouth of the Rhine has made the country into a gateway between the inland capitals of Europe and

FACT BOX

THE COUNTRY
Official name: Kingdom of the Netherlands
Capital: Amsterdam
Seat of Government: The Hague
Land regions: Dunes and Polders, Sand Plains in east, Southern Uplands
Land area: 14,405 sq mi (37,310 km), including 1,261 sq mi (3,265 km²) of inland water
Climate: Temperate maritime with cool summers and mild winters. Most rainfall during summer months
Main rivers: Rhine, Maas, Waal, Lek, IJssel
Highest elevation: Vaalser Berg 1,053 ft (321 m)

Lowest elevation: Prins Alexander Polder 21.7 ft (6.6 m) below sea level

THE GOVERNMENT
Form of Government: Constitutional monarchy
Head of State: King or Queen
Head of Government: Prime Minister
Administrative areas: 12 provinces
Legislature: Parliament (States-General): First Chamber 75 members, elected by provincial state parliaments for 6 years; Second Chamber 150 members, elected by the people for 4 years
Judiciary: High Court,

Courts of Appeal, district cantonal courts
Armed forces: Total strength: 103,600. Men must serve 14-17 months

THE PEOPLE
Population (1990): 14,752,000
Language: Dutch (also Frisian in Friesland)
Religion: Roman Catholic (38%), Protestant (30%), Muslim 2%), Jewish

THE ECONOMY
Currency: Dutch Guilder
Gross Domestic Product per person (1990): US$18,541
Annual Growth Rate (1985-90): 2.6%
Trade balance in US$

The **former Royal Palace** (*left*) in The Hague, built in 1640, was the residence of the Dutch monarchs until Louis Bonaparte moved the court to Amsterdam.

The Netherlands (*right*), often called Holland, is a small country located in northwestern Europe. The four main land regions consist of the sandy and infertile Dunes, the reclaimed lands called the Polders, the eastern Sand Plains, and the Southern Uplands. The marshy Delta area in the southwest is formed by the Maas and Schelde rivers, and by branches of the great Rhine.

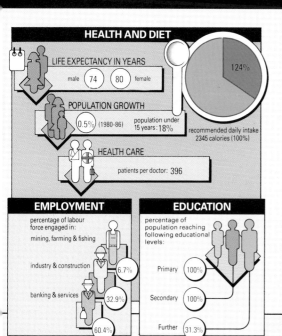

HEALTH AND DIET

LIFE EXPECTANCY IN YEARS
male 74 80 female

POPULATION GROWTH
0.5% (1980-86) population under 15 years: 18%

124%
recommended daily intake 2345 calories (100%)

HEALTH CARE
patients per doctor: 396

EMPLOYMENT
percentage of labour force engaged in:
mining, farming & fishing
industry & construction 6.7%
banking & services 32.9%
60.4%

EDUCATION
percentage of population reaching following educational levels:
Primary 100%
Secondary 100%
Further 31.3%

(1989): $3,611 mill.
Goods imported: Oil, machinery, food, livestock, chemical products, vehicles
Goods exported: Mineral fuel, chemicals, dairy products, electronic equipment, livestock
Trading partners: Belgium, Luxembourg, Germany, France, Great Britain, Italy, USA, Sweden
Transport: Length of railways (1988): 1,745 mi (2,809 km) Passenger miles (1988): 6,022 mill (9,692 mill km)
Communications: Number of daily newspapers (1986): 50 Circulation: about 4,518,000

the North Sea. The city of Rotterdam and the other major industrial cities north of the Rhine form a vast urban conglomeration known collectively as *Randstad Holland*.

To balance the spread of industrial and urban centres the Dutch have become very determined in their efforts to protect what remains of untouched countryside. The *Hoog Veluwe* in Gelderland in the centre of the country is a vast national park, where wild pigs and deer can be seen roaming through the forests or crossing the wide stretches of heathland. Many coastal areas have been preserved as sites of natural beauty and as tourist resorts.

People

THE DUTCH PEOPLE STEM FROM A mixed group of Germanic peoples – Frisians, Saxons and Lower Franks. At the beginning of the Christian era, Frisians occupied the northern coastal area, while Batavians lived in the Rhine delta. An influx of peoples followed the collapse of the Roman empire in the AD 400s, leading to the occupation of much land by the Franks. Thus the Dutch language evolved in many dialects and forms from the Old Low German used by the Franks, and it only achieved its final written form in the 1600s. In the northern province of Friesland, the much older language of West Frisian has survived, and is still officially recognized and taught in all the local schools.

The Dutch have been bold seafarers from the earliest times, and the country's golden age in the 1600s grew from its seaborne trade. In 1612, Dutch sailors founded New Amsterdam, later renamed New York, and established colonies in the West and the East Indies. The masterpieces of Dutch artists like Rembrandt (1606-69) express the splendours of that age.

Religious divisions

Holland has a strong religious tradition; 38 per cent of the population are Roman Catholics and 30 per cent are Protestants, belonging mainly to the denomination

Traditional clothes (*below*) are regularly worn by young and old in Marken and remoter parts of the Netherlands. Wooden clogs, left outside the doors of the spotlessly clean houses, prove practical footwear in muddy conditions.

Rich farmland (*right*), much of it wrested from the sea, covers almost two-thirds of the Netherlands' land area. The canals and waterways not only drain the land; they also provide a transport system for people and produce.

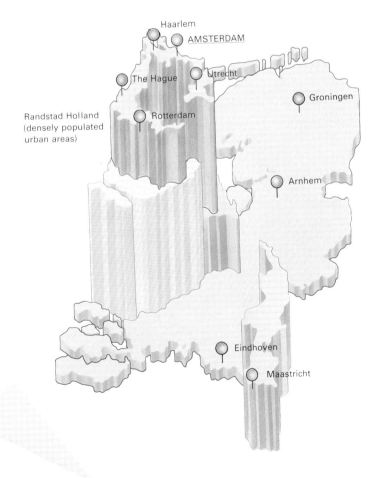

Persons per square

km	mile
More than 1,000	More than 2,590
501 to 1,000	1,296 to 2,590
201 to 500	520 to 1,295
101 to 200	261 to 519

Major cities

The Netherlands (*left*) ranks among the most densely populated nations on Earth. The majority of its population lives in the cities and towns of the western part of the country, in the great conurbation known as *Randstad Holland*.

Superb seagoing ships, like this man-of-war (*above*), enabled the Netherlands to build a maritime empire during the 1600s. Dutch trading companies set up colonies in southern Africa, Indonesia, and the Americas.

Indonesians (*above*) from the old Dutch empire play a useful role in their adopted country. The Netherlands today has an excellent record in race relations, and the contribution of nationals from overseas is valued.

Winter ice (*below*) enables the Dutch people to use their waterways as roads. The climate is generally mild; but sharp frosts in winter are a common occurrence, and people use skates to travel to and from work.

known as the Dutch Reformed Church. The division between the faiths used to be quite clearly marked, with Protestants living in the northern provinces and Catholics in the south, separated from each other by the Rhine and Maas rivers. These divisions first emerged during the long religious wars which overwhelmed Holland during its struggle for independence from Spain in the 1500s and 1600s. Today, although the geographic boundaries are not so clear, the cultural differences still run through many aspects of public life: both denominations have their own schools, hospitals, social amenities and political parties. But the rigid separation of former days has largely vanished, thanks especially to the progressive spirit of the Roman Catholic Church in Holland, and the trend towards increased tolerance, particularly among the young.

During the boom period of the 1960s and 1970s, Holland welcomed an influx of *gastarbeiddderen* (guest workers) to meet the demands of industrial expansion. Most of these newcomers came from Turkey and Morocco. However, the country has also become the home of a number of people from the former Dutch colonies of Suriname, the Netherlands Antilles, the Moluccan Islands and Indonesia. Some fled from political oppression, others were attracted by the prospect of better wages and a higher standard of living. Today these immigrant groups account for about five per cent of the total population. The Netherlands' race relations have in general proved a model of tolerance. Difficulties have been on the whole tactfully resolved.

Randstad Holland

With a population of nearly 15 million, the Netherlands has one of the densest concentrations of people in the world. There are more than 1,000 inhabitants per square mile (390 per square kilometre) and nine out of ten of these live in the towns. As a result the urban areas have spread out in all directions. Numerous well-maintained national parks and nature reserves provide ample scope for recreation, but the Netherlands offers very little in the way of wild untouched countryside. The rural way of life too, has mostly disappeared, except for a few isolated areas.

The most densely populated area is a strip of land stretching in an arc from Utrecht and Hilversum in the northwest, to Dordrecht in the southwest. This massive built-up area is *Randstad Holland*, an urban spread similar to the eastern seaboard of the USA. This whole region has come to serve as a link between the highly industrialized European hinterland and the coast, and it handles an intense concentration of trade, industry and shipping.

Amsterdam

AMSTERDAM, THE CAPITAL OF THE Netherlands, is a paradoxical city, an intriguing mixture of opposites. At once chic and casual, sophisticated and scruffy, this internationally important trading centre exudes the relaxed, friendly confidence of a successful small town. It is even built on a paradox: its elegant houses were raised on countless wooden piles in an unpromising muddy marsh at the mouth of the Amstel River. It is a tolerant place that welcomes new ideas while basking in the afterglow of its golden age during the 1600s.

Amsterdam traces its origins back to a fishing village founded in the 1200s, at the junction of the Amstel and IJ rivers. A dam built at this time made the city a centre for the transfer of cargoes. The city's name means "dam of the Amstel". Amsterdam grew rapidly after the 1580s, when it became a centre for international trade and banking.

Damrak, the main street, leads to the Dam Square, site of the startlingly grimy royal palace and the *Nieuwe Kerk* (New Church) which leads a double life as an art gallery. Damrak continues as Rokin, lined with shops and restaurants, ending at the *Munt Plein* (Mint Square), from which you can glimpse the tourist-hungry Rembrandtsplein. To the west of Damrak runs Kalverstraat, a crowded and unpleasant pedestrian shopping street, whose only redeeming features are the wonderful Historical Museum and some intriguing little bars hidden away in tiny alleys running off the western side. South of Kalverstraat runs Leidsestraat, invigorating for the unwary, as the tramlines plough right through the pedestrian area. Leidseplein is the centre of the leisure industry, the home of many of Amsterdam's 30 cinemas, the *Stadsschouwburg* (City Theatre), and a good proportion of its more than 1,200 bars. In the winter there is even an open-air ice rink. Only a few minutes farther south is the Museum Quarter, which combines culture with high-class shopping. The public museums, including the Rijksmuseum (home of Rembrandt's *Night Watch*) and the Van Gogh Museum, cluster round Museumplein. The world-famous Concertgebouw faces the Rijksmuseum across the square. Cultural ideas are frequently exchanged: music students often perform under the Rijksmuseum arches. To the west of the museums runs the P.C. Hoofstraat, with its fashionable clothing and shoe stores.

Amsterdam's bright yellow trams crisscross the city, but the residents mostly prefer to cycle. They snake nonchalantly through the traffic, talking earnestly to a friend perched on the carrier behind the *achterop* (saddle), or effortlessly transporting a ludicrously huge item of furniture, or even taking the dog for a brisk scamper. Alternatively, a canal trip can provide a taste of the city, and offers a superb view of the canalside houses.

But to get the most out of Amsterdam, you should walk: stroll along the gracious canals, fringed with lime trees and lined with tall, narrow town houses, each supporting a different gable. You will soon realize that there are no high buildings and that the light and the skyline are much the same as when the elegant houses were first built. The houses have narrow facades but are deep and roomy inside. (You can see this at Anne Frank's House, where the doomed Frank family hid from the Nazis in World War II). Frugal merchants built this way to avoid paying tax levied on the frontage.

Built to house the servants who worked in the grand canal houses, the nearby Jordaan district is crossed by tiny cobbled streets, full of snug bars, little shops, unlikely small industries and romantic bohemians.

Architecture buffs should proceed even further northwest to the Spaarndammerbuurt to see the workers' housing (still in use) designed in 1915 by Michel de Klerk of the Amsterdam School. In the south of the city lies the Oud-Zuid district, laid out in Art Deco style by H. P. Berlage (1856-1934).

Streetlife

The essence of Amsterdam can be savoured by observing the streetlife. As most of the city's more than 695,000 inhabitants live in cramped apartments, they like to socialize in the city's bars and cafés. Most authentically "Amsterdam" are the so-called "brown cafés", small crooked rooms with tobacco-impregnated walls, bathed in soft light filtered through stained glass windows; here you can drink, read, play chess or billiards, or just sit and relax.

You can also listen to the city: you will hear the background carillons from the many churches; the insistent clamour of the tram bells; and the evocative tinkling of the street organs (often drowned out by the ferocious rattling of the brass collecting tray by the organ grinder). It is considered bad luck and bad form to pass by without parting with some small change.

To see Amsterdammers in action, go with them to market; the most famous is the daily Albert Cuypmarkt, a sprawling, busy and cosmopolitan market specializing in food and clothing. Its specialities from Suriname and Indonesia hint at the Netherlands' colonial past; Turkish and Moroccan food reflect the needs of the city's community of guest workers. Waterlooplein, in the old Jewish quarter of the city, was once the biggest and best street market in Europe, and is still worth a visit for its astounding amount of interesting ironmongery.

Amsterdam's many canals (*far left*) drain the city's marshy foundations. There are over 62 miles (100 kilometres) of canals, housing nearly 3,000 licensed houseboats. Every night, the canal water is drained into the harbour and replaced.

Haircuts (*left*) are offered in Amsterdam's Vondel Park on the Queen's official birthday. Like New York's Central Park, Vondel Park is the venue for concerts, festivals and plays in the summer months.

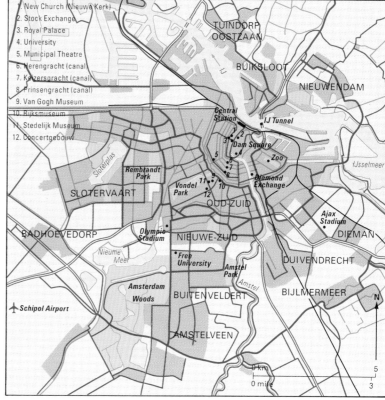

1. New Church (Nieuwe Kerk)
2. Stock Exchange
3. Royal Palace
4. University
5. Municipal Theatre
6. Herengracht (canal)
7. Keizersgracht (canal)
8. Prinsengracht (canal)
9. Van Gogh Museum
10. Rijksmuseum
11. Stedelijk Museum
12. Concertgebouw

Amsterdam's bicycles (*left*) far outnumber family cars. There are few things which cannot be carried on one.

The *Magerebrug* ("skinny" bridge) (*far left*) is a wooden drawbridge spanning the river Amstel.

Amsterdam (*above*) resembles the wheel of a bicycle, with the larger canals arranged in concentric rings around the centre. Smaller canals radiate outwards like the spokes of the wheel. The city's canal system contributes to its relaxed pace of life,

and literally reflects its elegant buildings. The Netherlands' capital boasts a sophisticated economy, but tourists flock to Amsterdam to visit major cultural attractions such as the Rijksmuseum, the Stedelijk Museum and the Van Gogh Museum.

The North Sea

BETWEEN THE STRAIT OF DOVER AND the Norwegian Sea lies the shallow, often turbulent North Sea. Covering about 218,178 square miles (565,078 square kilometres), the North Sea separates Britain from mainland Europe. But as recently as the end of the last Ice Age, about 10,000 years ago, it was above sea level, as evidenced by the moraine (iceborne sand and gravel) on its floor. These materials were the sea's chief mineral resources until the late 1960s and early 1970s, when deposits of natural gas were discovered, together with oil reserves, between Scotland and Norway.

The exploitation of these high-quality fossil fuels posed special problems. Although the water is shallow, with an average depth of 100 feet (30 metres) in the south and 394 feet (120 metres) in the north, the North Sea often suffers from stormy conditions. The platforms for extracting gas and oil from under the sea had to be of a design different from any used before. Built of steel or concrete, they had to withstand hurricane-type gusts of wind, and waves that could tower 80 feet (24 metres) high.

The main beneficiaries of the fossil fuels were Britain and Norway. In 1986, Britain, with 13 oil-producing offshore fields, was the world's fifth largest producer, with Norway in 14th place. Production had passed its peak by 1990, though the rigs will continue to yield oil until well after the year 2000.

Exploitation and the environment

The North Sea rigs have caused surprisingly little pollution. Despite some accidents, such as the 1988 fire on the Piper Alpha platform, when 167 people were killed, conservationists estimate that less than one per cent of the oil spillage entering the sea comes from the oil rigs.

The North Sea has been under greater threat from other sources. It is a major spawning ground for many fish species, including cod, haddock, herring, mackerel, plaice, sole, and whiting, yielding a catch of about 2.72 million tonnes a year. But 100 years of overfishing have led to the serious depletion of several species.

The North Sea is also a busy seaway, with industrial cities around its shores and on the rivers that empty into it. It has long been a dumping ground for sewage, oil, and industrial and other wastes. The effects of pollution have been measured in fish, shellfish, seabirds, and sea mammals. In 1988 thousands of seals died of a virus that produced pneumonia symptoms. Though experts were divided, many argued that the epidemic was caused partly because toxic wastes have damaged the seals' immune systems.

The map (*right*) of the North Sea shows the chief oil- and gas-fields, the pipelines used to transport the fuels to the land, and the main fishing areas. Also shown are the national zones agreed by the countries bordering the sea for the extraction of the oil and gas. To establish the ownership of the deposits, a north-south boundary was fixed as a line equidistant between the coasts of Britain and mainland Europe. The borders in the eastern North Sea were more difficult to fix and involved long negotiations. The leading gas-fields are in the south, where the gas was distilled from deeply buried coal beds formed in the Carboniferous period, about 300 million years ago. The light gas seeped upwards and was trapped in permeable rock layers. The oil and gas in the central and northern North Sea are of more recent origin. They formed from the remains of plants and bacteria in the Jurassic period, about 200 million years ago.

Sources of pollution in the North Sea are shown in the map (*bottom right*). The oil and gas industry has caused little pollution as compared with the dumping of industrial wastes, the disposal of sewage, and many years of overfishing.

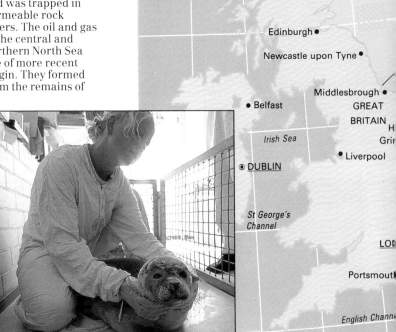

The seals in the North Sea were hit in 1988 by a virus which may have been caused by pollution. Workers at a nursery (*above*) in the Waddenzee, in the northern Netherlands, were among environmentalists who treated the symptoms of the virus. Despite their efforts, many seals died.

Shetland Is

Orkney Is

Aberdeen •

Dundee •

Edinburgh •

Newcastle upon Tyne •

Middlesbrough •

GREAT

BRITAIN

• Belfast

Irish Sea

Grir

• Liverpool

⊚ DUBLIN

St George's Channel

LOI

Portsmout

English Chann

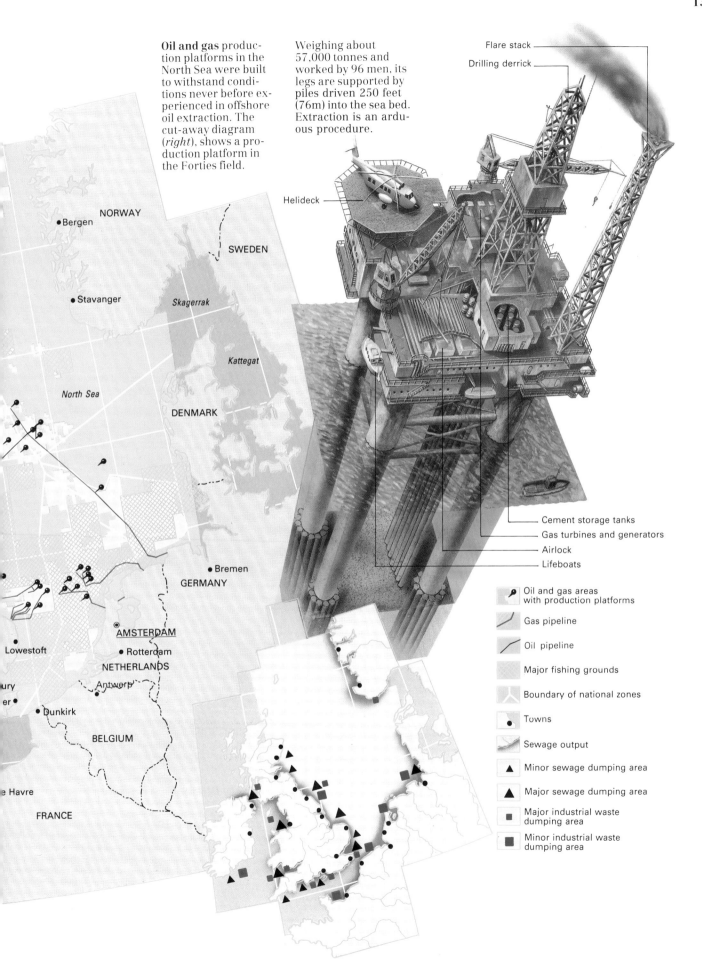

Oil and gas production platforms in the North Sea were built to withstand conditions never before experienced in offshore oil extraction. The cut-away diagram (*right*), shows a production platform in the Forties field.

Weighing about 57,000 tonnes and worked by 96 men, its legs are supported by piles driven 250 feet (76m) into the sea bed. Extraction is an arduous procedure.

Flare stack

Drilling derrick

Helideck

Cement storage tanks

Gas turbines and generators

Airlock

Lifeboats

NORWAY
Bergen

SWEDEN

Stavanger

Skagerrak

Kattegat

North Sea

DENMARK

Bremen
GERMANY

AMSTERDAM

Lowestoft

Rotterdam

NETHERLANDS

Antwerp

Dunkirk

BELGIUM

Havre

FRANCE

Oil and gas areas with production platforms

Gas pipeline

Oil pipeline

Major fishing grounds

Boundary of national zones

Towns

Sewage output

Minor sewage dumping area

Major sewage dumping area

Major industrial waste dumping area

Minor industrial waste dumping area

BELGIUM

Belgium, together with the Netherlands and Luxembourg (the Benelux nations), lies at the heart of the European Community. But this heart is divided across its centre by Europe's most fundamental language frontier. On one side, the language and culture derive from the Germanic-speaking tribes who swept into Europe in the 400s; on the other live people whose mother tongue is French, one of the so-called Romance languages originating from Latin. This division between Dutch-speaking Flanders and French-speaking Wallonia has long been a source of friction for Belgium.

In size, Belgium is one of Europe's smallest countries, covering an area of only 11,783 square miles (30,519 square kilometres). However, it is also one of Europe's richest and most densely populated. Situated between powerful neighbours, and separated from Great Britain by a narrow strip of sea, it has benefited from its geographical position to become an important centre of industry and commerce from medieval times to the present day. But for the same reason it has also been a battleground between warring nations, especially during the two world wars.

Despite its small size, Belgium is a place of many and varied landscapes, from the dunes and beaches of the northern coast to the forest-clad mountains of the Ardennes. Its fertile soil supports a thriving agricultural sector, while the development of new industries in the north counterbalances the decay of older ones, such as coal and steel, in the French-speaking south. Criss-crossed by many navigable waterways, and possessing one of the world's finest road systems, it is a country that makes life easy as well as pleasant for the tourist.

Belgium's eventful history has endowed it with a rich artistic and architectural heritage. It is a country where the towns sometimes seem like wonderful museums, and contain churches and galleries filled with priceless art treasures. It is also noted throughout Europe for its delicious food, especially in the capital, Brussels.

In 1958, Brussels played host to the 1958 World's Fair, symbolized by its futuristic emblem, the **Atomium** (*left*). Since then, the city has become a torchbearer of international cooperation, and is today the home of many European institutions, such as the European Commission, the Benelux economic union, the North Atlantic Treaty Organization (NATO), and the European Atomic Energy Community (Euratom). An entire neighbourhood of the city, called the Cité Européenne, has been specially built to accommodate many of these European institutions.

Belgium Today

UP TO THE TIME OF ITS INDEPENDENCE in 1831, Belgium and its inhabitants were ruled by many different foreign masters. The popular uprising in 1830 against the absolute rule of the Netherlands paved the way for Belgium's independence the following year. In 1831, a National Congress issued a parliamentary constitution and elected Prince Leopold of Saxe-Coburg as king of Belgium. The present king, Baudouin I (b.1930), has ruled since 1951. He carries out mainly formal state duties and advises the government but does not take an active part in the business of government. According to the constitution, no minister in Belgium's constitutional monarchy may take any initiative whatsoever without the approval of the monarch, but the king for his part may not make any political decisions without the backing of parliament. Harmony typifies the relationship of King and government.

Two cultures
The Belgian political scene is dominated by the long-standing conflict between the Flemings and the Walloons. Efforts by these two groups to preserve their separate identities have sometimes verged on civil war. The conflict runs like a thread through the political, social and cultural life of the country. Both peoples have their own political parties, their own schools and their own cultures. In order to protect this status, Belgium revised its constitution in 1970-71 and in 1980, moving from a centralized unified state to a federal state with autonomous regions. This regionalization primarily affected communications and the media, edu-

King Baudouin/ Boudewijn I (*above*), King of Belgium, leaves the state opening of Parliament. Monarch since 1951, his role is mainly advisory and official.

FACT BOX

THE COUNTRY
Official name: Kingdom of Belgium
Capital: Brussels
Land regions: Coastal and Interior Lowlands, Kempenland in NE, Central Low Plateaus, Ardennes in SE
Land area: 11,783 sq mi (30,519 km²)
Climate: Temperate oceanic. Cool summers, mild winters
Main rivers: Schelde, Meuse, Demer, Sambre
Highest elevation: Botrange Mountain 2,277 ft (694 m)
Lowest elevation: Sea level along the coast

THE GOVERNMENT
Form of Government: Constitutional monarchy

Head of State: King
Head of Government: Prime Minister
Administrative areas: 9 provinces, divided into 589 communes
Legislature: Parliament: House of Representatives (212 members, elected by the people); Senate (182 members, elected by the people, provincial councils and other senators). 4-year terms
Judiciary: Court of Cassation, regional courts of appeal, district courts. Special courts (labour, commerce, military)
Armed forces: Total strength: 92,400. Men must serve 10 or 12 months after age 18

THE PEOPLE
Population (1990): 9,938,000
Language: Dutch, French (both official), German (regional)
Religion: Roman Catholic (89%), Protestant, Jewish

THE ECONOMY
Currency: Belgian franc
Gross Domestic Product per person (1990): US$19,807
Annual Growth Rate (1985-90): 3.5%
Trade balance Belgium-Luxembourg in US$ (1989): $1,589 mill
Goods imported: Machinery, motor, vehicles, chemicals, mineral oil, cotton, food products

The imposing **Palais de Justice** (*left*), or law courts, is one of Brussels' most important landmarks. The broad Rue de la Régence, in the foreground, runs northeast towards the Palais de Roi, residence of Belgium's monarch.

The Kingdom of Belgium (*right*) is a small, thickly populated industrial nation in northwest Europe. Fertile lowlands cover much of its area, but in the southeast rise the forest-covered hills of the Ardennes.

cation, energy supply, employment policy and some parts of economic policy.

Politics and government
Belgium's parliament consists of two houses, the 212-member House of Representatives and the 182-member Senate. Members of Parliament are elected to serve four-year terms. Executive power lies in the hands of the prime minister, who is head of the government, and a cabinet known as the Council of Ministers, which must include equal numbers of Dutch-speakers and French-speakers. Dutch is the official language of education and public communications in Flanders, while French enjoys the same status in Wallonia. Eastern Wallonia contains a small German-speaking area.

For administrative purposes, the country is divided into nine provinces, each with an elected council, and a governor appointed by the king. Each province consists of a number of *communes* (cities and towns), whose voters elect a local council. The king appoints the mayor of a commune on the basis of the recommendation of its council. The Court of Cassation is the country's highest court. Five regional courts hear appeals of lower court decisions.

Climate and terrain
Belgium enjoys a moderate climate with cool summers and mild winters. Temperatures range from a January average of 35°F (2°C) to a July average of 64°F (18°C). Despite its small size, the country boasts a wide variety of landscapes, from the dunes and treeless plains of the Coastal and Interior Lowlands and the Central Low Plateaus to the wooded hills of the Ardennes. As in the Netherlands, sea walls and drainage canals preserve the coastal lowlands from flooding, and the fertile soil yields abundant harvests.

In northeastern Belgium, the Kempenland or Campine is a mining and industrial area where birch forests grew in former times. These have largely been cleared to make room for fast-growing evergreens. The centre of the country consists of fertile flatlands, and includes the capital, Brussels. In southeastern Belgium the Ardennes region offers visitors a beautiful landscape of undulating, forest-covered country, intersected by winding rivers, containing deer and wild boar. The country's major rivers include the Demer, the Schelde, the Sambre and the Meuse (or Maas). Together with a large canal network, these also serve as arteries of transport.

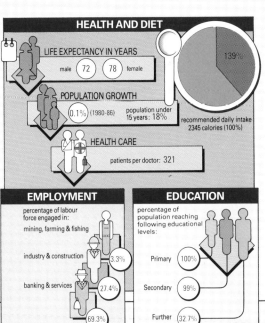

HEALTH AND DIET

LIFE EXPECTANCY IN YEARS
male 72 78 female

POPULATION GROWTH
0.1% (1980-86)   population under 15 years: 18%

139%
recommended daily intake 2345 calories (100%)

HEALTH CARE
patients per doctor: 321

EMPLOYMENT
percentage of labour force engaged in:
mining, farming & fishing   3.3%
industry & construction   27.4%
banking & services   69.3%

EDUCATION
percentage of population reaching following educational levels:
Primary   100%
Secondary   99%
Further   32.7%

Goods exported: Iron and steel, machinery, transport equipment, pharmaceutical products, chemicals, processed foods, glass products, textiles
Trading partners: EC countries, USA
Transport:
Length of railways (1988): 2,217 mi (3,568 km)
Passenger miles (1988): 3,944 mill (6,348 mill km)
Communications:
Number of daily newspapers (1989): 35
Circulation (1989): 2,149,438

A TOURIST TRAVELLING THROUGH Belgium can hardly fail to notice that people in Liège speak a completely different language from those of the coastal resort of Knokke, and that even within Brussels the language varies. In some places French is spoken, in others Dutch is the universal language. Everywhere, signs in both languages testify to a linguistic and cultural divide that runs across the country like an invisible ravine. About one-third of the population are French-speaking Walloons, living in the south of the country, while more than half are Dutch-speaking Flemings, who live in the north.

A linguistic frontier running east-west, to the south of Brussels, separates the two language groups. The capital is a bilingual area, although it is located within the Flemish region. French is most commonly spoken in the city centre while Dutch is more predominant in the outlying areas. The city's status has long been a source of disagreement between the Flemings and Walloons, and a problem for successive governments. Dual-language road signs bear silent witness to the persistent conflict.

The roots of conflict

Despite the clear separation into language regions, the country has endured political and social tensions, fuelled by the language problem, since its origin more than 150 years ago. The conflict was already in evidence at that time, when French was the official language. This was to the clear disadvantage of the Flemings, who suffered discrimination and suppression. In the 1800s, Wallonia's coal mines and heavy industry made it the country's political and economic centre, while a majority of the Flemish population consisted of peasant farmers and domestic servants.

Between 1873 and 1898, laws were enacted recognizing Dutch as a language to be used in schools, in the courts, and for official business. However, the Flemings remained a disadvantaged group until the 1960s, when cutbacks in the coal industry began to take effect. With the steel crisis of the 1970s, Wallonia declined in wealth to become the country's poor relation.

Meanwhile, the self-confidence and wealth of the Flemings increased, since massive commercial and industrial development in the north altered the economic balance in the country to their advantage. In the 1960s, they held mass demonstrations to demand political equality and cultural independence.

After numerous clashes, reforms were introduced in 1970-71 and 1980. As a result, Parliament altered the constitution to give each language group as much self-rule as possible through its own cultural council.

Belgium's separation into Flanders and Wallonia, together with the cultural independence of these regions, was written into the country's basic law; the capital of Brussels received special status as a dual-language area.

A federal state

These reforms were the first steps on the path to decentralization which led, in 1988, to Belgium's conversion into a federal state. The new constitution failed to bring stability to the political system. Elections in 1991 strengthened the power of regionally-based parties. But the extensive political and economic autonomy now enjoyed by the language regions has yet to bring the conflict to an end.

Many problems remain, however, especially on the economic front, where the greater economic strength of the Flemings provides a potential source of future conflict. The success of the reforms will depend to a great extent on whether the central government can contain Belgium's language conflict and prevent it from developing into a virtual economic war.

Mass demonstrations by Walloons (*right*) in the 1960s marked bitter tensions between Belgium's two language groups. Demands by Flemings for political equality have been largely met, but differences remain.

Belgium (*below right*) ranks as one of the most thickly populated countries in the world. About 95 per cent of its people live in cities and towns. The country's linguistic divide (*bottom*) runs through the centre, with French-speaking Wallonia in the south, and Dutch-speaking Flanders in the north.

Dutch and French signs in Brussels (*above*) signal Belgium's language divide.

Population density
per square mile / per square km

per square mile	per square km
1,296 to 2,590	501 to 1,000
520 to 1,295	201 to 500
261 to 519	101 to 200
130 to 260	51 to 100

Metropolitan areas

Ostend · Bruges · Ghent · BRUSSELS · Kortrijk · Antwerp · Mechelen · Louvain · Hasselt · Liège · Charleroi · Namur

BRUSSELS

Language regions

- Dutch (Flemish)
- French (Walloon)
- German

The Mons region (*left*) of French-speaking Wallonia reflects the decay of a declining industrial area. The commercial supremacy of Wallonia yielded with the steel crisis of the 1970s to the Dutch-speaking north.

Antwerp's *Grote Markt* (*above*) reflects the new-found prosperity of Flanders. Centuries ago, Antwerp's harbour ensured its position as an important commercial centre; the city's architectural glories witness to its former success, and Antwerp has continued to profit from shipbuilding and repairing. However, it has recently benefited even more from the new steel and petrochemical industries that have made Flanders their base.

Brussels

ALTHOUGH BELGIUM'S CAPITAL CITY celebrated its millennium in 1979, Brussels has been a place of settlement for far longer than 1,000 years. On the east side of the city, archeologists have found that a large Stone Age community flourished there some 7,000 years ago. Located in Belgium's Central Low Plateaus, modern Brussels owes its foundation to the Senne River. Some time before AD 900, French-speaking settlers built a fort on the river to protect their territory from Flemish (Dutch) rivals. Because the Senne formed part of a system of waterways linking western Germany and northern France, *Bruocsella* ("town on the brook") had become a prosperous trade centre by the 1000s. But although the city owes its existence to the Senne, it has shown the river little gratitude. Today, the river follows an underground course as the city's main sewage channel.

By the 1200s, Brussels was famous throughout Europe as a trading place and a centre of the wool industry. The skill of its craftsmen in producing fine carpets, tapestries, lace and other textile goods was reflected in the wealth of its merchants. Over the centuries, it aroused the greed of many conquerors, and the city came under Burgundian, Spanish, Austrian, French and Dutch rule. In 1830, the performance of a patriotic song in Brussels' Theatre Royal de la Monnaie led to the revolution in which Belgium threw off Dutch rule. The theatre still stands, and is today the city's leading opera house. In 1831, Brussels became capital of the new nation.

A capital twice over

Since that time Brussels has increased in size, in importance and in wealth. Its metropolitan area houses nearly one million people, making it the largest city in Belgium. It endured German occupation in both world wars. Today it is a capital twice over, acting as the headquarters of the European Community (EC) and the North Atlantic Treaty Organization (NATO). It can thus claim to be the "capital of Europe". To the demands of its own large business community, Brussels adds those of the many thousands of employees of EC agencies. Massive office blocks, luxury hotels, glittering stores and wide expressways dominate much of the city. Manufacturing plants produce ceramics, drugs, processed foods, paper and textiles.

The Grand' Place

But at the heart of Brussels lies a reminder of its ancient heritage. This is the magnificent square now called the Grand' Place, and known in the Middle Ages as the *Grote Markt* ("great marketplace").The picturesque buildings fronting the Grand' Place

date from the late 1690s, when they housed the guilds (trade organizations) of the city's merchants and craftsmen. They replaced earlier buildings destroyed by French artillery in 1695. Only the nearby *Hotel de Ville* (town hall), dating from the mid-1400s and one of Europe's most beautiful buildings, survived the three-day bombardment. A statue of St. Michael, the city's patron saint, still tops its graceful spire.

The Grand' Place is seen at its best on Sunday mornings, when it houses flower and bird markets. During the *Ommegang* ("walk around") pageant in July, citizens parade around the square in costumes of the 1500s. On any fine day, a table outside one of its many cafes provides a superb view of the golden scrollwork and sculptured decorations of the guild houses.

The oldest inhabitant

A maze of small streets runs off the Grand' Place, named after the traders they once housed: Herb Market Street, Pepper Street, Herring Street, Cheese Market Street, and others. In this district, the traveller may meet the city's "oldest inhabitant". Dating from the early 1600s, the *Manneken-Pis*, a fountain incorporating the bronze figure of a small boy, is Brussels' best-known landmark and symbolizes the city's spirit of cheerful independence.

The Grand' Place (*above*), at the heart of Brussels' "lower city", hosts a popular flower market on Sundays. The elegant houses lining the square date from the 1600s, and were built to house the offices of the city's merchant guilds.

The Cité Berlaymont (*right*) is the headquarters of the European Commission, the body which administers the European Community (EC). Brussels is also the headquarters of NATO, and a major business centre.

Brussels lace, or *point-de-gauze* (*below*), is one of the city's most famous products. On the left, a plaque marks the residence of Victor Hugo, author of *Les Misérables*, who lived in Brussels during his exile from France.

Northwest of the Grand' Place lies the oldest and most splendid of Brussels' many fine churches: St. Michael's Cathedral. Founded in the 1000s, and rebuilt from the 1200s, the cathedral is renowned for its stained-glass windows dating from the early 1500s.

Brussels may have been built on trade, but its people have always had an eye for beauty, as shown by the magnificent collections housed in the Royal Museum of Fine Arts and the city's other great galleries. Flemish art flourished during the 1300s-1700s, and some of its greatest masters included Memling, the van Eycks, the Brueghels and Rubens.

French and Dutch culture blend in Brussels' buildings and artistic heritage. It is a pity that this harmony is not always reflected in the relations between its French- and Dutch-speaking citizens. The visitor will see that all public notices are in both languages. A constitutional amendment in 1967-71 made the metropolitan area officially bilingual. Brussels' Free University, founded in 1834, now has separate French- and Dutch-speaking faculties. French-speaking Walloons predominate in Brussels, but the city lies just north of a line dividing the Walloon provinces of south and west Belgium from the Flemish (Dutch-speaking) provinces of the north and east.

Brussels (*right*) became capital of Belgium after the country gained independence from the Netherlands in 1831. The city lies in Belgium's Central Low Plateaus. Together with its surrounding metropolitan area, Brussels contains a population of some 989,877, and constitutes one of Belgium's three economic regions. Brussels is a bilingual (two-language) area, and lies on the boundary line between French-speaking Wallonia and Dutch-speaking Flanders.

The many small cafes of Brussels (*left*) add a relaxed flavour to life in Europe's "capital city". Brussels also enjoys an enviable reputation as one of the gastronomic centres of Europe. Special dishes include beef stewed in beer.

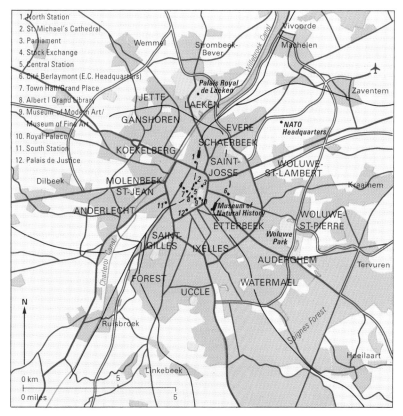

1. North Station
2. St Michael's Cathedral
3. Parliament
4. Stock Exchange
5. Central Station
6. Cité Berlaymont (E.C. Headquarters)
7. Town Hall/Grand Place
8. Albert I Grand Library
9. Museum of Modern Art/Museum of Fine Art
10. Royal Palace
11. South Station
12. Palais de Justice

LUXEMBOURG

THE GRAND DUCHY OF LUXEMBOURG contains two main geographical regions: the Oesling in the north and northwest, and the area called the *Bon Pays* (in French) or *Gutland* (in German) in the south. The Oesling is part of the Ardennes mountains, an upland region with its highest point being the Buurgplaatz, which reaches 1,834 feet (559 metres) near the northern border. The plateau is dissected by the River Sûre and its tributaries which flow through winding valleys overlooked by wooded slopes often topped by medieval fortresses.

The lower Bon Pays region also has many castles. Here the higher land is wooded, while the lower parts are fertile farmland. The River Alzette flows from south to north across the Bon Pays. The area in the east, known as "Little Switzerland", is cut by the valleys of the Ernz Blanche and Ernz Noire rivers. It is a bizarre landscape, with rocky pinnacles, cliffs, caves and deep ravines.

Most of Luxembourg has a mild, moist climate. Winters are cold and snowy, especially in the highest parts of the Oesling. In the southeast, the Moselle valley, which forms the boundary with the Federal Republic of Germany, has a mild climate and is known for its fruity Moselle white wine.

The people

The population is unevenly spread. The most densely populated areas include the capital, which contains more than one-fifth of the population, the industrial zone in the far south, and the farming regions of the Bon Pays. The Oesling is sparsely populated. Most of the people are Roman Catholics of German origin. But foreigners, mainly migrant Italian workers and European civil servants, who live in the capital, make up about a quarter of the population.

Three languages are spoken: French, German and Letzeburgesch, a Moselle Frankish dialect similar to German and incorporating many French words, which became the third official language in 1984. Most people speak Letzeburgesch, which is a unifying force in this small country, though they usually write in French or German. Luxembourg's newspapers are printed in German, while the French language predominates in cultural, legal, political and religious affairs.

The economy

Rich deposits of iron ore in the south led to the establishment of a major iron and steel industry in the late 1800s. This industry, dominated by a giant concern known as ARBED, has long been the most important sector in the country's economy, and iron and steel are the leading exports. However, rising wage costs and fierce competition from abroad led to the closures of many fac-

tories in the 1970s and 1980s. As a result, Luxembourg has reduced its dependence on heavy industry.

Since the 1960s, Luxembourg has attracted many small and medium-sized businesses. Besides the growing number of service industries, the chief growth areas have been in high technology, chemical and plastics industries, including the production of tyres. Agriculture now employs only 6 per cent of the workforce.

The capital Luxembourg, which contains the Grand Ducal Palace, home of the monarch, is a city of banks, bridges (totalling around 110), and bureaucrats, and houses many European institutions, which make a special contribution to the economy. It is a major international financial centre and its banking sector now employs almost as many people as the steel industry. Banking has become important largely because of the enthusiasm of Luxembourgers for a Single European Market (which allows free exchange of goods and capital, and standardized tax legislation), and their ability to think on a European scale. The government's liberal attitude to economic and financial affairs, and its favourable tax laws, have encouraged this development. Many companies avoid paying taxes that most European countries impose by using Luxembourg as an accommodation address.

The capital

The city of Luxembourg, with its population of about 76,000, occupies a picturesque position on a rocky plateau overlooking the valleys of the Alzette and Petrusse. It is now a lively, cosmopolitan city, though it retains

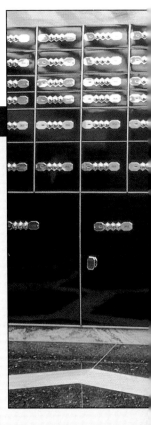

Industry

Luxembourg is a tiny country, but its industrial power far exceeds its size. Steel manufacture has for many years underpinned the economy, and continues to do so; all the steel and pressed-steel mills are conveniently located near open-cast iron-mining districts. So efficient is the industry that the miniature state is in the top 20 of the world's crude steel producers, and has by far the highest output per person.

Since the 1970s, however, the world has seen a relative decline of steel, but the country has kept abreast of new developments. Luxembourg today is home to many high technology industries, producing electronic equipment, computers and data-processing machines. Above all, its central location and unswerving allegiance to the idea of a European Community have made it an international financial centre of major importance within the community.

The city of Luxembourg (*above*), capital of the Grand Duchy of Luxembourg, is situated on a plateau high above two river gorges. Its Old Town contains many fine buildings; but Luxembourg is above all an important centre of the European Community, being the seat of both the European Parliament and the European Court of Justice. Painted signs over an old shop front (*above*) attest to Luxembourg's continuing prosperity.

A Luxembourg bank (*left*) and the stock exchange (*below*) indicate Luxembourg's importance as an international financial centre. Banking has almost overtaken the metal industry as the country's most important activity.

much of the charm of a small provincial town. The Pont Grande-Duchesse-Charlotte (Grand Duchess Charlotte Bridge), which leaps the River Alzette at a height of 278 feet (85 metres) with a span of 755 feet (230 metres), is literally "a bridge to Europe". It leads from the Old Town to Kirchberg, a modern new town of wide boulevards, built in 1966 to accommodate the European quarter and the numerous European institutions. Kirchberg is the seat of the Secretariat of the European Parliament, the European Court of Justice, the European Court of Auditors, the European Investment Bank, and the European Coal and Steel Community. About 6,000 civil servants work in Kirchberg, and Luxembourg competes with Brussels and Strasbourg for the title of "capital of Europe".

But despite their European outlook, the people of Luxembourg retain an independent spirit, expressed in the words of their national anthem, *"Mir welle bleiwe wat mir sin"* ("We want to remain what we are").

LUXEMBOURG IS ONE OF WESTERN Europe's smallest countries, yet it has played a major role in the continent's recent history. With Belgium and the Netherlands, it helped to found Benelux, an economic union which, in 1961, became the world's first totally free labour and goods market. It was also a founder member of the North Atlantic Treaty Organization in 1949 and of the European Economic Community in 1957. The country's charming old capital, also called Luxembourg, is the headquarters of the European Court of Justice and other West European institutions. It is also an international financial centre, with more than 100 banks in operation.

The people often call their land-locked country the "green heart of Europe" and it contains much beautiful scenery. In the north is an upland region called the Oesling, an extension of the Ardennes mountains of Belgium, while the south is called the *Bon Pays*, or *Gutland*, two terms meaning "Good Land". One spectacular area in east-central Luxembourg, between Echternach and the brewing town of Diekirch, is known as "Little Switzerland". Attractive landscapes, romantic castles, ancient ruins perched on hilltops, and towns steeped in medieval atmosphere attract many tourists to Luxembourg.

Government and education
Luxembourg is a grand duchy. Under its constitution of 1868, it is a hereditary monarchy, with a grand duke (or duchess) as head of state. The grand duke's duties are now mainly ceremonial and the grand duchy is a parliamentary democracy, with representatives elected by popular vote.

The Chamber of Deputies consists of 60 members elected for five-year terms. Voting is compulsory for everyone aged 18 and over. The Cabinet consists of a minister of state, who is president of the government, and at least three other ministers. Luxembourg also has a Council of State, an advisory body made up of 21 members appointed for life by the monarch. The leading political parties in recent years have been the Christian Social Party and the Socialist Workers Party.

Luxembourg's position in the heart of Europe is reflected in its educational system, which lays special emphasis on language studies. Administered by the state, local government, and religious institutions, education for Luxembourgers is compulsory from the ages of 6 to 15. German is usually the language used for teaching primary school pupils, with French increasingly employed later on. The Luxembourgers' own dialect, Letzeburgesch, is also in everyday use.

History
Luxembourg became an independent state in AD 963, when Duke Siegfried, Count of Ardennes, built the castle of Lucilinburhuc, a Saxon word for "little fortress", on the site of the present capital. In the 1300s and 1400s, the country provided four Holy Roman emperors. One of them, Charles IV, raised Luxembourg to the status of a grand duchy in 1354.

The country later came under a succession of foreign powers, including Burgundy, Spain, France and Austria. After the defeat

FACT BOX

THE COUNTRY
Official name: Grand Duchy of Luxembourg
Capital: Luxembourg
Land regions: Ardennes (Oesling) in the north, Bon Pays (Gutland) in the south
Land area: 998 sq mi (2,586 km²)
Climate: Temperate and moist, with cool summers. Winters are cold and snowy in upper regions, mild in Bon Pays
Main rivers: Moselle, Alzette, Sûre, Clerf
Highest elevation: Buurgplaatz 1,835 ft (559 m)
Lowest elevation: On Moselle river, 435 ft (133 m) above sea level

THE GOVERNMENT
Form of Government: Constitutional monarchy
Head of State: Grand Duke or duchess
Head of Government: Prime Minister
Administrative areas: 3 districts, divided into 12 cantons and communes
Legislature: Chamber of Deputies (60 members), elected by the people for 5 years. Advisory Council of State (21 appointed members) also has some legislative functions
Judiciary: Superior Court of Justice (court of appeal, court of cassation), district courts, courts of

Justices of the Peace
Armed forces: Voluntary service. Total strength: 800 men

THE PEOPLE
Population (1990): 367,000
Language: French, German, Letzeburgesch
Religion: Roman Catholic (about 95%), Protestant

THE ECONOMY
Currency: Luxembourg franc
Gross Domestic Product per person (1990): US$27,330
Annual Growth Rate (1985-90): 5.1%
Trade balance Belgium-Luxembourg in US$ (1989): $1,589 mill

Buurgplatz
1,835ft
(559m)

Troisvierges
Ardennes Mountains
Clervaux
Hosingen
GERMANY
Wiltz
Vianden
Sûre
Bourscheid
Diekirch
Ettelbruck
Berg
Echternach
Redange
Attert
Mersch
Larochette
Wasserbillig
Junglinster
Mertert
BELGIUM
Bon
Steinfort
Pays
Grevenmacher
Capellen
LUXEMBOURG
Hesperange
Pétange
Sanem
Remich
Differdange
Bettembourg
Esch-sur-Alzette
Dudelange

N

0 km   10   20
0 miles   10

FRANCE

Luxembourg's 24-storey Centre Européen (*above*) acts as one of the nerve centres of the European Parliament, the European Court of Justice, and several international organizations. Thus tiny Luxembourg ranks as one of the three "capitals" of the European Community.

Luxembourg (*above right*), one of Europe's smallest countries, contains rolling hills in the north and industrial regions in the south.

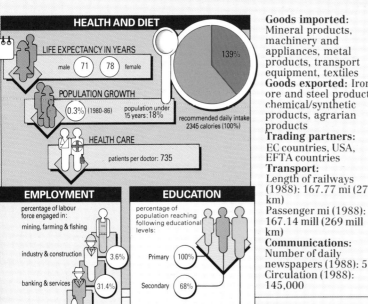

HEALTH AND DIET

LIFE EXPECTANCY IN YEARS
male 71   78 female

POPULATION GROWTH
(0.3%) (1980-86)   population under 15 years: 18%

139%
recommended daily intake 2345 calories (100%)

HEALTH CARE
patients per doctor: 735

EMPLOYMENT
percentage of labour force engaged in:
mining, farming & fishing
industry & construction   3.6%
banking & services   31.4%
65%

EDUCATION
percentage of population reaching following educational levels:
Primary   100%
Secondary   68%
Further   3.4%

Goods imported: Mineral products, machinery and appliances, metal products, transport equipment, textiles
Goods exported: Iron ore and steel products, chemical/synthetic products, agrarian products
Trading partners: EC countries, USA, EFTA countries
Transport: Length of railways (1988): 167.77 mi (270 km)
Passenger mi (1988): 167.14 mill (269 mill km)
Communications: Number of daily newspapers (1988): 5 Circulation (1988): 145,000

of Napoleon I of France, the Congress of Vienna in 1815 confirmed Luxembourg as a grand duchy and a member of the German Confederation, though technically under Dutch control, because the king of the Netherlands was also the grand duke of Luxembourg. In 1839, the larger, western part of the country became a part of the newly independent country of Belgium and is now the Belgian province of Luxembourg. It was not until 1867, after unsuccessful attempts by the French Emperor Napoleon III to take possession of the grand duchy, that Luxembourg became fully independent.

On the death of William III of Orange in 1890, the personal union with the Netherlands was ended because William's successor, Wilhelmina, could not become head of state under Luxembourg's constitution (though a constitutional amendment in 1912 allowed women to succeed). Duke Adolphus of Nassau-Weilburg became grand duke in 1890 and the present grand duke, Jean, who succeeded in 1964, is his descendant in direct line.

Germany occupied the country during World Wars I and II. Part of the "Battle of the Bulge" (1944-45) was fought in northern Luxembourg, resulting in severe damage to the region. After the war, however, the country became one of the most prosperous in Europe.

FRANCE

In 1989, France celebrated the 200th anniversary of the great revolution which laid the foundations of today's republic. The French Revolution signalled more than the end of France's old regime; it also marked the birth of the modern age. With its tumultuous past, varied landscapes and mixed population, France embodies all of Europe's many facets, but during the course of its history the French people have developed a strong national awareness, mingling traditional and modern attitudes and lifestyles.

The second largest country in Europe after Russia, France's geographical position confers many advantages. Its long coastline takes in the Atlantic Ocean and the Mediterranean Sea, giving it a mild climate, while its fertile soils provide superb conditions for agriculture. Overseas possessions such as Martinique enjoy equal status with mainland France.

France has often been one step ahead of other countries; it developed a unified, centrally governed state relatively early, and the absolute monarchy of Louis XIV (1638-1715) became, in its time, the model emulated by all the ruling houses of Europe. In contrast, the ideals of the French Revolution, symbolized by the national motto *Liberté, Egalité, Fraternité* (Liberty, Equality, Fraternity), set the standards for the modern democracies of the world. Today, France attracts both admiration and criticism, but its contributions to literature, art, cinema, medicine and many other fields are almost without equal.

French sophistication, or *savoir-vivre*, attracts admiration far beyond the country's borders. Almost every French person can discuss food and wine with great expertise. The products of French vineyards are rivalled only by those of France's cheesemakers.

This relaxed way of life, however, embraces more than just eating and drinking. It implies taking things easy, taking pleasure in the social contacts made at the pavement cafe, when playing *boules* (bowls) or when buying groceries. And it means making full use of personal freedoms without constraining one's individuality.

There is a common belief that Paris and France are one and the same thing, and such buildings as the **Sacré Coeur Basilica** *(left)*, atop Montmartre, certainly embody the scale and majesty of the nation's capital. While the metropolis on the Seine is certainly the centre of France's government and economy, the wide range of terrain and of local cultures, ranging from the misty coasts of Brittany to the high mountain pastures of the Haute-Savoie, makes plain that the capital does not speak for all of France.

France Today

THE BICENTENNIAL OF THE FRENCH Revolution, celebrated lavishly on July 14, 1989, symbolized the coming of age of France's republican political system. But if France today enjoys stable democratic government under the leadership of a president, political life maintains an energetic tension between competing philosophies.

The nation-state
Following the Revolution, a succession of 16 different constitutions produced the widest possible variety of forms of government. This French nation-state, despite internal divisions or changes of government, has deep roots in the fabric of society. One manifestation of this unity is the national anthem, *La Marseillaise*, composed in 1792. It rings out at state receptions as well as at strikes and demonstrations.

Unity also stems from the country's well-developed educational system, which provides the same level of instruction throughout the country. Education is compulsory until age 16, and about 85 per cent of children attend public schools. There is also a system of private schools, mainly run by the Roman Catholic Church. Education at the university level is free, and special schools, known as the *Grandes Écoles*, prepare students for careers in the civil service, the armed forces and other fields.

The notion of the inviolable nation-state holds the key to France's tradition of centralism. For centuries the centralized state acted as a counter to regional power, which represented a possible threat to the relationship between citizen and state. The recent policy of regionalization has slightly changed this situation.

With an area of 210,026 square miles (543,965 square kilometres), mainland France (including Corsica) is the largest state in western Europe. In addition, it administers the overseas territories of Guadeloupe and Martinique in the Caribbean; Réunion and Mayotte in the Indian Ocean; New Caledonia, French Polynesia and the Wallis and Futuna Islands in the South Pacific Ocean; French Guiana in South America and Saint-Pierre and Miquelon in the North Atlantic Ocean.

France is divided into 96 departments in the mother country and several more in the overseas territories. A locally elected council handles the administration of each department, while a commissioner, known as a prefect, represents the interests of the national government. Since 1960 there has been an intermediate level of authority — 21 planning regions elected by the people and a president elected by each council.

The constitution
France is a democratic, parliamentary republic with a two-chamber parliament, consisting of the National Assembly and the Senate. The present constitution dates from 1958, when the crisis over the Algerian war of independence brought down the Fourth Republic. Under President General Charles de Gaulle (1890-1970), the Fifth Republic came into being, and the new constitution enhanced the powers of the President.

Following the constitutional amendment of 1962, the President is elected for a period of seven years. He appoints the prime minister and the Council of Ministers. The

FACT BOX

THE COUNTRY
Official name: Republic of France
Capital: Paris
Land regions: N Plains, Brittany-Normandy Hills, NE Plateaus, Rhine Valley, Aquitanian Lowlands, Central Highlands, French Alps/Jura, Mediterranean Lowlands, Rhône-Saône Valley, Corsica
Land area: 210,026 sq mi (543,965 km²)

Climate: Warm summers, cool winters. Warmer climate on Mediterranean coast
Main rivers: Loire, Garonne, Rhône, Seine
Highest elevation: Mont Blanc 15,771 ft (4,807 m)

Lowest elevation: Sea level along the coast

THE GOVERNMENT
Form of Government: Parliamentary presidential republic
Head of State: President
Head of Government: Prime Minister
Administrative areas: Mainland: 21 regions, divided into 96 municipal departments
Legislature: National Assembly (577 members, 5-year terms) and Senate (319 members, 9-year terms)
Judiciary: Court of Cassation, Courts of Appeal, Court of Assizes. Lower courts
Armed forces: Total

strength: 458,960.
Conscription: Men must serve 12 months

THE PEOPLE
Population (1990): 56,612,000
Language: French
Religion: Roman Catholic (85%), Muslim (4%), Protestant (2%)

THE ECONOMY
Currency: French franc
Gross Domestic Product per person (1990): $21,107
Annual Growth Rate (1985-90): 2.4%
Trade Balance in US$ (1987): −$14,513 mill
Goods exported: Machinery, mineral oil, chemicals, automobiles
Goods exported: Machinery, chemicals,

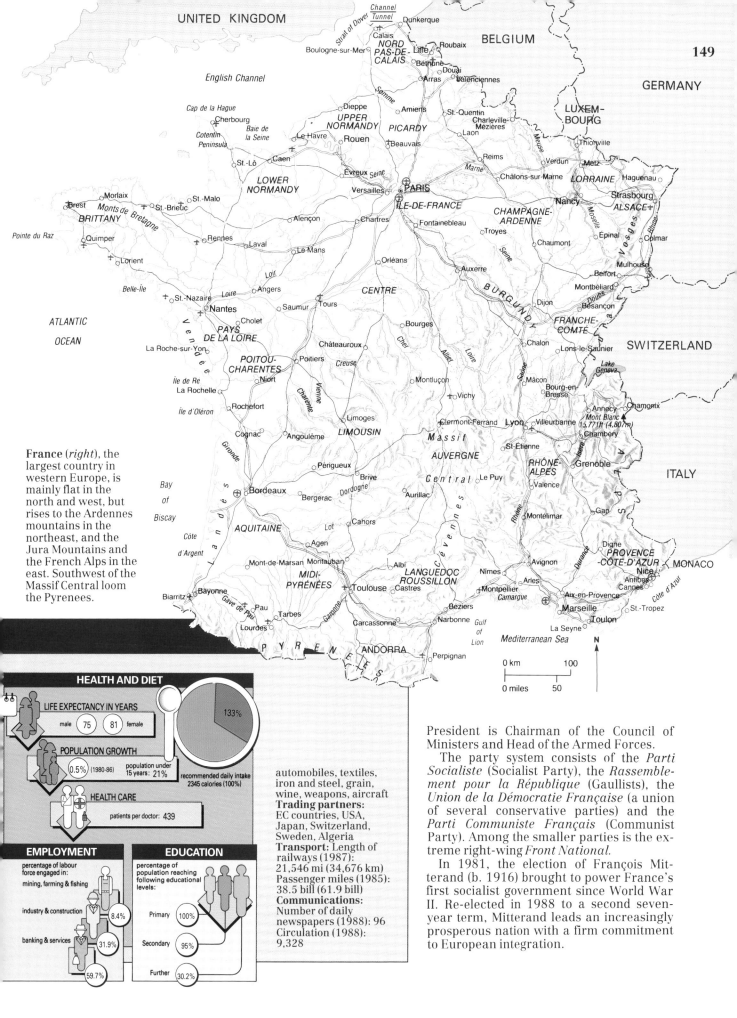

UNITED KINGDOM

Channel Tunnel

Strait of Dover

BELGIUM

GERMANY

LUXEM-BOURG

English Channel

Dunkerque
Calais
Boulogne-sur-Mer
NORD PAS-DE-CALAIS
Lille
Roubaix
Béthune
Douai
Arras
Valenciennes

Cap de la Hague
Cherbourg
Baie de la Seine
Cotentin Peninsula
Dieppe
Amiens
St-Quentin
Charleville-Mézières
Laon
UPPER NORMANDY
PICARDY
Reims
Verdun
Metz
Thionville
LORRAINE
Hagueneau
Strasbourg
ALSACE

St.-Lô
Caen
Le Hâvre
Rouen
Beauvais
Évreux Seine
Châlons-sur-Marne
Nancy
Épinal
Colmar

Morlaix
St.-Malo
St-Brieuc
Versailles
PARIS
ÎLE-DE-FRANCE
Chartres
Fontainebleau
CHAMPAGNE-ARDENNE
Troyes
Chaumont
Vosges
Mulhouse
Belfort

Brest
Monts de Bretagne
BRITTANY
Rennes
Alençon
Le Mans
Orléans
Auxerre
Dijon
Montbéliard
Besançon
FRANCHE-COMTÉ

Pointe du Raz
Quimper
Laval
Loir
Angers
Saumur
Tours
CENTRE
Bourges
Cher
Chalon
Lons-le-Saunier
Doubs
SWITZERLAND

Lorient
Belle-Île
St.-Nazaire
Nantes
Cholet
Loire
Châteauroux
Poitiers
Creuse
Montluçon
Allier
Mâcon
Bourg-en-Bresse
Lake Geneva

ATLANTIC OCEAN
PAYS DE LA LOIRE
La Roche-sur-Yon
POITOU-CHARENTES
Niort
Vienne
Vichy
Clermont-Ferrand
Lyon
Villeurbanne
Annecy
Chamonix
Mont Blanc 15,771ft (4,807m)

Île de Ré
La Rochelle
Île d'Oléron
Rochefort
Charente
Limoges
LIMOUSIN
Angoulême
Cognac
Brive
Périgueux
Massif Central
AUVERGNE
St-Étienne
RHÔNE-ALPES
Chambéry
Grenoble
ITALY

Bay of Biscay
Gironde
Bordeaux
Bergerac
Dordogne
Aurillac
Le Puy
Valence
Gap

Côte d'Argent
Landes
AQUITAINE
Lot
Cahors
Agen
Cévennes
Montélimar
Digne

Mont-de-Marsan
Montauban
MIDI-PYRÉNÉES
Albi
LANGUEDOC ROUSSILLON
Castres
Nîmes
Avignon
Aix-en-Provence
PROVENCE -CÔTE-D'AZUR
Nice
Antibes
Cannes
MONACO

Biarritz
Bayonne
Gave de Pau
Pau
Tarbes
Lourdes
Toulouse
Carcassonne
Narbonne
Béziers
Montpellier
Camargue
Arles
Marseille
Toulon
St.-Tropez
Côte d'Azur

PYRENEES
ANDORRA
Perpignan
Gulf of Lion
La Seyne
Mediterranean Sea

N

0 km   100
0 miles 50

France (*right*), the largest country in western Europe, is mainly flat in the north and west, but rises to the Ardennes mountains in the northeast, and the Jura Mountains and the French Alps in the east. Southwest of the Massif Central loom the Pyrenees.

HEALTH AND DIET

LIFE EXPECTANCY IN YEARS
male 75   81 female

133%

POPULATION GROWTH
0.5% (1980-86)
population under 15 years: 21%
recommended daily intake 2345 calories (100%)

HEALTH CARE
patients per doctor: 439

EMPLOYMENT

percentage of labour force engaged in:
mining, farming & fishing
industry & construction   8.4%
banking & services   31.9%
59.7%

EDUCATION

percentage of population reaching following educational levels:
Primary   100%
Secondary   95%
Further   30.2%

automobiles, textiles, iron and steel, grain, wine, weapons, aircraft
Trading partners:
EC countries, USA, Japan, Switzerland, Sweden, Algeria
Transport: Length of railways (1987): 21,546 mi (34,676 km) Passenger miles (1985): 38.5 bill (61.9 bill)
Communications: Number of daily newspapers (1988): 96 Circulation (1988): 9,328

President is Chairman of the Council of Ministers and Head of the Armed Forces.

The party system consists of the *Parti Socialiste* (Socialist Party), the *Rassemblement pour la République* (Gaullists), the *Union de la Démocratie Française* (a union of several conservative parties) and the *Parti Communiste Français* (Communist Party). Among the smaller parties is the extreme right-wing *Front National*.

In 1981, the election of François Mitterand (b. 1916) brought to power France's first socialist government since World War II. Re-elected in 1988 to a second seven-year term, Mitterand leads an increasingly prosperous nation with a firm commitment to European integration.

THE LANDSCAPE OF FRANCE REVEALS natural riches around every corner, and the diversity of French agriculture and settlement reflects the variety and the fertility of the natural environment. Much of France escaped the effects of the Ice Age, so the landscape is mellow, with gentle hills, plateaus and valleys carved by rivers. But the soft curves of the plains give way to imposing mountains, great river gorges and beautiful beaches, making the landscapes of France among Europe's loveliest.

Diverse regions

In the southeast and southwest lies some of the country's most spectacular scenery. The snowy peaks of the French Alps and Jura Mountains provide a natural border between France, Italy and Switzerland. The majestic peak of Mont Blanc reaches 15,771 feet (4,807 metres), ranking not only as the highest point in France, but also in Western Europe. The lofty Pyrenees mountains in southwest France form the frontier between France and Spain.

France's west coast receives the great waves of the open Atlantic along the sandy shores of the Bay of Biscay, while further north, steep cliffs plunge almost vertically into the sea on the Channel coast of Brittany. Intriguing features of this craggy coastline include mysterious fields of megaliths, or standing stones, notably at Carnac, and outcrops of pink granite rock. The lowlands flanking the Bay of Biscay hold pine forests, rolling plains, sand dunes and the almost endless vineyards of Bordeaux.

The Paris Basin, or the Île de France, forms the heart of the country. Layers of sedimentary rock underlie this large trough, and geologists recently revealed the existence of oil deposits beneath the city of Paris itself. The Seine River drains this large circular area, and forested hills enclose its flat, rolling fertile plains.

East of Paris, a series of rocky ridges resemble the upturned edge of a huge saucer, and the chalky uplands around Reims support the vineyards of the famous Champagne country. The northern plains extend to the Belgian and German borders, where the forested Vosges Mountains and the Belfort Gap open France to the east. The steep slopes of the Rhine valley define France's boundary with Germany. Its valley provides fertile farmland, while trees and vines cover the higher slopes.

The highlands of the Massif Central, covering the southeastern part of France, are one the country's most arresting natural features. Its pleasantly rolling hills and plateaus are the eroded remains of an ancient mountain chain, worn down to stumps

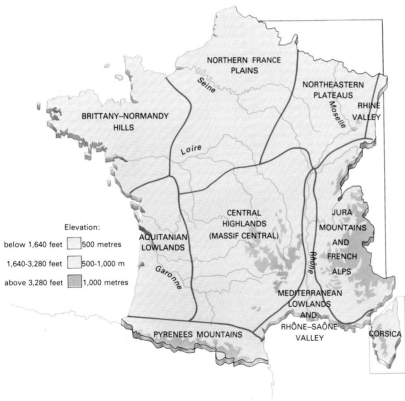

Elevation:

below 1,640 feet — 500 metres
1,640–3,280 feet — 500–1,000 m
above 3,280 feet — 1,000 metres

NORTHERN FRANCE PLAINS

BRITTANY–NORMANDY HILLS

Seine

Loire

NORTHEASTERN PLATEAUS

RHINE VALLEY

Moselle

AQUITANIAN LOWLANDS

CENTRAL HIGHLANDS (MASSIF CENTRAL)

Garonne

JURA MOUNTAINS AND FRENCH ALPS

Rhône

MEDITERRANEAN LOWLANDS AND RHÔNE–SAÔNE VALLEY

CORSICA

PYRENEES MOUNTAINS

Red-roofed buildings (*right*) huddle around the chapel of Sons Brancion, situated amid the rolling fields and forests of western France, in the department of Saône-et-Loire. In the distance, a line of hills borders the green expanse.

France's land regions (*left*) range from the high Alps, Jura and Pyrenees mountain ranges to the fertile lowlands of the Paris basin. The Massif Central consists of rounded hills, the eroded remnants of volcanic mountains. With such a long coastline, the Atlantic Ocean and the Mediterranean Sea naturally exert a great influence on France's climate. In Provence, along the Mediterranean coast, dry conditions limit cultivation, but olive trees and fragrant herbs cling to the hillsides.

over millions of years. The upper reaches of the Loire River, the longest in France, dissect the remnants of these extinct volcanoes, which form perfectly symmetrical domes, some as high as 6,000 feet (1,800 metres).

Climate and vegetation

The diversity of the French landscape plays a decisive role in the climate of each region. Westerly winds from the Atlantic give coastal regions a rainy climate with cool winters and mild summers. In contrast, the less exposed southwest enjoys a Mediterranean climate with hot, dry summers and mild winters. The Alps help to shield the sunny Riviera coast from cold north winds for much of the year. East of the Atlantic coast, a more continental climate prevails, with hot summers, cold winters and medium rainfall throughout the year. Heavy winter snows and rain fall in the Alps and Jura mountains.

The natural forests of France, particularly in the basin regions, were early victims of man's agricultural activities. But today, forests cover some 20 per cent of the country, especially in mountain and upland areas, making France one of the most forested European nations. In most areas, local climate influences the natural vegetation. In Normandy, dense hedgerows, known as *bocage*, protect fields from the sea breezes. In contrast, the south of France boasts a profusion of herbs, succulents and aromatic plants. Bush and scrub vegetation – *maquis* and *garrigue*, rockrose, laurel, lavender and thyme – now grows in place of depleted forests of cork oak trees and cypresses. Olive trees give the area a Mediterranean flavour, but forest fires often ravage the hills of southern France, causing severe damage.

Rugged peaks (*left*) present a bleak outlook in the French Alps adjoining Switzerland. Here lies Mont Blanc, at 15,771 feet (4,807 metres) France's highest mountain. Many ski resorts thrive on the lower Alpine slopes.

French "cowboys" (*right*) herd the famous wild horses of the Camargue, a vast marsh area at the delta of the Rhône River. Until recently, the Camargue was an unspoilt wilderness but much of it has now been drained.

People

TO THE REST OF THE WORLD, THE French nation seems to present a unified whole. All its people share the riches of the French language, but a close look at the country's demographic structure reveals that France is anything but unified.

Like its landscape, great variation characterizes the population of France. In terms of lifestyle, social manners and the way they see themselves, the people of the Midi (Mediterranean south), the Auvergne, Normandy, Savoie and Aquitaine, are worlds apart. In addition to quite marked regional differences, France has a number of ethnic minorities – Bretons, Basques, Catalans, Corsicans, Alsatians and Flemings – who insist on their own cultural and social independence.

For hundreds of years, the centralized state system prevented the fragmentation of France in the face of its great ethnic diversity. Central control ensured that any efforts towards regional autonomy on the part of minorities met with strong opposition. However, central administration also fostered the growth of national institutions, and a strong pride in being French. Today French government policies of regionalization encourage local customs.

Immigrants to France

Following World War II, the ethnic spectrum of France's population broadened considerably. Guest workers from Europe's poorer nations, especially Portugal, contributed to this first, but a greater influx came after France's withdrawal from its colonies in the 1950s. In terms of numbers, North African immigrants from the countries of the Maghreb – Algeria, Morocco and Tunisia – form the largest components of an immigrant community that also comprises significant groups of West Africans, Vietnamese and Caribbean peoples. As the countries of the Maghreb achieved independence, many thousands of their inhabitants migrated to France, mostly to find work. North Africans sometimes suffer discrimination in employment and housing, and extremist politicians like *Front National* leader Jean-Marie Le Pen urge that France should cease to accept any more immigrants. However, France's traditional tolerance and openness works against racism; North Africans now enjoy enhanced civil and political rights, but many other problems remain to be solved.

Linguistic diversity

The different dialects and languages used throughout the land reflect France's ethnic and cultural diversity. Neither Roman occupation, Frankish conquerors, nor the centralized state ever managed to standardize the French people.

In ancient times, a Celtic people called Gauls lived in what is now France. The French language first developed with the Roman invasion of the country under Julius Caesar (58-51 BC), when the Gauls adopted the Latin tongue of the Roman soldiers; but the arrival of Germanic tribes in the AD 400s brought new linguistic influences. Today, the French language belongs to the Romance, or Latin-based, group of languages. Catalan, known in France as *langue d'Oc*, also belongs to the Romance group of languages, and is spoken as an everyday tongue by some 12 million people in France and Spain. In France, the language flourishes in the Languedoc and Roussillon regions.

In Alsace and parts of Lorraine, the areas flanking Germany, the German language remains alive in the form of the Alamannic dialect. In some French Alpine regions, in Monaco, and on Corsica the people speak a mixture of French and Italian.

Some of the inhabitants of western Britanny still speak Breton, a Celtic language similar to Welsh. But an independent language prevails most strongly in the Basque region of the Pyrenees. Basque is the oldest European language, and one of the few not derived from Indo-Germanic or Latin roots. Around 500,000 Basques live in France and some 2,500,000 in Spain.

A religious procession (*above*) in St Tropez on the Côte d'Azur keeps alive France's Roman Catholic faith. France does not recognize an official religion, but Roman Catholics make up most of the population.

Flanked by cheering crowds, cyclist Laurent Fignon (*left*) completes a leg of the 1989 Tour de France. The gruelling 24-day race, one of France's top sporting events, draws cyclists on a course right around France.

Under shady trees in Bordeaux, a group of old men (*below*) deliberate over cards. Bordeaux is world-renowned as one of France's major wine centres, and its prosperity lends a stately air to its parks and boulevards.

Population structure and movement

France today contains a population of about 57 million people, but in spite of rapid population growth during the late 1800s, the country until recently had one of the lowest birth rates in Europe. This trend was only reversed in the later 1900s, prompted by government measures to encourage larger families, especially after World War II. Between 1950 and 1989, the population increased by about 15 million.

Because of its large land area, population density in France is low in comparison with that of neighbouring countries, and its distribution is very uneven. The greatest concentration of people – about 20 per cent of the entire population of France – live in the Paris metropolitan area, one of the largest metropolitan areas in the world. Apart from its importance as a centre of government and business, Paris is also the heart of French culture and civilization.

Besides Paris, industrial cities such as Marseille, Lyon, Toulouse and Nice act as magnets for people from the less developed regions, while the southern coast is also increasingly popular. Today, Nice is a centre for high-technology research, and its pleasant climate also makes it an attractive retirement area. This migration contributes to the unequal regional distribution of people so typical of modern France.

On patrol in Paris's Palais de Chaillot near the Eiffel Tower, two *gendarmes* (*below*) – members of the national police force – reflect France's new multiracial society. Immigrants from former French colonies now make up a large part of the population.

Folk dancers on stilts (*right*) in the town of Brive-la-Gaillarde enliven a summer festival. Despite a history of state centralization, France today gives more encouragement to its rich spectrum of regional cultures and customs.

Paris

"PARIS? PARIS IS THE EIFFEL TOWER, with its spire reaching to the heavens," sang the famed French *chanteur* Maurice Chevalier; and for many this structure is more than a lasting tribute to engineering skill, dominating a city of monumental architecture and feather-light dreams. The tower's familiar tapering outline, formed by 7,000 tonnes of ironwork, floats as lightly as lace against the skyline.

Erected in 1887-89 for the Universal Exhibition marking the centenary of the beginning of the Revolution, the Eiffel Tower was intended to stand only for the duration of the exhibition, but the development of radio-telegraphy saved it from demolition: its height of 986 feet (300.51 metres) made it an ideal transmitting station.

A harmonious whole

On a clear day, the tourist (some 3,000,000 of whom mount the Eiffel Tower each year) has an incomparable view of Paris. Below lies the Seine River with its many bridges. From the hill of Montmartre, haunt of painters, to that of Montparnasse, the heart of the bohemian Latin Quarter, the romantic city extends its charms for all to see. A huge white arch, known as La Grande Arche, located in the futuristic business complex of La Defense, provides another spectacular view of the city. On the horizon to the east lies the impressive theme park, Euro-Disneyland, opened in 1992.

Yet it is typical of Paris that the symbol of this ancient city, whose history stretches back to Roman times, should be a comparatively modern structure like the Eiffel Tower. At once richly medieval and vividly contemporary, Paris has never been static, but has continually been subjected to grandiose building and town planning schemes. The broad boulevards of the 1800s, which now typify the city's smartest quarter, were planned partly to discourage would-be revolutionaries from constructing barricades across their width. In peace or war Paris's architects built not in isolation but with a view to creating a harmonious whole.

The famous sights of Paris range from the Sainte Chapelle, built in the 1300s by King Louis IX (St Louis) to house the relic of the Crown of Thorns, to the "secular temple" of the Panthéon, designed as a church but converted after the Revolution to a burial place for Republican heroes. Few people can forget their first walk along the broad chestnut-lined avenue of the Champs Élysées, with the Arc de Triomphe, built in 1806-36 as Napoleon's memorial to his Great Army, at the western end. The Hotel des Invalides, ordered by Louis XIV as a home for disabled soldiers, was built in 1676; one of the world's finest military museums, it houses Napoleon's tomb.

Notre Dame Cathedral (*above*) dominates the old quarter of Paris from its island in the Seine. The *quais*, or riverbank streets, that line the Seine are the haunt of open-air booksellers (*bouquinistes*) and their clients.

A cafe (*below*) at the top of the Champs Élysées, Paris's most famous avenue, offers tourists a fine view of the Arc de Triomphe. This commemorates the army of Napoleon Bonaparte (1769-1821) and was completed in 1836.

Foremost among Paris's medieval structures is the Cathedral of Notre Dame, begun in 1163. A masterpiece of Gothic design, this majestic building glories in a magnificent rose window, some 30 feet (9.5 metres) in diameter; above it rises an open arcade, guarded by grotesque gargoyles, and two great towers.

The most impressive secular building in Paris is probably the Palais du Louvre. Originally a fortress, dating from about 1200, this became a royal residence in the mid-1300s, under Charles V, and was elaborated by successive rulers until today it extends for half a mile (0.8 kilometres) along the Seine. In 1793, it became "The Museum of the Republic", and is now one of the world's largest art museums, housing such masterpieces as the *Venus de Milo* and Leonardo's *Mona Lisa*. In 1989, the Louvre acquired a fascinating architectural addition in the form of a transparent pyramid.

The living and the dead

As much a part of Paris as its great buildings is the spirit of its everyday life. The city was noted for its lively cafes as early as 1715, when these were said to number 300, and today residents and tourists alike enjoy sitting at tables on the *terrasses* (covered areas outside the cafes) to chat and watch the street life. Such a break may give

The Eiffel Tower
(*left*), symbolizes Paris
for millions of tourists.
A temporary structure
built as part of the
1889 Exhibition, it has
become an enduring
landmark for Pari-
sians and visitors
alike.

A fire-eater (*above*)
gives a display of his
art outside Paris's
famed modern art
complex, the Centre
Pompidou.

visitors strength to tackle the numerous obligatory sights, and perhaps also the street
markets, which trade in food, flowers,
clothes, books, stamps – and even a bird
market with blatantly dyed finches.

The vital, bustling city of Paris contains
within itself a fascinating smaller city – for
the dead. This is Père Lachaise cemetery,
an elaborately designed graveyard of 116
acres (47 hectares) dating from the early
1800s. This contains the mortal remains of
numerous celebrated persons, including
writers such as Molière (1622-73) and La
Fontaine (1668-94). Since then, many other
writers, musicians and artists have been
buried here, from Proust to Wilde, and from
Chopin to the rock idol Jim Morrison.

Paris has its underworld, too: its eleg-
antly refurbished Métro (underground railway), its remarkable – and visitable – sew-
ers and, above all, its Catacombs. The sew-
ers, dating from the 1800s, are known
worldwide as the fictional haunt of the
"Phantom of the Opera". Equally forbidding, and sinister, but far more ancient, are
the Catacombs – underground passages
beneath Montparnasse dug out as long ago
as Roman times. Here, a macabre tour
through skull-lined galleries leads to a vast
ossuary (container for human bones) hold-
ing the debris of more than six million
skeletons.

Paris (*right*), one of
the world's loveliest
cities, is the capital
and largest city of
France. Set on the
banks of the Seine, its
centre contains wide
avenues, pleasant
sidewalk cafes, eleg-
ant shops and numer-
ous historic monu-
ments, with industrial
areas occupying the
outskirts. A centre of
the arts, Paris offers
tourists and residents
an unrivalled range
of art treasures, and
also boasts elegant
shops, very fine res-
taurants and a whole
range of exciting
nightlife.

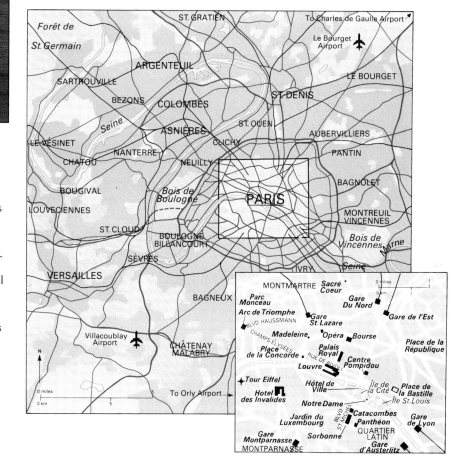

French Style

POPULAR IMAGES OF THE FRENCH include that of a red-faced, well-covered man, enjoying an appetizing meal while savouring through his ample moustache a good glass of wine. Another "typical" French person is the dark and elegant woman, neatly and fashionably dressed, and behaving with perfect confidence and social ease. These images embody two of the most remarkable characteristics of the French, best described by French phrases that have entered the English language – *savoir-vivre* ("know how to live" – an appreciation of the good things of life) and *savoir-faire* ("know-how"). It says much of the quality of French life that many such expressions have been taken over by English-speakers, such as *bon viveur* (someone who lives well), *gourmet* (a lover of good food), *haute cuisine* (sophisticated cooking), *haute couture* (high fashion), *chic* (elegant) and *panache* (style or flair).

From at least the 1700s, the lifestyle and culture of the French have represented a civilized ideal to which many other countries have aspired. Until comparatively recently, French rather than English was the main language of the West, and certainly the one which anyone wanting to be thought of as "educated" needed to know. The French language has a far smaller vocabulary than English, and is governed by stricter rules. Yet it is this very precision, combined with its elegance, that has made it seem so sophisticated to foreigners. In other words, even the language of the French is a reflection of the good taste and high culture for which this nation is famous.

French cooking

An aspect of French culture which continues to enjoy an undisputed reputation for excellence is the country's food and wine. Although other people might eat and drink as well as the French, they cannot boast such internationally known cooks as Carême, Escoffier and Bocuse, or so many famous wines as Burgundy, Bordeaux and Champagne; neither can they claim to have influenced food fashions so greatly. Such is the fame of French gastronomy abroad that many foreign restaurants try to make their dishes seem more appealing and sophisticated by giving them French names.

Foreigners take French cooking so seriously because the French themselves regard it as much more than a means of nourishing the body. Bocuse compared cooking to an opera, and many other Frenchmen have considered it as a form of philosophy, notably Anthelme Brillat-Savarin (1755-1826), a French politician, who wrote an influential book entitled *The Philosopher in the Kitchen*. The French approach to food tells just as much about the

A customer (*below*) ponders a purchase of ducks at a market in Bordeaux, south-west France. French cuisine relies on fresh natural produce, and many people scorn the mass-produced items popular in food stores of other countries.

A stylish couple (*right*) relax at one of Paris's many restaurants. French style owes much to a belief that pleasure is a serious business, to be undertaken with care, correctness, and a proper respect for the formalities.

A shop window (*below*) presents a graceful display of goods. This establishment, founded in 1761, continues an enduring tradition of elegance that has endowed French consumerism with its distinctive style.

A French working man (*bottom*) samples a mouthful of bread warm from the bakery. In France, bread is baked daily at thousands of small *boulangeries*, where loaves traditionally appear in numerous different forms.

Fashion models (*left*) display the latest modes at a show in the Tuileries, Paris. *Haute couture* (high fashion) stems from the "creations" of top designers to become a worldwide, billion-dollar industry. Many design houses, such as Chanel and Dior, also market related products such as perfume and other "accessories". To most people, France is a byword for all that is *chic* (stylish) in women's clothing. Yet French people buy clothes sparingly.

national mentality as does the American fondness for "fast food". Eating, say the French, should never be a hurried experience but a celebration of life. This was excellently illustrated in a recent and highly successful movie, *Babette's Feast*, in which a French refugee from Paris in the late 1800s finds a home in Denmark, and transforms the outlook of a group of dour, down-to-earth and mean-spirited country-folk by means of the delights of a leisurely meal, crammed with French delicacies.

High fashion

A number of parallels can be drawn between French food and French fashion. France is almost as celebrated for its *couture* (fashion) as for its *cuisine* (cooking): the Spring fashion shows in Paris are still the most influential in the world, and, if one were asked to name a handful of fashion designers, it is the names of Frenchmen such as Yves Saint-Laurent, Pierre Cardin and Christian Dior that immediately spring to mind. Yet, curiously, statistics show that the French as a whole spend less money on clothes than many other nations.

Just as the essence of French food lies less in complex, extravagant sauces than in careful preparation of simple ingredients, so too do the French have the ability to look chic while wearing the simplest of clothes. The French were the inventors of denims (the word refers to cloth from the town of Nîmes), and still pride themselves on the elegant cut of their jeans. They have also the ability to adapt brilliantly the fashions of other countries: just as the French borrowed from Japanese food in the creation of their highly influential *nouvelle cuisine*, so too in fashion have they been able to transform the lumpy kilt and casual sports jacket of Britain into the smartest of clothes. Ultimately the French believe that to be fashionable requires a certain state of mind. As the celebrated *couturier* Yves Saint-Laurent himself said, "'Chic' lies less in the clothes than in the spirit."

The inimitable style and flair of the French are revealed in many other aspects of their culture, from the elegant display of a grocer's shop to their very individual movies. French cinema has always been noted for the beauty of its images, and for its ability to make interesting the simplest of stories. Take, for instance, such a movie as Eric Rohmer's *Claire's Knee*, which deals for its entire length with a man's searching for the right psychological moment in which to touch a girl's knee. To make a witty, beautiful, intellectually stimulating, and sensual movie out of a story in which the only action is the eventual fondling of this knee requires a quality which the French have in abundance. And that is *panache*.

French Wines

THE FRENCH NOT ONLY ENJOY THEIR wine; they also take it very seriously. For the making and marketing of wine counts as one of France's main economic concerns. Symbols of excellence throughout the world, the famous vintages of Champagne, Burgundy and Bordeaux command impressive prices at top auction houses. But these represent only the most glamorous part of an industry that, directly or indirectly, involves one in ten of all French workers.

The wine trade employs a wide range of people, from peasant farmers in the south (the Midi), cultivating a few acres of vines, to Paris businessmen exporting fine wines around the world. In between come various kinds of wine merchant, makers and suppliers of accessories from pruning knives to fermentation tanks, makers of barrels and vats, sellers of insurance, printers of labels – and a host of others. In France, a whole industry depends on the vine, regulated by a network of government bodies. These are dedicated to raising standards, seeing that wine is properly made and accurately labelled, and encouraging growers to upgrade their vineyards and to improve wineries.

Change for the better
Recent decades have seen important changes in French wine. The wide plains of the Midi, once entirely devoted to the cultivation of rather poor-quality grapes, are being abandoned – for domestic consumption has fallen sharply. The average intake in the late 1960s stood at 24.6 gallons (112 litres) per person per year; today it has fallen to 17.6 gallons (80 litres), and the quality is far higher. In France, wine has increasingly become a mealtime drink to be savoured, rather than a tipple at bars.

This change in drinking habits at first led to a glut of wine, causing a problem (shared with Italy) known in the European Community as the "wine lake". Cheap, poor-quality wine from the southern half of France helped to fill this lake until the EC bureaucrats decided to drain it away by paying growers to give up grape farming, and encouraging those who remained to plant better grapes, cultivate more suitable land, and make better wine.

Wine grades
Such wine has a good chance of attaining one of the official quality categories. Highest of these is "*Appellation d'Origine Contrôlée*" (AOC), which indicated that the wine has been made according to set standards and in a particular location, and has passed a tasting test. The lowest, but still approved, category is designated "*vins de pays*" (country wines). More modest than AOC-rated wines, these require the grower

to obey rules establishing the kinds of vine cultivated, the quantity grown per acre, and the methods used in production.

French wine laws are based on the concepts of location and yield. Champagne, for example, must come not only from a certain region, but even from certain vineyards within that region. Unless listed as part of the Champagne appellation, the land may not be used to grow grapes and make champagne wine. And only a certain amount of wine can come from each acre of vines. For the French believe, unlike their German neighbours, that in the case of wine "more" means "worse".

The *Appellation d'Origine Contrôlée* vineyards are found all over wine-growing France. They vary considerably in status and quality: "AOC" on a label is no guarantee of excellence, for some wine regions are better than others, and within each area some producers fare better than others. All the AOC label tells the consumer is that the minimum standards have been met.

Creation of the "*vin de pays*" category has led to the improvement of ordinary wines and wine areas. Government-sponsored advertizing has trained consumers to regard these wines as authentic and properly made. Thus growers can charge more for them than for the "*vin de table*", which has no particular place of origin.

Wine benefits
Wine is a very simple natural product, but one which needs much care to make well, and still more care to make predictably. It also combines (unlike other agricultural industries) the growing of the raw material and its processing into a saleable product, with the two activities happening close to

Two workers in the vineyards of Château Haut-Brion, Bordeaux region (*above*), help bring in the harvest. Bordeaux's cooler Atlantic climate, mineral-rich bedrock and poor topsoil make it a prime wine region.

Wine regions

Geography has made France the source of many of the world's greatest wines. The country lies at just the right latitude to receive good sunshine for ripening the grapes, yet is not too hot — except in parts of the south. Too much heat allows fermentation to get out of control. Modern refrigeration technology can avoid this, but too much sun will still lead to inferior wine. The best French wines still come from the cooler areas: Bordeaux,

close to the Atlantic; Burgundy with its Côte d'Or ("golden ridge"); Champagne on the cool northern chalk plains; Alsace behind its sheltering hills. Further south, fine wines come from the Rhône Valley. But in the Mediterranean

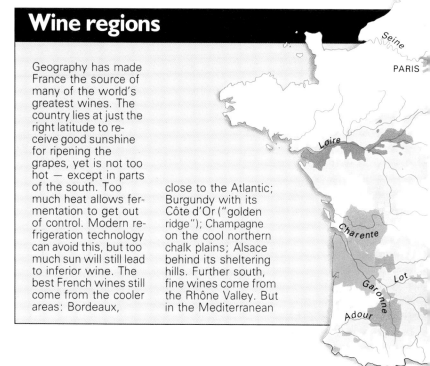

A typical wine château (*right*) consists of a modest house (1) surrounded by vineyards (2) from which the grapes are taken to the crusher (3). A fermenting vat (4) receives the liquid, while the residue is squeezed in a hydraulic press (5). The new wine ferments further in stainless steel vats in an adjacent building (6) and is then transferred to oak barrels (7). Bottling (8) takes place in a separate room.

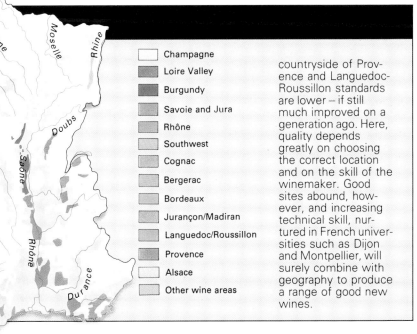

Champagne
Loire Valley
Burgundy
Savoie and Jura
Rhône
Southwest
Cognac
Bergerac
Bordeaux
Jurançon/Madiran
Languedoc/Roussillon
Provence
Alsace
Other wine areas

countryside of Provence and Languedoc-Roussillon standards are lower – if still much improved on a generation ago. Here, quality depends greatly on choosing the correct location and on the skill of the winemaker. Good sites abound, however, and increasing technical skill, nurtured in French universities such as Dijon and Montpellier, will surely combine with geography to produce a range of good new wines.

each other. Concerned about the movement of people from the countryside to the towns, the French authorities value this characteristic of the wine industry, which not only benefits local people but also offers them a number of different careers. Wine also brings benefits in the form of tourism, for wine-lovers around the world flock to see the fabled places where the great wines are made, particularly the so-called "*châteaux*" (vineyard estates).

However, growers' cooperatives, rather than the more glamorous châteaux, account for most French wine. These organizations unite hundreds, or even thousands, of farmers, each of whom may own only a few vines. Together, they can afford modern wine-making techniques and specialist staff to make, bottle and market the wine. Good cooperatives actively promote their wine on export markets, and represent an effective means of raising local standards and, as a result, farmers' incomes.

Monaco

The Monaco Grand Prix (*below*), a thrilling road race through the steep streets of the town, is held every year, and forms a highlight of the motor racing circuit.

THE INDEPENDENT PRINCIPALITY OF Monaco, the second smallest state in the world, perches atop a rocky promontory overlooking the Mediterranean Sea. Its land area of three-quarters of a square mile (1.9 square kilometres) includes the capital Monaco, the community of La Condamine around the harbour, and the town of Monte Carlo, sprawling along the southern fringe of the French Maritime Alps. Up until 1959, Monaco embraced some 370 acres (150 hectares). Extensions to this area, formed by dumping material into the sea, make up the Fontvieille industrial area.

A constitutional monarchy since 1911, Monaco today claims the title of one of the richest countries in Europe. Yet, little more than a century ago, a travelogue described this region as "among the poorest areas of the French Riviera". Monaco's territory includes remains from prehistoric times, but traces its origins to 600 BC, when Phoenician sailors used this strategic location to construct a harbour. The name of the principality may derive from the name of one of their gods – Melkart. During Roman rule, the harbour was extended to form the *Portus Herculis Moneci*.

It was not until the high Middle Ages that Monaco again emerged into the spotlight. In 1191, Holy Roman Emperor Henry VI (ruled 1165-97) granted Genoa possession of Monaco in return for supporting his territorial interests in Italy. The rivalry in Italy between the Guelphs, supporters of the Pope, and the Ghibellines, supporters of the Emperor, spilled over in the 1200s into the city-state of Genoa. In 1297, Francesco Grimaldi, who as a supporter of the Guelphs

FACT BOX

THE COUNTRY
Official name:
Principality of Monaco
Capital: Monaco
Land area: 0.73 sq mi
(1.9 km²)
Climate:
Mediterranean with mild, moist winters and hot, dry summers
Highest elevation:
Chemin des Revoires
535 ft (163 m)
Lowest elevation: Sea level along the coast

THE GOVERNMENT
Form of Government:
Parliamentary monarchy
Head of State: Prince
Head of Government:
Minister of State (and 3 councillors)
Administrative areas:
4 districts

Legislature: National Council, consisting of 18 members, elected for 5 years
Judiciary: Supreme Tribunal, Court of Revision, Criminal Tribunal, Court of Appeal, lower courts
Armed forces: No compulsory military service

THE PEOPLE
Population (1990):
28,000
Language: French, Monégasque
Religion: Roman Catholic (about 90%)

THE ECONOMY
Currency: French franc
Gross Domestic Product per person (1991): n.a.

Annual Growth Rate:
n.a.
Trade balance in US$:
n.a.
Goods imported:
Consumer goods of all kinds
Goods exported:
Cosmetics and pharmaceutical products, electronics, synthetic materials, tinned food, beer, dairy goods
Trading partners: EC countries (about 70%)
Transport: Length of railways: 1.05 mi (1.7 km), operated by the French National Railways
Communications:
Number of daily newspapers (1984): 2
Circulation (1979):
11,000

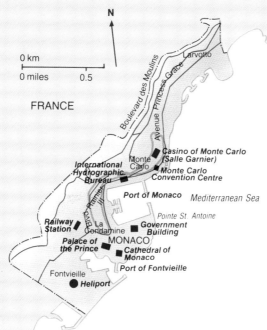

rate lasted until 1860, when France again took over. In return, Monaco gave France the towns of Menton and Rocquebrune.

The economy
Since that time, Monaco's boundaries have remained unchanged. It has always maintained a very strong association with France, and the French franc serves as the principality's currency. A French civil servant, chosen by the ruling prince, heads the government, and under the terms of a treaty concluded in 1918, Monaco will automatically come under French rule if the ruling prince produces no male heir. In 1956, the marriage of Prince Rainier III to the American film actress Grace Kelly (1929-82) turned the world spotlight on Monaco's ruling family.

In the past, political confusion brought poverty to the principality, and to escape

had to flee Genoa, arrived in Monaco. In subsequent years, the aristocratic Grimaldi family severed their links with Genoa, and strengthened their rule of Monaco.

During the 1500s and 1600s, dissension within the Grimaldi family led to several changes of sovereign. However, the family retained permanent power, and in 1659 adopted the status of princes.

In 1792, the Monégasques – as the people of Monaco call themselves – declared the principality a republic, and a year later, revolutionary France seized the territory. At the Congress of Vienna in 1815, Monaco regained its independence, but placed itself from that time onwards under the protection of the Kings of Sardinia. This protecto-

Across the entrance to the port (*above left*) lies the town of Monte Carlo, largest of the three towns which make up the tiny principality of Monaco. The green-roofed Casino is one of Monaco's chief attractions, but favourable tax laws draw many foreign residents.

Monaco (*top*) occupies a rocky stretch of Mediterranean coastline along the French Riviera, surrounded on three sides by France.

The Royal Palace (*above right*), in the old town, is the seat of the Grimaldi family, rulers since the 1500s.

this situation, Prince Charles III (1818-89) founded the Société des Bains de Mer in 1861. As the operator of Monaco's famous casino, and most of its beaches, hotels and clubs, this became a key institution.

Today, summer tourism plays a vital role. The fine harbour attracts many yachts and the Monaco Grand Prix is one of the highlights of the international automobile racing calendar. Only about 15 per cent of the population are native Monégasques; the rest are Americans, British, Italians or others, who reside in Monaco because of its lack of income tax.

Today, the principality is also a major industrial and administrative centre, with numerous small and medium-sized businesses in the fields of cosmetics, foodstuffs, textiles and electronics. The state printing works is known far beyond Monaco's boundaries, and collectors prize the principality's colourful postage stamps. The Oceanographic Museum, set up by Prince Albert I (1848-1922), enjoys a worldwide reputation.

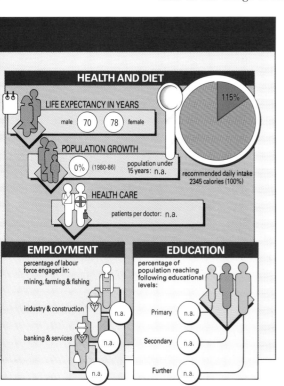

THE PRINCIPALITY OF ANDORRA, located high in the Pyrenees mountains separating France and Spain, represents one of the geographical and political oddities of Europe. The landscape of Andorra comprises the Valira valley basin, partly forested and hemmed in by steep, rocky mountains.

The centres of settlement lie in the triple valley complex of Valira del Norte, Valira del Orient, and the main Valira valley. Joined by the two side valleys near the capital, Andorra la Vella, the Valira basin runs southwards towards Spain. Road access is considerably easier from Spain than from France, since the difficult Envalira Pass (Puerto de Envalira) is often snowbound in winter. The pass crosses the main crest of the Pyrenees at a height of 7,900 feet (2,408 metres).

History

Andorra's origins date from a union between the remnants of Visigothic tribes, Basque conquerors and the original Celtic-Iberian population. The valleys formed a significant stronghold to the rear of the Spanish bishopric of Seo de Urgel, created in 795, and located in the Spanish March. During the long period of Muslim rule in Spain, Andorra strengthened its economic and cultural links with Christian Europe.

The principality's current status derives from the Treaty of Lérida of 1278, an agreement (*Paréage*) dividing dominion between France (then represented by the Counts of Foix), and Spain, whose interests were upheld by the Bishop of Urgel. This treaty remains in force today, a curious reminder of

Lying high in the Pyrenees, Andorra (*right*) nestles in a junction of three valleys. The inhabitants, formerly farmers, now derive their prosperity from Andorra's role as a tax-free shopping centre.

The wildlife of the Pyrenees (*far right*) inhabit one of Western Europe's last wild areas. The mountains present a barrier to human activity, allowing a variety of species to flourish. Stands of fir trees cling to the rocky slopes.

the days of feudalism. Today the President of France and the Bishop of Urgel act as co-princes of Andorra.

Andorra's feudal structure, dating from the Middle Ages, embraces both high and low level jurisdiction. The *Questia*, an annual tribute paid by the Andorrans, is handed over to the agents of the co-princes. In alternate years, the president and the bishop each receive small sums of money, and every other year, the bishop receives six hams, six cheeses and 12 chickens.

While France represents Andorra in international affairs, a parliament carries out domestic government. Members are elected for four-year terms; half are replaced every two years. The country's official language is Catalan, but French and Spanish are in

FACT BOX

THE COUNTRY
Official name: Principality of Andorra
Capital: Andorra la Vella/Andorre La Vieille
Land area: 179 sq mi (464 km²)
Climate: Dry and sunny; heavy snowfall in winter
Main rivers: Valira del Norte, Valira del Orient, Madriu
Highest elevation: Coma Pedrosa 9,665 ft (2,946 m)
Lowest elevation: 2,756 ft (840 m) above sea level

THE GOVERNMENT
Form of Government: Principality
Head of State: Sovereignty is jointly held by Bishop of Urgel

(Spain) and President of France (co-princes)
Head of Government: Head of Executive Council
Administrative areas: 7 "Valleys" (parishes)
Legislature: Executive Council (28 members, elected for 4 years)
Judiciary: Judges of the Peace and Judges of Appeal. Higher courts in France and Spain
Armed forces: People's militia; every man between 16 and 60 must have a gun

THE PEOPLE
Population (1990): 47,000
Language: Catalan (official), Spanish, French

Religion: Roman Catholic (99%)

THE ECONOMY
Currency: French franc, Spanish peseta
Gross domestic Product per person n.a.
Annual Growth Rate: n.a.
Trade balance in US$: n.a.
Goods imported: Consumer goods of all kinds
Goods exported: Electrical energy, cattle, sheepskin, ceramics, wood
Trading partners: Mainly France and Spain
Communications: Number of daily newspapers: n.a.

common use. Andorra's outstanding political problem is the definition of its borders, which after many centuries still remain provisional in nature.

The economy

Andorra's mountainous landscape permits only small-scale agricultural use, restricting farming to terraced, irrigated areas in the valleys. From the 1400s, pastoral agriculture formed the foundation of the national economy. Flocks of sheep enabled the mountain-dwelling Andorrans to maintain their independence, and many also earned a living smuggling goods over the high mountain passes.

Before Spain's entry into the European Community (EC), Andorra's low taxes pro-vided Spanish shoppers with a cheap source of spirits, tobacco and electronic goods. Large discount stores today dominate the streets of the capital but, since Spain's entry into the EC in 1986, commercial regulations have deprived Andorra of much of this income. As a result, the principality has increased its efforts to develop other sources of income, in particular its tourist facilities. Tourism now counts as Andorra's biggest source of income, and the rugged landscape ensures its popularity as a ski resort. In 1991, Andorra joined the EC customs union, giving it equal access to the entire EC market. The little principality has also begun to expand its banking sector, to encourage its development as a financially attractive area for foreign companies.

1. Pyrenean ibex (goat)
2. Brown bear
3. Griffon vulture
4. Imperial eagle
5. Ptarmigan
6. Snow finch
7. Pyrenean desman
8. Alpine salamander
9. Turk's cap lily
10. Pyrenean squil
11. Crocus
12. Pyrenean snakeshead
13. Scots pine
14. Mountain pine

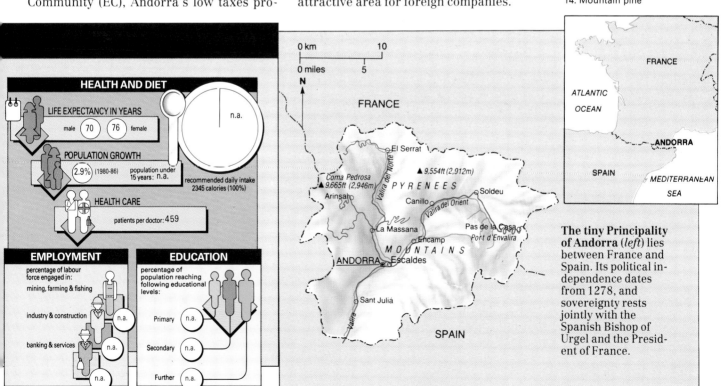

HEALTH AND DIET

LIFE EXPECTANCY IN YEARS

male 70   76 female

n.a.

POPULATION GROWTH

2.9% (1980-86)   population under 15 years: n.a.

recommended daily intake 2345 calories (100%)

HEALTH CARE

patients per doctor: 459

EMPLOYMENT

percentage of labour force engaged in:

mining, farming & fishing

industry & construction   n.a.

banking & services   n.a.

n.a.

EDUCATION

percentage of population reaching following educational levels:

Primary   n.a.

Secondary   n.a.

Further   n.a.

0 km   10
0 miles   5
N

FRANCE

El Serrat

Coma Pedrosa
9,665ft (2,946m)

▲ 9,554ft (2,912m)

P Y R E N E E S

Arinsal

Canillo

Soldeu

Valira del Orient

La Massana

Pas de la Casa
Port d'Envalira

Encamp

M O U N T A I N S

ANDORRA   Escaldes

Sant Julià

Valira

SPAIN

FRANCE

ATLANTIC
OCEAN

ANDORRA

SPAIN

MEDITERRANEAN
SEA

The tiny Principality of Andorra (*left*) lies between France and Spain. Its political independence dates from 1278, and sovereignty rests jointly with the Spanish Bishop of Urgel and the President of France.

S pain, Europe's third largest nation, covers most of the Iberian Peninsula, extending southwestwards from the forbidding barrier presented by the Pyrenees mountains. Much of the country consists of a high plateau, the Meseta, with mountains and fertile plains fringing its outer edge. Spain's population is low in comparison with its area, so much of the countryside, such as the **La Mancha region** (*left*), with its famous windmills, appears wild and desolate.

Spain has always been very different from the rest of Europe. Indeed, the regions within its own borders also vary dramatically. Castile is the centre of Spain, but regions such as Catalonia, Andalusia, Galicia and the Basque country give Spain a lively and cosmopolitan mix of cultures.

The country's long and turbulent history has endowed it with many special characteristics. Cities like Granada and Córdoba boast monuments from the years of Arab rule, while the dramatic paintings of El Greco (c.1541-1614) and the Escorial palace outside Madrid speak of the glories of Spain's Golden Age during the 1500s and 1600s. Today, an annual invasion of more than 40 million tourists heads for the resorts of Spain's Mediterranean coast.

Christopher Columbus sailed from Spain in 1492 to discover the New World. The development and exploitation of these new American territories brought Spain enormous wealth. However, the expense of ruling a huge empire, coupled with crippling wars in Europe, dissipated Spanish wealth so that the country eventually became isolated from Europe.

In the 1900s, the long rule of the dictator Francisco Franco (1892-1975) stifled innovation, and his death opened the way to fundamental changes. In 1975, the country returned to democratic government, with King Juan Carlos I (b. 1938) as constitutional monarch.

Today, Spanish society has blossomed, yet there remains a wide gap between the down-to-earth peasant life in many of the provinces and the trendy prosperity that marks the big cities. Spain's economy began to grow in the 1950s, with the growth of tourism, but only in the 1980s did prosperity and industrial growth seem more than a distant dream. Spain now boasts one of the highest rates of economic growth in the world. In 1986, Spain joined the European Community (EC) and voted to remain within the North Atlantic Treaty Organization (NATO). The overall impression Spain gives is of a nation with a new zest for life whose people look forward confidently to a prosperous future within the wider context of a united Europe.

GENERAL FRANCISCO FRANCO, DICTATOR of Spain ever since his victory in the Spanish Civil War (1936-39), died in 1975. The funeral ceremonies had scarcely ended before the first whispers of freedom breathed over the nation. As early as 1947, Franco had declared that a king would succeed him, fully expecting any monarch to continue his own repressive policies. But the sudden change from dictatorship to monarchy and democracy brought with it dramatic political, social, and cultural reforms.

A new Spain

Franco's designated successor was Prince Juan Carlos, the grandson of the exiled King Alfonso XIII, who fled from Spain in 1931. The young prince was crowned King Juan Carlos I, just two days after the death of the dictator. Spain's first king for 44 years announced prophetically: "Today marks the beginning of a new era for Spain." In fulfilment of that prophecy, Spain has left behind the years of dictatorship, and is today a stable parliamentary democracy, with the king as head of state. The 1978 Constitution defines the nation as a social welfare and constitutional state. One former foreign minister of Spain gave the king complete credit for the country's startling transformation. He described the king "without any doubt as the driving force behind the changes".

When Juan Carlos came to the throne, Spain was reeling under a succession of strikes and terrorist attacks mounted by Basque separatists. Its economy was ill-equipped to meet the challenge of foreign competition, and the king's initial attempts

at reform met with deep suspicion and misunderstanding. One of his first moves was to appoint Adolfo Suárez González as his prime minister. Suárez, like the king, favoured a democratic form of government. Franco had banned all political parties except the *Movimento Nacional* (National Movement), the powerless party founded by the dictator. The new Spanish monarchy ended this ban, and the ban on independent trade unions. In the 1977 elections, voters faced a choice of parliamentary candidates for the first time since 1936. The Union of the Democratic Centre, headed by Suárez, won the largest number of seats in the *Cortes* (parliament).

In 1978, Spain's voters approved a new Constitution based on democratic principles. In 1981, Suárez resigned as prime minister and was succeeded by Leopoldo Calvo Sotelo. More democratic reforms followed in breathtaking succession, including measures to relax censorship, free the remaining political prisoners, and legalize divorce. The government in Madrid encouraged regional authorities to assume greater control as a step towards eventual autonomy and regional parliaments.

In 1982, Spain joined the North Atlantic Treaty Organization (NATO). At the end of that year, the left-wing Socialist Workers' Party won a majority of the seats in parliament. The party's leader, Felipe González, became prime minister, and head of Spain's first socialist government since 1939.

In 1981, a group of Civil Guard officers staged an armed rising against the government, and occupied the Cortes. The king appeared on television in a dramatic appeal

FACT BOX

THE COUNTRY
Official name: Kingdom of Spain
Capital: Madrid
Land regions: Meseta, N Mts, Ebro Basin, Coastal Plains, Guadalquivir Basin. Balearic Is, Canary Is, towns of Ceuta and Melilla (N Africa)
Land area: 194,899 sq mi (504,782 km²), incl. Balearic Canary Is., Ceuta and Melilla
Climate: Inland regions: hot summers, cold winters; dry. Coastal plains and Balearic Islands: Mediterranean. N. mountains: oceanic
Main rivers: Tajo, Guadiana, Ebro, Duero, Guadalquivir
Highest elevation: Pico

de Teide 12,198 ft (3,718 m) on Canary Islands
Lowest elevation: Sea level along the coast

THE GOVERNMENT
Form of Government: Parliamentary monarchy
Head of State: King
Head of Government: Prime Minister
Administrative areas: 17 autonomous regions, 52 provinces
Legislature: Chamber of Deputies (350 members) and Senate (248 members), elected for 4 years.
Judiciary: Civil and military law. Supreme Court, appeal, provincial, local, military courts

Armed forces: Total strength: 320,000.
Conscription: Men must serve 12-16 months after age 21

THE PEOPLE
Population (1990): 38,925,000
Language: Castilian (official). Catalan, Basque, Galician spoken by minorities
Religion: Roman Catholic (about 99%)
Gross Domestic Product per person (1990): US$12,476
Annual Growth Rate (1985-90): 4.9%
Trade balance in US$: (1990): $7,200 mill
Goods imported: Mineral oil, minerals, machinery, grain,

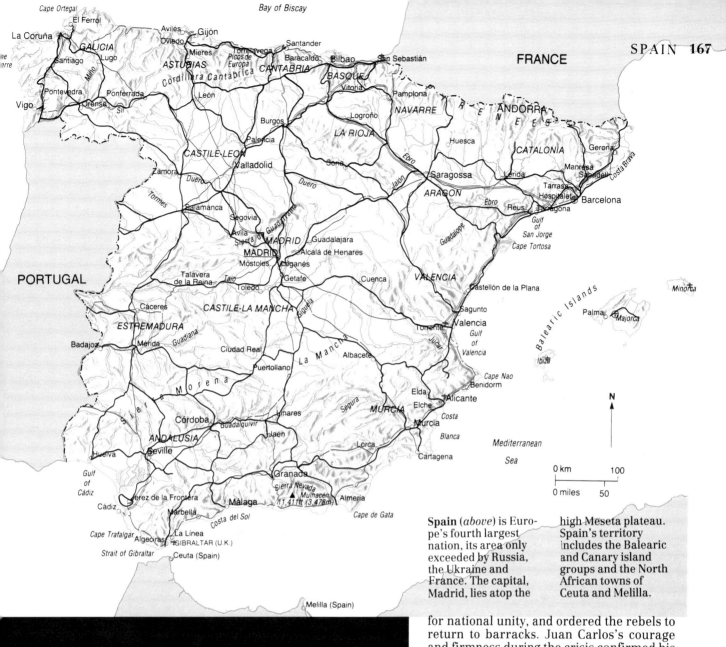

Bay of Biscay

Cape Ortegal

FRANCE

PORTUGAL

Balearic Islands

Mediterranean Sea

N

| 0 km | | 100 |
| 0 miles | 50 | |

Spain (*above*) is Europe's fourth largest nation, its area only exceeded by Russia, the Ukraine and France. The capital, Madrid, lies atop the high Meseta plateau. Spain's territory includes the Balearic and Canary island groups and the North African towns of Ceuta and Melilla.

for national unity, and ordered the rebels to return to barracks. Juan Carlos's courage and firmness during the crisis confirmed his credentials as an upholder of democracy, and he also became a symbol for the reconciliation of a significantly divided country.

The new European

Spain joined the European Community in 1986, setting an international seal of approval on its democracy, and obtaining wider access to the European market. In 1992, Spain hosted a number of major international events, notably the Summer Olympic Games (held in Barcelona) and the World's Fair (held in Seville).

In social terms, Spanish women took advantage of new freedoms and a measure of legal equality, to enter the workplace in large numbers. Spaniards are officially 99 per cent Roman Catholic, but only about one-third of the people still follow the strict teachings of the Church. People of all faiths enjoy complete religious freedom and there is no state religion.

HEALTH AND DIET

LIFE EXPECTANCY IN YEARS

male 73 79 female

POPULATION GROWTH

0.5% (1980-86) population under 15 years: 24%

134%

recommended daily intake 2345 calories (100%)

HEALTH CARE

patients per doctor: 315

EMPLOYMENT

percentage of labour force engaged in:

mining, farming & fishing

industry & construction 16.9%

banking & services 31.2%

51.9%

EDUCATION

percentage of population reaching following educational levels:

Primary 100%

Secondary 98%

Further 29.6%

chemical products
Goods exported: Cars, citrus fruits, olives/olive oil, wine, iron and steel, textiles
Trading partners: France, Great Britain, Germany, Italy, Netherlands, USA, Mexico, Saudi Arabia
Transport: Length of railways (1989): 8,433 mi (13,573 km) Passenger miles (1988): 9.7 bill (15.6 bill km)
Communications: Number of daily newspapers (1988): 102 Circulation (1988): 2,967,000

SPAIN IS THE FOURTH LARGEST COUNTRY in Europe in area, after Russia, Ukraine and France, occupying about five-sixths of the Iberian Peninsula. Portugal takes up the western coastal strip, and the tiny state of Andorra and the British Crown Colony of Gibraltar remain separate entities. In addition to the North African enclaves of Ceuta and Melilla, Spain's sovereign territory also includes the Canary Island off the northwest coast of Africa, and the Balearic Islands in the Eastern Mediterranean.

Spain has an area of 194,899 square miles (504,782 square kilometres). The landscape falls into seven distinct regions: the Meseta, the Northern Mountains, the Ebro Basin, the Coastal Plains, the Guadalquivir Basin, the Balearic Islands, and the Canary Islands.

The Meseta, the largest land region, is a huge, dry plateau, slashed with valleys, gorges and low ranges of mountains, such as the Sierra de Guadarrama north of Madrid. The Meseta takes up most of the Spanish mainland and is surrounded by ranges of steep protective mountains, such as the Sierra Nevada in Andalusia and the Cantabrian mountains in the north. The yellowish-brown soil covering the Meseta discourages cultivation, so agriculture has traditionally relied on the raising of sheep and goats. Forests clothe many of the low hills, remnants of Spain's ancient forest cover, but most of the plains sprout only occasional shrubs and flowering plants. This inland region is sunny and hot in summer, and experiences generally cold winters. Madrid stands in the centre of the Meseta, at the very heart of Castile, and is Europe's highest capital city. Most of Spain's major rivers rise in the Meseta, and the longest of these is the Tajo (Tagus), flowing 626 miles (1,007 kilometres) through eastern Spain and Portugal into the Atlantic.

The mountains

The Northern Mountains stretch across the whole of northern Spain from the Atlantic Ocean in the west to the coastal plains in the east. They include the Galician, Cantabrian and Pyrenees ranges. The mountains rise steeply out of the sea, and the region's generally wet and cool climate supports the forests cloaking the lower slopes.

The Pyrenees, at an average height of 3,500 feet (1,070 metres), form a grim barrier that has effectively sealed Spain off from the rest of Europe for much of the nation's history. Only three reliable passes breach the wall of the Pyrenees, but for centuries the mountains have been home to the Basque people. Occupying both sides of the Franco-Spanish border, more than 500,000 Basques live in France, and about 2,500,000 in Spain. South of the Basque

Below 1,640 feet	500 metres
1,640-3,280 feet	500-1,000 metres
Over 3,280 feet	1,000 metres

FRANCE

N

NORTHERN MOUNTAINS

EBRO BASIN

Ebro

MESETA

PORTUGAL

Tajo

COASTAL PLAINS

GUADALQUIVIR BASIN

Guadalquivir

BALEARIC ISLANDS

0 km 200
0 miles 100

Spain (*above*) occupies most of the Iberian Peninsula. The Meseta, a high plateau, dominates the landscape, rimmed by mountains and fertile plains. In the northeast, the high Pyrenees divide Spain from France.

The Cantabrian mountains (*right*), in the northern region of Asturias, form part of the chain that includes the Picos de Europa and the Pyrenees ranges. Much of northern Spain consists of forested mountains.

country lies the autonomous region of La Rioja, famous for its fine table wines.

In the Ebro Basin, in northeastern Spain, broad plains cradle the Ebro River on its 565-mile (909-kilometre) course from the Cantabrian Mountains to the Mediterranean. The dryness of the region calls for extensive irrigation, and reservoirs storing winter rainfall have transformed this area into one of the most fertile in the country. Hydroelectric power furnishes a quarter of Spain's energy needs, and major dams on the Ebro near Lérida power the industries of Catalonia.

Coastal plains fringe Spain's Mediterranean coast, and include the regions of Catalonia, Valencia, Murcia and Andalusia. Catalonia was perhaps the earliest part of Spain to be influenced by northern Europe, particularly by its immediate neighbour, France. Catalonia's capital, the industrial centre and seaport of Barcelona, ranks as Spain's second city. The resort area of the Costa Brava, like its southern neighbours the Costa Blanca and the popular Costa del Sol, attracts millions of visitors annually through a combination of fine sandy beaches and almost year-round sunshine. The rolling, forested hills often stretch all the way down to the sea. Farther south, Valencia and Murcia's coastal plains rank among Europe's major fruit-growing areas.

The Sierra Nevada, rising above the castle of Calahorra, (*above*) divides southern Andalusia from the Mediterranean. Many of its peaks are snow-covered, and the highest, Mulhacén, reaches 11,411 feet (3,478 metres). With a landscape of rolling hills and plains, **Andalusia** (*below left*) is one of Spain's most picturesque areas, but it also endures a hot, dry climate. The **Costa Brava** (*below*) on the coast of Catalonia, is one of Spain's major resort areas.

Andalusia

Non-Spaniards commonly regard Andalusia as the region that is most typically Spanish. In fact, it is the part of Spain that least resembles Europe, as well as the last portion of Spain to be ruled by the Arabs. Andalusia's hot, arid climate seems to have more in common with North Africa, and many of the towns of Andalusia still display glories dating from the days of Arab rule. These include Granada, with its palace of the Alhambra, and Córdoba, with its mosque converted into a cathedral.

The snow-capped Sierra Nevada range rises in Andalusia at the edge of the Meseta, and runs to a length of 60 miles (95 kilometres). The mountains soar to 11,411 feet (3,478 metres) at Mulhacén, the highest point on the Spanish mainland.

The Guadalquivir Basin covers the southwestern part of Spain. At its heart is the Guadalquivir River, flowing across Andalusia to empty into the Gulf of Cadiz, some 360 miles (580 kilometres) from its source. This hot region is extremely fertile, thanks to irrigation, but the Huelva area also contains deposits of iron ore.

The Balearic Islands rise invitingly in the Mediterranean, from 50-150 miles (80-240 kilometres) off the Spanish mainland. There are five major islands, Majorca, Minorca, Ibiza, Formentera and Cabrera. Majorca, the largest of them, is by far the most fertile and the most popular of these holiday islands.

The Canary Islands lie in the Atlantic Ocean, some 60-270 miles (96-432 kilometres) off the northwest coast of Africa. They include seven major islands. The three largest are Tenerife, Fuerteventura, and Gran Canaria. The islanders claim to live in a climate of eternal spring and, as a result, thrive on tourism.

People

A TRAVELLER DRIVING THROUGH PARTS of inland Spain today may wonder if he is passing through a deserted country. Some of the hamlets seem to be completely abandoned, particularly in the central Meseta region. Although Spain's population has more than doubled since 1900, density in rural areas is very thin, amounting to 203 persons per square mile (78 per square kilometre). A substantial majority of the people live in towns and cities.

The great rush into the cities began in the 1960s, when Spain began a long-overdue economic expansion. The heady prospect of full employment and rising wages lured many workers away from the impoverished provinces into the mushrooming suburbs of the industrial centres. Sadly, this unplanned expansion sometimes destroyed the substance and character of many of the older cities and towns.

The 1900s also saw millions of Spaniards leave their homes to seek employment in France, Switzerland, Germany and other wealthier European nations, where they settled as immigrant workers. The wages they sent home provided a major boost to the Spanish economy. However, in the 1980s, Spain's booming economy drew many migrants back to their homeland.

Spaniards seem to be blessed with a longer lifespan than their counterparts in most other European countries. Spanish men live for an average of 74 years, and the figure for women is 80 years old. But this does not mean that Spain is a land of old people. Until recently, the average age of the population was dropping because of the high birthrate. But during the 1980s the tradition of large families declined in popularity, partly from a yearning for better standards of living and partly from the reduced influence of Roman Catholicism.

Regional groups

Today, Spain's official language is Castilian, which is spoken by most of the people. This reflects the cultural and political domination exerted by Castile since the union of the crowns of Castile and Aragon in the 1400s. But as a result of its ancient heritage, the nation consists of several distinct regions, each fiercely proud of its own language, cultural traditions, and aspirations for independence.

The most vociferous demands for separate nationhood come from the Basques, of whom roughly 2,500,000 live in Spain. The Basque provinces, known to the Basques as *Euskadi*, lie in the north of the country, and about 500,000 Basques live in neighbouring France. Capital of the Basque region is Bilbao, an industrial and financial centre located on the Bay of Biscay. The Basque tongue, also called *Euskera* or *Euskara*, is un-

related to any other European language. Since 1959, the terrorist attacks of ETA (Basque Homeland and Freedom) have reinforced Basque demands for independence.

The people of Catalonia, in northeastern Spain, constitute a large and vocal minority, and the prosperity of their province reinforces their calls for greater autonomy. The Catalan language is similar to the *langue d'Oc* of southwestern France, and Catalan is widely spoken in Catalonia, where it is the official language. The Catalan capital is Barcelona. Catalonians share their history and tongue with the Balearic Islands, for Catalonians are traditionally a seafaring people.

A third strong regional group lives in Galicia, in the northwest corner of the country. This fairly isolated region was settled centuries ago by Celtic peoples and was

Local pottery (*left*) burdens the donkey of a pedlar in Toledo, central Spain, making a colourful display to entice the attention of tourists seeking souvenirs. Some 40 million tourists visit Spain annually, and the country depends on the income from tourism. Until the growth of the tourist industry in the 1960s, many Spaniards were forced to migrate north to work in France or Germany. Today, tourism employs hundreds of thousands of Spaniards.

the last area of Spain to succumb to the Arab invasion in the 700s. The town of Santiago de Compostela, where the bones of St James the Apostle are alleged to rest, has been an important focus for pilgrims since the Middle Ages. Galicians speak a dialect akin to Portuguese, and keep alive their independent cultural identity.

Since Franco's demise, all these regions enjoy varying degrees of home rule. Spanish government policy today favours the granting of measures of autonomy to the various regions, reversing the repressive centralism enforced under Franco.

The Spanish way of life

Ways of life vary from region to region. Basques have their own distinctive costume, reserved nowadays for ceremonial occasions, but the Basque black beret is famous all over the world. Vestiges of Arabic influence

In a Madrid street (*above*), sunlight casts a golden glow over a seller of nuts. In spite of problems caused by the great movement of population to the cities since the 1960s, Spanish urban life retains much of its relaxed quality.

An elderly country-man (*left*), in the Picos de Europa region of Asturias, sets out to tend his garden. His black beret, originally associated with the Basques of northern Spain, forms part of the traditional dress of the rural worker.

still prevail in the southern region of Andalusia. Visitors to the region enjoy the haunting sound of flamenco music and the spectacle of its exciting accompanying dance, created by the Gypsies of Andalusia.

With increased prosperity since the 1960s, the pains and pleasures of modern urban life have largely transformed Spanish society and culture. *Siestas* (afternoon naps) are largely being discarded, but *fiestas* (feast days) remain to be enjoyed. And most people still like to take a *paseo* (walk) before their evening meal. They often do not eat until 11 o'clock at night.

Today, Spain is also home to hundreds of thousands of foreigners, many of whom live along the sunny Mediterranean coast. But the foreign population also includes tens of thousands of Moroccan Arabs, mostly illegal immigrants, who eke out a miserable existence on low-paid manual labour.

Madrid

THE CHARM OF MADRID LIES NOT IN ANY of its physical attributes, but in its extraordinary vitality, a quality which has been recognized since the 1600s, when the city first emerged as a major metropolis. Though dating back probably to a Roman settlement built over a prehistoric site, the place had little identity until the time of the Arabs, who constructed a fortress or *Alcazar* on top of a long, steep ridge rising above the River Manzanares (the site is now occupied by a gigantic royal palace, put up after 1743, when a fire destroyed the Alcazar). After its conquest by the Christians in 1083, Madrid slumbered, and was just a dreary provincial town until 1561, when Philip II decided to make the place the permanent centre of his court. But after his first enthusiasm, the king devoted less energy to the new capital than to the construction of the nearby monastery and palace of El Escorial, directly underneath the Sierra de Guadarrama north of Madrid.

A growing city
Under Philip II's successors, Madrid began to expand at a prodigious rate. In the early 1600s it boasted a population greater than that of most European cities, and a cultural life unrivalled anywhere in the country. Madrid saw the publication in 1605 of a novel that was to place Spain on the literary map of Europe – *Don Quixote* by Miguel de Cervantes (1547-1616). Shortly afterwards, the painter Diego Velázquez (1599-1660), one of the most outstanding of Western artists, moved from Seville to Madrid, a gesture which was to be imitated by many of his colleagues from the south. At the same time Madrid's appearance was radically transformed, and numerous imposing buildings and squares were constructed, many of which still survive. One of Madrid's main tourist attractions from this period is the Plaza Mayor, a grand arcaded square where activities ranging from the burning of heretics to bullfighting took place.

The commercial heart of Madrid meanwhile grew up around the nearby Puerta del Sol, a square which at one time marked the southeastern boundaries of the city. Whereas the Plaza Mayor is today mainly a magnet for tourists, the Puerta del Sol is still the noisy and animated meeting-place which one traveller of the 1600s likened to a "bay in the sea, always in agitation".

Urban reform
With the rapid growth of Madrid, the city came to encompass great extremes of wealth and poverty. The crime and stench of Madrid became infamous, but it was not until the enlightened reign of Charles III (1759-88) that a programme of urban reform was finally introduced, including the

installation of a sewerage system. Among Charles' other achievements was the conversion of a royal estate on the eastern outskirts of the city into a public park (the Retiro) which is still one of the great municipal parks of Europe. It was Charles, too, who instigated the building of the Prado, which was soon to achieve its position as one of the world's major art museums.

When Spain became a fashionable tourist destination in the early 1800s, tourists tended to visit Madrid largely for the same reason that they do so today – to go to the Prado. The city itself attracted them less, lacking as it did the picturesque qualities they associated with Spain. For it was a town in the process of rapid industrialization, containing a population described by one British traveller as "the most extraordinary vital mass to be found in the entire world". In the course of the century, Madrid's population was to grow from under 200,000 to half a million. Today it has reached more than three million.

Cultural achievement
In the early years of this century much of the old centre of Madrid was destroyed by the construction of the Gran Vía. But the city's cultural life meanwhile experienced a period of remarkably vitality. Many of the city's leading writers and artists – such as

The Retiro Park (*above*), with its statue of King Alfonso XII, once formed part of the extensive royal estates. Today, it is a beautiful, formal garden, and includes a large boating lake and a celebrated botanical garden.

A student artist (*right*), uses a Madrid pavement to make a chalk copy of Velázquez's masterpiece, *Las Meninas* (The Maids-of-Honour). The original painting hangs in Madrid's famous art gallery, the Prado Museum.

The Plaza de España (*left*) stands in the heart of Madrid, but looks west across the Manzanares River toward the plains of Castile. The wide streets and high-rise buildings are typical of this bustling and still-growing city.

Madrid (*below*) and its city centre invite the tourist to stroll along its many fine avenues. It also contains a wealth of memorable sights and impressive monuments. These include The Edificio de España, the Palacio Real and Teatro Real, the Church of San Francisco and the sumptuous Cathedral of San Isidro, the Bellas Artes and the world famous Prado Museum, the austere Palace of Justice, the Archeological Museum, and the National Library.

the poet Federico García Lorca, the painter Salvador Dali, and the film-director Luis Bunuel – became associated with the Residencia de Estudiantes, a pioneering educational institution. The cultural excitement of these years was brought to an end by the Civil War of 1936-39, after which Madrid became a sad and somnolent place. Significantly, many of the city's celebrated cafes were turned into banks.

With the death of Franco in 1975, Madrid reverted back to its animated former self, and came once again to play an important role in the modern world. The massive thoroughfare now known by its original name of the Castellana has been embellished in recent years with a splendidly imaginative and graceful series of buildings. Madrid has also become a great centre of fashion, a place known all over Spain for its "*Movida*" or young trendsetters. Above all Madrid is once more the city where – in the words of Hemingway – "nobody goes to bed until they have killed the night." To experience the full vitality of Madrid you need only visit the Castellana on a summer night, for then you will find a vast mass of people of all ages strolling, talking and enjoying themselves almost until the break of day. No other city in Europe can claim to have such an intensive street life as this historic Spanish capital.

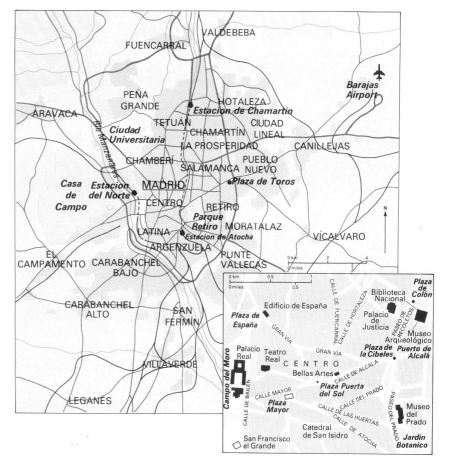

Fiestas

A TOURIST VISITING SPAIN FOR THE first time cannot fail to be struck by the country's appetite for constant festivals or *fiestas*, occasions marked by a degree of high spirits hardly known in other European countries. They have long been a feature of Spanish life, and an English traveller to Spain in the 1830s, Richard Ford, was not alone in wondering how the Spaniards managed to support themselves, "as every day seems a holiday."

At all times of the year, in every part of Spain, some major festival is taking place. But the character of these festivals changes considerably from one region to another: those of Valencia and Catalonia feature an abundance of fireworks and bonfires; those of Andalusia in the south glory in the sound of castanets and guitars, and the swirl of polka-dotted dresses. Andalusia is perhaps Spain's most festive and, in many ways, most "typical" region.

Spain's festival year begins in earnest in February, with carnivals taking place in numerous towns, most notably in the Andalusian port of Cádiz. Here the streets are packed with gaily costumed people re-enacting historical events in a richly humorous way. Much of the humour is deeply disrespectful of authority, and it is perhaps not surprising that during the repressive era of Franco's dictatorship, carnivals were banned entirely.

Holy Week

The fooling around and high spirits of the carnivals give way at Easter to the more solemn and spectacular celebrations of *Semana Santa* (Holy Week). In Spain's Holy Week Processions – the most famed and exciting in Europe – the joyful and the gloomy aspects of the Spanish character come vividly together in celebration of the death and resurrection of Christ and the anguish of the Virgin Mary. These celebrations differ considerably from region to region, but most include long lines of "penitents" – men and boys wearing cloaks and pointed hats not unlike those associated with the Ku-Klux-Klan in America. Some of these "penitents" take part as a genuine act of penance, going barefoot and carrying heavy crosses (once they would even wear chains and beat themselves); but others take part simply through a fondness for dressing up. Finer details of the Holy Week processions, such as the precise way in which an image should be dressed or carried, may mean little to tourists, but the sheer delight of the spectacle, and the transformation of an entire town into a vast stage set, peopled with thousands of actors, cannot fail to make a lasting impression.

In Seville, where Holy Week is celebrated more lavishly than in any other part of Europe, Easter is no sooner over than the *Feria* (fair) begins. The Seville *Feria* – Spain's most famous – traces its origins to a medieval market for horses and cattle. Today it is simply a non-stop, week-long party taking place in colourful, striped marquees decorated with paper lanterns and streamers. The women of Seville, traditionally frustrated at not being able to act as Penitents during the Holy Week, dress up in vividly coloured flamenco or gypsy costumes, featuring long trains, polka dots and silk shawls. A continual round of singing and dancing takes place in the marquees, accompanied by the drinking of much sherry. However, you will rarely see any coarse behaviour, for the Sevillians believe that enjoying yourself requires considerable art and style.

Bullfights

An essential element of the Seville *Feria* is the daily bullfight, a sport in which the Spanish love of ritual is at its most evident. Numerous foreigners, such as the American writer Ernest Hemingway, have enthused about the beauty, bravery and skill of this sport; but an equally large number – and a growing number of Spaniards too – have condemned it as being little more than savage butchery, and have called for its abolition. The main attraction of bullfighting stems from the pageant and ritual of the occasion, the animation of the crowd, the colour of the participants' costumes, and the playing of the band at key times. But occasionally, moments of pure, inexplicable magic may sometimes occur, as when the matador, whose task is to kill the already weakened bull with his sword, carries out a particularly daring or elegant movement, inspiring the whole audience to gasp in astonishment or even to shed tears.

Wearing colourful dresses, dancers (*above right*) at the *Feria de Cabello* in Jerez swirl to the haunting, rhythmic tones of flamenco music. Flamenco music was born in Andalusia, and its origins lie in gypsy songs.

Hooded penitents (*right*) walk in procession through Seville each year during Holy Week. Some 100 processions take place, punctuated by the singing of *saetas* (laments). The lavish Seville *Feria* follows soon afterwards.

Pilgrimage to the past

Of all the festivals in Spain, if not in Europe, the most remarkable and well-attended is probably the pilgrimage to El Rocío. This takes place at Whitsun, only a short time after the Seville *Feria*. An isolated hamlet lying about 60 miles (96 kilometres) from Seville, El Rocío marks the place where, in the Middle Ages, a miraculous image of the Virgin came to light. Even earlier, however, the region appears to have been the centre of a fertility cult. Today, pilgrims dressed in flamenco costume travel to El Rocío from all parts of Spain, many carrying their belongings in ox-drawn wagons resembling those of America's Wild West. The celebrations combine elements of Holy Week and of the *Feria*, perfectly blending religious and secular elements. Here you leave the everyday modern world to enjoy a sleepless week of constant, anarchic activity, set in a haunting landscape of sand dunes and marshes that many believe to possess a special spiritual energy. It is hard indeed to return to reality after such an experience. Fortunately for the lover of fiestas, Spain leaves you with little time for serious reflection. For the summer months lie ahead, and with them come a wider range of festive activities than ever. No wonder that the Spaniards sometimes feel that they suffer to enjoy themselves.

The pilgrimage to El Rocío (*left*) in Andalusia is one of Spain's oldest religious festivals, and pilgrims traditionally arrive in wagons often decorated with coloured streamers. The celebrations last for several days.

Human "castles" (*right*), rising precariously above cheering crowds, are a regular feature of fiestas in Catalonia. Fireworks, giant puppets and Catalan music and dance also add to the exuberant atmosphere.

Balearic Islands

THE BALEARIC ISLANDS, A GROUP OF Spanish islands located in the Mediterranean, lie about 124 miles (200 kilometres) off the east coast of Spain. A combination of beautiful scenery, magnificent beaches and a mild winter climate attract millions of visitors from all over the world each year.

The Balearics cover an area of 1,935 square miles (5,014 square kilometres) and boast a population of about 685,000. The archipelago includes five major islands and more than 100 uninhabited rocky islets. The main islands are Majorca (Mallorca in Spanish), Minorca (Menorca), Ibiza (Iviza), Formentera, and Cabrera. Ibiza and Formentera are also known as the "pine islands", a term derived from the Greek word for a variety of juniper tree. The islands are actually the tops of sunken mountain peaks, the eastern extension of a range that plunges into the Mediterranean from mainland Spain. The main urban centre and administrative capital of the islands is beautiful, bustling Palma on Majorca, the largest of the islands.

The story of the islands

Romance tinges the long history of the islands. It was here that Hercules reached the western frontiers of the ancient world to snatch the Golden Apples of the Hesperides from the Tree of Life. In the 1900s, a Catalan writer and artist described the island chain as a "lotus land where men are never in a hurry, women never grow old". Some 800 years ago, Raymond Lully, the great scholar of Arabic and Chaldean studies, brought intellectual lustre to his native Majorca. And much later, in the 1800s, the composer Frederic Chopin and the novelist George Sand wintered on the island. Poets, artists, musicians and philosophers still gather regularly on Majorca.

Dotted here and there throughout the islands are a number of massive square or circular stone towers called *talayots*. These mysterious prehistoric structures testify to once-flourishing Bronze and Iron Age cultures. Phoenicians and Greeks originally invaded the islands, followed later by the Carthaginians. In 123 BC, the Carthaginians were driven out by the Romans, who founded the city of Palma.

After the Roman empire disintegrated, the Balearics fell under the control of invaders; first the Vandals, then the Visigoths and, in AD 789, the Arabs. In 1235, James I of Aragon sailed from mainland Spain to sweep the Arabs from the islands. In 1262, he bequeathed Majorca to his younger son as an independent kingdom. But in 1348, Peter IV reunited the islands with Aragon. From that time on, almost without interruption, the Balearics belonged to Aragon, and later to Spain.

A village (*right*) nestles among trees on a hillside in Majorca (also called Mallorca), largest of the Balearic Islands. Coastal mountains, where terraced cultivation has been carried on for centuries, surround a fertile plain.

An elderly resident (*far right*) of Formentera, southernmost of the main Balearics, is shaded by a sun-hat as she takes a *paseo* (walk). *Mallorquin*, the dialect of the islands, is a blend of Catalan, Provençal and Italian.

An ornate, carved portico (*below*) reflects the sunlight in an ancient street in Ciudadela, Minorca. The island was a British possession in the 1700s, when its chief town, Mahón, was an important naval base.

Sun, sea and sand (*right*) bring swarms of tourists every year to the beaches of Majorca. The balmy western Mediterranean climate of the Balearics, with hot, dry summers and mild winters, has made the islands a mecca for holiday-makers all the year round. Although the tourists flock to the beaches of the Balearics, the islands contain impressive historical sites, including Bronze Age settlements and the Gothic cathedral of Palma.

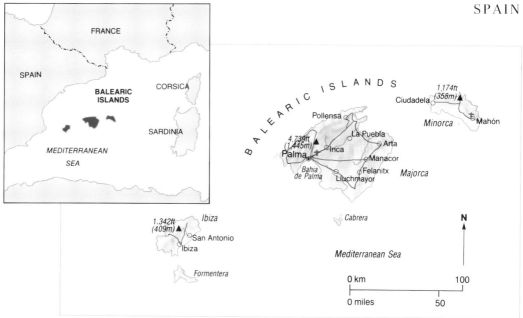

The Balearic Islands, (*above*) located off the eastern coast of Spain comprise five main islands, and a host of small, uninhabited islets. The history of the islands began with the ancient Iberians, but many invaders have ruled the Balearics.

The Balearics are actually the peaks of mountains rising from the Mediterranean floor. Majorca is the largest island, while Ibiza and Formentera are the least inhabited. The Balearic group forms a province of Spain.

The islands today still betray some Arabic touches, such as the many Arabic place names. The Moors originated Majorca's distinctive terrace cultivation, while the desolate windmills found on the island also date from Moorish times. In the 1200s, victorious Catalans settled in the Balearics. Not all of the Moors were driven out at this time. The Catalans enslaved those who remained, but over a number of generations, their descendants mingled with the growing Catalan population.

Majorca's official language is Spanish, but many older islanders still speak *Mallorquin*, an east Catalonian dialect. Quite distinct in sound and vocabulary from the Catalan of mainland Spain, Mallorquin incorporates elements of Provençal and northern Italian dialects. Variants of this dialect persist on Minorca and Ibiza, and reflect Spain's linguistic diversity.

The face of the islands

Majorca still clings to its reputation as "the pearl of the Mediterranean", in spite of the high-rise apartments and hotels clustered along its beaches. Picturesque secluded bays are never far away from the bustle of the tourist resorts. In the northwest of the island, a tree-covered crest rises at Puig Mayor to an impressive 4,740 feet (1,445 metres). A lower range of hills, called the Sierra de Levante, dominates the eastern flank. Between these heights, undulating fertile plains in the centre of the island support a variety of crops, particularly almonds, figs, olives, oranges, and grapes.

The smaller island of Minorca, some 25 miles (40 kilometres) northeast of Majorca, has changed less over the years than its larger neighbour. The rugged coastline fringes a central chalky plateau. A few stark slate hills rise in the north to a height of 1,180 feet (360 metres). In the 1700s, the British, who occupied the island for a period of some 66 years, developed the island's agriculture and road system.

Tourism plays a major role in the economy of the Balearics. While Majorca became a major resort for northern Europeans during the 1960s and 1970s, Ibiza, formerly a haunt of pirates, and the long undiscovered island of Formentera, now also rank as tourist destinations.

Gibraltar

THE BRITISH COLONY OF GIBRALTAR, A peninsula jutting from the southeastern coast of Spain, has an area of 2.3 square miles (6 square kilometres). Almost all of this is occupied by a huge mass of limestone, the "Rock of Gibraltar", rearing up like the head of a great lion that guards the sea gate between the Mediterranean and the North Atlantic. Its sheer cliffs rise to around 1,400 feet (426 metres) on the north and east. From the peaks – when they are not shrouded by the thick haze of the "Levanter", the easterly wind off the Mediterranean – one may look north as far as the Sierra Nevada of Spain, or south to the Atlas and Rif Mountains of Morocco.

All over the world, people speak of "the Rock" as a symbol of strength and security. To the ancients it was one of the "Pillars of Hercules", created by the hero-god to mark the rift he tore between Europe and Africa. Thus he created the Strait of Gibraltar, the channel linking the Mediterranean with the Atlantic. The Phoenicians were the first to recognize the strategic importance of this "Key to the Mediterranean". They established on the Rock a trading colony that jealously guarded the Strait.

Conquest and siege

In AD 711 the Moors of North Africa seized the Rock from Gothic Spain. Their leader, Tariq ibn Ziyad, ordered a fortress built high on the hillside looking west over Algeciras Bay. The "Moorish Castle" that now stands above Gibraltar Town incorporates only fragments of Tariq's stronghold, but his name lives on: over the centuries, from European pronunciation of Jebel al Tariq ("Tariq's Mountain"), the Rock got its modern name. Spain re-established ownership in 1462, but from the 1500s its rule was challenged by the rising maritime power of Britain. In a surprise attack in 1704, an Anglo-Dutch force took Gibraltar on behalf of the Archduke of Austria. But the invaders' British commander raised the flag of his own country, withstood a Franco-Spanish siege, and saw British possession of Gibraltar recognized in 1713.

The Rock was swiftly developed as Britain's major western Mediterranean base. Huge breakwaters were built to protect the western anchorage and the military dockyard at its southern end. In 1779-83 the British garrison withstood one of history's greatest sieges, an artillery duel by land and sea. The defenders tunnelled shot-proof "galleries" deep into the Rock, which can still be seen today.

Naval power based on Gibraltar played an important part in defeating two great dictators: Napoleon Bonaparte in the 1800s, and Adolf Hitler in the present century. During World War II, warships from

A Barbary ape (*below*) suns itelf high up on "the Rock". It is the only wild monkey found in Europe, where Gibraltar is its sole habitat. Legend says that when the apes depart, British rule on the Rock will end.

Fishermen (*bottom*) prepare their nets on a beach in the shadow of the mighty Rock of Gibraltar. The civil population of about 35,000 imports almost all its food, since Gibraltar lacks any farm-land for raising crops or livestock.

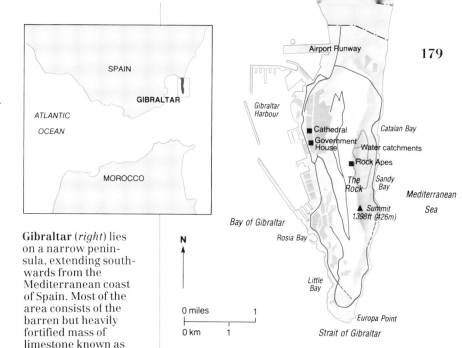

An ocean-going vessel (*left*) awaits repair in dry dock at Gibraltar's main shipyard. A vital naval base for centuries, Gibraltar maintains extensive port facilities, although prosperity depends also on trade and tourism.

On Summit Ridge (*below*), the highest part of the Rock, metal sheeting drains rainwater into catchment tanks with a total capacity of 15,000,000 gallons (68,190,000 litres); there is no other natural water supply.

Gibraltar (*right*) lies on a narrow peninsula, extending southwards from the Mediterranean coast of Spain. Most of the area consists of the barren but heavily fortified mass of limestone known as the Rock of Gibraltar.

Gibraltar fought through vital supply convoys to Malta. In 1942, the Rock was the command centre for the Allied landings in Northwest Africa.

In the early 1960s, Spain renewed its claim to the territory, restricting travel overland to Gibraltar, and in 1967 closed the border, after the native Gibraltarians (most of mixed Spanish, Portuguese, Maltese and Italian stock) voted massively in favour of remaining "British". It was not fully re-opened until 1985.

Gibraltar remains a British naval and air base, but its modern prosperity stems also from its development as a trade centre and tourist resort. As well as a warm, dry climate and fine beaches, it offers tax-free, duty-free shopping. With the establishment of the Single European Market in 1992, Gibraltar hopes to attract new investment from other European states.

In the past, however, "free trade" in Gibraltar meant smuggling, and the skill of Gibraltarians in "stinging" both revenue officers and buyers won for them the nickname of "Rock Scorpions". Because Gibraltar Town is built on rock terraces ascending a steep hillside, its inhabitants are also called "Rock Lizards", and many speak "Rock English", an odd mixture of English and Spanish.

The Rock's most famous "natives" are its Barbary apes, shaggy-haired creatures about the size of a large dog. Gibraltar is their only European habitat, but whether they arrived naturally from North Africa or were brought in by man is not known. They wander freely over the upper Rock, and legend has it that British rule will endure only as long as the apes remain. In September 1944, at a critical period of World War II, Winston Churchill found time to send a firm directive to his Colonial Secretary: "The establishment of apes on Gibraltar should be 24 ... every effort should be made to reach this number as soon as possible and maintain it thereafter." The colony is periodically strengthened by new stock from North Africa.

Apart from St Michael's Cave, a fantastic natural labyrinth of underground lakes and stalactites, most of the "sights" of Gibraltar stem from its warlike past. The rock-cut galleries begun during the great siege were extended into some 30 miles (48 kilometres) of tunnels during World War II, when the massive reservoirs excavated below the rainwater catchment areas of the eastern summit were expanded to hold 15,000,000 gallons (68,190,000 litres). Less well-known is the mighty "Rock Buster" cannon. When it was cast in 1872, this was the biggest gun ever made; it is a fitting emblem of "Fortress Gibraltar".

PORTUGAL

Portugal, a small but ancient country occupying the western strip of Europe's Iberian Peninsula, faces towards the Atlantic Ocean. Its location, and the fact that Spain, a much larger and more populous country, covers the rest of the peninsula, long ago encouraged it to develop a strong maritime tradition and empire. In the late 1400s and early 1500s, Portugal pioneered Europe's age of discovery, opening up routes to the east round the tip of Africa, and across the Atlantic to Brazil. This led to the establishment of colonies in Asia, Africa and South America. Portugal's importance dwindled in the late 1500s, but part of its empire, especially in Africa, remained until the 1960s and 1970s.

The hardy but hospitable Portuguese derive their ancestry from the ancient Iberians, who lived there more than 5,000 years ago, as well as from many other groups, ranging from Phoenicians and Carthaginians to North African Muslims. Since the 1960s, many blacks from Portugal's former African possessions have also made their homes there. A strongly Roman Catholic country, Portugal enjoys numerous religious festivals, processions and pilgrimages, notably at Fàtima, in the district of Santarém, where the apparition of the Virgin Mary to three children in 1917 established it as a leading place of pilgrimage for all Catholics.

Today, Portugal's unspoilt coastline and beaches, pleasant climate, beautiful old towns and villages, friendly people, and fascinating history and culture have made it attractive to increasing numbers of tourists. From its northern town of Porto, where port wine comes from, to the sunny province of Algarve in the extreme south, the country offers a variety of interests far greater than its size. These include distinctive folk music and dance, colourful festivals, historic sites, delicious seafood and choice wines.

Part of the European Community since 1986, Portugal only achieved its present status as a democratic republic with the revolution of 1974, when it threw off the rule of dictators who had imposed an oppressive regime from 1926. The fight for democracy, combined with damaging wars in the former colonies of Angola and Mozambique, weakened Portugal's already fragile economy. Today it is struggling to improve its people's standard of living, but remains one of Europe's poorest countries. Many Portuguese, like these **fishermen** (*left*) near Mira on the Atlantic coast, are forced to seek a livelihood as "guestworkers" in other European lands, but most return with their savings to retire in "*na minha terra*" (my own country).

Portugal Today

DURING THE 1500s, PORTUGAL'S monopoly of the spice trade made it the richest country in Europe, with an empire stretching from Brazil to China. Today, Portugal is one of Western Europe's poorest nations, but it boasts a strong democratic political system, and a high rate of economic growth. Its hardworking, friendly people once produced famous discoverers and explorers. Today, Portugal looks to Europe, and its people are more likely to be farmers, fishermen or computer operators.

Modern Portugal entered the world stage in April 1974, when young military officers of the Armed Forces Movement overthrew the longstanding dictatorship established by Antonio Salazar (1889-1970), which had ruled the country for nearly half a century. In a coup dubbed "the revolt of the captains", the officers set up a provisional government, abolished the secret police and restored the political and civil rights of the people. Political parties soon emerged to lobby for votes. The April revolution, which took the red carnation as its symbol, sadly led to clashes between opposing political groups, but for the most part, Portugal returned peacefully to democracy.

This new atmosphere extended to Portugal's colonial empire, and the new government immediately opened negotiations with nationalist movements. In 1974, Portuguese Guinea, in Africa, gained its independence, taking the name of Guinea-Bissau. The following year saw a number of other African possessions achieve freedom from the mother country, including Angola, Cape Verde, Mozambique, and São Tomé and Principe. In 1976, Indonesia annexed Portuguese East Timor in the East Indies. Under the terms of an agreement signed between Portugal and China, control of the tiny territory of Macao – a Portugese colony since 1557 – will pass to China in 1999.

The political system

In 1976, the people of Portugal participated in the first free elections for more than 50 years. The assembly that emerged from these elections framed a new constitution, envisioning a socialist society.

As a result of new electoral laws, voters today elect a parliament and the country's president. The president serves a maximum two terms of five years, acting as head of state, head of the armed forces, and head of the Supreme National Council of Defence. These offices were significant until 1982, since before that date the armed forces retained an advisory role in the government. The prime minister, usually the head of the majority party in the Assembly of the Republic (parliament), is appointed by the president to head the government.

The 250-member, one-chamber Assembly sits for a four-year term. Candidates are elected by proportional representation, in which political parties obtain seats in proportion to their total vote.

After 1976, Portugal had several different governments. The two largest political groups by far are the Social Democratic Party (PSD) and the Socialist Party (PS). The PSD claims to be a centrist party, while the more leftist PS, which first governed Portugal after the 1976 elections, is a social-democratic party. In 1986, veteran PS leader Mario Soares was elected President.

FACT BOX

THE COUNTRY
Official name: Republic of Portugal
Capital: Lisbon
Land regions: Coastal Plains, Northern and Southern Tablelands, Central Range
Land area: 35,553 sq mi (92,082 km²), including Azores and Madeira island groups. Mainland: 34,340 sq mi (88,941 km²)
Climate: Mild, increasingly Mediterranean towards the South. Spring and summer: warm and dry; autumn and winter: cool with heavy rainfall
Main rivers: Tagus (Tajo), Douro, Guadiana, Mondego, Sado

Highest elevation: Estrela 6,539 ft (1,993 m)
Lowest elevation: Sea level along the coast

THE GOVERNMENT
Form of Government: Parliamentary republic
Head of State: President
Head of Government: Prime Minister
Administrative areas: 22 districts with further divisions
Legislature: National Assembly with 250 members, elected by the people to 4-year terms
Judiciary: Supreme Court. Lower courts of appeal, district and local courts. Military courts

Armed forces: Total strength: 73,600, plus reservists. Conscription: men must serve 12-15 months in army or 18-20 months in navy or air force

THE PEOPLE
Population (1990): 10,337,000
Language: Portuguese
Religion: Roman Catholic (about 95%)

THE ECONOMY
Currency (1989): Escudo
Gross Domestic Product per person (1990): US$5,670
Annual Growth Rate (1985-90): 4.6%
Trade balance in US$ (1990): –$2,253 mill

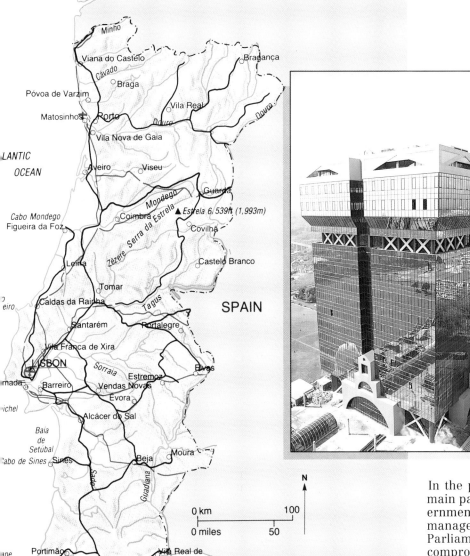

Portugal (*far left*) is the westernmost nation in continental Europe. Outside the flatlands of the west and south coasts, Portugal's terrain consists mainly of plains broken by heavily forested mountain ranges. The Tagus River divides north and south. Portugal's territory also includes the Azores and Madeira island groups – situated far out in the Atlantic – and the tiny colony of Macao in China.

The Amoreiras shopping and office complex (*left*) makes a startling addition to the skyline of Lisbon. EC membership has brought new investment to Portugal, but despite a high rate of growth, the country ranks as one of Western Europe's poorest.

In the past, the even balance between the main parties led to a series of coalition governments. But in the late 1980s, the PSD managed to achieve an absolute majority in Parliament without having to resort to the compromise of a coalition.

Education

Elementary education is compulsory for children from the ages of 6-14. Enrollment is high, but secondary education is not compulsory, as children from poorer families often enter the workforce. Portugal has ten universities, four of which opened after the 1974 revolution. The country's oldest university, located in Coimbra since 1537, was originally founded in Lisbon in 1290.

From 1959 until 1986 the country belonged to the European Free Trade Association (EFTA). However, in 1986, Portugal received a boost to its economy, as well as approval for its political evolution, when the country joined the European Community (EC). Portugal is also a member of the North Atlantic Treaty Organization (NATO).

Portugal faces the future with the confidence of a true democracy. The country's problems stem mainly from an economy still based heavily on agriculture. Inflation and unemployment still loom, but the growth of new industries led the World Bank and the International Monetary Fund (IMF) in 1989 to rank Portugal 23rd among industrial nations.

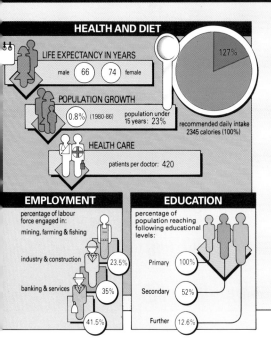

HEALTH AND DIET

LIFE EXPECTANCY IN YEARS
male 66   female 74

127%
recommended daily intake 2345 calories (100%)

POPULATION GROWTH
0.8% (1980-86)   population under 15 years: 23%

HEALTH CARE
patients per doctor: 420

EMPLOYMENT

percentage of labour force engaged in:
mining, farming & fishing   23.5%
industry & construction   35%
banking & services   41.5%

EDUCATION

percentage of population reaching following educational levels:
Primary   100%
Secondary   52%
Further   12.6%

Goods imported: Mineral oil, machinery, motor vehicles, grain
Goods exported: Textiles, yarns, machinery, chemicals, cork, fish, fish products, wood, wine, olive oil, resin, pyrite
Trading partners: Great Britain, Germany, USA, France and other EC countries
Transport: Length of railways (1989): 2,931 mi (4,717 km)
Passenger miles (1988): 3,390 mill (5,456.2 mill km)
Communications: Number of daily newspapers (1988): 35
Circulation (1988): 859,000
495,000

THE LAND OF PORTUGAL CONSISTS OF A strip 94-125 miles (150-200 kilometres) in width, running along the Atlantic edge of the Iberian Peninsula. From the lower Minho River, which forms the border with Spain in the north, it extends south across the western roof of the Iberian Highlands – the Meseta. The Serra da Estrela, an extension of the Castilian plateau, makes up the Central Range, and includes Portugal's highest mountains, which rise to more than 6,000 feet (1,830 metres). The Serra da Estrela divides Portugal into two parts: the north consists of the mountainous terrain of High Portugal and the central Portuguese hills, while the south is mainly flat with low hills. The Coastal Plains, which cover the western and southern coasts, are generally low-lying, with broad sandy beaches occasionally broken by a steeper coastline featuring rugged, deeply fissured rocks.

Northern Portugal

The northern part of High Portugal, which lies between the rivers Minho and Douro, is also known as the Northern Tablelands, and marks a continuation of the mountain terrain of Galicia. But age has eroded these mountains to form an undulating landscape of hills and valleys, cut through with rivers. The Douro in particular cleaves deeply into the land to form a narrow, sunny valley, where vines are cultivated on steep slate terraces, yielding the grapes used in the manufacture of Portugal's famous port wine. Near the coast, small villages nestle in meadows and fields, fringed with oak and beech woods. The higher, mainly forested mountain area in the northeast allows little agriculture except in the valley sides and bottoms, while the high plateaus, which rise to 1,640-2,460 feet (500-750 metres) and are overlooked by mountain ranges, have no vegetation other than bush forests and barren heathland.

South of the Douro, High Portugal continues with the gently sloping plateau of Beira, a hilly region some 2,000-3,300 feet (600-1,000 metres) in height, covered with olive groves and the Mediterranean shrubland known as *maquis*. The dividing line of the Serra da Estrela consists of bare granite uplands, formed in the Ice Age, which reach a height of almost 6,600 feet (2,000 metres).

The broad coastal plain lying to the west slopes gently towards the sea, ending in a thinly covered coast marked with lagoons. Farmers cultivate rice in the flat river valleys, and corn in the higher and drier areas. Lines of trees protect the fields against erosion by wind. Towards the south, this coastal strip narrows and merges with the hills of the Estremadura region in the interior of the country. This intensively farmed landscape features large villages set in olive

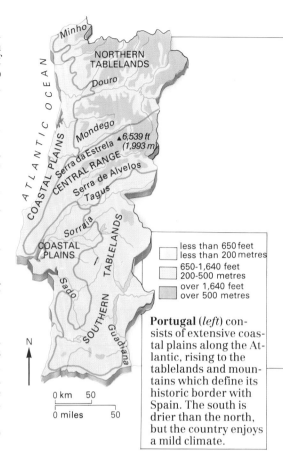

Portugal (*left*) consists of extensive coastal plains along the Atlantic, rising to the tablelands and mountains which define its historic border with Spain. The south is drier than the north, but the country enjoys a mild climate.

	less than 650 feet / less than 200 metres
	650-1,640 feet / 200-500 metres
	over 1,640 feet / over 500 metres

The extensive pine forests (*above*) around Coimbra in wooded northern Portugal yield resin used for making pitch and turpentine, as well as timber for building and furniture. Pines make up 40 per cent of woodlands.

Sandy beaches (*right*) clear waters and warm summers make the Algarve region, on the southern coast, a popular holiday centre. Southern Portugal is hot and dry, but the influence of the Atlantic ensures a friendly climate.

groves, vineyards and cornfields. Rugged, bare chalk hills reach up from here to a height of some 2,300 feet (700 metres).

The Ribatejo lowland consists of a wide depression on the lower Tagus River, filled with sediments from the river. This is one of the most fertile regions in Portugal, and yields olives, vines and rice. The land is still sinking, which quite often results in earthquakes. The most serious of these occurred in 1755 and almost completely destroyed Portugal's capital of Lisbon.

Southern Portugal

In southern Portugal, the landscape consists of wide plateaus – a low-lying continuation of the Meseta of New Castile. Endless wheat fields, interrupted by fallow land covered with *maquis*, dominate this monotonous, gently hilly country, which develops into wide fields and bogs near the coast.

The rolling pastures and cropland (*top*) at the northern foot of the Serra de Monchique in southern Portugal typify the dry conditions and large farms of this region. In the north, forests and small farms predominate.

The Douro River (*above*), across which steams a freight train, is one of Portugal's most important waterways. The Douro, which empties into the Atlantic at Porto, waters one of the country's chief wine regions.

Only the higher hills and sierras still carry the remains of the former oak and pine forests. Towards the south, the low plateaus merge gradually into the highland of the High Algarve. This deeply cut region includes countless rounded hills bare of tree cover, and therefore very prone to erosion. Intensively cultivated fields and bush maquis dominate the landscape, while the southern coastal fringe and the Lower Algarve produce a range of fruits, including almonds, olives, figs, oranges and carobs.

The Atlantic Ocean strongly affects the climate, which becomes more Mediterranean towards the south. With decreasing rainfall from north to south, the country enjoys very warm summers, but only in the south are the winters short and mild – the higher mountain areas in the north may lie under snow for weeks at a time. The coastal area, however, is mild all year round.

People

SOMEONE ONCE DESCRIBED PORTUGAL as "a sunny state of mind by the sea". Such a description might be apt, but the amazing physical, cultural, and economic variety of this small, gentle country belies the generalization. The creaking oxcarts of Trás-os-Montes, the backward interior region "behind the mountains", is a world away from the cosmopolitan ambience of Lisbon, the capital. The citizens of bustling Porto (Oporto) have a proverb that says "Coimbra sings, Braga prays, Lisbon shows off, and Porto works". There may be some truth behind this sentiment, for the people of northern Portugal are generally more conservative and businesslike than the people of the sun-drenched Alentejo and Algarve regions of the south.

Life in the cities

Porto is one of Portugal's busiest commercial centres. Although off the tourist track, it is a picturesque city with a population close to 1,700,000 people. Today it is a major financial and banking centre, but for centuries its name was linked to the wine trade. In the 1700s, English companies established themselves in Porto to buy and ship port wine, thereby cementing the longstanding political and economic links between Portugal and Britain.

Coimbra, home of the second oldest university in Europe, boasts steep cobbled streets, and traces its roots to Roman times. Along with its academic atmosphere, Coimbra keeps alive a strong tradition of *fado*, a popular form of Portuguese song. Usually accompanied by the guitar, *fado* laments life's hardships in tones heavily spiked with *saudade*, or bittersweet nostalgia. *Fado* can be joyous, as in the *fado corrida*, sung after bullfights, but traditions vary from region to region. The *fado* of Coimbra is serious and intellectual, accompanied only by a slow, rhythmic beat. International audiences came to know *fado* through the songs of Amalia Rodrigues.

Braga's flower-filled thoroughfares frame the greatest Holy Week procession in Portugal and reinforce the city's claim to be the "Portuguese Rome". The Portuguese are strongly Roman Catholic, and there are only small minorities of Protestants, Jews and Muslims. Holy days fill much of the calendar, and most people take their religious duties seriously. One of the greatest Roman Catholic shrines stands at Fàtima, a village about 65 miles (105 kilometres) north of Lisbon. It was there, on May 13, 1917, that the Virgin Mary is said to have appeared to three shepherd children, prophesying world peace. The figure allegedly appeared six times. Ever since, thousands of pilgrims from all over the world converge on Fàtima on the 12th and 13th of each month, from May to October, to pay their devotions.

Lisbon

The Portuguese capital, Lisbon, is the nerve centre of the nation. Covering a semicircle of low hills, on the north bank of the Tagus (Tajo) river, it offers an irresistible blend of old and new. Some say that Ulysses first landed here, but archaeologists prefer to date its birth at about 5000 BC. However, most of the present city is less than 250 years old.

On the morning of November 1, 1755 (All Saints Day), one of the most terrible earthquakes in history struck Lisbon. The Tagus drained to its muddy bed before huge tidal waves swept in from the Atlantic to drown the city and many of its inhabitants. Many more were wiped out by the fires that raged in the ruins. When it was all over, more than 60,000 people had perished and two-thirds of Lisbon had been destroyed.

The men who rebuilt the city, directed by the then prime minister, the Marquis of Pombal (1699-1782), were artists of imagination. They introduced the wide, graceful boulevards, mosaic pavements, and perfectly proportioned buildings that are a feature of modern Lisbon. Sadly, a major fire, in the summer of 1988, gutted many fine old buildings from this period.

A fisherman at Nazaré (*below*), on Portugal's central Atlantic coast, repairs his nets in time-honoured fashion. Traditionally a seafaring people, Portuguese fishermen still sail far across the Atlantic to net their deep-sea catch.

An elevator in Lisbon (*right*) indicates the steepness of some of the hills over which Portugal's capital sprawls. The present city, with its picturesque streets, arose from the rubble of the catastrophic earthquake of 1755.

Today's metropolis covers some 32 square miles (84 square kilometres). The 25th of April Bridge, which spans Lisbon's wide natural harbour, is one of the longest suspension bridges in the world. The *Baixa*, or Low Town, is a low, flat district that lies next to the harbour. A leisurely, old-world quality permeates its elegant shops. The oldest quarter of Lisbon, known as the *Alfama*, is of Moorish origin, and its tangle of cobbled alleys and steep streets provides a fascinating experience for the visitor.

Lisbon's population of more than 2.1 million includes many former inhabitants of Portugal's African colonies, and the diversity of the city's population reflects its importance as a port. Mild winters and hot summers encourage a stroll along the tree-lined Avenida da Liberdade, or through elegant parks where the calls of peacocks and other exotic birds fill the air.

The *Alfama* (*below left*), where these men gather after work, is Lisbon's oldest quarter. Its steep, narrow streets restrict traffic, retaining the charm of this former Moorish town. Above lies the fortress of São Jorge.

An old woman (*above left*) in the vineyards of the Douro region of northern Portugal displays the charm and warmth for which the people of Portugal are famous. Much of the country's population still live in rural areas.

At Tomar (*below*), the Thanksgiving procession takes place every four years. Religion plays a major part in the lives of Portuguese people. The shrine at Fàtima, near Lisbon, has become a major pilgrimage site for Roman Catholics.

"The object of travel", declared Doctor Samuel Johnson (1709-84), "is to reach the Mediterranean." Even before he made this assertion, privileged people from many parts of the world had begun to make the "Grand Tour" of Europe: the educational pilgrimage for young aristocrats, by way of Europe's major cities to Italy, long regarded as the birthplace of modern Western culture. The British poet Lord Byron (1749-1832) "fell immeasurably in love" with Italy. Goethe, the great German poet, celebrated "the land where the lemon-trees bloom . . . where the gold oranges glow in their dark foliage". Even the American Mark Twain was moved to remark that "the Creator made Italy to a design by Michelangelo" (he also hung outside his Venetian lodgings a sign: "Beware of the Doge"!). Today, millions of tourists every year follow in the footsteps of these famous figures.

Perhaps no other country has so rich a mixture of pleasures to offer. Italy has landscapes for all tastes and seasons: the majestic Alpine peaks of the north; the lakes and the fertile Po Valley of upper Italy; the quiet olive groves and verdant rolling countryside of **Tuscany** (*left*); the wooded Apennine Mountains that form Italy's "backbone"; the coastal plains of the Adriatic and the more rugged western coast, where Vesuvius dominates the bright blue Bay of Naples; the harsh, sun-baked hills of the south; the mountainous island of Sardinia; and, lying like a great rock about to be kicked by the toe of the Italian "boot", savagely beautiful Sicily.

It is impossible to travel far in Italy without being reminded of the country's profound influence upon Western culture. The proud ruins of temples and theatres, triumphal arches celebrating military glories, and roads and aqueducts reflecting civil prosperity, all these stand as symbols of the mighty Roman empire which, at its height, embraced most of the known world. Florence, Venice, Mantua and other ancient cities of Italy embody the spirit of the Renaissance, the "new learning" that marked the transition between the medieval and modern worlds.

Whatever one seeks in Italy – peaceful countryside; lively tourist centres for skiing, swimming, sailing or simply lazing in "sunny Italy"; great centres of art and music (for Italy is the home of opera) – one will find added pleasure in the nature of the vivacious Italian people. This is expressed in their obvious enjoyment of the small pleasures of everyday life: a good meal, the company of family and friends, and, happily for the traveller, a tradition of open-mindedness and warm hospitality.

Italy Today

ITALY IS AN ANCIENT LAND BUT A young nation. It did not become a united state until the establishment of the monarchy in the 1860s-70s. From 1922 until its defeat in 1943 during World War II, it was under authoritarian Fascist rule. In 1946 a popular referendum transformed the monarchy into a republic (*Repubblica Italiana*). A new constitution, proclaiming "a democratic republic founded on work", came into effect in January 1948.

Although democratic institutions were quickly established, many political and social crises have troubled Italy since then. There have been some 50 changes of government; the result not only of fierce disagreement between the government and opposition parties, but also of strife within the various parties forming the ruling coalitions. Among Italy's many problems are a large public sector debt; periodical inflation of a weak currency; a clumsy administrative system and inadequate public services; and an economic imbalance between the prosperous north and the poorer southern regions. The opposition of the powerful labour unions to governmental anti-inflation policies has led to frequent strikes. The outrages of politically inspired terrorists and of organized crime (dominated by the infamous Mafia) have tarnished Italy's image worldwide.

President and premier

The Italian head of state is the president, who is elected for a seven-year term by the majority vote of members of parliament and delegates from the regional councils. He appoints the premier from among the members of parliament (who must approve his choice), has the power to dissolve parliament, and is commander of the armed forces. Parliament consists of two houses with equal legislative powers: the Senate, with 320 members, and the Chamber of Deputies, with 630 members. All the deputies and 315 of the senators are elected for a five-year term under a system of proportional representation (where the party's size reflects the number of votes won). The remaining five senators are life senators nominated by the president. The government consists of the premier and the members of his Cabinet. The premier chooses his own Cabinet ministers, subject to the approval of both president and parliament.

Italy's political instability stems largely from its complex electoral system and its large number of political parties. Coalition governments, formed by the union of two or more parties, are the rule, and, since the premier may be removed from office at any time by a parliamentary vote of censure, inter-party disagreements lead to frequent changes of government. Some legislative continuity is preserved, however, by the fact that when a government falls, many Cabinet members retain their posts under its successor. Further, since 1946, the majority of Cabinet positions have been held by members of Italy's largest political party, the *Democrazia Cristiana* (DC; Christian Democratic Party). However, the strength of the opposition parties, such as the Communists (now the Party of the Democratic Left), is such that the DC has almost always had to rule in coalition with smaller parties: the Liberals, Republicans,

---

FACT BOX

THE COUNTRY
Official name: Italian Republic
Capital: Rome
Land regions: Alpine Slope, Po Valley, Adriatic Plain, Apennines, Apulia/SE plains, W Uplands/Plains, Sicily, Sardinia
Land area: 116,314 sq mi (301,252 km²)
Climate: Mediterranean in central and S, cold winters in N
Main rivers: Po, Arno, Tiber, Volturno
Highest elevation: On Mont Blanc 15,521 ft (4,731 m)
Lowest elevation: Sea level along the coast

THE GOVERNMENT
Form of Goverment:

Parliamentarian republic
Head of State: President
Head of Government: Prime Minister
Administrative areas: 20 regions, divided into provinces and communes
Legislature: Chamber of Deputies (630 members) and Senate (315 elected and 5 appointed members). 5-year terms
Judiciary: Constitutional Court, courts of cassation, courts of assizes, lower courts
Armed forces: Total strength: 386,000. Conscription: men must serve 12 months (army/air force) or 19

months (navy) after age 18

THE PEOPLE
Population (1990): 57,576,000
Language: Italian
Religion: Roman Catholic (99%)

THE ECONOMY
Currency: Italian lira
Gross Domestic Product per person (1990): US$18,575
Annual Growth Rate (1985-90): 3.0%
Trade balance in US$ (1988): – $11,551 mill
Goods imported: Crude oil, motor vehicles, textile yarns, machinery, metals
Goods exported: Clothing and shoes, machinery, motor

Map labels

SWITZERLAND
AUSTRIA
FRANCE
Aosta
VALLE D'AOSTA
PIEDMONT
Turin (Torino)
Cuneo
Maritime Alps
Savona
MONACO
San Remo
Gulf of Genoa
Ligurian Sea
Lake Maggiore
Lake Como
Varese
Busto Arsizio
Novara
Vercelli
Pavia
Asti
Alessandria
Piacenza
Cremona
Monza
Milan (Milano)
Bergamo
Brescia
LOMBARDY
Lecco
Como
Lake Garda
Bolzano
TRENTINO-ALTO ADIGE
Trento
Dolomites
Cortina d'Ampezzo
Carnic Alps
FRIULI-VENEZIA GIULIA
Udine
Pordenone
Treviso
Vicenza
VENETIA
Verona
Padua (Padova)
Venice (Venezia)
Trieste
SLOVENIA
Mantova
Adige
Rovigo
Gulf of Venice
CROATIA
Po
Parma
Reggio nell'Emilia
Modena
Ferrara
EMILIA
Bologna
Ravenna
Forlì
Adriatic Sea
Genoa (Genova)
LIGURIA
La Spezia
Carrara
Massa
Viareggio
Pisa
Lucca
Pistoia
Prato
Leghorn (Livorno)
Arno
Florence (Firenze)
TUSCANY
Siena
SAN MARINO
Rimini
Pesaro
Ancona
MARCHES
Piombino
Elba
Pianosa
Grosseto
CORSICA (France)
Monte Cristo
UMBRIA
Perugia
Assisi
Terni
Viterbo
ABRUZZI
Ascoli-Piceno
L'Aquila
Pescara
Chieti
LATIUM
Tiber
VATICAN CITY
ROME (ROMA)
Anzio
Latina
MOLISE
Campobasso
San Severo
Cassino
Gulf of Manfredonia
Foggia
CAMPANIA
Caserta
Benevento
Cerignola
Barletta
Andria
Bari
APULIA
Altamura
Naples (Napoli)
Gulf of Gaeta
Ponza
Ischia
Torre del Greco
Salerno
Castellammare di Stabia
Capri
BASILICATA
Potenza
Matera
Brindisi
Lecce
Strait of Otranto
Gulf of Taranto
Taranto
ALBANIA
Punta Caprara
Sassari
Olbia
Alghero
Nuoro
Tirso
Oristano
SARDINIA
Iglesias
Cagliari
Capo Carbonara
Capo Spartivento
Strait of Bonifacio
Capo Santa Maria di Leuca
Rossano
Gulf of Policastro
Cosenza
CALABRIA
Crotone
Catanzaro
Tyrrhenian Sea
Lipari Islands
Stromboli
Ionian Sea
Vulcano
Mediterranean Sea
Egadi Islands
Trapani
Marsala
Palermo
Messina
Reggio di Calabria
Strait of Messina
Capo Spartivento
SICILY
Agrigento
Gela
Mount Etna
Catania
Augusta
Syracuse (Siracusa)
Ragusa
Capo Passero

Scale: 0 km 100 200
0 miles 100

N

Italy (*left*) stretches from the Alps to the Mediterranean Sea. Its northern half contains the beautiful lakes and the fertile Po Valley while the south tends to be hotter and drier.

Body text

Social Democrats and, increasingly since the 1960s, the left-wing Socialists. In the early 1990s, the increasing influence of regionally-based organizations reflected public dissatisfaction with the established political parties.

Italy has a system of local government based on its division into 20 regions, which are in turn divided into provinces and again into communes. Each region, province and commune has its own elected council. Although most power rests with the national government, the regional councils exercise significant local legislative and administrative powers. Many of the regional councils are dominated by left-wing parties. Thus, the democratic sharing of power also creates further difficulties for the national government.

The fact that the Italian state survives, and still preserves great potential for economic, social and cultural development, owes much to the character of the Italian people. Italians complain bitterly of their country's cumbersome and sometimes corrupt bureaucracy, of the poor quality of their transport, health or education services, and of their ponderous system of justice. Yet Italian society, in spite of its great political, social and regional divisions, retains much of the splendid vitality that once built a mighty empire.

Infographics

HEALTH AND DIET

LIFE EXPECTANCY IN YEARS
male 70 female 76

139%
recommended daily intake 2345 calories (100%)

POPULATION GROWTH
0.2% (1980-86)
population under 15 years: 19%

HEALTH CARE
patients per doctor: 345

EMPLOYMENT
percentage of labour force engaged in:
mining, farming & fishing 10.7%
industry & construction 32.7%
banking & services 56.6%

EDUCATION
percentage of population reaching following educational levels:
Primary 97%
Secondary 76%
Further 24.7%

vehicles, textiles, chemicals, fruits and vegetables
Trading partners: Germany, France, USA, Great Britain, Netherlands, Austria, Switzerland
Transport: Length of railways (1990): 12,176 mi (19,595 km)
Passenger miles (1986): 26,932 (43,343 mill km)
Communications: Number of daily newspapers (1988): 73
Circulation (1988): 6,005,000

Land

ITALY, A LARGE COUNTRY IN SOUTHERN Europe, consists of a mountainous peninsula with a shape often likened to that of a high-heeled boot. It extends for some 700 miles (1,130 kilometres) southward from the Alps into the Mediterranean Sea. Its territory includes the large Mediterranean islands of Sicily, lying off the "toe" of the "boot", and Sardinia , and a number of smaller islands, notably Elba, Ischia and Capri. It is bordered to the north by the Alps, which it shares with France, Switzerland, Austria and, to the northeast, Slovenia. Its coasts, totalling 2,685 miles (4,321 kilometres) in length, lie along the Ligurian and Tyrrhenian seas to the west, the Mediterranean to the south, the Ionian Sea to the southeast, and the Adriatic Sea to the east. The independent states of the Vatican City, at Rome, and San Marino, near the Adriatic coast, lie within Italy's borders.

The Alpine regions

Nearly 80 per cent of Italy's terrain is mountainous or hilly. The highest peaks lie in the northern region, the Alpine Slope, where the Italian sector of the Mont Blanc (known as Monte Bianco in Italian) massif, at the junction of the French and Swiss borders, rises to 15,521 feet (4,731 metres). Here, alpine scrub at the higher elevations yields to meadowland and then to evergreen and deciduous (leaf-dropping) forest. In the Alpine region, below the Swiss border, lies the beautiful lake district, where lemon and orange groves, palm trees and magnolias grow in sheltered areas around Lakes Maggiore, Como and Garda. Here, winters are generally mild, with an average January temperature of 39°F (4°C) at Salo on Lake Garda. In the higher regions, the winter months are cold and wet, increasing in severity towards the the east, where the permanent snow line comes as low as 8,300 feet (2,530 metres) and rainfall may exceed 40 inches (102 centimetres) per year.

Below the Alpine foothills lies Italy's most fertile and densely populated region, the Po Valley, a wide, flat plain some 17,000 square miles (44,000 square kilometres) in area. The forests that once covered this land have been cleared by man to make way for the intensive cultivation of cereals, rice and potatoes. The Lombardy Plains, famous for their poplar trees, contain great cities where art and industry flourish. Here, summers are generally warm and pleasant, although winters may be severe in the higher central regions, and rainfall generally exceeds 30 inches (76 centimetres) per year. The Adriatic Plain, to the east, receives much less rain. A limestone region, it is underlaid by a system consisting of numerous underground channels which drain off much of its water.

The columns (*right*) of an ancient temple rise in a meadow at Paestum, south of the Gulf of Salerno. Here, in spite of earthquakes, remains of Greek settlement have endured for more than 2,000 years.

The Italian landscape (*far right*) consists of eight distinct land regions. These include the Alpine Slope, the Po Valley, the forest-covered Appenine Mountains, Apulia and the southeastern plains, the Western Uplands and Plains, Sicily, and Sardinia – both islands.

Graceful cypress trees (*above*) shade a sun-baked road in the hill country of Tuscany, northwestern Italy. The warm summers and light rainfall of this region provide ideal conditions for the cultivation of vines.

An ancient fortress (*right*) at Sirmione, once the stronghold of the rulers of Verona, frowns down on Lake Garda, largest of the lakes of northern Italy. The lake district lies in the beautiful south-central Alpine region.

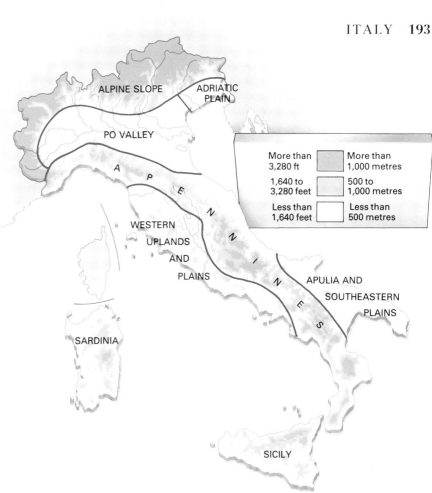

The Apennine Mountains form Italy's backbone. They extend along the greater part of the peninsula, from the Alpine northwest, across central Italy, and into Sicily. The Apennines are most rugged in the northwest, which contains the famous marble quarries of Carrara and Massa, but the highest peaks are in the central Apennines, east of Rome, where the Gran Sasso d'Italia reaches 9,560 feet (2,914 metres). The plateaus of the central region provide good pastureland, but farther south rainfall decreases and the rocky, sun-baked slopes are barren. An active volcanic region near Naples includes Vesuvius, while the southern Apennines are subject to earthquakes of sometimes terrifying intensity.

Uplands and plains

Between the Mediterranean (Tyrrhenian) coast and the north-central curve of the Apennines lie Italy's Western Uplands and Plains. The low, rolling hills and river valleys of the northern area, extending across Umbria and Tuscany, are second only to the Po Valley in agricultural importance. In the southern part of the region, the coastal plain centring on the cities of Rome and Naples, are the Pontine marshes. A fertile part of the Roman *campagna* (countryside) in early times, they were later abandoned; for many centuries men struggled to re-

claim them, but the drainage system was not completed until the 1930s. Drainage of the marshes improved the Roman climate, which is notably mild in spite of the influences of the cold northerly wind called the *tramontana*, and the hot *sirocco*, the southern wind from the Saharan regions that affects much of southern Italy.

East of the Apennines, in the "heel" of the Italian boot, north and east of the Gulf of Taranto and extending as far north as the Biferno River, lies the region of Apulia and the Southeastern Plains. Three lowland areas – the Capitanata Plain, around Foggia, to the north; the Adriatic coast around Lecce, to the east; and the Taranto plain in the southwest – fringe the Apulian plateau. The limestone plateau is semi-arid because much of its water is carried away by a system of underground channels which honeycomb the limestone rock. The surrounding plains, however, are fertile. Large quantities of olive oil are produced here with the aid of water brought from the Sele River, an Apennine stream flowing to the Gulf of Salerno, by the Apulian Aqueduct. This vital public work was constructed in 1905-28. A 9-mile (14.5-kilometre) long tunnel carries water beneath the Apennines and distributes it throughout the Apulian provinces by way of a 143-mile (230-kilometre) aqueduct and a system of side channels.

People

IN 1860-70, THE DECADE IN WHICH Italy became united, the nation had about 28,000,000 inhabitants. Since then the population has doubled in size, the highest rate of increase occurring in the 1930s-70s. Thus, Italy is densely populated, with 493 persons per square mile (190 per square kilometre). But this overall figure obscures regional differences in population growth and distribution. Some 40 per cent of the total population is concentrated in the Po Valley, which constitutes only 16 per cent of the total area, and the coastal areas are generally more densely populated than the mountainous interior.

The industrialized north, despite its falling birth rate, has the highest population density; the south, where the birth rate is comparatively high, is sparsely populated. This is largely attributable to the mass migration of workers from south to north after World War II; a movement that reached its peak in the 1960s, when some 2,500,000 persons are estimated to have moved from south to north. Government-sponsored programmes for the economic development of the southern regions have slowed the rate of migration. During the earlier part of this century, many Italians left home for foreign countries: to North and South America in the earlier 1900s, to the African colonies of the "new Roman Empire" in the 1910s-30s, and to the United States, Canada and Australia after World War II.

Race, language and religion
The Italian race has been formed over many centuries by an amalgamation of the original inhabitants of the Apennine peninsula, the Ligurian peoples, with various immigrant races. The "typical" Italian, black-haired, with olive skin and dark eyes, does indeed predominate in modern Italy, but there are a number of significant ethnic variations. The Arabs and Normans who successively occupied those areas have left their traces in southern Italy and Sicily. Many people of Greek and Albanian stock are found in Calabria and Sicily, while in Friuli-Venezia Giulia, in the Slovenian border region, Slav elements are clearly distinguishable. People of German descent form a majority in South Tyrol province in the Trentino-Alto Adige region.

Similar variations are apparent in the Italian language. Italian itself is a *Romance* language, largely derived from Latin. It emerged as a separate language from around AD 1000, deriving its standard modern form from the educated speech of Tuscany, the tongue of Dante Alighieri and other major Italian writers. There exist also some 100 regional dialects, influenced by the languages of former conquerors or immigrants: German in northern

A meeting of friends (*below*) at a cafe table in a Tuscan town leads to a leisurely chat. Although they profess to be lovers of the countryside, some 72 per cent of Italians live in urban areas, where cafes form important social centres.

Members of a religious community (*right*) enjoy a peaceful walk. Although more than 95 per cent of Italians regard themselves as Roman Catholics, the great power formerly wielded by the Church has diminished.

A Roman lady (*left*) hangs out her washing from a tenement window. For centuries large apartment blocks have housed many of the city's people. Many Italian cities, especially in the north, now suffer from overcrowding.

A lady of Calabria (*below left*), the region at the "toe" of Italy, listens to the serenade of an accordion band. Internationally, Italy is more often associated with grand opera than with more humble music-making.

Italy; French in Piedmont; French, Spanish and Arabic in Sicily. As in other countries, dialects are gradually falling out of use because of the standardizing influence of the mass media. German remains an official language in South Tyrol, while many communities in the Dolomites speak a Latinate tongue called *Ladin*, similar to Swiss *Romansh*.

More than 95 per cent of the Italian people are Roman Catholics. Italy is the "homeland" of the Roman Catholic Church, and its buildings, clergy and ceremonies characterize the urban and rural landscape. However, the enormous political and social power that the Church exercised in the past has significantly diminished, although most Italians still preserve great respect for the Church.

Local loyalties

The people of modern Italy have much in common with each other. There is their religion, however diluted; their increasingly standardized language; and a national character typified by good humour, close family relationships, and a great love of good art, food and sport. All Italians are at one in cheering on the *Azzuri* (blue shirts) at a *calcio* (soccer) international. But Italy was, until the later 1800s, a collection of small independent states; political unification and improvements in inter-regional communications have not yet succeeded in removing all regional differences.

These differences are not simply political or economic, although economic inequality contributes to the stereotypical views of each other held by north and south. Many northerners condemn southerners as idle, grubby peasants, and are portrayed in turn by the southerners as heartless, greedy barbarians. Italian society is basically urban in character – 72 per cent of its population live in towns or cities – and has been so since the days of Imperial Rome. Although Italians profess a delight in the countryside they are townspeople at heart. The people of the various regions, and in particular those of the former great city-states – Florence, Genoa, Milan, Pisa, Venice, and others – cherish their individual identities and strive to preserve their dialects, traditions, festivals, local foods and wines.

Rome

LEGEND CLAIMS THAT THE DAY OF Rome's foundation, April 21, 753 BC, also saw the murder of one of the city's founders, Remus, by his brother Romulus. Thereafter, violence continued to stain her history, at least in the ancient period; the republic that bloodily replaced the first kings ended in dictatorship and anarchy, leading to the autocratic rule of the emperors. Under the Empire, the words *"Civis Romanus sum"* ("I am a Roman citizen") were the proudest boast a man could make – but the pride of the Roman citizen rested on a foundation of slavery and destruction. "They make a desert, and they call it peace!" remarked a contemporary historian of Rome's method of dealing with conquered territories. Yet that oppressive empire gave to the Western world the foundations of its modern governmental, legal and military systems, as well as its languages and arts. And it left some of the noblest monuments of the ancient world. Today, the vestiges of ancient Rome stand proudly in the heart of the modern city.

Imperial remains

Rome, it is said, was not built in a day; and, equally truly, a lifetime is not long enough to appreciate the city. Perhaps the most impressive monument of imperial Rome is the Colosseum, near the long street called the Via del Corso at the heart of modern Rome. This vast amphitheatre, built in AD 72-80, symbolizes the city's eternity: for the Romans say that when the Colosseum falls, Rome will fall with it – and the end of the world will follow.

The many-tiered shell of marble and red "travertine" stone that encloses the Colosseum's vast arena has survived frequent pillage and misuse: popes raided its fabric to build St Peter's and other churches; generals used it as a fortress; and businessmen as a fertilizer factory. From AD 80 until the 400s, it was the scene of gladiatorial combats, wild-beast shows and, very probably, the execution of Christian martyrs – but some scholars assign the latter atrocities to the Circus Maximus, the great chariot-racing oval. These ancient sports arenas have their modern counterpart in the huge Sports Palace of the EUR (Universal Exhibition of Rome) in the city's most modern quarter, begun under the dictator Benito Mussolini (1883-1945) in 1938 and finally completed in 1976.

West of the Colosseum lies the Forum, a complex of ruins marking the commercial and religious centre of the ancient city; and the Imperial Fora (plural of forum), the civic centres raised in self-glorification by Julius Caesar and his successors. The largest is the Forum of Trajan (ruled AD 98-117), centred on a column 131 feet (40

metres) in height. A striking series of sculptures, containing some 2,500 figures carved in low relief, spirals up Trajan's Column. But the column, like many of Rome's ancient monuments, is often almost hidden from view by protective sheeting. Air pollution, caused by modern Rome's seething traffic, poses a critical threat to these historic structures.

Living on the past

Modern Rome is not an industrial city, although there is a factory complex to the northwest, while to the southeast lies Cinecittà, the internationally famous movie-making "city". But tourism remains central to Rome's economy, so in a sense Rome may be said to live on her past.

Certainly, her more recent building schemes hardly match the glories of the Empire and Renaissance. Italy's political rebirth in the 1800s is commemorated at the termination of the Via del Corso, at the Capitoline Hill, by the Victor Emanuele Monument, an elaborate white edifice that Romans mock as "the Typewriter". Many medieval houses were destroyed in the creation of this monstrosity. Mussolini's grandiose town-planning schemes of the 1920s and 1930s demolished more historic buildings and created a traffic system that recalls the original function of the Corso – a track along which wild horses were raced.

Rome's Colosseum (*above*), containing places for more than 70,000 spectators, opened in AD 80 with a performance that lasted 100 days. This involved fights to the death between human participants and some 5,000 wild animals of different kinds.

The Piazza Navona (*right*), a traffic-free zone, covers the site of an ancient race course, and ranks as one of Rome's most popular meeting places. The Fountain of Neptune looks across to the church of S Agnese in Agone, built in the 1600s.

The Spanish Steps (*left*), built in 1726, climb up to the church of S. Trinita dei Monti. Here tourists and Romans alike come to see and be seen, sitting on the steps and watching the interplay of light over the Eternal City.

The city of Rome (*below*), for centuries the heart of the Roman Empire and capital of the world, retains its magic to the present time. The River Tiber runs through the city, which includes such famous landmarks as St Peter's Square; the Colosseum, where Roman emperors watched battling gladiators and wild beast shows; the Spanish Steps, a popular resting place for tourists; the Piazza del Popolo, hub of modern Rome; the Opera House; and the Roman Forum, the administrative and legal centre of ancient Rome.

However, two of Rome's most famous tourist meeting places, the Trevi Fountain and the Spanish Steps, have survived the attentions of self-glorifying rulers. The visitor who tosses a coin into the Trevi, best-known of Rome's many fountains, is said to thus guarantee a happy return to the city – and the large sums dredged weekly from the fountain go towards the upkeep of Roman orphanages. Located between the Piazza di Spagna and the Via Condotti with its world-famous fashion shops, the Spanish Steps have long been the haunt of some of Rome's less conventional visitors, from the "bohemians" of the 1800s to the "hippies" and "punks" of today.

Delightful idleness

The tourist who lounges in the sunlight on the Spanish Steps, or sits outside one of the many cafes with a glass of wine or a dish of *cassata* (the ice-cream pudding that ranks as Rome's favourite delicacy), can relax and watch the world go by, content to follow an aspect of Roman life recorded as long ago as AD 100 by the writer Pliny the Younger (AD 62-114). Pliny noted the Roman talent for what modern Italians call *dolce far niente* ("delightful idleness"). For although few cities have experienced more than Rome, few people know better than the Romans how to rest from their labours when the work is done.

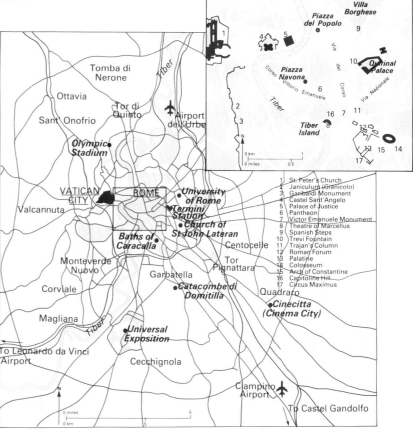

Art and Culture

PACKED WITH IMPORTANT MONUMENTS of art and architecture, Italy has for centuries between the cultured tourist's principal destination in Europe. Some visitors wonder how the creators of this grandiose past could possibly be ancestors of present-day Italians, with their evident interest in fun, food and fashion. Others believe that the Italians have probably always been like this, and that their culture is saved from being oppressive thanks to this intensely human quality.

Italy's *classical* (ancient Greek and Roman) heritage, with its emphasis on the human figure, has profoundly influenced its culture. In the centuries that followed the collapse of the Roman Empire in the AD 400s, memories of the classical tradition persisted more strongly in Italy than in any other country. The painter Giotto (c. 1267-1337), for example, depicted figures of substance and real-life proportions, just as you would find in classical art, long before the Renaissance style became established.

The Renaissance

Giotto came from Florence, as did his two major writer contemporaries Dante (1265-1321) and Petrarch (1304-74). Both these authors were deeply learned men, and yet a sense of humour, an interest in food and drink, and an obsession with love underlie even such sophisticated and complex works as Dante's celebrated *Divine Comedy*. This epic journey through Hell, Purgatory and Heaven is enlivened with sharp and witty descriptions of the poet's contemporaries;

Presentation of the Virgin (above) by Titian can be seen at Venice's Accademia Gallery. Venetian artists concentrated on effects of light and colour rather than the "heroic" mood of Florence and Rome.

Bernini's *The Ecstasy of St Teresa* (*below left*) dramatizes religious experience in the dynamic Baroque style. Sculptor, architect and painter, Bernini created this work at Rome for Pope Urban VIII.

The Ducal Palace (*below*) at Urbino, finished in 1474, reflects the "complete man" of the Renaissance. In addition to the duke's living quarters, it included a stateroom, library, theatre, galleries and

two chapels. Two stair towers framed the original arcaded courtyard, while later additions included an audience hall to the north, and a "secret garden" in a second courtyard.

Botticelli's *Primavera* (*left*), at the Uffizi in Florence, reveals the painter's interest in classical myth. Painters before the Renaissance concentrated on religious rather than "pagan" themes.

Michelangelo's *Creation of Adam* (*above*) one of the glories of Vatican City's Sistine Chapel, shows God imparting life to the first man. A leader of the Italian Renaissance, Michelangelo was also a great sculptor, poet and architect whose work has powerfully influenced the development of Western art.

and in the last part of the work, Dante's beloved Beatrice guides the poet in a tour around Heaven.

In the 1400s, Florence's heady cultural life developed into what we now know as the Renaissance – an outpouring of artistic, literary and scientific talent fired by an interest in classical culture. An amazing number of great artists and architects lived and worked in the city, from Masaccio (1401-28) to Botticelli (1444-1510). Little of this intensive cultural activity would have happened without financial backing, and this was amply provided by the great Florentine banking family, the Medicis.

In the early 1500s, the period of the so-called High Renaissance, Florence lost its cultural predominance. This was an age dominated by a handful of geniuses, one of whom, Leonardo da Vinci (1452-1519), was active mainly in and around Milan. Scientist, painter, architect, inventor and mathematician, Leonardo was the proverbial "Renaissance man", whose diversity of talents has never been matched. However his influence as an artist was relatively limited during his lifetime, certainly in comparison to that of his two great contemporaries, Raphael (1483-1520) and Michaelangelo (1475-1564). Both these artists were summoned to work in Rome, which under Pope Julian II developed into Europe's major centre of artistic patronage; for the next 300 years Rome was to be a Mecca for artists, who came to work there from all over the world.

Rome's only serious rival, culturally, politically and economically, was Venice, where from around 1500 there evolved a thriving and highly distinctive artistic tradition. Whereas the paintings of Raphael and Michelangelo stand out for their powerful drawing and composition, those of Titian (c. 1490-1576), their great Venetian contemporary, are striking for their colour and lifelike flesh tones – so realistic that one critic wrote that you could see the blood flowing through the veins of the figures.

In the field of music, Monteverdi (1567-1643), perhaps the greatest of Italy's early composers, was the first major exponent of opera, a musical form which in its outpouring of sentiment could hardly be more Italian. With its mingling of drama, singing, and spectacular scenic effects, it was also an art form totally in keeping with the next great phase of Italian art – the Baroque.

Baroque and after

The Baroque style was born in Rome, where it found its most perfect expression in the sculpture of Gianlorenzo Bernini (1598-1680), the dynamic architecture of Borromini (1599-1667), and in the vast ceiling paintings of artists such as Pietro da Cortona and Ignazio Pozzo. The last great exponent of the Italian baroque spirit was G-B Tiepolo (1696-1770).

Italian art declined with the death of Tiepolo, and Italy came to attract artists largely for the monuments of its past. The legacy of Italy's past overwhelmed most of the Italian artists, writers and musicians of the 1800s. The greatest achievements of this period were often inspired by this past, above all in the operas of Rossini, Bellini, Verdi and Puccini. Puccini continued to compose in a lush romantic vein well into the present century.

The group of Italian writers and artists known as the Futurists made an attempt early this century to break away from Italy's past, and did so in a perverse and often humorous way, as with Marinetti's *Futurist Cookery Book*. Yet Italy's strong classical tradition has been behind most of the finest Italian achievements this century, from the haunting arcaded landscapes of de Chirico to the Roman-inspired engineering works of G.A. Nervi. Finally, it is appropriate that in the recent reaction to abstract painting, resulting in a return to classical, human values, Italy should have played a leading part.

Sicily and Sardinia

ROUGHLY TRIANGULAR IN SHAPE, THE island of Sicily lies off the southwestern "toe" of Italy, from which it is separated by the Strait of Messina. With an area of 9,926 square miles (25,708 square kilometres), it is the largest and most populous island in the Mediterranean Sea. Together with a number of smaller islands, notably Pantelleria, Ustica, and the Lipari and Egadi groups, it constitutes one of the 20 political regions of Italy. The citizens of its nine provinces elect a 90-member Sicilian parliament and also send representatives to the parliament in Rome.

Geographically, Sicily is an extension of the Apennine mountains, and about 85 per cent of its area is hilly or mountainous, rising to 11,122 feet (3,390 metres) in the snow-capped peak of Mount Etna, an active volcano, on the east coast. The plain of Catania, south of Mount Etna, is the island's only large lowland area. Although frequently troubled by earthquakes, it is Sicily's main area of settlement, for its soil is enriched by deposits of volcanic ash and produces good harvests of olives, grapes, citrus fruits and cereals. The mountainous interior was once densely forested, but centuries of over-cutting have left most of the mountain slopes bare and subject to erosion. The climate is generally mild, with average temperatures of 45°F (7°C) in winter and 79°F (26°C) in summer. But rainfall is scanty, and the hot, dry *sirocco* wind sometimes causes summer droughts.

Outside influences

Although the Strait of Messina is only some 2 miles (3 kilometres) wide at its narrowest point, the traveller who takes the ferry from the mainland to Sicily finds himself in a society strikingly different from that of Italy. The Sicilian character is a result of centuries of conquest, by Greek colonists as early as the 700s BC, then by Carthaginians, Romans, Germanic tribes, Byzantines, Muslims from North Africa, Normans, French, Germans and Austrians. The traces left by these conquerors on Sicily's language and culture are immediately apparent. Sicilian dialects incorporate Arabic, Greek and other European tongues. Sicily's landmarks range from Greek remains at Agrigento and Syracuse to the architectural wealth of Palermo, the Sicilian capital, with its Moorish, Norman, Byzantine, Renaissance and Baroque temples and palaces.

Less obvious is the effect that long years of foreign domination have had on the Sicilian character. Over the centuries, the Sicilians became a secretive, inward-looking people, valuing personal and family honour above any wider sense of community, and distrusting outside authority. The Mafia, now known worldwide as a criminal

The harbour at Alghero (*below*) in Sardinia provides a picturesque backdrop for a stroll. Many of the people speak Catalan, a Spanish dialect. The Spanish influence can be seen in the architecture of the island.

The Sardinian coastline (*right*) has a rugged beauty – but the island has few resources. Tourism offers a chance of development, but the construction of holiday facilities has aroused resentment among local people.

organization, had its origins in Sicilian resistance to foreign rule. Its tradition of *omerta* ("law of silence"), which forbids cooperation with "foreign" forces of law and order, still greatly affects Sicilian life.

It has been hard for Sicily to adjust to the modern world. The Italian government's "Green Plans" of the 1950s-60s only partly succeeded in breaking down the traditional structure of Sicilian landholding, with a few great landowners and a multitude of poor tenant farmers. From the early 1900s, thousands of young Sicilians emigrated to the United States and other foreign countries. Even today, many leave for the industrial cities of northern Italy. Thus, Sicily loses the young and ambitious who might help in her modernization. Industrial development, although spurred on by the discovery of oil around Ragusa and Gela, and the construction of a refinery at the port of Augusta, remains limited.

Sardinia

Sardinia, Italy's other large island, is the second biggest island in the Mediterranean, with an area (including a number of smaller islands) of 9,301 square miles (24,090 square kilometres). It lies in the Tyrrhenian Sea, more than 100 miles (160 kilometres) west of the Italian mainland and some 9 miles (14 kilometres) south of the French

Sardinians (*below*) and **Sicilians** (*above right*), like many island people, have a long history of conquest. The legacy of outside influences is clearly reflected in their regional dialects, and also in their food and way of life.

An ancient theatre (*left*) stands on a hill overlooking the Golfo di Catania at Taormina, situated on the north-east coast of Sicily.

island of Corsica. It is divided into four provinces, each named after its major town: Cagliari (which contains the island's capital), Nuoro, Oristano and Sassari.

About 90 per cent of the island is mountainous, rising to 6,017 feet (1,834 metres) in Punta La Marmora in the east-central area. The only extensive lowland region is the Campidano plain of the southwest, where citrus fruits, olives, cereals, grapes and almonds are grown. Elsewhere, large herds of sheep (amounting to more than 30 per cent of Italy's stock) and goats are grazed. Deforestation has been extensive, but there are large areas of cork trees in the northeast. Cork is a leading export, as are a wide variety of minerals.

Like Sicily, Sardinia has a long history of foreign conquest, and it shares many of the problems of the larger island. Like the Sicilians, its people tend to distrust foreigners and to cling to tradition. Drainage projects have not yet completely eradicated the malaria that has long been the scourge of the island, and industrial development remains limited. A major hope for the future may lie in tourism, although the development of an increasingly popular tourist centre on the Costa Esmeralda (Emerald Coast) of the northeast has aroused some resentment among Sardinians, who contrast the visitor' luxurious lifestyle with their own poverty.

Vatican City

THE VATICAN STATE, OR VATICAN CITY, is the smallest independent country in the world, occupying a mere 109 acres (44 hectares) – the size of an average city park. Yet its ancient city walls contain the spiritual and administrative centre of the Roman Catholic Church (the largest of all the Christian Churches) as well as buildings and art treasures of unique historical value and remarkable beauty. St Peter's Church, or Basilica, ranks as one of the world's most important buildings, acting as a church, museum and architectural masterpiece.

Origin of the city state

The Vatican Hill was once the site of the emperor Nero's public gardens and circuses, where many Christians met their deaths. By the AD 100s a Christian shrine had been set up on the hillside, marking the grave of the apostle Peter. In the 300s the first Christian emperor, Constantine, built a *basilica* (palatial church) over the original shrine. As time passed, many other buildings sprang up within an encircling wall.

Today, Vatican City includes not only the magnificent basilica of St Peter's with its splendid square, but also the Apostolic Palaces and administrative offices, including the Curia (in which popes are elected), the Vatican Museums, housing the archives and library, the Vatican Gardens, and several other sizeable buildings. Beyond the city walls, the Vatican State also contains the church of St John Lateran, which serves as the pope's cathedral when fulfilling his role as Bishop of Rome. The Vatican's other possessions outside its city walls consist of the basilicas of Santa Maria Maggiore and

San Paolo (both also in Rome), and the pope's official summer residence at Castel Gandolfo 12 miles (20 kilometres) southeast of the Italian capital.

The present St Peter's Basilica – the Vatican City's most visited attraction – ranks as the largest Christian church in the world; it is also undoubtedly one of the most handsome, designed first by Antonio da Sangallo and later by Michelangelo between the 1530s and 1560s. Much of its ornate carving is by Bernini, who also designed the impressive double colonnade surrounding St Peter's Square. The Vatican Museums contain a fine collection of ancient Roman statuary, and a number of priceless works of art by such masters as Fra Angelico, Raphael, Titian and Leonardo Da Vinci. Some of Michelangelo's last and best paintings adorn the ceiling and one wall of the nearby Sistine Chapel. The artist is said to have completed the entire work while lying on his back on precarious scaffolding near the ceiling.

The administration

The pope's dual role as both head of the Roman Catholic Church and Bishop of Rome includes the responsibility for the legislative, executive and judicial affairs of the entirely independent Vatican State. The state's borders and the sovereignty of the pope were recognized in the Lateran Treaty of 1929. The Cardinal Secretary of State is responsible for foreign affairs: the Vatican maintains international relations through ambassadors (known as *nuncios* or *pronuncios*) in about 80 countries throughout the world.

Pope John Paul II (*below*), born 1920 as Karol Wojtyla, was elected in 1978. He is the only Pole to have held the office. The pope is the spiritual head of the Roman Catholic Church and the Bishop of Rome.

FACT BOX

THE COUNTRY
Official name:
The State of Vatican City
Land area: 109 acres (0.44 km²)
Main river: Tiber

THE GOVERNMENT
Head of State:
Pope
Head of Government:
Governor (internal affairs)/Cardinal Secretary of State (foreign affairs)
Judiciary: Supreme Tribunal of the Signature, Tribunal of the Sacred Roman Rota (religious cases); civil courts
Armed forces: Swiss Guard (papal personal guard). Total strength: 120 men

THE PEOPLE
Population (1990):
about 1,000
Language: Italian
Religion: Roman Catholic

THE ECONOMY
Currency: Vatican lira/Italian lira
Transport: Length of railways (1987): 0.53 mi (862 m)
Communications:
Number of daily newspapers (1988): 1 Circulation: 70,000

The colourful uniform of the Swiss Guard (*above*) was, it is said, designed by the great Renaissance artist Michelangelo.

Vatican citizens

Most of the Vatican City's population are nuns and priests who work in administrative posts on behalf of the Church. Day-to-day administration of the City is the responsibility of the Governor, to whom the colourfully dressed Swiss Guard (the pope's official bodyguard) reports. This corps of 120 men have been charged with the duty of protecting the pope since the 1500s. The Vatican administers civil law only; criminals are handed over to the Rome police.

Nearly 4,000 employees commute each day into the City to maintain such operations as the City's railway communications centre, its postal organization (including the printing of postage stamps), its telephone and telegraph systems, water supply, lighting and street-cleaning amenities, and its health care services and law courts. The Vatican's famous banking system also employs a number of people in its mint, and in its investment and licensing offices. Non-resident workers come into the Vatican to work on its radio station and its daily newspaper, *Osservatore Romano*. Some act as guides, security guards or cleaners in the museums, archives and library. The state also depends economically on bequests and donations to the Church.

The Vatican City (*below*) lies entirely within the city of Rome, Italy's capital. The world's smallest independent country, it contains large blocks of accommodation for its citizens. The gardens of Pope Leo IV cover half of the city's area while the Chapel and St Peter's Basilica lie in the southeast.

1 Vatican Museums
2 Pinacoteca Art Gallery
3 Greenhouses
4 Summer Palace of Pius IV
5 Old Observatory
6 Tapestry Workshop
7 Governor's Palace
8 Ethiopian College
9 Wall of Leo IV
10 Radio Station
11 Railway Station
12 Mosaic Factory
13 Sacristy
14 Sistine Chapel
15 Papal Palace

16 Swiss Guards' Barracks
17 Polyglot Press
18 Post Office
19 Belvedere Courtyard
20 Citizens' Apartments

0 metres 200
0 yards 220

St. Peter's Square (*top*), the splendid piazza dominated by St Peter's Basilica, is the destination of several thousand pilgrims every Easter Sunday. The pope delivers his Easter message from a balcony.

Cardinals and bishops (*above*) gather in the Sistine Chapel during a bishop's synod. Cardinals from all over the world carry the collective responsibility for the election of popes.

San Marino

THE "MOST SERENE" REPUBLIC OF SAN Marino is a tiny independent state entirely surrounded by Italy. It lies in the northeastern foothills of the Apennine Mountains, 12 miles (19 kilometres) from the Adriatic Sea. San Marino ranks as Europe's third smallest state after the Vatican City and Monaco. The capital, San Marino City, lies on the upper slopes of Mount Titano, a mountain which has three major peaks. Three medieval towers, linked by a curtain wall, crown these points. The highest peak reaches 2,478 feet (755 metres). These three towers symbolize the country, appearing on its flag as well as on the postage stamps which are prized by collectors all over the world.

San Marino was traditionally founded by, and named after, Saint Marinus, a Christian stonemason, who took to the mountains in the early 300s to escape religious persecution. In the following centuries a succession of religious communities established themselves in the rugged country, which claimed the status of an independent republic in the 1300s. The pope recognized the independence of San Marino in 1631. The San Marinese celebrate their national day on the eve of Saint Marinus' day, September 3, with colourful parades, music, dancing and festivities of all kinds.

The world's oldest republic

Despite the fact that Italy has always surrounded it and dominated it politically and economically, San Marino boasts a proud tradition of independence. This, in part, reflects its forbiddingly mountainous terrain. Its constitution dates from 1262 and is still

FACT BOX

THE COUNTRY
Official name: Republic of San Marino
Capital: San Marino
Land regions: Rugged mountain terrain throughout the country
Land area: 24 sq mi (61 km²)
Climate: Mild climate with ample rainfall. Winter temperatures can fall below freezing
Main rivers: Ausa, Fiumicello, San Marino, Marano
Highest elevation: Mount Titano 2,478 ft (755 m)
Lowest elevation: Ausa river 164 ft (50 m) above sea level

THE GOVERNMENT
Form of Government: Parliamentary republic

Head of State: 2 captains-regent, serving for 6 months
Head of Government: Regents and Congress of State
Administrative areas: 10 districts (*castelli*)
Legislature: Grand and General Council with 60 members, elected to 5-year terms
Judiciary: Supreme court "Council of Twelve", office of captains-regent, civil and criminal appeals judges, district courts
Armed forces: Military service not obligatory, but all citizens between ages 16 and 55 can be called upon to defend the state. Small unit "milizia" with 180 men as honorary guard

THE PEOPLE
Population (1990): 23,000
Language: Italian
Religion: Roman Catholic (94%)

THE ECONOMY
Currency: Italian lira
Gross Domestic Product per person: n.a.
Annual Growth Rate: n.a.
Trade balance in US$: n.a.
Goods exported: Stamps, tiles, wood, machinery, ceramics, wine, wool, hides, chemicals, textiles, furniture
Trading partners: Mainly Italy
Communications: Number of daily newspapers (1988): 6

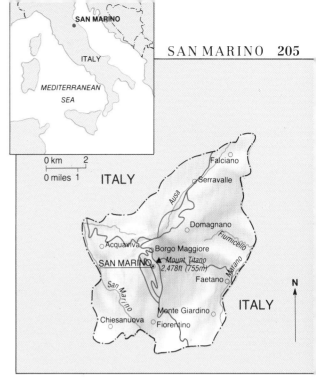

in force. The establishment of San Marino's independence made it unusual in comparison with many of its neighbouring states, nearly all of which were absorbed into the kingdom of Italy during the unification that took place in the late 1800s.

The Grand and General Council, which has 60 members elected for five-year terms, governs the country. From among its members, two "captains-regent" appoint the heads of the 10 government departments. Together with these 10, the captains-regent form the Congress of State, or Cabinet. Political parties are much the same as those in Italy and power is usually in the hands of a coalition of political parties. Women obtained the vote only in the 1960s.

Trading agreements

In 1861, during the period of Italian unification, San Marino entered into an agreement with Italy. The larger country guaranteed both protection and financial assistance in return for customs and excise benefits and a monopoly on San Marino's salt and tobacco imports. The country also earns part of its living by allowing special tax advantages to companies registered inside it, and by printing and selling postage stamps.

Tourism is the country's major source of income: the capital has many historic buildings and attracts well over two million visitors every year. Locally made jewellery, silks, leather goods and ceramics fill the numerous souvenir shops. Sweet dessert wine made from local grapes can be found in the restaurants and hotels. Ceramics, leather and textile industries flourish in the suburban areas surrounding the capital.

The San Marinese

Around a quarter of the population lives in the countryside where, although the soil is generally rocky and poor, the mild climate and ample rainfall enable farmers to grow a variety of crops. Barley, wheat, vegetables and fruit constitute the main harvests; herds of cattle and sheep graze on the hill slopes, producing milk, cheese, butter, wool and hides for tanning. Quarries export stone and lime to Italy, and supply the raw materials for the tile industry.

Culturally, the people are virtually identical with the Italians of the surrounding region. They speak Italian and belong to the Roman Catholic faith. Educational facilities have much in common with those of Italy and many San Marinese students finish their schooling at colleges and universities over the border in Italy.

The walled city of San Marino (*above left*), capital of the small nation that forms an enclave in northeastern Italy, is spectacularly situated on Mount Titano. San Marino has been an independent republic for almost 700 years.

San Marino's picturesque setting (*above*) and sunny summer weather attract more than 2 million visitors every year.

The independent state of San Marino (*top right*) lies entirely within Italy. Most of the country clings to the rugged hillsides of the Apennine mountains.

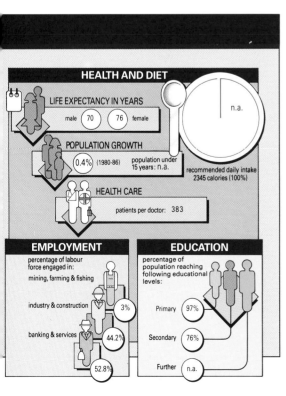

Malta

REPUBBLIKA TA' MALTA

THE REPUBLIC OF MALTA CONSISTS OF the Mediterranean islands of Malta, Gozo and Comino, as well as the much smaller uninhabited islands of Cominotto and Filfla. Malta's capital, Valletta, lies on the east coast. Two-thirds of the entire population of the country live there, crowded onto its long, thin peninsulas and spreading inland. The islands represent the tops of submerged mountains that connect Sicily and North Africa: their position at the centre of the Mediterranean has provided landfall for sailors of all centuries, from Odysseus (legendarily detained here by the nymph Calypso) to Saint Paul (shipwrecked here) and the Allies in World War II.

Malta's early history

The first human settlements date from the New Stone Age, about 5,000 years ago. These people left "Mother Goddess" statues and remains of what appear to be temples at Tarxien, Hagar Qim, Muajdra and Hal Saflieni. In ancient times the islands were occupied by Phoenicians, Carthaginians, and Romans. Byzantines, Arabs and Normans were among the rulers of Malta in the Middle Ages. Finally, in AD 1530, the Holy Roman Emperor Charles V gave Malta to the Knights of the Order of St John of Jerusalem (the Knights Hospitallers, whose emblem was what is now called the Maltese Cross) after they had been driven by the Turks from the island of Rhodes. It was the Knights who built the massive fortifications still visible at Valletta, and many churches in the country, thoroughly establishing the Roman Catholic faith which today remains the predominant religion of the population.

Napoleon Bonaparte seized Malta on his way to Egypt in 1798, only to lose it again to the English two years later. The English thereafter retained control of Malta for more than 150 years, and their influence is still widespread.

Malta was particularly valuable as a naval base for the Allies during World War II, and the heroism of its people was recognized with the remarkable award of a British medal of honour (the George Cross) at the end of the war. However, even when independence was granted in 1964, it was a further 10 years before Malta joined the British Commonwealth.

In many ways, Malta today is neither European nor African: in political terms, the country is determinedly neutral and is thus quite prepared to have friendly relations both with Italy to the north and Libya to the south. To some extent this reflects the fact that the population of Malta is itself a mixture of the various strands of its historical past. Even the national language, which only attained a written form during the 1900s, is a compound of western Arabic with many Italian and a few Greek words. English, however, is also an official language.

The economy

Malta's soil is rocky, founded on porous limestone bedrock, and relatively infertile. Natural resources are few, but the climate is comparatively mild, although sea winds may attain considerable force. Rainfall of more than 20 inches (480 millimetres) per year is the average. Nearly half the population of Malta is engaged in agriculture, cultivating their terraced fields on the rugged

FACT BOX

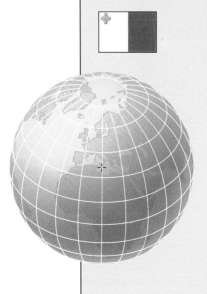

THE COUNTRY
Official name: Republic of Malta
Capital: Valletta
Land regions: Plateau in W, hilly crests and basins in N, il-Ghasel lowland in NE, hill country in S and SW
Land area: Total: 122 sq mi (316 km²). Malta 95 sq mi (246 km²), Gozo 26 sq mi (67 km²), Comino 1.1 sq mi (2.8 km²)
Climate: Mediterranean with dry, hot summers and mild winters
Main rivers:
Highest elevation: Bingemma Heights 829 ft (253 m)
Lowest elevation: Sea level along the coast

THE GOVERNMENT
Form of Government: Parliamentary republic
Head of State: President
Head of Government: Prime Minister
Administrative areas: 6 districts
Legislature: House of Representatives (69 members serving 5-year terms)
Judiciary: Criminal, civil, special courts
Armed forces: Voluntary Total strength: 751 men

THE PEOPLE
Population (1990): 353,000
Language: Maltese, English
Religion: Roman Catholic (98%)

THE ECONOMY
Currency: Maltese lira
Gross Domestic Product per person (1990): US$6,559
Annual Growth Rate (1985-90): 6.1%
Trade balance in US$ (1989): – $640 mill
Goods imported: Semi-manufactured/manufactured goods, fuel, machinery, motor vehicles, chemical products, food
Goods exported: Textiles, potatoes, vegetables, edible oil, flowers, wine, tobacco
Trading partners: Great Britain, Germany, Italy
Communications: Number of daily newspapers (1988): 3

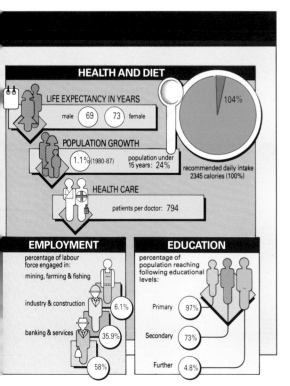

HEALTH AND DIET

LIFE EXPECTANCY IN YEARS

male 69   73 female

104%

POPULATION GROWTH

1.1% (1980-87)   population under 15 years: 24%

recommended daily intake 2345 calories (100%)

HEALTH CARE

patients per doctor: 794

EMPLOYMENT

percentage of labour force engaged in:

mining, farming & fishing

industry & construction   6.1%

banking & services   35.9%

58%

EDUCATION

percentage of population reaching educational levels:

Primary   97%

Secondary   73%

Further   4.8%

Malta (*top right*) lies roughly halfway between Italy and North Africa. Many Europeans have holiday homes on the islands.

Projecting balconies (*above left*) enable the tenants of this apartment building in Valletta to take the air. Old high-rise buildings house many of the inhabitants of Malta and Gozo.

Brightly-painted boats (*above right*) throng one of the many fine natural harbours that have made Malta a centre for Mediterranean shipping since the island was colonized by the Phoenicians.

hillsides. Locally grown produce includes cauliflowers, onions, grapes, potatoes, tomatoes and wheat, as well as milk, pork and poultry.

To make a living, many of the population work at the shipbuilding and repair yards, as well as in construction, light manufacturing industry or tourism. Residents include a number of retired Britons attracted by relatively low rates of taxation.

Malta is nominally ruled by a president, although the prime minister of the 69-member House of Representatives actually holds executive power as the leader of the Cabinet. Education is free and compulsory for children between the ages of 6 and 16, in both public and religious (Roman Catholic) schools. The University of Malta is located in Msida, near Valletta. Instruction at all levels is in both English and Maltese.

The main tourist attractions include some outstanding examples of Baroque and Renaissance art and architecture. More than 750,000 tourists, on average, visited the islands each year during the 1980s.

GREECE

All visitors to Greece comment on the exceptionally rich blue of the sky, the glimmering turquoise of the sea, and the whiteness of the houses, rocks and sand. The country's landscape has a wild and natural beauty, being for the most part dominated by rugged hills and mountains, and numerous intricately shaped islands. Long sea inlets reach into the rocky coastline creating deep bays between rocky promontories. But Greece is not a gentle land, and its working people have always had to struggle for their survival and means of livelihood.

Many of the principles of Western democratic government, aesthetic ideals, scientific and philosophic analysis and inquiry have their roots in this one small country. To the casual visitor it may seem that modern Greece is still directly connected with the splendid monuments of Mycenae and Tiryns described by Homer, the open-air theatres were performances of works by Sophocles and Euripides took place, and the graceful temples of Greek gods and goddesses.

But the thread of continuity has been broken many times during the intervening centuries, especially during the long years of Turkish occupation when the Greek sense of independence and pride suffered greatly. Nevertheless, Greece is a country where the past is dramatically visible in the shape of its monuments of classical architecture and art, and in the legends of the gods and heroes which still provide vivid insights into human nature.

For modern Greeks, this classical ancestry can represent a burden as well as a source of pride. Acclaimed as the inventors of the concept of democracy, many Greeks have had to live for generations in extreme poverty, often suffering from political oppression – quite the opposite of the democratic ideal.

Because of its favourable location in the eastern Mediterranean, Greece long ago became a bridge between Europe, Asia and Africa, and a link between the cultural forces of East and West. However, in recent centuries this strategic position has proved to be more of a source of weakness than strength, and the country has suffered from numerous invasions and occupations by foreign powers.

A visitor to Greece cannot fail to appreciate the fine scenery and the archaeological splendours that the country has to offer, but it would be a pity to concentrate on these things and to ignore the complexities and qualities of the Greek people themselves. They are a highly individualistic nation: hospitable yet aloof, and bound by a strong sense of tradition.

SINCE GREECE GAINED INDEPENDENCE from Turkish domination in 1829, the country has seldom been free from political and economic difficulties. During the first part of this century, the country was divided between a political group who supported a republic, and royalists who wanted a monarchy. During World War II, bands of freedom fighters (*andartes*), mainly led by Communists, fought bravely against German occupation. After the war, the old antagonism re-emerged, shifting to confrontations between the Communists and the pro-royalty faction. A bloody civil war resulted, lasting from 1946 to 1949. The Western powers provided massive military aid to the royalists, who in 1952 were able to proclaim the restoration of the monarchy.

A precarious stability was maintained for the next decade, but this relied on a policy of outlawing the Communist Party and any left-wing movements which might be seen as a threat to the ruling regime.

The rule of the Colonels

The year 1963 saw the emergence of the Centre Union Party under the leadership of the former liberal George Papandreou, but on the eve of new elections in 1967 a group of junior army officers staged a takeover and martial law was declared. During the seven years of what became known as the "Colonels' Regime", the constitution was suspended and civil rights severely limited. In 1974, conflict in Cyprus ended the regime, following Turkey's invasion of the island to protect the Turkish Cypriot minority. The elder statesman Constantine Caramanlis (b.1907) became the leader of the "New

Democracy " party which, as a successor of Greece's right-wing parties, formed a civil "Government of National Unity". However, most Greek people voted against the restoration of the monarchy and for the creation of a democratic republic.

Under the 1975 constitution the president was to be elected every five years by a two-thirds majority, and this ensured a strong governmental power base. Political life began to get back to normal, and the left was reintegrated into the political system.

The Papandreou scandal

The 1981 election produced a clear winner in the shape of the Pan-Hellenic Socialist Movement (PASOK), which under Andreas Papandreou (b. 1919) gained around 48 per cent of the vote, and went on to form the first Socialist government in Greek history. However, after eight years of rule the image of Greece's leaders had been tainted by corruption and scandal which shattered the ideals of the people and brought the political life of several politicians to an abrupt end. The Greek people seem to now favour a policy of "catharsis", the cleansing of the state and administrative machinery.

Certain fundamental features of the Greek political system and culture were personified in the figure of Papandreou. In the shape of PASOK he created a modern and well-organized party, but at the same time he led his party in an autocratic fashion, purged opponents from its ranks, and established a dangerous "cult of personality" in Greek politics.

The 1989 elections ended Papandreou's rule over the country. The so-called "New

In traditional uniform (*above*), an *evzone* (soldier) stands on guard at the tomb of the country's Unknown Warrior. The soldier's tasselled cap and pom-pommed slippers derive from Albanian traditional dress.

FACT BOX

THE COUNTRY
Official name: Republic of Greece
Capital: Athens
Land regions: Central Pindus, Thessaly, Salonika Plain, Macedonia-Thrace, Peloponnesus, SE Uplands, Ionian and Aegean Islands, Crete
Land area: 50,949 sq mi (131,957 km²)
Climate: Mediterranean (mild, wet winters, hot, dry summers). Continental in N mountains.
Main rivers: Vardar, Aliakmon, Pinios, Arakhthos
Highest elevation: Olympus 9,570 ft (2,917 m) above sea level
Lowest elevation: Sea level along the coast

THE GOVERNMENT
Form of Government: Parliamentarian republic
Head of State: President
Head of Government: Prime Minister
Administrative areas: 52 *nomoi* (departments) plus Mount Athos (self-governing)
Legislature: National Assembly with 300 members, elected to 4-year terms
Judiciary: Special Supreme Tribunal. Jurisdiction divided into administrative, criminal and civil law
Armed forces: Total strength: 214,000 Conscription: men must serve 21 months in army, 25 months in

navy and 23 months in air force after age 21

THE PEOPLE
Population (1990): 10,046,000
Language: Greek
Religion: Greek Orthodox (97%) Muslim (1%)

THE ECONOMY
Currency: Drachma
Gross Domestic Product per person (1990): US$6,566
Annual Growth Rate (1985-90): 1.8%
Trade balance in US$ (1987): − $8,823 mill
Goods imported: Manufactured goods, mineral oil/oil products, machinery, water vehicles, chemical products, iron and steel

Orestias

BULGARIA

MACEDONIA

Komotini

Serrai Drama Xanthi

Kilkis Kavalla

Vardar Struma Alexandroupolis

(Axios)

ALBANIA

Florina Yiannitsa *Thasos*

Kastoria Thessaloniki (Salonika)

Veroia

Kozani Katerini *Khalkidhiki* *Samothraki*

Peninsula Mount

Mount Olympus ▲ Gulf Athos ▲

9,570ft (2,917m) of Moudhros

Salonika *Limnos*

Ioannina

Strait of Otranto Trikkala Larisa

Pinios

Kardhitsa Volos TURKEY

Kerkira Othris Northern Sporades

(Corfu) Mountains

Paxoi Arta Lamia Skopelos

Gulf of Evvoia Skiros Mitilini

Lesbos

Agrinion Evvoia Kimi

Levkas Levadheia Khalkis Aegean Khios

Ithaki Thivai Sea Khios

Ionian Marathon (Chios) 0 km 100 200

Kefallinia Elevsis Megara ATHENS (ATHINAI) Samos 0 miles 100

(Cephalonia) Patrai Piraeus Samos

Sea (Patras) Andros N

Zakinthos Korinthos Tinos Ikaria Patmos

(Zante) (Corinth) Saronic Siros Mikonos Leros

Pirgos Gulf Kea Kalimnos

Gulf Peloponnesus Kithnos Paros Kos

of Tripolis Serifos Naxos Kos

Kiparissia Argos Gulf Sifnos Amorgos Astipalaia Rodhos

Kalamai of Simi

Sparti Argolis Ios Tilos Rhodes

Gulf Milos Sikinos Lindos

of Thira

Messini Gulf Anafi Karpathos

of Kithira

Mediterranean Laconia Kasos

Sea of Crete

Sea Andikithira

Khania (Canea) Iraklion (Candia)

Rethimnon Sitia

Crete

Greece (*right*) is a
small country, and is
divided by mountains
and water into a large
number of separate
regions. Its territory
includes the large is-
land of Crete and
about 450 other is-
lands which make up
20 per cent of its area.

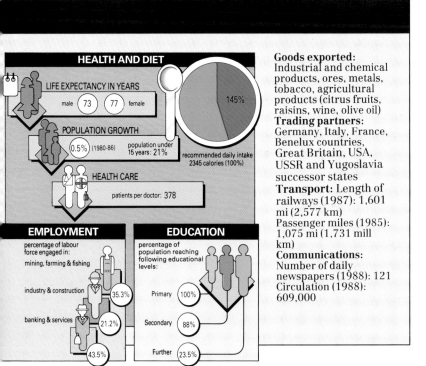

HEALTH AND DIET

LIFE EXPECTANCY IN YEARS

male (73) (77) female

145%

POPULATION GROWTH

(0.5%) (1980-86) population under
15 years: 21%

recommended daily intake
2345 calories (100%)

HEALTH CARE

patients per doctor: 378

EMPLOYMENT

percentage of labour
force engaged in:

mining, farming & fishing

industry & construction 35.3%

banking & services 21.2%

43.5%

EDUCATION

percentage of
population reaching
educational
levels:

Primary (100%)

Secondary (88%)

Further (23.5%)

Goods exported:
Industrial and chemical
products, ores, metals,
tobacco, agricultural
products (citrus fruits,
raisins, wine, olive oil)
Trading partners:
Germany, Italy, France,
Benelux countries,
Great Britain, USA,
USSR and Yugoslavia
successor states
Transport: Length of
railways (1987): 1,601
mi (2,577 km)
Passenger miles (1985):
1,075 mi (1,731 mill
km)
Communications:
Number of daily
newspapers (1988): 121
Circulation (1988):
609,000

Democracy" group became the leading
party, supported by a left-wing coalition.

The Communists today still represent a
powerful force in Greek politics, in spite of
the fact that their proportion of the vote has
remained stagnant at around 10 per cent
since 1974. Their influence is particularly
strong among the trade unions, which are
nevertheless divided along party lines. In a
country with a small pool of employees and
few socialist traditions, this has led to a
weakening in the representation of workers' interests. The same can be said for
broad areas of public life, and in the universities and professional associations.

In terms of foreign policy, Greece's ties
with the West have shaped all its activities.
Greece joined NATO in 1952, and became a
full member of the European Community in
1981, having been an associate member
since 1961. In 1988 Papandreou initiated a
Greco-Turkish dialogue, bringing hope that
peace might eventually take the place of the
constant disputes that have characterized
these two countries for so long.

DISTINCTIVE FEATURES OF THE GREEK landscape include rugged mountains (which cover much of the mainland), dramatic coastal areas where long fingers of land stretch into the clear blue sea, and clusters of islands scattered over the waters of the Aegean, Ionian and Cretan Seas. Nearly 450 islands make up some 20 per cent of the entire land region of Greece, but there are many more tiny islets in Greek territorial waters. Except for a few districts in Thessaly, no part of the country is more than 50 miles (80 kilometres) from the sea. Although the total area of Greece is much smaller than that of Portugal, the deeply-carved bays and long tongues of land give it a length of coastline greater than that of Spain and Portugal together.

Mountains and uplands cover some 70 per cent of the entire land area, including the islands (which are themselves the tips of submerged mountain ranges). Deforestation and the resulting process of erosion have greatly affected the quality of the soil. In the upland regions this tends to be poor, stony and either bare of any vegetation, or covered with thorny scrub plants typical of the Mediterranean *maquis*.

Land regions

In the complexity of its contours and in the variety of its natural features, Greece can be said to surpass every country in Europe. The mountain ranges and the sea divide the country into numerous land regions, while each of the many islands has its own unique qualities and differences.

In terms of geological structure Greece can be separated into two areas. On the western side of the mainland, parallel to the coast, there runs the complex system of the Pindus Mountain Range, which forms the backbone of the Balkan Peninsula, and rise to heights of over 7,800 feet (2,400 metres). Composed mainly of limestone and sandstone, these are a continuation of the Dinara Planina mountains of Yugoslavia, and run through the Peloponnesus.

The eastern side of the country features a geologically ancient range, consisting of a continuation of the Pelagonian and Rhodope mountains of the north. Both of the mountain systems of Greece have been lowered, elevated and distorted by massive geological movement, and shifts in the Earth's crust continue to this day, making Greece an active earthquake zone.

The upland regions are unproductive as agricultural land or as pasturage, but on the lower slopes of the mountains some villages have combined small-scale shepherding and the raising of livestock with the cultivation of orchards, tobacco and cereal crops. However, such communities are becoming increasingly deserted since the

younger generation tends to move to the towns or other countries in search of a more prosperous future, and often only the old men and women are left behind to carry on an almost forgotten way of life.

Although the plains and the lowlands of Greece are not as appealing to the eyes of a tourist, they have always been a focus for settlement and agricultural development. The plains of Thessaly are known as the "bread basket" of Greece, and the plains of Salonika in the northeast are an important centre of agricultural production.

Climate

Greece enjoys a characteristic Mediterranean climate with hot dry summers followed by mild wet winters. But the climate varies greatly in the different regions, depending on altitude and location. The north and inland regions experience quite cold winters and very hot summers, and in the mountain regions snow and freezing temperatures are common. The southern islands, most of the Peloponnesus and the Attic Peninsula have seasons that are less extreme in their variations. During the summer the dry wind from the north, the *meltemi*, may cause some discomfort. The western side of the mountains receives most of the annual winter rainfall, and the east of the country tends to be much drier.

A mountain landscape (*above left*) in the Peloponnesus, the rugged southern Greek peninsula, where the ancient town of Mystra (Mistras) clings to the hillside. Mystra was a major city of the later Byzantine empire.

The Greek coastline (*right*), rocky and arid, remains unchanged since Homer's hero Odysseus sailed the "wine-dark sea". In the background, however, we see a modern phenomenon: hotels and apartments.

Vegetation

The vegetation of Greece resembles that of southern Italy, but also has many features in common with Asia Minor. From sea level to a height of about 1,500 feet (460 metres), oranges, olives, vines and other typical Mediterranean crops flourish. The cypress tree is still a classic feature of the landscape, and the air is scented by the aromatic herbs typical of the scrubby *maquis*.

In the higher regions, the natural vegetation formerly consisted of oak, chestnut, beech and plane trees, as well as coniferous varieties, but Greece has suffered severely from the loss of its original forests. The destruction of the country's once dense forests started in ancient times, when the Greeks used the wood for shipbuilding and fuel. Today, the delicate ecosystems of the islands and much of the high mainland regions have been disrupted by the ravages of herds of goats and by the felling of trees for use as building materials and fuel. Nowadays only some 20 per cent of the country is forested, and these areas are particularly threatened by the modern danger of annual forest fires. Once they have started, these are very hard to contain and can destroy vast stretches of forest, leaving little more than naked rock. It takes several decades for a forest to be re-established, and inevitably many are lost for ever.

Vineyards and olive groves (*above*) make a pattern of cultivation in a fertile valley in Crete. Crete has a generally mild, dry climate, but the hot *meltemi* wind from the north may make the late summer oppressively hot.

Mouse Island (*right*) lies just off the coast of Corfu. Known in Greek as Pontikonisi, it is said to be the boat which brought the legendary Odysseus back to Ithaki and was turned to stone by Poseidon, the god of the sea.

People

GREECE'S INHABITANTS NUMBER ABOUT 10 million, of whom about 95 per cent are Greek. Minorities such as Macedonians, Turks, Albanians and Bulgarians make up the other 5 per cent.

Due to the high birth rate, the population has increased by about 20 per cent since 1940. This dramatic increase has helped to generate several waves of emigration, linked to the commercial and political development of the country.

The pattern of emigration

During the 400 years of Turkish domination, many Greeks left their native land to found business colonies in Vienna, Odessa and Alexandria. Then, during the early 1900s, many more left the country to find their fortunes in the USA. Political refugees went into exile after the civil war in 1945, and during the early 1960s many Greek workers settled in Western Europe, especially in West Germany. However, since the 1970s the number of emigrants has been falling.

Although modern Greeks see themselves as the descendants of the early Hellenistic races, other influences, including Slavic, Albanian and Italian, have left their mark over the course of centuries. However, Greeks have a strong presence, and in spite of geographical separation, they have maintained their cultural identity and developed a very definite national consciousness.

The unifying language and religion

Almost all Greeks speak modern Greek, a language which developed from classical Greek. And almost all of them belong to the Greek Orthodox Church, which occupies an important position as the state religion. Its influence pervades all aspects of both private and public life, although the effects of modernization and industrialization have brought about a change in people's values.

Greek Orthodox festivals are an important part of people's lives. In Greece, the most important holiday is Easter. Religious services accompany processions, dancing, fireworks and ample good food. A feast of lamb is traditional on Easter Sunday. Most Greeks give presents on St Basil's Day, which falls on New Year's Day, rather than on Christmas Day.

The Greek way of life

Greek food combines Mediterranean fruit and vegetables with lamb, chicken and fish. Typical dishes such as *dolmathes* (vine leaves stuffed with rice and minced meat) and *moussaka* (a delicious baked dish of aubergine and lamb) can be found all over the country. Other specialities include kebabs (pieces of meat cooked on skewers over charcoal) and tangy *feta* cheese. Olive oil also features largely in many Greek dishes.

The family unit influences all of Greek life. The family group provides protection and respect but in return requires certain responsibilities from each member of the family. Traditionally, the husband takes care of external affairs while the wife's duties revolve around caring for the family. In this respect, the position of Greek women is deeply rooted in a very definite patriarchal society. In the past, women were rarely seen alone in public and seldom participated in local affairs and decisions. However, these rigid roles have gradually become relaxed.

Until recently, the position of Greek women was also undermined by the priorities given to motherhood and marriage rather than education and professional qualifications. Although supposedly forbidden by law, the Greek dowry system (*prika*) still operates in several regions. This often takes the form of the gift of a house from the parents of the bride to the groom. In the past it was common for the father and brothers in a family to work towards a dowry for the daughter, so that the bride could be married in accordance with her standing. Also, it was customary for all the girls in one family to marry in order of age, starting with the eldest, and for brothers to remain single until all their sisters were married.

The *kafenion*, or coffee house (*above*), forms a social centre for Greek townspeople, in particular for the menfolk, traditionally great talkers and arguers. Women still occupy a secondary place in more conventional Greek society.

This shopkeeper (*left*) on the Ionian island of Corfu (Kerkira), off western Greece, has on display many of the ingredients of *horiatiki*. This is the traditional Greek salad, with olives and other vegetables, and *feta* cheese.

A kiss (*right*) is given to a priest distributing bread at a religious festival. Most Greeks belong to the Greek Orthodox Church and most communities have their own saint, whose festival is celebrated with prayer and feasting.

These traditional family customs are becoming increasingly old-fashioned and have almost died out in the cities. They are also far less widespread even in rural areas than they were in the past. The family unit is beginning to lose its importance, especially in urban areas, and there is an unmistakable move towards smaller families. Old social structures are breaking down and the attitudes towards women have undergone change. Today, many Greek women work outside the home so that they can better the often poor financial situation of the family.

The insufficient opportunities and lack of work in the countryside has in recent years led to a very rapid process of urbanization in Greece. In 1920, over 60 per cent of Greeks lived in rural areas. But, by 1981, this figure had dropped to 30 per cent, with over 3 million people living in the Greater Athens area – about one-third of the population.

By contrast, the mountain villages and islands have become desolate, with only old people remaining in residence. The dramatic population trend is reflected by centralization in and around the capital city, Athens. People flock in to find employment in industry and commerce. Athens also acts as the political and administrative centre of the country. Greece's second largest city, Thessaloniki, has also experienced a rapid population growth.

Elderly neighbours (*below*) enjoy a chat on Crete, largest and most independent of the Greek islands.

In recent decades, many islanders have moved to Athens or gone abroad.

Athens

THE CITY OF ATHENS UNIQUELY intertwines the past with the present. Hectic traffic hoots its way through the narrow streets; modern factories and apartment blocks dominate large areas; much of the city dates back no further than the 1830s, when major rebuilding followed Athens' selection as capital of the new Greek kingdom after the War of Independence. Yet this modern city boasts the *agora* (marketplace) where Socrates taught philosophy some 2,200 years ago; the open-air theatre where drama in both its tragic and its comic forms was invented in the early fifth century BC; and wherever you go, you will probably catch a view of the Parthenon, the majestic "temple of the Maiden" and greatest glory of ancient Athens, towering above the bustle and traffic.

Athens traces its history back some 5,000 years, when the ancient Greeks established a settlement on the great flat-topped hill which became known as the *Acropolis*, the "high city". Over the centuries, the city spread out below the hill, taking the name of Athens from its patron goddess Athena. During the fifth century BC it became the cultural centre of Greece, attracting philosophers, dramatists, poets, historians, statesmen and architects whose works have influenced the West until the present day.

The hill of the gods
The golden age of Athens comes forcibly to mind when you visit the Acropolis, where the ruins of a dramatic array of temples and public buildings have survived the ravages of time. Early in the history of Athens, the hill ceased to be a dwelling site, and was dedicated to the glory of the gods. A huge Persian army sacked the city in 480 BC, destroying the temples of the Acropolis; but 33 years later, under the leadership of Pericles, the Athenians began to rebuild. It is the great structures of this period that dominate the Acropolis today, including the monumental gateway of the Propylaea, the restored Temple of Athena Nike, and the vast. Theatre of Dinoysus, the birthplace of European drama. Loftiest and loveliest of all stands the marble temple of Athena, the Parthenon, with its massive columns and celebrated friezes. Like other buildings on the Acropolis, the Parthenon suffered serious damage during the Ottoman Turkish occupation. In 1801 the British statesman Lord Elgin purchased some of the finest sculptural decorations and removed them to London. The "Elgin Marbles" remain on display in the British Museum, in spite of recent Greek demands for their return.

Originally, the buildings of the Acropolis were brilliantly coloured with paint and gilding. This decoration faded centuries ago, but the golden patina of age gave a warm hue to the stone until comparatively recently. The pallid colouring of the marble today is a recent and tragic phenomenon – in the past 25 years, chemical pollution has done more damage than 20 centuries of recorded time. In an attempt to save the glorious ruins, entrance to the buildings has been forbidden, and many statues have been removed to the Acropolis Museum for protection, to be replaced by replicas cast in concrete.

Life of the marketplace
The Acropolis may represent the most dramatic vision of ancient Athens, but everywhere in the city you encounter echoes of the past. Visit the famous "flea market" of the Monastiraki in quest of bargains, and you will find blacksmiths plying their trade as they have done for 2,600 years in the street of their patron god,

Hephaestos. Turn a corner, and you come to the Agora, the ancient marketplace, once the centre of Athenian life, dedicated not only to trade but to athletic displays, dramatic competitions and the discussion of philosophy. Here the philosopher Socrates (470-399 BC) taught his pupils; here, some 450 years later, Saint Paul preached Christianity to the Athenians. Archaeologists have uncovered the Agora's shops and temples, preserving the remains of public buildings such as the *stoas* (covered arcades). The Stoa of Attalus, built between 159 and 138 BC, was restored in the 1950s, and now forms a museum.

Modern Athens too has its great squares humming with life, most notably Syntagma ("Constitution") Square, the city's administrative centre. Here the *Evzones*, or Presidential Guards, patrol Parliament House in their very distinctive uniforms, including the

The majestic Parthenon (*left*), temple of the goddess Athena, dominates the Athenian skyline from its site atop the hill called the Acropolis. Erected between 447 and 432 BC, the marble building measures 237 × 110 ft (72 × 34 m). Sadly, chemical pollution now threatens the fabric of the Parthenon and other classic Greek buildings.

Embroidered cloth (*far left*) is sold by an Athenian street vendor. For centuries, Greek handicraft workers have been noted for fine embroidery.

Young Athenians (*below left*) enjoy a social gathering at a *taverna* (restaurant-café). Here, one may take one's choice from a number of tasty dishes, and dance to *rebetika* and *bouzouki* folk music.

fustanella, a short kilt said to derive from the garb of Roman legionaries. The Athenian *kafenia* (coffee houses) continue to encourage the art of conversation so popular in the city's golden age, but many prefer the **tavernas** (restaurant-cafés), where you may listen to *rebetika* (folk songs) and dance to *bouzouki* music. The steeply slanting streets of the Plaka district contain numerous delightful *tavernas*, specializing in Greek delicacies, but the best *bouzouki* music is probably to be found in the port area of Piraeus.

The Athens festival

Perhaps the ageless spirit of Athens is better captured by a visit to the Odeon of Herodes Atticus, built in about AD 170. In this vast theatre, seating up to 5,000 people, classic Greek tragedies (as well as more modern works) are still performed during the annual Athens Festival of music and drama. On a hot summer evening, the audience is seated splendidly, if not very comfortably, on marble benches, with 32 steeply raked rows curving in a semi-circle around the stage. The audience and language are modern, the white marble facing of the seats reflects the work of contemporary restorers; but some 2,000 years ago an Athenian audience sat in this same theatre to watch perhaps the same play. Here in Athens the past is never very far away.

Athens (*right*), connected to its port of Piraeus, was once the intellectual and artistic treasure-house of the world. Sights include the Parthenon (9), Stoa of Attalus (6), Erechtheum (8), Theatre of Dionysus (10), Odeon (11), Temple of Zeus (12) and Hephaesteum (7). Athens University (1) and Parliament (2) reflect modern history, while other treasures can be found at the Archaeological Museum (3), the Benaki Museum (4) and the Byzantine Museum (5).

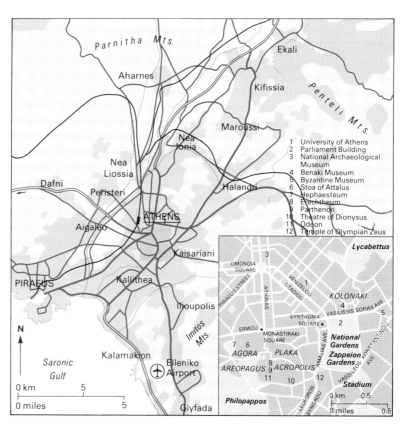

1 University of Athens
2 Parliament Building
3 National Archaeological Museum
4 Benaki Museum
5 Byzantine Museum
6 Stoa of Attalus
7 Hephaesteum
8 Erechtheum
9 Parthenon
10 Theatre of Dionysus
11 Odeon
12 Temple of Olympian Zeus

Crete and Rhodes

CRETE, THE SOUTHERNMOST GREEK island in the Mediterranean Sea, is the largest of the Greek islands. About a fifth of Crete's 500,000 inhabitants live in or near the island's main city, Iraklion.

Apart from the fascinating archaeological sites all over the island, Crete's beautiful landscape and colourful traditions attract many visitors every year. Tourists enjoy the awe-inspiring views from the Cretan mountains, the spectacular Samaria gorge, and the peace and tranquility offered by the remote beaches of the southern coast.

Early Crete

The first major civilization in the region of Greece centred on Crete as long ago as 3000 BC. It is known as the Minoan culture, named after King Minos, the legendary ruler of Crete. The Minoans were expert sailors, skilful builders and sophisticated craftsmen who grew wealthy from trade. The remains of elaborate buildings, such as the palace of Knossos on Crete, provide evidence of the Minoans' prosperity and building skills. They had a system of writing but scholars do not know what language they spoke, except that it was not Greek. The Minoans dominated the Aegean world until about 1450 BC when the nearby volcanic island of Thira exploded. Experts believe that this catastrophe and its after-effects weakened the Minoan civilization and brought it to an end.

The palace of King Minos at Knossos, a few miles southeast of Iraklion, contains Crete's most important Minoan remains. The English archaeologist, Sir Arthur Evans, started unearthing the enormous palace in 1900 and had it partially rebuilt. He showed that the king's residence was surrounded by palatial villas containing frescoes and plaster reliefs. These include scenes of "bull-dancing" (in which young men and women were depicted leaping over bull's backs) as well as many maritime themes. The superb and unforgettable archaeological museum in Iraklion now houses most of the treasures of the palace. The rest of Crete also contains sophisticated Minoan settlements, especially at Ayia Triadha in the south.

Crete's historical roots

Following the Romans, the Arabs and the Venetians, Ottoman Turks conquered Crete in 1669. The Christian Orthodox religion was outlawed. But the Cretans continued to speak Greek and failed to follow the new religion – Islam – with any fervour. Oppressed both by a change of official faith and by the burden of taxes, many Cretans fled to the mountains to take up the struggle against Turkish occupation.

After gaining its autonomy in 1898, Crete became a part of Greece in 1913. The island's Muslim inhabitants were uprooted in the compulsory exchange of populations in 1923, but the Turkish influence is still apparent in the architecture of some of the cities – in Rethimnon, for example, once the island's intellectual and cultural centre.

Crete's position, midway between Europe and North Africa, made it of vital strategic importance in World War II. German paratroops landed on Crete in 1941 and, after ten days, the British troops stationed there were driven off the island. Many Cretans, who played a passionate role in the struggle against the incoming forces, inflicting considerable losses on the invaders, had to flee to the mountains. Many villages were razed to the ground and the inhabitants killed during the resistance campaign. It was not until May 1945 that the occupying Germans forces finally withdrew.

Evening light adds a warm glow to the harbour at Khania (Canea) (*centre*). The port has been settled since Minoan times and is now the economic focus of western Crete.

Playful dolphins (*right*) decorate the walls of the Queen's Apartments in the Palace of Knossos on Crete. The frescoes were painted onto wet plaster, a technique which gives the images a vibrant quality.

Rhodes

Rhodes, the largest of the Dodecanese islands, lies just 12 miles (19 kilometres) from the southwest coast of Turkey. Its well-watered slopes support oleanders (the rose-like shrubs which give the island its name "island of roses"), cedars and pines.

Rhodes was once the site of the Colossus of Rhodes, one of the Seven Wonders of the Ancient World. This immense bronze statue towered over the harbour until an earthquake felled the giant in 224 BC.

Historic sites
- Mycenaean sites
- Byzantine sites
- Castle of the Knights of St John

More than 1,640ft — More than 500m
650 to 1,640ft — 200 to 500m
Less than 650ft — Less than 200m

Rodt
Ialysos
Maritsa
Kamiros • Kalavardha
Kastellos
Monolithos
Pheraklos
Lindos
Kattavia

0 km 20
0 miles 10

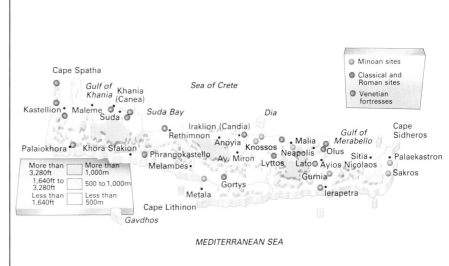

The islands of Crete (*above*) is situated far to the southest of the Greek mainland. Crete separates the Mediterranean from the Aegean. It was the home of the ancient maritime Minoan civilization 5,000 years ago.

Recent political events

The civil war which broke out in Greece after the end of World War II began to affect Crete in 1947. Government troops landed, marking the start of the battle against Cretan partisans. The latter were forced to surrender in the Samaria gorge.

In the 1963 elections, the vast majority of Cretans voted for Georgios Papandreou (1888-1968) who promised a liberal revitalization of Greece. In 1967 a group of military officers (who became known as "the Colonels") seized power in Greece, but the Cretans held on to their liberal beliefs. In recent elections the Cretans have voted for the socialist PASOK party of Andreas Papandreou (b. 1919), the son of Georgios.

Economy

The tourist trade provides employment for a large number of Cretan people, both in the hotel trade and in the provision of services and food. Cretan specialities include a number of seasonal dishes. In winter and spring, snails and *horta* – wild grass that tastes like spinach – are traditional delicacies. Some local people make a living selling traditional Cretan crafts such as the huge terracotta storage jars which can be seen all over the island.

The island contains useful deposits of iron ore and lignite (brown coal) in the west, and Iraklion has a growing food-processing industry. Other plants manufacture building materials, soap and leather goods.

The mountainous nature of the island makes it difficult to farm. Most agriculture is concentrated in the fertile river valleys between the upland areas. Typical Mediterranean crops such as olives, citrus fruits and grapes are grown, but recently, horticulture has become more profitable.

In 1310, the island became a base for the Knights Hospitallers of St John. Many of the fine old buildings of the original medieval town have survived, surrounded by formidable enclosing walls. Turkish forces invaded the island in 1522, claiming it for almost four centuries. Decorative mosques stand as reminders of the period of Turkish rule. Rhodes became part of Greece in 1947.

Thousands of tourists visit Rhodes each year.

The massive walls of the Residence of the Grand Master, a crusader castle (*above*) rise above the town of Rhodes. The Knights of St John occupied the island in 1310 until they were driven out by the Turks in 1522.

Mediterranean Sea

MANY MILLIONS OF VISITORS FLOCK every year to the countries of the Mediterranean with their sunny beaches, fascinating landscapes, historic sights, ancient monuments and elegant, treasure-packed cities. Superabundantly endowed by nature with a delightful climate, beautiful scenery, attractive vegetation and delicious food, the Mediterranean region has earned the title of Europe's paradise playground. Here from the earliest times, peoples and cultures from Europe, Asia and Africa have taken root, leaving fascinating traces. Everywhere, the sun shines for most of the year, and winters are mild. But the economic climate may become considerably less agreeable, as many experts are now warning.

An inland sea
The Strait of Gibraltar, formed about 5.5 million years ago, connects the Atlantic Ocean with the Mediterranean, which would otherwise be an inland sea. Without the Atlantic inflow, the almost tideless Mediterranean would simply evaporate within 1,000 years (as it has done in the past). The ocean waters flow into the Mediterranean, cleansing and renewing it. But this cleansing process is not strong enough to dispel the effects of human activity. Pollution is beginning to leave a stain on the deceptively clear waters of the Mediterranean. Natural vegetation and wildlife is at risk almost everywhere: development for tourism and industry eats into the natural habitats, while sea creatures suffer from effluents in the water. Even at Gibraltar, where sea and ocean meet, dolphins are becoming comparatively rare, while many other species, such as mud turtles, have been pushed to the edge of extinction.

About 360 million people already live in the Mediterranean region, and each year an influx of tourists causes the coastal population to double. Tourist complexes have gone up everywhere but, until relatively recently, little thought has been given to the problems arising from this huge popularity. Tourism is a major source of valuable foreign exchange, but in most Mediterranean countries the space available for development is vanishing fast, and most existing resorts are already packed during the holiday season.

Industry and tourism
Industry has played a big part in fouling the coastal waters of the Mediterranean. Indeed, many local communities in the region are beginning to consider tourism as a better source of employment than industry. Tourism relies on labour-intensive activity at a time when automation is reducing jobs in industry. And it is undeniably cleaner than most industrial processes. But here the problem is that the sheer pressure of

Mikonos (*right*) displays many of the features that make the islands of Greece among the most sought-after holiday places in the world. Fine beaches, a sunny climate and picturesque surroundings attract millions of visitors yearly. But the Mediterranean is virtually an inland sea, lacking the tides that cleanse and renew ocean resorts. The sheer popularity of the Aegean islands is creating serious problems for the region's ecology.

numbers is threatening the natural landscape. With almost all sites on the northern Mediterranean either being developed or earmarked for development, businessmen are beginning to look towards the comparatively underdeveloped North African coastline.

Countries such as Morocco are said to be "sitting on a goldmine" in terms of tourist potential. But such development will inevitably add to pollution. Industrial catastrophes, such as the oil slick that nearly inundated the Moroccan coastline in January 1990, can overwhelm an already perilous ecological situation. Today many believe that the Mediterranean, once the heartland of Western civilization, and now Europe's sunshine playground, faces environmental disaster unless steps are taken immediately. Pollution figures are hard to come by, but tourists themselves are beginning to react adversely, not only to crowded conditions, but also to recent outbreaks of pollution-caused disease at certain resorts. A UN statistic suggests that the region may receive as much as 100 billion gallons of sewage each year, much of it untreated.

The future of the Mediterranean
Some experts predict the destruction of the Mediterranean environment within 50 years unless the building boom is controlled. The environment is a finite resource, they insist, and must be protected. Yet almost all of the coastline is a potentially attractive site for development. The outlook for the 1990s is sombre, suggesting a saturated market with many tourists beginning to look elsewhere as buildings multiply and destroy the landscape, and the quality of the beaches continues to deteriorate.

Ecologists urge the need for a new approach. And already signs of a change can be seen. In Spain's Albufera, for example, an area that began to be developed as a huge tourist complex by speculators in the 1960s, the land has been cleared of buildings, and replanted with natural vegetation. Now it is a bird sanctuary for avocets, marsh harriers, and other threatened species. Such sanctuaries would continue to attract large number of visitors, but their establishment would benefit rather than threaten the endangered ecology of the region.

Benidorm (*top far right*), one of Spain's most popular resorts, has become seriously overcrowded in recent years. The Spanish government is attempting to reduce landscape destruction caused by tourism.

Perast (*above far right*), set in Kotor Bay on the Dalmation coast, enjoys the status of a national monument. Its tranquil atmosphere and comparatively unspoilt landscape reflect its remote situation.

The Mediterranean seaboard (*left*) attracts millions of tourists every year with its warm weather and sunny beaches. But this popularity has worsened pollution problems arising from industrial developments around ports.

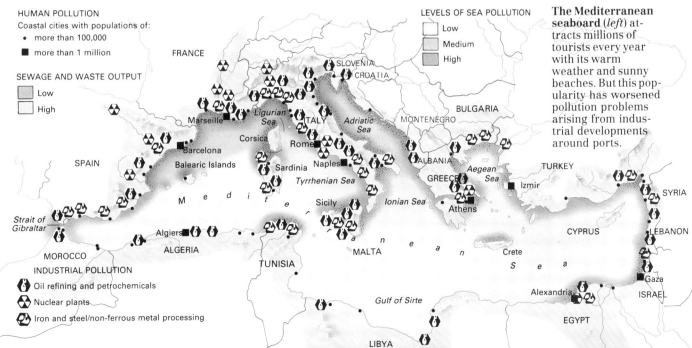

HUMAN POLLUTION

Coastal cities with populations of:

- • more than 100,000
- ■ more than 1 million

SEWAGE AND WASTE OUTPUT

Low

High

LEVELS OF SEA POLLUTION

Low

Medium

High

INDUSTRIAL POLLUTION

Oil refining and petrochemicals

Nuclear plants

Iron and steel/non-ferrous metal processing

FRANCE

SLOVENIA

CROATIA

BULGARIA

MONTENEGRO

Marseille   *Ligurian Sea*   ITALY   *Adriatic Sea*

Corsica   Rome

SPAIN   Barcelona

Balearic Islands   Sardinia   Naples   ALBANIA

Tyrrhenian Sea   GREECE   *Aegean Sea*

TURKEY

Izmir

Sicily   *Ionian Sea*

Athens

SYRIA

Strait of Gibraltar

Algiers   M e d i t e r r a n e a n   S e a

MOROCCO   ALGERIA   MALTA

Crete   CYPRUS   LEBANON

TUNISIA   Gaza

Gulf of Sirte   Alexandria   ISRAEL

EGYPT

LIBYA

Albania

THE REPUBLIC OF ALBANIA LIES ALONG the coast of the Adriatic Sea on the western side of the Balkan Peninsula. To the south, the country borders Greece. Albania's eastern and northern borders are shared with the Yugoslav successor states of Montenegro, Serbia and Macedonia. The narrow Strait of Otranto separates Albania from Italy.

Albania's landscape is rugged, and mountains cover some 70 per cent of its total area of 11,100 square miles (28,748 square kilometres). The central uplands, heavily forested with oak, elm and coniferous trees, flatten out towards the west into a marshy coastal plain. In the south, the mountains extend down to the Adriatic, forming the cliffs of the Albanian (or Ionian) Riviera.

People and history

Like their Balkan neighbours, the people of Albania are Slavic in origin. Ethnic Albanians make up 98 per cent of the country's population, and there are also small minorities of Greeks and Macedonians. Many ethnic Albanians – predominantly Muslims – live in the neighbouring territory of Kosovo, which forms part of the former Yugoslavia, but is claimed by Albania. Since Kosovo was annexed by Serbia in 1990, its inhabitants have suffered severe repression and discrimination.

The people of Albania call their nation *Shqiperi* (Land of the Eagle). It is a name well-suited to this mountainous country, which has only recently emerged from more than 50 years of isolation enforced by its former Communist government.

Albania's isolation has its origins in both tradition and recent events. As a bridgehead for conquerors of the Balkans, it has undergone invasion and has fiercely resisted foreign domination for more than 2,000 years. Albania's national hero, Scanderbeg (Gjergi Kastrioti Skerbeu, 1403-68), whose personal arms now form the national flag, led the resistance against the Ottoman Turks. Turkish rule from the later 1400s lasted until the Balkan Wars of 1912-13, when the larger Balkan nations' attempts to seize parts of Albania's territory further strengthened Albanian distrust and dislike for all foreigners. This was increased by successive occupations of the newly-independent nation by both the Central and Allied powers during World War I.

A measure of unity was imposed under Ahmed Beg Zogu (1895-1961), who was president from 1925 and King Zog I from 1928 to 1939. In 1939, Fascist Italy occupied Albania and declared it part of the Italian empire; German occupation followed in 1943-44.

Hoxha: heir to Scanderbeg

During World War II, Albania found a new national hero. In 1944, the Communists of the National Liberation Front (NLF), led by Enver Hoxha (1908-85) set up a Communist government in Tiranë, Albania's capital.

Hoxha cut off Albania from the rest of the world, and introduced policies to make the country economically self-reliant. After Hoxha's death, Albania's government sought to reform the economy and end their country's self-imposed exile. In May 1990, religious worship – banned by the Communists since 1967 – was permitted again.

FACT BOX

THE COUNTRY
Official name:
Republic of Albania

Capital: Tiranë
Land regions:
Mountainous
throughout, apart from
coastal plain
Land area: 11,100 sq
mi (28,748 km²)
Climate:
Mediterranean along
the coast, moderate in
the mountains
Main rivers: Buenë,
Drin, Mat, Shkumbin,
Vijosë
Highest elevation:
Mount Korabit 9,026 ft,
(2,751 m)
Lowest elevation: Sea
level along the coast

THE GOVERNMENT
Form of Government:
Parliamentary republic
Head of State:
President
Head of Government:
Prime Minister
Administrative areas:
26 districts, divided
into localities
Legislature: People's
Assembly with 250
members, elected by
the people for 4 years
Judiciary: Supreme
Court, 26 district courts
Armed forces: Total
strength: 42,000 plus
reservists.
Conscription: men
must serve 2 years in
army or 3 years in navy
or air force

THE PEOPLE
Population (1990):
3,250,000
Language: Albanian

Religion: Sunni Muslim
(70%), Greek Orthodox
(about 20%), Roman
Catholic (about 10%).

THE ECONOMY
Currency: Lek
**Gross National Product
per person (1987):**
US$710
Annual Growth Rate:
n.a.
Trade balance in US$:
n.a.
Goods imported: Iron
and steel, farming
machinery, mining
equipment, vehicles,
textiles, grain
Goods exported:
Mining products
(chromite, copper ore
etc.), tobacco, hides,
wool, fruit

Bajram Curri

North Albanian Alps

Drin

Lake Scutari

Shkodër   Puke   Kukës

Mount Korabit
▲9,026ft (2,751m)

Lezhë   Rrëshen   Peshkopi

Gulf of Drin

Burrel

Cape Rodonit   Krujë

MACEDONIA

Adriatic

Erzen   TIRANË

Durrës

Sea   Kavajë   Elbasan

Shkumbin   Librazhd   Lake Ohrid

Karavastas Lagoon   Lushnje   Pogradec
Gramsh

Lake Prespa

Semani   Stalin   Devoll

Fier   Berat

Korçë

Sazan

Corovode
Osum

Cape Gjuhëzes   Vlorë   Vjose

Ersekë

Tepelene

Përmet

GREECE

Gjirokaster

Drin

Sarande

N

0 km _____ 50
0 miles _____ 50

Albania (*right*), lying on the Balkan Peninsula of southeastern Europe, is one of the continent's most inaccessible and underdeveloped nations. Most of the country is mountainous; on the northern border with Montenegro the North Albanian Alps rise to around 8,500 feet (2,590 metres). The only significant flat land lies along the Adriatic coast. These rugged mountains contain important mineral resources.

The Byzantine church in Apollonia (*above*) is a place of worship for Greek Orthodox Christians. However, most Albanians are Sunni Muslims. From 1967-90, Albania's rulers banned all religious worship. Apollonia itself was an important city of Illyria, an ancient culture which formerly covered much of the area of modern Albania. The Albanian people are the last descendants of the Illyrians.

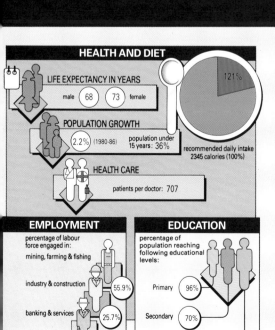

HEALTH AND DIET

LIFE EXPECTANCY IN YEARS

male (68)   (73) female

121%

POPULATION GROWTH

(2.2%) (1980-86)   population under 15 years: 36%

recommended daily intake 2345 calories (100%)

HEALTH CARE

patients per doctor: 707

EMPLOYMENT

percentage of labour force engaged in:

mining, farming & fishing

industry & construction   55.9%

banking & services   25.7%

18.4%

EDUCATION

percentage of population reaching educational levels:

Primary   96%

Secondary   70%

Further   7.2%

Trading partners: Former Yugoslavia, Czechoslovakia, Romania, Poland, Italy, France, Greece, Germany, China **Transport:** Length of railways (1991): 316 mi (509 km) **Communications:** Number of daily newspapers (1988):2 Circulation (1988): 145,000

However, popular demands for greater freedom and multi-party democracy, grew rapidly. Riots took place in Tiranë, and many thousands of Albanians attempted to migrate to Italy and Greece in search of greater opportunity.

In 1991, opposition parties were legalized. Democratic elections in that year returned the Communists to power. However, the declining economy forced the government to hold new elections in March 1992, when the Democratic Party of Albania, the main opposition group, won a large majority.

The economy

Today, Albania ranks as Europe's poorest country. Industry is not well developed, and farming is the most important sector of the economy. Albania has important mineral resources, including chromite (chromium ore), iron, copper, cobalt and nickel. In addition, there are deposits of oil and natural gas. Under the Communists, agriculture and industry were state-run. In the early 1990s, economic reforms included the removal of price controls and the rapid privatization of farmland.

FORMER YUGOSLAVIA

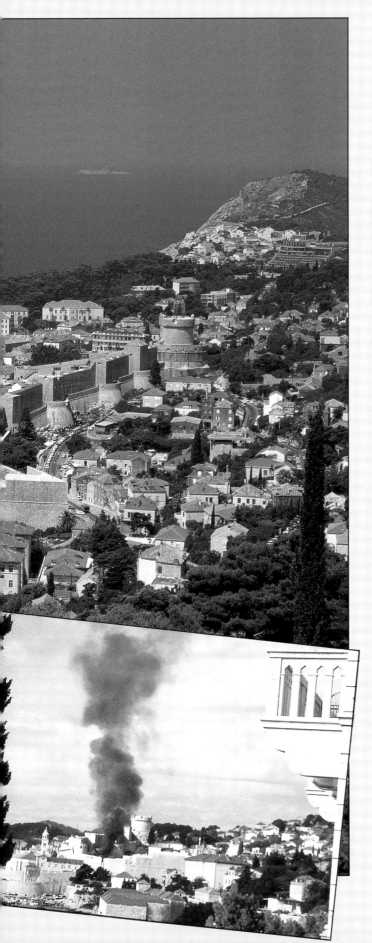

ontrasts dominate the landscape of Yugoslavia, the "land of the Southern Slavs". These geographical disparities mirror the ethnic, cultural and religious differences that divide the region's inhabitants. A violent process of separation into independent nations has split asunder the six constituent republics of former Yugoslavia. The tourist paradise of **Dubrovnik** (*left*) on the Dalmatian coast typifies the tragic effects of the conflict (*inset*).

The region's coastline is the steepest and rockiest in the Mediterranean; but inland lie vast areas of flatland, perhaps matched in Europe only by the plains of neighbouring Hungary. Zagreb, capital of strongly Roman Catholic Croatia, boasts the ancient cathedral of St Stephen – but it also contains one of Europe's finest mosques. Belgrade, capital of Eastern Orthodox Serbia, saw the construction of the huge San Marko cathedral in the 1980s, yet Serbia's most venerable monasteries are situated in Kosovo, an area mainly occupied by Muslim Albanians.

As its name indicates, Yugoslavia was dominated by Southern Slavic peoples: Serbs (about 36 per cent of the population), Croats (20 per cent), Slovenes (eight per cent) and Macedonians (six per cent). Muslim Slavs, most of whom lived in Bosnia-Hercegovina, formed about nine per cent of the population. Serbs and Croats are closely related despite their religious and cultural differences. The principal language, Serbo-Croat, is spoken by both groups but has two written forms: Croatian uses the Roman alphabet, while Serbian uses the Cyrillic (Russian) script.

Yugoslavia's cultural differences are rooted in history. The northwestern part of the region, consisting of Slovenia and Croatia, was for centuries ruled by the Catholic monarchs of the Habsburg empire. But Serbia, Bosnia-Hercegovina, Macedonia and Montenegro formed part of the Muslim Turkish Ottoman empire. As a result, there is now a broad division between an area of Western, Catholic-based culture, and an area where Eastern Orthodox, or Muslim, beliefs prevail. In 1990, when Yugoslavia began to disintegrate, Catholic Slovenia and Croatia led the rush to independence.

However, cultural and religious differences are not alone responsible for the conflict that erupted in July 1991. More important was the civil war of 1941-45, when pro-German Croats were savagely opposed by mainly Serb Chetniks (Royalists) and Partisans (Communists). Dreadful atrocities, amounting almost to genocide, left an enduring legacy of hatred on both sides.

Break-up of a nation

YUGOSLAVIA IN ITS MODERN FORM dates only from 1945. It was then that General Tito (Josip Broz), victorious leader of the Communist Partisans against German and Italian forces in World War II, proclaimed the Federative People's Republic of Yugoslavia. The following year, a constitution was adopted establishing a federation of six republics (Slovenia, Croatia, Bosnia-Hercegovina, Serbia, Montenegro and Macedonia) and two autonomous regions (Vojvodina and Kosovo).

Under Tito, who remained Yugoslavia's leader from 1945 until his death in 1980, the country consisted of a socialist federal republic. Although a Communist, Tito tried to make Yugoslavia independent of the Soviet Union. In 1948 he successfully defied the Soviet dictator Josef Stalin, and throughout the 1950s followed a policy of non-alignment, siding with neither the Communist powers nor the democratic Western nations. Tito's style of Communism gave Yugoslavia's peoples a fair amount of self-rule and personal freedom (they were allowed, for example, to travel abroad), and a standard of living superior to that of other Communist nations.

However, as head of both state and party, Tito gathered all political power into his own hands. Politicians who forfeited his good will were summarily dismissed: in 1971 Croatian Communist leaders supporting independence for their state were expelled from the party, and some Serbian leaders suffered the same fate soon afterwards. As a result, leaders of the League of Communists of Yugoslavia (LCY) took steps to prevent Tito from preparing the way for a

successor who would inherit all his powers.

Thus in 1974 a new Constitution led to the weakening and general reduction of the dictatorial powers of the head of state and party leader, granting a much greater measure of independence to individual states and their leaders. The government was now headed by the Presidency, a nine-member council formed by Tito himself and by one representative of each of the six republics and two independent provinces. After Tito's death in 1980, the Presidency was reduced to eight members, each of whom in turn served a one-year term at its head.

Economic crisis

Unfortunately, this decentralization of government led to slow and clumsy decision-making, since lengthy negotiations took place before the requisite unanimous decisions could be reached. This time-consuming process made it impossible to introduce urgently needed reforms in political and economic life. During the apparently prosperous 1970s Yugoslavia had largely depended on foreign loans, and by 1988 the nation's foreign debt stood at some $20,000 billion. Living standards fell, unemployment rose, and by early 1989 inflation had climbed above 500 per cent. At last the federal government took drastic action, devaluing the dinar by a factor of 10,000. But even the replacement of 10,000 old dinars by one new dinar brought only temporary success.

Economic disaster reinforced the opinion of the federation's two most economically stable republics, Croatia and Slovenia, that

FACT BOX

THE COUNTRY
Official name: Socialist Federal Republic of Yugoslavia (until 1991)
Capital: Belgrade
Land regions: Coastal Region, Interior Highlands, Pannonian Plains
Land area: 98,766 sq mi (255,804 km²)
Climate: Central European in most parts (cold winter, hot summers); Mediterranean along the coast (mild winters, hot summers)
Main rivers: Danube, Sava, Drava, Neretva, Morava
Highest elevation: Mount Triglav 9,393 ft (2,863 m)
Lowest elevation: Sea level along the coast

THE GOVERNMENT
Form of Government: Socialist federal republic
Head of State: President of 9-member council (Presidency)
Head of Government: Prime Minister
Administrative areas: 6 federal republics, 2 autonomous provinces
Legislature: Federal Assembly: Chamber of Republics and Autonomous Provinces (88 members) and Federal Chamber (220 members)
Judiciary: Civil, criminal and military courts, Supreme court in each republic; lower courts
Armed forces: Total strength: 214,100

Conscription: men must serve 12 months

THE PEOPLE
Population (1987): 23,411,000
Language: Serbo-Croat, Slovene, Macedonian (official). Magyar and Albanian spoken by minorities
Religion: Serbian-Orthodox (41.5%), Roman Catholic (31.8%), Muslim (12.3%)

THE ECONOMY
Currency: Dinar
Gross National Product per person (1987): US$2,480
Annual Growth Rate (1973-85) 2.7%
Trade balance in US$ (1986): − $1,109 mill

their only hope of prosperity, democratic pluralism, and closer alliance with Western Europe, lay in independence from Yugoslavia. In 1990, Slovenian leaders, supported by their Croatian allies, declared their desire to secede. But these moves towards independence were strongly opposed by Serbia, under the authoritarian President Slobodan Milosevic. More than half a million Serbs lived in Croatia, and 1.3 million lived in Bosnia-Hercegovina, so that the break-up of Yugoslavia would split the Serbian nation into three parts. Milosevic threatened to wage war rather than to allow this to happen.

Former Yugoslavia (above) is located on the northwestern part of the Balkan peninsula. The federation of six republics began to disintegrate in 1990, with the secession of Slovenia and Croatia.

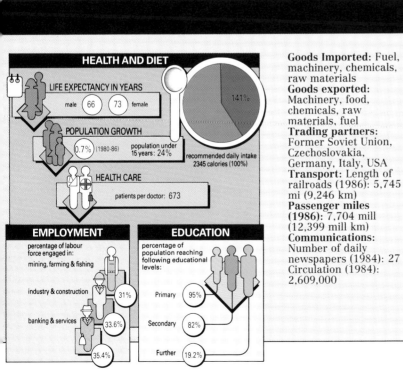

HEALTH AND DIET

LIFE EXPECTANCY IN YEARS

male 66 73 female

141%

POPULATION GROWTH

0.7% (1980-86)   population under 15 years: 24%

recommended daily intake 2345 calories (100%)

HEALTH CARE

patients per doctor: 673

EMPLOYMENT

percentage of labour force engaged in:

mining, farming & fishing

industry & construction   31%

banking & services   33.6%

35.4%

EDUCATION

percentage of population reaching following educational levels:

Primary   95%

Secondary   82%

Further   19.2%

Goods Imported: Fuel, machinery, chemicals, raw materials
Goods exported: Machinery, food, chemicals, raw materials, fuel
Trading partners: Former Soviet Union, Czechoslovakia, Germany, Italy, USA
Transport: Length of railroads (1986): 5,745 mi (9,246 km)
Passenger miles (1986): 7,704 mill (12,399 mill km)
Communications: Number of daily newspapers (1984): 27 Circulation (1984): 2,609,000

In 1989 Serbia had already used brutal measures to destroy the independence of Vojvodina and Kosovo. In June 1991, when Slovenia and Croatia declared independence, the Serbian-controlled Federal Army marched into Slovenia and, when forced to retreat, moved the war into Croatia. Meanwhile, two other former Yugoslavian republics, Bosnia-Hercegovina and Macedonia, declared independence, leaving only Serbia and Montenegro from the former Yugoslavian state. In May 1992 the war spread to Bosnia–Hercegovina, where Serbian units battered the ancient towns of Sarajevo and Mostar, and displaced whole populations. Trade sanctions were imposed on Serbia by the UN, after numerous earlier cease-fires proposed by the UN and the EC had failed. In June 1992, UN forces managed to enter Sarajevo to give some relief to its people from Serbian blockade.

Serbia

HISTORICALLY AND GEOGRAPHICALLY, the landlocked eastern republic of Serbia occupied a dominant position in Yugoslavia. With a population of some 9,400,000 persons in an area of about 34,116 square miles (88,361 square kilometres), it was the largest of the former federal republics and the site of the federal capital, Belgrade.

The Slavic people known as Serbs settled in the area, then the Roman province of Illyria, in the 6th century AD. In the Middle Ages Serbs controlled a prosperous Slav empire, but this broke up after the Ottoman Turks defeated the Serbs at Kosovo Polje in 1389. However, through centuries of Turkish rule the Serbs maintained their nationalist spirit, and at last, after risings in 1804 and 1815, Serbia achieved self-government. In 1878 the Treaty of Berlin, resulting from Turkey's defeat in war with Russia, recognized Serbia as an independent nation.

The region was occupied by Austria during World War I, but Serbia emerged on the winning side. In 1918 it took the lead in the formation of the Kingdom of the Serbs, Croats and Slovenes, to which it brought its territories of Bosnia-Hercegovina, Macedonia and Kosovo. This was the first manifestation of Yugoslavia in its modern form. Other regional nationalities resented Serbian domination, and civil war broke out after German invasion in 1941. Serbia was partitioned between a Fascist Croatia, Hungary and Bulgaria. The Allies supported the Communist-dominated guerillas (Partisans) under Josip Broz (Tito).

This background accounts to some extent for the Serbs' tendency to regard both the Yugoslavian kingdom of 1918-45 and the Communist federation set up under Tito after World War II as their own state. Serbs outside Serbia itself, in Bosnia-Hercegovina, Croatia and Macedonia owe their main loyalty to Serbia. But although Serbs have always been the largest ethnic group in Yugoslavia, they only made up some 40 per cent of the total population.

After World War II, Serbia became one of the republics of Communist Yugoslavia, and it included in its territory two autonomous regions, Vojvodina and Kosovo – once the cultural heartland of the Serbian people.

FACT BOX

Name in use: Serbia: Federal Republic of Yugoslavia (with Montenegro)
Capital: Belgrade
Land area: 34,461 sq mi (88,361 km²)
Land regions: Lowlands in N, yielding to hills S of Danube river; mountainous in NE (Timok) and S (Kosovo)
Climate: Continental, with hot dry summers, cold winters

Highest elevation: Daravica 8,712 ft (2,656 m)
Lowest elevation: Danube c.130 ft (40 m)
Government: Presidential republic
Head of state: President
Population (1991): 9,721,177
Languages: Serbian (official), Albanian, Hungarian
Religions: Eastern Orthodox, Muslim
Currency: Yugoslav dinar
GDP per person: n.a.

The church (*top*) at Gradac dates from the Middle Ages. Religion divides Orthodox Serbs from Croatian Catholics and Bosnian Muslims.

Frescoes (*above*) in Gracanica monastery illustrate the achievements of Serbian Renaissance art. The monastery lies on Serbia's western border.

Belgrade's Republic Square (*above*), with its cafes, statues and National Theatre, was a popular meeting place for the many tourists who once flocked to Yugoslavia. Capital of Serbia and largest city of the former federation, Belgrade is sited on the confluence of the Save and Danube rivers.

A water mill at Kunzin, Kosovo (*right*) grinds corn for the locals. Muslim Albanians form the bulk of Kosovo's population, and have suffered at the hands of Serbian nationalists.

Albanians make up about 90 per cent of its population of some 1,600,000; Serbs account for less than 10 per cent, but maintain a very strong attachment to the region. As Eastern Orthodox Christians, they regarded the mainly Muslim Albanians as "foreigners" with no real right to Kosovo. In the 1960s-70s, efforts were made to fully integrate the Albanians into the Yugoslavian state, but in the early 1980s the Albanians demanded that Kosovo should be made an independent republic. There were serious riots, and harshly repressive policies returned.

In 1988-89 there were again serious civil disturbances in Kosovo and also in Vojvodina. The nationalist leaders of Serbia, headed by Slobodan Milosevic, aware that Yugoslavia was likely to break up into several states, set out to end the "artificial partition" of Serbia. In 1990, a new Serb consistution removed the last vestiges of autonomy from Kosovo and Vojvodina.

After Serbia's first free elections, in December 1990, when nationalist parties achieved power, Milosevic was elected President. His policy was to preserve as much as possible of a Serbian-dominated Yugoslavia, and he used Serbian-dominated Federal Army to support Serbian nationalist guerillas' activities in Croatia from mid-1991 and later in Bosnia-Hercegovina. Serbia has earned condemnation from such bodies as the EC and the UN for apparently initiating much of the violence.

By summer 1992, there was a growing anti-war movement in Serbia, many feeling Milosevic's actions were inhumane and disastrous for Serbia. Nevertheless, despite fears that the conflict would spread to Kosovo and Macedonia, Milosevic continued his attempts to consolidate a rump Serbia-Yugoslavia.

Vojvodina and Kosovo

The autonomous region of Vojvodina was part of the empire of Austria-Hungary, passing to the Kingdom of Serbs, Croats and Slovenes at the end of World War I. At that time only about one-third of its people were Slavs; about one-quarter were German and about the same number Hungarian. Today, there are only about 9,000 Germans in Vojvodina's population of just over 2,000,000. Immigration has brought the Serbian proportion up to some 55 per cent. Hungarians (about 20 per cent) and Croats (about 5 per cent) are the largest minorities, but there are representatives of more than 20 other nationalities, notably Slovakians, Romanians and White Russians.

Kosovo has been called "the poorhouse of Yugoslavia". It is over-populated, its agricultural methods are outdated, and about 40 per cent of its workforce is unemployed.

Montenegro

"FREEDOM LIVES IN THE MOUNTAINS," is a proverb of the people of Montenegro – a saying that has proved true in the history of this small state in southwest Yugoslavia. Its name, either as Montenegro or, in Serbo-Croation, Crna Gora, means "Black Mountain", and its rocky ranges have long offered its inhabitants a base for resistance to would-be conquerors. Its ancient capital of Cetinje was a "nest of freedom" on the slopes of Lovcen, a 5,740-foot (1,570-metre) peak in the Dinaric Alps. The Lovcen looks out over the Gulf of Kotor on the state's scenic Adriatic coast, whose charms for many centuries attracted foreign visitors. In ancient times they came as Greek, Roman or Turkish invaders; in modern times as tourists from all over Europe.

Warlike past

In the Middle Ages Montenegro formed part of the Serbian Empire. In the later 1300s, when the Empire fell to the Turks, many Serbs fled to the mountains of Montenegro, where an independent state, ruled from 1516 by a prince-bishop, was formed. Although the Turks occupied much of Montenegro after the 1520s, its people resisted so stoutly in their mountain strongholds that they preserved a great deal of their independence. This was officially recognized by Turkey in 1799.

In the 1800s and early 1900s Montenegro had two outstanding rulers. The first, Prince-Bishop Peter II Njegos (ruled 1830-51), was a philosopher and poet who continued and strengthened a tradition of close alliance, both cultural and political, with Russia. The tiny Slav state's alliance with its great Slavic neighbour gave rise to a semi-humorous Montenegrin boast that "We and the Russians number many millions".

Peter's successor abandoned the traditional title of bishop and ruled as prince and lord. He was followed by Montenegro's second outstanding modern ruler, Nicholas I Njegos, who ruled first as prince (1860-1910) and then as king (1910-18). A reformer and modernizer, he was a party to the Treaty of Berlin (1878) which extended Montenegro's boundaries and won it full international recognition as a sovereign state. He gained more territory by his successful

A Montenegrin peasant (*below left*) tends her flock in an olive grove.

The Lovcen (*below*), a typically inaccessible peak rising from the Adriatic coast to a height of 5,770ft (1,759m), forms part of the Dinaric Alps. It overlooks the Gulf of Kotor and symbolizes Montenegro's independence.

Fisheries (*right*) on the Dalmatian coast use traditional methods unchanged for generations.

FACT BOX

Name in use: Montenegro; Federal Republic of Yugoslavia (with Serbia)
Capital: Podgorica
Land area: 5,387 sq mi (13,812 km²)
Land regions: Narrow coastal strip; karst and chalk highlands in W; Woodlands E of Tara river, slate-bearing mountains in E
Climate: Hot dry summers, mild rainy winters
Highest elevation: Durmitor 8,272 ft (2,522 m)
Lowest elevation: Sea level
Government: Presidential Republic
Head of state: President
Population (1991): 616,327
Languages: Serbo-Croat (official), Albanian
Religions: Eastern Orthodox, Muslim
Currency: Yugoslav dinar
GDP per person: n.a.

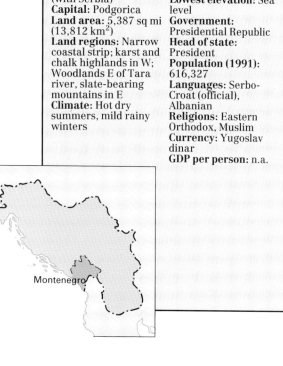

Montenegro

opposition to Turkey in the Balkan Wars of 1912-13, but was decisively defeated in 1915 when he led Montenegro against Austria-Hungary in World War I. The country was occupied, Nicholas fled abroad (dying in exile in 1921), and at the war's end the Montenegrin National Assembly decided to abolish its own monarchy and join the Kingdom of the Serbs, Croats and Slovenes.

Between World Wars I and II Montenegro was a province of Yugoslavia. During World War II, however, its mountains became a stronghold for Tito's Partisans. One of its leaders in resistance to German and Italian occupation was its greatest modern cultural figure, the author Milovan Djilas. After the war its brave resistance (and also Djilas's close friendship with Tito) won Montenegro the status of one of the six constituent republics of Tito's Yugoslavia.

Montenegro today

Montenegro is the smallest and least populated of the Yugoslavian republics, with about 600,000 people living in an area of 5,387 square miles (13,812 square kilometres). Around 62 per cent of its people are Montenegrins, most belonging to the Eastern Orthodox Church, nine per cent are Serbs, 15 per cent are Muslims, and about five per cent are Albanians. Its capital, formerly Titograd, has resumed its pre-1945 name of Podgorica.

The republic's economy is under developed. It contributed only a tiny proportion of former Yugoslavia's total wealth and has few industries. About half of the total work force is employed in agriculture. Its other major source of income, tourism, has been hard hit by the civil war.

Montenegro's first free elections were held in December 1990 and, in contrast to those in most other parts of Yugoslavia, did not result in defeat for the Communists. The Communist League took 83 of the 125 parliamentary seats and Reform Communists won 17 seats; the remaining 25 seats were shared between Muslim and Albanian minority parties. This result tended to confirm the republic's historic alliance with Serbia, where Reform Communists (Socialists) had won power.

Momir Bulatovic of the Communist League was elected President of Montenegro in December 1990. He emerged as a staunch adherent of President Slobodan Milosevic of Serbia, true to the old saying that "Serbia and Montenegro are like two eyes in the same head". But although Montenegro supported Serbia in demanding the preservation of the Yugoslavian federation, it has followed a far less militaristic path than the belligerent nationalist policies of its northern neighbour during the destructive and bloody civil war.

Macedonia

MANY TOURISTS WHO HAVE TRAVELLED through Yugoslavia on the way to Greece have looked on Macedonia, southernmost of the former Yugoslav republics, as simply a hot and dusty stretch on their road to more popular resorts. Yet the largely untouched landscapes around Macedonia's three great lakes, Ohrid, Prespa and Doiran, are a natural paradise. As well as its lovely lakes, Macedonia boasts wild mountain scenery, notably in the Bistra Mountains and in the Sar Mountains, where there are winter sports resorts.

Before the civil war, an increasing number of foreign tourists had begun to discover these pleasures. Lake Ohrid in particular attracted many with its clear waters and fine beaches, ringed by mountains. Many old, well-preserved buildings, including medieval churches and monasteries dating from the periods of Byzantine and Bulgarian rule, stand along its shores. In the town of Ohrid, once capital of the Kingdom of Bulgaria, the former Cathedral of Sant Sophia, dating from the 800s, contains medieval wall paintings now restored after being covered with mortar by the Turks, whose Islamic religion forbids pictures of the human figure.

The heart of a great Greek empire in ancient times, homeland of Alexander the Great, Macedonia originally covered areas in northern Greece and Southwestern Bulgaria. Between the 900s and 1200s it was ruled sometimes by the Byzantines and sometimes by the Bulgarians (who still claim the Macedonians to be a Bulgarian people). But by the 1300s it had become a Serbian possession. Following the defeat of Prince Lazar of Serbia by the Turks at the battle of Kosovo Polje in 1389 it then became part of the Ottoman Empire.

Turkish rule ended with the Balkan Wars of 1912-13, as a result of which Macedonia was divided into three parts. The largest, Vardar Macedonia, went to Serbia; Bulgaria got Pirin Macedonia; the remainder went to Greece. This division still troubles the politics of the Balkan area. In 1919, as "South Serbia", Vardar Macedonia was taken by Serbia into the newly formed Kingdom of the Serbs, Croats, and Slovenes (modern Yugoslavia).

FACT BOX

Official name: Republic of Macedonia
Capital: Skopje
Land area: 10,030 sq mi (25,713 km^2)
Land regions: Mountainous between rivers Crni Drim and Vardar; isolated mountain valleys with gorges and high passes
Climate: Dry summers, heavy precipitation in mountains

Highest elevation: Korab 9,066 ft (2,764 m)
Lowest elevation: Vardar-Tal c.328 ft (100 m)
Government: Presidential republic
Head of state: President of the Republic
Population (1991): 2,033,964
Languages: Macedonian (official), Serbo-Croat, Albanian
Religion: Eastern Orthodox, Muslim
Currency: Dinar
GDP per person: n.a.

Macedonia

A marketwoman at Ohrid (*above*) uses primitive scales to weigh produce. The ancient town borders Lake Ohrid, the largest and deepest in the Balkans.

A paved street in Skopje (*right*) testifies to an ancient continuity of urban life.

Bulgarian occupation during World War II drove many Macedonians to join Tito's Partisans. Then, in 1946 the Communist regime established Macedonia as one of the six independent republics of the Yugoslavian federation. The Macedonian language, which resembles Bulgarian and is written in Cyrillic letters, was recognized as a separate language and the republic's official tongue.

Since the Balkan Wars, however, both Greece and Bulgaria have feared that Macedonian nationalism threatens the historic Macedonian territories they hold. Greece denies that a "Macedonian" national minority exists within its borders; Bulgaria emphasizes the "Bulgarian" history of Macedonia. This, along with a desire to emphasize independence from their powerful neighbour Serbia, has made Yugoslav Macedonias strongly nationalistic.

The Macedonians' sense of national identity had led to clashes with the state's Albanian population, who make up nearly 20 per cent of the republic's population of some 2,000,000 persons. These are mostly immigrants from the neighbouring region of Kosovo. The state also has a sizeable (perhaps 300,000 strong) minority of Gypsies, but the problems they present are economic and social rather than political.

Macedonia today

Macedonia is one of the least economically developed regions of former Yugoslavia. It is rich in agriculture, growing cereals, fruits and vegetables, tobacco and cotton, but its industrial development has suffered serious setbacks as a result of unwise investment in huge metallurgical projects.

The republic's first free elections were held in November 1990, when more than 80 per cent of voters participated. No party got an overall majority, but in a further poll the front runner was the nationalist, anti-Communist, Internal Macedonian Revolutionary Organization (IMRO), which gained 37 parliamentary seats. The former Communist Party, now the Party for Democratic Change, won 31 seats. The Albanian Party for Democratic Prosperity (hampered by a voting system that handicaps national minorities) won 25 seats, just beating the Socialist Alliance of Reform Forces.

January 1991 saw the appointment as President of Kiro Gligorov, a former comrade in arms of the Communist leader Tito, by a large majority of parliamentary votes. Gligorov's declared aim was to keep Macedonia independent from Serbia and to keep his state out of the Serbian-Croatian conflict. In October 1991 Macedonia declared its independence from the Yugoslav federation.

The monastery church of St Panteleimon (*above left*), near Skopje, was built in 1164 and contains fine Byzantine frescoes. Most Macedonians are Eastern Orthodox Christians, but have been independent of the Serbian Orthodox church since 1967.

Paprika is harvested (*below*) on the plains of Pelagonyia. Poorly developed in economic terms, Macedonia's rich soil supports crops including vines, tobacco, cotton, mulberries and rice.

Bosnia-Hercegovina

IN OCTOBER 1991, BOSNIA-HERCEGOVINA declared its independence from the Federal Republic of Yugoslavia. Since that time, it has suffered terribly at the hands of Serbian militias and the Serbian-dominated Federal Army, which have all but destroyed its ancient cities and displaced its multi-ethnic population.

Before the tragic civil war that has devastated former Yugoslavia, the territory had a special charm of its own. It had a flourishing agriculture and was rich in timber and minerals. Its capital of Sarajevo was a centre of Muslim culture and learning, and many fine mosques, ancient and modern, stood there and elsewhere.

Bosnia-Hercegovina was the central unit of the six republics that made up the Yugoslavian federation and, like the federation as whole, was peopled by a variety of races and religions. About 44 per cent of its people were Bosnian (Slavic) Muslims, some 31 per cent were Serbs, and around 17 per cent were Croats.

Although there are no hard and fast divisions of settlement, the Bosnian Muslims lived mainly in the central areas, the Serbs in the east and along the northern border with Croatia, and the Croats in the west. Thus the Muslims were in a sense at the heart of the nation. Traditionally they formed a buffer between the Croats and Serbs. Both Croatia and Serbia had for centuries hoped to take control of Bosnia-Hercegovina, either to rule it themselves or to divide it between them.

Turkish rule

Bosnia, the northern part of the republic, was originally part of Serbia, but gained independence in AD 960. It came under Hungarian domination in the 1100s-1200s, when Christianity was introduced, and from 1353 was briefly an independent kingdom, to which parts of Croatia and Dalmatia belonged. In 1463 it was taken by the Turks.

Hercegovina, to the south, was originally independent but underwent periods of both Serbian and Bosnian rule in the 1200s-1300s, finally falling to the Turks in 1482. Bosnia and Hercegovina were then united as a province of the Ottoman Empire, becoming a predominantly Muslim area bet-

Sarajevo (*far right*), capital of Bosnia-Hercegovina, was the official residence of the Ottoman Turkish Pasha from 1583-1878 and contains numerous mosques. Most of Bosnia-Hercegovina's 1.9 million Muslims belong to the Sunni branch of Islam. In the summer of 1992, the city suffered merciless attack (*right*) from Serbian forces and the fighting has reduced the civilian population to desperate straits. Much of the attractive city has been destroyed.

FACT BOX

Official name: Republic of Bosnia-Hercegovina
Capital: Sarajevo
Land area: 19,940 sq mi (51,129 km^2)
Land regions: In S karst mountains with scattered woodland; to N wooded ore mountains, karst regions with fertile valleys, riverine valley of Save in N
Climate: Intermediate Mediterranean and continental
Highest elevation: Plocno 7,308 ft (2,228 m)
Lowest elevation: Sea level
Government: Presidential republic
Head of state: 7-member presidency
Population (1991): 4,366,000
Language: Serbo-Croat (official)
Religion: Muslim (44%), Eastern Orthodox (31%), Roman Catholic (17%)
Currency: Dinar
GDP per person: n.a.

Bosnia and Herzegovina

Mostar (*below*), chief town of Hercegovina, spans the Neretva river with its Turkish Bridge, built in 1566.

ween Eastern Orthodox peoples to the east and Roman Catholics to the west.

From 1878 Bosnia-Hercegovina came increasingly under the rule of Austria-Hungary, which finally took it from the Turks in 1908. Slovene, Croatian and Serbian nationalists all opposed Austro-Hungarian rule. On June 28, 1914, the Bosnian Serbian patriot Gavrilo Princip (1894-1918) assassinated Archduke Francis Ferdinand, heir to the throne of Austria-Hungary, in Sarajevo, capital of Bosnia-Hercegovina, thus triggering off World War I.

At the end of World War I, Bosnia-Hercegovina was taken by Serbia to become part of the Kingdom of the Serbs, Croats and Slovenes – which from 1929 was called Yugoslavia. During World War II most of the territory was controlled by the pro-German "Independent Croatian State" set up by the Ustase (Croatian Fascist movement). Tito's Communist Partisans has provisionally founded the Federal People's Republic of Yugoslavia in 1943, and at the war's end in 1945 Bosnia and Hercegovian became one of its six member republics.

National and religious conflict

For centuries, Bosnian Muslims, Croat Roman Catholics, Serbian Orthodox Christians, and a large Jewish community, lived fairly peacefully together in Bosnia-Herce-

govina. But World War II stressed national and religious differences between the area's "three nations". It was the scene of major fighting between Tito's Partisans and German and Italian occupation forces.

The divisions between these communities were apparent in the republic's first free elections, in November-December 1990, when its peoples voted along national and religious lines. Thus, the strongest party was the Muslim Party of Democratic Action; the Serbian Democratic Party was second; the Croatian Democratic Union took third place. However, all three parties had stated that they wished to preserve Bosnia-Hercegovina as a constituent republic of Yugoslavia. The Muslim president, Alija Izetbegovic, tried to keep his state neutral in the conflict between Serbia and Croatia.

When, in October 1991, Bosnia-Hercegovina declared its wish to become independent, the decision was fiercely opposed by the Serbian Democratic Party, and Serbia threatened to use the Federal Army to "protect Serbian areas". This threat was tragically realized in March 1992, when the full power of the Serbian-backed Federal Army was turned against non-Serbian communities, especially in Sarajevo.

Attempts by international agencies to bring an end to the carnage were of no avail, and today the state is in ruins.

Croatia

CROATIA LIES IN THE NORTHWESTERN part of former Yugoslavia, south of Slovenia, and covers three historic regions: Croatia proper, Dalmatia and Slavonia. A long coastal strip, extending southwards from the Istrian peninsula down the Dalmatian coast to the ancient port of Dubrovnik, connects in the north with the main body of Croatia. Beyond lies the territory of Slavonia, between the Drava and Sava rivers.

History

The Croats, whose name means "mountaineers", began to settle in what was then the Roman province of Illyria in the fifth century AD. Their territory was an independent state from 925 until 1091, when it was conquered by Hungary. Except for a period of Ottoman Turkish rule in 1526-1699, it was part of the Kingdom of Hungary until 1867, when it became a territory of the Habsburg Empire of Austria-Hungary. In 1918 it joined with other territories to form the Kingdom of Serbs, Croats and Slovenes (modern Yugoslavia).

Slavonia, also under Turkish domination in the 1500s-1600s, was joined to Croatia under Hungarian rule in the early 1700s. Dalmatia, the Adriatic coastal region, was divided between Croatia and Serbia in the 900s-1000s, but came increasingly under the control of the powerful maritime Republic of Venice, which ruled it in the 1400s-1700s. In 1815 it was taken by Austria, remaining part of Austria-Hungary until that empire's collapse at the end of World War I. In 1919, along with most of what is now the Croatian part of Istria, it became part of Croatia.

Another part of Croatia with a complex and, in the 1990s, significant history is Krajina, along the western and northern border of Bosnia and Hercegovina. In the 1500s the Habsburgs settled this area with peasants, mostly Serbians, who were intended to form a defensive barrier against the Turks who then held Bosnia. The "Emperor's Borderers" maintained semi-independence, supported by Austria, in this area until the late 1800s. In January 1992 Krajina was declared an "independent Serbian republic".

Croats against Serbs

Croats make up the great majority of the population of modern Croatia, accounting for about 3,700,000 out of a total of some 4,760,000 persons. They consider their language, Croato-Serbian, which they write in Roman letters, to be a separate form of the Serbo-Croatian tongue spoken by Serbs, Montenegrins and most Bosnians, who use the Cyrillic (Russian) script.

Most Croats are Roman Catholics,

At Vinkovci *(below)*, in eastern Croatia, a militiaman tries to console a woman standing in the ruins of her home. Fighting between Croats and Serbs has devastated much of Croatia, and a UN-supervised truce has not halted the conflict.

Zagreb *(right)*, capital of Croatia, is dominated by the historic Roman Catholic cathedral of St Stephen. The city's origins lie with Slavic tribes who settled here in the AD 600s. Until 1557, Zagreb consisted of two separate towns.

FACT BOX

Official name: Republic of Croatia
Capital: Zagreb (Agram)
Land area: 22,050 sq mi (56,538 km²)
Land regions: In N Croatian-Slavonian mountains and riverine valley between Drava and Save; highlands in W; narrow coastal strip with islands in S
Climate: Mild continental in W, mediterranean along coastal strip
Highest elevation: Dinara 6,005 ft (1,831 m)
Lowest elevation: Sea level
Government: Presidential republic
Head of state: President
Population (1991): 4,763,941
Language: Croato-Serb
Religion: Mainly Roman Catholic
Currency: Dinar
GDP per person: n.a.

Croatia

A market in Zagreb
(above) offers produce
from local farms and
smallholdings
untouched by the civil
war raging elsewhere.
Croatia's economy is
the most highly
developed of the six
republics of the for-
mer Yugoslavia.
However, the impact
of civil war and the
transition to a free-
market economy has
produced economic
hardship. Croatia's
tourist industry, once
an economic main-
stay, has completely
collapsed.

whereas the Serbs, who form the second
largest population group (about 600,000),
belong to the Eastern Orthodox Church.
Croatia also contains smaller groups of
Slovenes, Bosnian Muslims, Italians and
Slovaks.

The present bitter conflict between
Croats and Serbs stems partly from a his-
torical wish for independence on the part of
the Croats, partly from the events of World
War II, and partly from political and social
disagreement after 1945. Serbs are embit-
tered by memories of 1941-45, when the
Ustase, the Croatian Fascist movement led
by Ante Pavelic, set up an "Independent
Croatian State" suppported by German and
Italian occupation forces. Many thousand
Serbs, Communists and non-Communists
alike, were cruelly put to death, along with
Gypsies and Jews.

In post-World War II Yugoslavia, Croats
felt that the economic policies of the central
government in Belgrade meant that
Croatia's wealth was being taken to support
other republics. They claimed that Serbs in
Croatia were unfairly favoured, being appointed to a high proportion of the most important posts in the republic's administration, judiciary and police.

Civil war

Open warfare in Croatia began late in 1990.
Serb extremists violently seized control of
some areas and declared their independence from Zagreb, Croatia's capital. From
early 1991 such localized activities grew
into a real military offensive against
Croatia, in which Croatian Serbs were supported by the Yugoslav Federal Army. The
battles, with increasing numbers of military
and civilian casualties, were at first mainly
in western Slavonia and on the southern
Dalmatian coast, where the destruction of
the ancient city of Dubrovnik aroused
worldwide concern.

Later, fighting moved to eastern Slavonia,
where the fall of Vukovar, near the Serbian
border, in November 1991, revealed
Croatia's military weakness in the face of
Serb partisans backed by the Federal Army.
Croatia's independence was recognized by
Germany in December 1991, but other EC
nations held back until early 1992.

Early in 1992 a United Nations Peacekeeping Force was sent to Croatia, but had
little success. Meanwhile, destruction has
been widespread: villages have been destroyed, farmland devastated, and towns
battered. Thousands of people have lost
their homes and possessions. The damage
to Croatia's economy, before the fighting
rivalled in prosperity only by that of Slovenia, has been immense. A massive influx of
refugees from Bosnia-Hercegovina had worsened the country's problems by July 1992.

Slovenia

FORMERLY A CONSTITUENT PARTNER OF the Federal Republic of Yugoslavia, Slovenia declared its independence from the federation on June 25, 1991. The Serbian-controlled Yugoslavian Federal Army attempted to prevent this by military action, and on July 2 the Slovenian capital of Ljubljana was bombed. However, the European Community succeeded in imposing a cease-fire, resulting in the withdrawal of the Federal Army (which had suffered reverses in the fighting). Slovenia proclaimed its full independence on October 8, and all Yugoslav army units had withdrawn from Slovenian territory by October 26, International recognition of the new state came in January 1992.

Landscape and history
Slovenia was the most northerly of the six constituent republics of former Yugoslavia, occupying an alpine area to the northwest. Most of the region is mountainous, with lower lands along the coast, along the Sava river, and towards the Pannonian plains. Extensive woodland and attractive limestone landscapes encouraged tourism until the recent conflict that has engulfed the former country of Yugoslavia. The Istrian coast, too, drew increasing numbers of visitors with its Mediterranean-Italian character.

FACT BOX

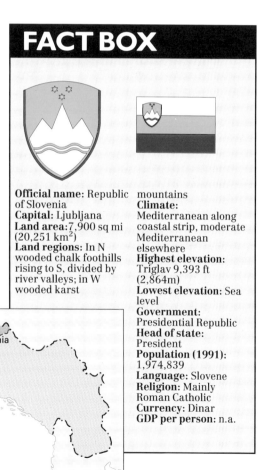

Official name: Republic of Slovenia
Capital: Ljubljana
Land area: 7,900 sq mi (20,251 km²)
Land regions: In N wooded chalk foothills rising to S, divided by river valleys; in W wooded karst mountains
Climate: Mediterranean along coastal strip, moderate Mediterranean elsewhere
Highest elevation: Triglav 9,393 ft (2,864m)
Lowest elevation: Sea level
Government: Presidential Republic
Head of state: President
Population (1991): 1,974,839
Language: Slovene
Religion: Mainly Roman Catholic
Currency: Dinar
GDP per person: n.a.

Piran (*left*), a tourist resort in northwestern Istria on the Gulf of Trieste, was an important Adriatic base in the Middle Ages, and later a key trading area commanding the northern Adriatic region.

Triglav (*above*) ranks as the highest peak of the Julian Alps, in the north of Slovenia. The landscape is mainly mountainous, but descends to hilly country in the south, with fertile river valleys.

The great majority of the population, estimated at just under two million, are Slovenes, a Slavic people who settled the area in the 6th century AD. Western influence came early to the region, when missionaries from Salzburg converted the Slovenes to Christianity, introduced the Roman alphabet, and established a Western cultural orientation. The territory came under Frankish (Germanic) rule in the 800s.

In the late 1200s the region was taken by the Austrians, and remained under Austrian rule (finally that of the Habsburg empire of Austria-Hungary) until World War I, escaping the Turkish occupation undergone by many other parts of former Yugoslavia. In 1918 the ex-Austrian provinces that made up Slovenia joined the Kingdom of the Serbs, Croats and Slovenes. Although Slovenia perhaps foresaw difficulties with the Serbian-dominated kingdom, it feared both Italian advances from the Istrian region on the Adriatic, and "Germanization" from neighbouring Austria. Thus it joined the new state as the best way of preserving its territorial integrity and national identity.

After World War II Slovenia became one of six independent republics of the Yugoslavian Communist federation. Slovenian politicians were among the most enthusiastic supporters of Tito's regime. But after his death in 1980 it was Slovenia that led the way in calling for political reforms, especially in demanding that the federation should become a much looser association of independent republics. From the later 1980s this brought Slovenia into increasingly hostile confrontation with the Serbian leaders. Early in 1990 Slovenia's leaders withdrew from the League of Communists of Yugoslavia (LCY). This prepared the way for the end of Communist rule in Yugoslavia, and for the collapse of the federation.

Creation of the state

In Slovenia's first free elections in April 1990 the United Democratic Union (Democrats) obtained a working majority in parliament. The Democrats were a coaltion (different parties that have agreed to act together) between the Christian Democratic Party, the Democratic League, the Liberal Party, the Social Democratic Party, the Farmers' Association and the Green Party. The opposition was formed by the largest single party, the Democratic Reform Party (the former Slovenian Communist League). A former Communist, Milan Kucan, became president of the republic, with 58 per cent of the parliamentary votes, beating the Democrats' chairman Joze Pucnik. Lojze Peterle, leader of the Christian Democrats, became head of the government. In December 1990 nearly 90 per cent of the electorate voted in favour of Slovenian independence, which was formally declared on June 25, 1991.

The people today

Traditionally, the Slovenes are an ambitious and hardworking people. They have their own language, Slovenian (closely related to Serbo-Croatian) and, like the Croats, are mostly Roman Catholics. They have always differed in significant ways from the rest of the federal republic, and before independence they enjoyed the highest standard of living and the lowest rate of unemployment. Although Slovenes constituted only about eight per cent of forme Yugoslavia's total population, they were responsible for about 19 per cent of the nation's annual revenue and, with thriving factories (automobiles, textiles, chemical and metallurgical industries), some 20 per cent of its industrial output.

Unfortunately, the economy has been hard hit by the loss of foreign exchange caused both by war and by the end of a considerable income from tourism. Nor was the restructuring of a market economy successfully implemented. Eastern European markets were disrupted, and these losses could not be counterbalanced by exports to the West. Slovenia is paying dearly for its independence and its population faces a substantial drop in a standard of living that was once the envy of other Yugoslavs.

A wedding at Ljubljana (*above*) is celebrated in traditional style. Women guests wear embroidered white bonnets, with colourful tasseled shawls over white blouses.

Ljubljana's Grubarg Canal (*left*) brings old-world elegance to Slovenia's political and cultural capital.

THE REPUBLIC OF BULGARIA OCCUPIES about one-third of the eastern side of the Balkan Peninsula, and borders Turkey, Greece, Serbia, Macedonia and Romania. The country's Black Sea coastline runs for some 175 miles (282 kilometres). Bulgaria is mainly mountainous, particularly to the west, but fertile plains and valleys lie between the mountain ranges. As a result, Bulgaria's farms yield abundant crops and livestock.

The landscape is shaped by the Balkan Mountains, which climb up to 7,795 feet (2,376 metres) at Botev Peak – almost exactly in the middle of the country. Running for 385 miles (620 kilometres), the range divides the country into two halves. These have very different characteristics. The northern half – the Danubian Plateau – experiences a continental climate with cold winters, but warm and humid summers. The southern half – the Transitional Mountains and Lowlands – receives instead a more varied climate with cold winters and hot, dry summers. Up in the mountains, conditions change yet again, according to altitude and the distance inland. Over all the country the average temperature in July is 75°F (24°C). Average rainfall over the whole country is 25 inches (63 centimetres) but only the mountains receive considerable amounts of snow. The Black Sea has a special localised climate which tends to be mild in winter and hot in summer.

Northern Bulgaria

The Danubian Plateau represents a vast sheet of limestone covered in river-deposited silt. For this reason, it provides the country's most fertile farmland. The Danube River forms most of the border between Bulgaria and Romania to the north, and takes in several important tributaries – notably the Iskŭr and the Yantra. The limestone on its southern bank at times forms an impressive cliff up to 500 feet (150 metres) in height. The plateau is partly flat, especially up in the north, and partly undulating, especially towards the foothills of the Balkan Mountains. In the flatter areas – cut through by wet valleys and dotted with urban centres – fruit, vegetables and vines flourish. The drier uplands are used for the cultivation of wheat and maize. To the northeast are broad expanses of scrub grassland which provide pasture for sheep.

Most of the uplands that make up the Balkan Mountains are not particularly high. Taller peaks lie predominantly in the west, and some that reach 6,600 feet (2,000 metres) form the border with Macedonia and Serbia. In general the Balkans form lengthy ridges and small plateaus on which sheep graze or deciduous forests grow. In this way, although the Balkans appear on the map to be a barrier right across the middle of the country, there are in fact as many as 30 passes that allow traffic to flow with ease between the Danubian Plateau and the Transitional Mountains and Lowlands of southern Bulgaria.

Immediately south of the Balkan Mountains lie a number of lower parallel mountain chains. These are known as the Sredna Gora. Between the Balkans and these lower chains lies a zone of small basins. Because of their mild climate and sheltered position, these were settled by humans from an early date. It is in these fruitful basins that roses and vines are grown, and in one of them, the capital Sofia is located, at an altitude of 1,800 feet (550 metres). In and around Sofia, there are a number of mineral springs that some people believe have healing properties.

The Thracian Plain is also called the Maritsa Basin, and takes its name from the major river that runs right across Bulgaria by way of the country's second city, Plovdiv, forming a large part of southeastern Bulgaria. This is where several industrial and commercial cities are located and is the focus of Bulgaria's heavy industry and manufacturing. At the same time, extensive irrigation provides the means of intensive agriculture in the region. Fields of sunflowers and maize alternate with tobacco, vegetables, herbs and cotton.

Warm temperatures, sandy beaches and historic ruins, such as those at Nesebar (*below*), attract tourists from all over Europe to Bulgaria's Black Sea coast. However, pollution now poses a threat to coastal wildlife.

A small town (*right*) occupies a sheltered valley in the Transitional Mountains. The fertile valleys of this region support the growth of fruits and vegetables, including apples, grapes, tomatoes and watermelons.

Snowcapped peaks (*below*) rise above the Rila Mountains, part of the Rhodope Mountains of southern Bulgaria. The range includes the country's highest peak, and forms a barrier between Bulgaria and Greece.

Parallel rows (*bottom*) of ripening corn near Pleven on the on the Danubian Plateau illustrate the region's fertility. Most of Bulgaria's grain crops are grown here, aided by the high level of humidity during the summer months.

The mountainous south

The Rhodope Mountains occupy southern and southwestern Bulgaria, presenting a formidable barrier between Bulgaria and Greece. Coniferous forests and alpine meadows give this landscape an individual character that at one time was enthusiastically described by the poet Homer. At the northern tip lies the highest mountain in the country, Musala, at 9,596 feet (2,925 metres). In the Rila Mountains to the north lies the Rila Monastery, a historic shrine revered by all Bulgarians and now the site of the National Museum. In the peaks of the Pirin Mountains to the west – which may have been named after the ancient Slavonic god of thunder and of the harvest, *Peroun* – live bears, wolves and wild cats.

On the Black Sea coast, sandy beaches are interspersed with dunes, rocky cliffs and forest-covered hills. Broad expanses of reeds and water lilies mark the deltas of the Kamchiya and Ropotano rivers. On the Balkan foothills the vineyards reach right down to the sea. Farther north, monk seals bask on the rocks along the shore. They are among the rarest mammals in the world, but are threatened by the increasing pollution of the waters of the Black Sea. The large coastal resorts of Varna and Burgas have splendid beaches and parks, but they too are subject to pollution.

Bulgaria Today

IN THE EARLY 1990s, BULGARIA BEGAN the difficult transition from a Communist system – with a centrally-planned economy and rule by a single political party – to a democratic political system with a free-market economy.

Bulgaria's geographical position has long made it a bridge between Europe and Asia. In the AD 800s, the ancestors of the Bulgarian people ruled over a large part of the Balkans. This state was absorbed first into the Byzantine (Eastern Roman) empire, and later by the Ottoman Turks. An independent Bulgarian state did not reappear until the early 1900s, with the decline of the Ottoman empire. Bulgaria lost territory to Greece and Serbia during the Second Balkan War (1913), and even more after its defeat in World War I. Until World War II, the country was a mainly agricultural state ruled by a tsar (king). After World War II, Bulgaria underwent momentous changes, including the abolition of the monarchy and the seizure of power by the Communist Party.

Between 1946 – when the Communists first took power in Bulgaria following Soviet occupation during World War II – and 1990, the proportion of the population that lived in towns and cities rose from 20 per cent to 60 per cent. Within the same period, the capital, Sofia, experienced a population increase of 600 per cent. Much of the reason for this urbanization was the official policy of the Communist government towards state industrialization. This created some wealth, but workers' conditions remained poor, with low wages, and food, housing and consumer goods in short supply.

Floodlit at night (*right*), the Alexander Nevsky Cathedral towers above the buildings of central Sofia, the Bulgarian capital. The cathedral was built in the late 1800s after the Ottoman Turkish overlords were finally driven from the country.

Bulgaria (*far right*) lies in the southeastern corner of Europe. It has a coast on the Black Sea and contains a number of mountain ranges which run from west to east across the country. Almost all of its northern boundary with Romania is marked by the Danube river.

FACT BOX

THE COUNTRY
Official name: Republic of Bulgaria
Capital: Sofia
Land regions: Danubian Plateau, Balkan Mountains, Transitional Mountains and Lowlands, Rhodope Mountains
Land area: 42,823 sq mi (110,912 km²)
Climate: Mediterranean in S, with mild, moist winters and hot, dry summers. More continental in N with wider range of temperatures and more rain in summer
Main rivers: Danube, Iskŭr, Tundzha, Maritsa, Ogosta
Highest elevation: Musala Peak 9,596 ft (2,925 m)

Lowest elevation: Sea level along the coast

THE GOVERNMENT
Form of government: Socialist republic
Head of State: President
Head of Government: Prime Minister
Administrative areas: 8 regions plus city of Sofia
Legislature: National Assembly with 240 members, elected to 4-year terms
Judiciary: Supreme Court, 28 regional and 103 district courts
Armed forces: Total strength: about 129,000, plus paramilitary forces and People's Militia. Men must serve for 2-3 years

THE PEOPLE
Population (1990): 9,010,000
Language: Bulgarian. Minority languages (Turkish, Macedonian)
Religion: Bulgarian Orthodox (about 90%). Muslim, Protestant and Roman Catholic minorities

THE ECONOMY
Currency: Lev
Gross Domestic Product per person (1989): n.a.
Annual Growth Rate: n.a.
Trade balance in US$ (1988): $640 mill
Goods imported: Fuels, industrial equipment, metals, mineral oil, iron and steel, agricultural machinery

Recent upheaval

The "Gentle Revolution" of November 1989 saw the fall of Todor Zhivkov, head of state for the previous 27 years. Yet many of the Communist Party's former representatives, now under the banner of the Bulgarian Socialist Party, were again brought to power in the elections of June 1990, and matters did not immediately change for the better. The main support for the new government came from rural workers. It was, however, the candidate of the Union of Democratic Forces, a coalition of 16 opposition parties and factions, who was elected the new President of Bulgaria: Zhelyu Zhelev. In 1992, new elections brought Bulgaria's democratic coalition to power.

About 85 per cent of the people are of Bulgarian descent. Their ancestors were Slavs from southern Poland and what is now the Ukraine who arrived in the area around AD 500, or Bulgars, originally a nomadic people of Turkic or Tartar ethic background from Central Asia. The Bulgars arrived and were assimilated 100 years after the Slavs. These people speak Bulgarian, and for the most part belong to the Bulgarian Orthodox (Christian) Church (until 1990, religious practice, was officially discouraged by the Communist government). They write in the Cyrillic alphabet (originally devised by St Methodius, missionary to Bulgaria, and named after his fellow saint and brother, St Cyril). The literacy rate among Bulgarians is extremely high: about 95 per cent of people aged 15 or over can read and write. After compulsory state education between the ages of seven and 15, nearly all students go on to study at high school.

Minorities

The Turkish minority at present makes up some 10 per cent of the total population. Bulgaria belonged to the (Turkish) Ottoman empire between 1396 and 1878. Some parts remained in Turkish hands until 1908, and their oppressive rule has left the people very resentful. In 1985, the government began to enforce assimilation of the Turkish and other ethnic minorities (including Armenians, Macedonians, Russians and Gypsies). Turks were often obliged to change their names to Bulgarian ones, and not to speak Turkish in any public place or even read it in private. Their Islamic faith was also banned. These restrictive laws were revoked in 1990. For all Bulgaria's citizens, living standards remain among the lowest in Europe.

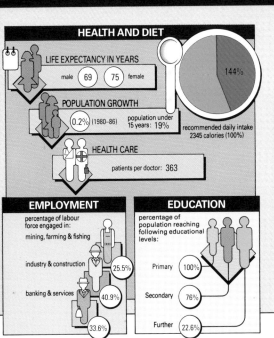

Goods exported: Cigarettes and tobacco, grapes, machinery, rose oil, wine, mining and oil refinery products

Trading partners: Russia, Ukraine, Czechoslovakia, Germany, Italy, France, Austria, Great Britain, Japan

Transport: Length of railways (1989): 2,848 mi (4,586 km) Passenger miles (1984): 4,720 mill (7,601 mill km)

Communications: Number of daily newspapers (1989): 14 Circulation (1989): 2,534,000

HEALTH AND DIET

LIFE EXPECTANCY IN YEARS
male 69   75 female

144%

POPULATION GROWTH
0.2% (1980–86)   population under 15 years: 19%

recommended daily intake 2345 calories (100%)

HEALTH CARE
patients per doctor: 363

EMPLOYMENT

percentage of labour force engaged in:

mining, farming & fishing — 33.6%

industry & construction — 25.5%

banking & services — 40.9%

EDUCATION

percentage of population reaching following educational levels:

Primary 100%

Secondary 76%

Further 22.6%

ROMANIA

ROMANIA LIES IN THE HEART OF eastern Europe, bounded by Moldova, Ukraine, Serbia, Hungary, and Bulgaria. Its sunny Black Sea coast, to the southeast, and its beautiful and varied scenery, attract many thousands of visitors every year.

Dominating the Romanian landscape are the Carpathian Mountains, which traverse the country from north to southwest, and separate the Transylvanian Plateau from the flatter and lower lands of Moldavia, Wallachia and Banat to the east and south. Another unmistakable feature is the rolling Danube River, which flows for 870 miles (1,400 kilometres) through Romania and in the south forms a natural border with Serbia and Bulgaria. To the northeast, near the coast, the river forms part of the border with Ukraine.

The Carpathians and Transylvania

The great arc of the Carpathian Mountain System encircles the Transylvanian Plateau. The Bukovina region lies in the Moldavian Carpathians near the border with Ukraine. It boasts fine ski slopes and dramatic scenery. Although the Eastern Carpathians are generally quite low, the Southern Carpathians – which are sometimes called the Transylvanian Alps – are truly alpine in character and size. In places, they reach heights of over 8,200 feet (2,500 metres). Romania's tallest mountain, Mount Moldoveanu, is in the Transylvanian Alps. It rises to a height of 8,343 feet (2,543 metres). These steep sided mountains, with their jagged crests, tower over the high plains below. They provide an ideal habitat for alpine flowers like the brilliant blue gentian and the edelweiss, and this is the only place in the world where *dianthus craioli* – a plant said to have magic powers – can be found.

Tourists flock to the Carpathians to walk and climb, and to appreciate the wealth of animal life: foxes, lynx, badgers, wolves and even bears still run wild here. Hikers can follow many signposted tracks over the peaks, up and down steep cliffs, through gorges and deciduous (leaf-shedding) and coniferous forests and over colourful mountain meadows. Lake Bicaz – formed behind a dam in the Eastern Carpathians – attracts both walkers and anglers. In fact, Romania is a paradise for anyone who enjoys fishing, with its rivers and lakes full of trout, carp, grayling, pike, barbel, perch, sheathfish and sturgeon. The Southern Carpathians provide a favourite haunt for winter sports enthusiasts.

Transylvania is probably best known as the home of the legendary Count Dracula. But the horror stories do not seem to fit in with the peaceful, picturesque landscape of this region. Beautiful towns, churches, vil-

"Dracula's Castle" (*below*), stronghold of the legendary vampire count, frowns down from a commanding height in the Transylvanian Alps (*right*) of south-central Romania. The story of Dracula, popularized by British writer Bram Stoker's famous novel of 1897, stems from the rule in Walachia during the 1400s of the notorious "Vlad the Impaler" (Prince Vlad Ţepeş), who executed both his Turkish enemies and his rebellious peasant subjects.

lages and farmsteads set among highlands and broad valleys make this a typical eastern European rural landscape. The fertile soil is intensively farmed for maize and wheat, and fruit and vines grow on the south-facing valley slopes.

Moldavia and Wallachia

In eastern Romania, at the foot of the Carpathians, lies Moldavia, which forms part of the Russian steppe land. The original steppe vegetation has disappeared, as the land is now intensively cultivated. Set in the wooded hills are many monasteries and churches, built in the 1300s and 1500s as fortified citadels of Orthodox Christianity. For Romania was for many centuries a front-line state in Europe's confrontation with the Muslim Ottoman empire. Wallachia lies in southern Romania. Its hilly landscape, crossed by many rivers, falls away to the Danube plains, which are covered with wheat fields. The eastern part of the region resembles the treeless, cultivated steppes of Russia.

The mighty Danube

In the west, the Danube breaks through the Banat Mountains at the Iron Gate, providing the force to drive a power station built by Romania and Yugoslavia. To the east, it is prevented from entering the Black Sea by

the Dobruja tableland, where excellent wines are produced. The Danube makes a detour to the north, where industrial effluent taints its flow as it turns eastwards and heads for the sea through Danubia, the region that bears its name. Near Galati, the river breaks up into a three-pronged delta, a region of rivers, islands, lakes, reeds, ponds and streams. Here, hundreds of species of birds, including cormorants, pelicans, wild geese, swans and herons, come to feed, rest and breed. Sadly, this natural sanctuary is threatened by environmental pollution.

Romania's 130 miles (209 kilometres) of Black Sea coast are ideal for recreation. Good weather is guaranteed from May to October, and the fine, sandy beaches stretch for 50 miles (80 kilometres). Here, modern tourist resorts stand alongside elegant, older spa towns such as Mamaia, Eforia and Mangalia.

Boatmen take their ease (*above*) at the Mouths of the Danube. The abundant wildlife of this area near the Black Sea is now threatened by industrial pollution.

Herds are watered in a stream in Walachia (*far left*), in the southern part of Romania. Women (*left*) stack the hay harvest to dry in the sun on the Moldavian Plains. Sparsely populated, this region contains some of the country's best farmland.

ROMANIA, A COUNTRY IN EAST EUROPE, lies southwest of the former Soviet Union and north of the Balkan Peninsula. Its name means "land of the Romans", for it derives its origins from the ancient Roman empire, of which it was once a part.

The political background

Romania came under Soviet control at the end of World War II. Under Red Army pressure, the country changed rapidly from a monarchy to a Communist state. The new Stalinist regime placed all sectors of the economy under state control, adopted a new constitution on the Soviet model and imposed its will through the Securitate, the hated secret police.

In 1965, Nicolae Ceausescu (1918-89) became the country's president. Calling himself *Conducator* (leader), he lived like an emperor, even appearing with a golden sceptre and an imperial orb. His extravagant lifestyle and that of his family – many of whom were given government posts – was in contrast to the ordinary people's poverty and desolation.

Although Romania belonged to COMECON and the Warsaw Pact (the trade and military alliances which linked the countries of Eastern Europe with the Soviet Union), it showed an independent spirit as far back as 1955. It refused to act as a producer of raw materials and agricultural goods for the Soviet Union, and maintained a fairly independent foreign policy which often criticized Soviet actions abroad. Under Ceausescu, Romanian industry entered a period of forced expansion, financed by Western credit and the exploitation of

the workforce. A balance of payments crisis in the early 1980s prompted the government to declare that it would pay back all its foreign debts. This led to rationing and great hardship for ordinary Romanians.

Economic hardships, and the harsh treatment of Germans and Hungarians, helped to bring down this brutal totalitarian government. Protests in Braşov in 1987 were followed by a popular uprising in December 1989. Starting in Timişoara, it soon spread to the whole country, with much bloodshed. A National Salvation Front took control, led by Ion Iliescu (b.1930). Ceausescu and his wife were tried and executed.

Elections held in May 1990 resulted in a massive victory for Ion Iliescu and the NSF. But some experts suggested that the whole revolution may have been "stage-managed" to replace one sort of socialist dictatorship with another.

However, although former Communists still occupy positions of power, the old Communist political structure has been overhauled. Romania's government has enacted far-reaching reforms to revitalize the country's stagnant economy. The privatization of formerly state-owned enterprises is a high priority for Romania's leaders. The country has even applied for membership of the European Community.

The economy

The Romanian economy, for many years one of the least developed in Europe, depended heavily on agriculture. However, efforts during the 1960s concentrated on the expansion of the industrial sector. This is now the country's largest employer and

FACT BOX

THE COUNTRY
Official name: Republic of Romania
Capital:
Bucharest
Land regions:
Transylvania (NW/centre), Bukovina, Moldavia (NE), Walachia (S), Banat (W), Dobruja (SE)
Land area: 91,700 sq mi (237,500 km²)
Climate: Continental with hot, sunny summers and cold winters. Plains warmer than mountain areas
Main rivers: Danube, Jiu, Oltul, Argeş, Ialomiţa, Siretul, Prut
Highest elevation:
Mount Moldoveanu 8,343 ft (2,543 m)
Lowest elevation: Sea level along the coast

THE GOVERNMENT
Form of Government:
Parliamentary republic
Head of State:
President
Head of Government:
Prime Minister
Administrative areas:
40 counties, divided into cities, towns and communes, plus city of Bucharest
Legislature:
Parliament: Assembly of Deputies 387 members) and Senate (119 members)
Judiciary: Supreme Court, county courts, local courts, military courts
Armed forces: Total strength: about 180,000. Men must serve between 16-24 months

THE PEOPLE
Population (1990):
23,272,000
Language: Romanian. Germans, Hungarians and other minorities speak own language
Religion: Romanian Orthodox (about 66%), Roman Catholic (about 7%). Muslim, Jewish, Protestant minorities

THE ECONOMY
Currency: Leu
Gross Domestic Product per person (1991):
US$1,164
Annual Growth Rate
n.a.
Trade balance in US$ (1989): $2,012 mill
Goods imported: Fuel, raw materials, metals, iron ore, coal, cotton, machinery, chemicals

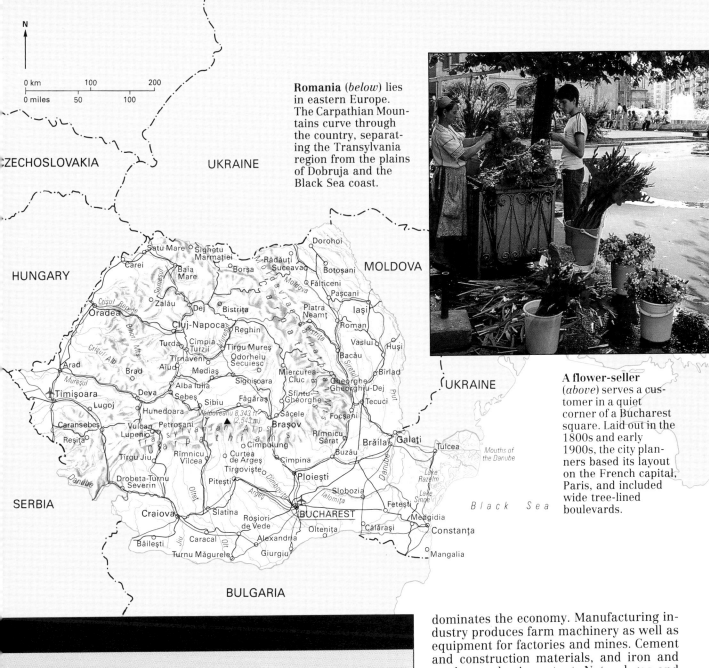

Romania (*below*) lies in eastern Europe. The Carpathian Mountains curve through the country, separating the Transylvania region from the plains of Dobruja and the Black Sea coast.

A flower-seller (*above*) serves a customer in a quiet corner of a Bucharest square. Laid out in the 1800s and early 1900s, the city planners based its layout on the French capital, Paris, and included wide tree-lined boulevards.

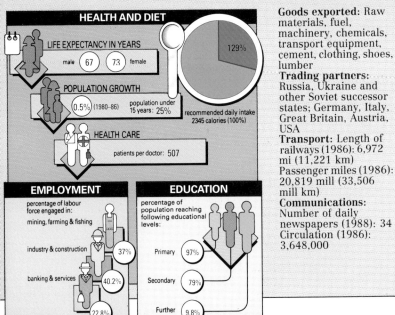

HEALTH AND DIET

LIFE EXPECTANCY IN YEARS

male 67 73 female

129%

POPULATION GROWTH

0.5% (1980–86) population under 15 years: 25%

recommended daily intake 2345 calories (100%)

HEALTH CARE

patients per doctor: 507

EMPLOYMENT

percentage of labour force engaged in:

mining, farming & fishing 37%

industry & construction 40.2%

banking & services 22.8%

EDUCATION

percentage of population reaching following educational levels:

Primary 97%

Secondary 79%

Further 9.8%

Goods exported: Raw materials, fuel, machinery, chemicals, transport equipment, cement, clothing, shoes, lumber

Trading partners: Russia, Ukraine and other Soviet successor states; Germany, Italy, Great Britain, Austria, USA

Transport: Length of railways (1986): 6,972 mi (11,221 km) Passenger miles (1986): 20,819 mill (33,506 mill km)

Communications: Number of daily newspapers (1988): 34 Circulation (1986): 3,648,000

dominates the economy. Manufacturing industry produces farm machinery as well as equipment for factories and mines. Cement and construction materials, and iron and steel, are also important. Natural gas and petroleum deposits have been developed, together with other minerals such as bauxite (from which aluminium is made), coal, copper, gold and iron ore.

Agriculture is still an important part of the economic life of the country. Cropland and pasture cover about 60 per cent of the land, while forests make up another 25 per cent. Grains, especially corn and wheat, rank as the largest crops. Grapes, fruit, potatoes and sugar beet are also grown. Sheep, cattle, horses, pigs and poultry are raised on the wide expanses of pasture. Like the other former Communist states of Eastern Europe, Romania is attempting the transition to a free market economy. This has led to hardship for the people, caused by rapidly increasing prices for food and energy, and decreased demand for the country's manufactured goods.

People

THE ROMANIANS ARE VERY DIFFERENT from other Eastern European peoples because they speak a "Romance" language – a language derived from Latin, the language of the Romans, who conquered part of the area (called Dacia) in AD 106. These origins make Romanian much closer to French, Spanish and Italian (also developed from Latin) than it is to Hungarian or Russian.

Early migrations

About 85 per cent of Romania's people are of Romanian ancestry. They are descended from Dacians who lived in the area before the arrival of the Romans, and a number of other tribes who invaded after the Romans left. These include the Goths, Huns, Slavs, Magyars, Tartars and Bulgars.

In the 1300s, the two principalities of Moldavia and Wallachia emerged, but were incorporated into the Ottoman (Turkish) empire. The Turks ruled for about 300 years until 1821. In 1859, Moldavia and Wallachia united and declared themselves to be the independent Kingdom of Romania in 1881. Moldavia was later split into two and the eastern half absorbed by the Soviet Union. In 1991, this territory – now known as Moldova – gained independence, with the Soviet Union's collapse. Moldova's Romanian majority strongly support reunification with Romania. However, the issue has led to conflict between Romanians and Moldova's Russian and Gagauz minorities.

Minorities

Romania's largest minority are the Hungarians, who make up eight per cent of the population. Germans make up another two per cent; there are also significant numbers of Gypsies, Jews, Turks and Ukrainians.

The Hungarians, Ukrainians and Turks all live quite close to the borders with their original countries. The German people live in several large areas within Transylvania. Gypsy people live in small groups in rural areas, and many still suffer from persecution from local people whose superstitious beliefs connect Gypsies with bad luck. The people of Moldova speak a language which is much like Romanian but written in Cyrillic script. Hungarians have lived in the west for centuries after Magyar tribesmen conquered Transylvania in the 800s and settled here to protect their border.

Germans and Hungarians

Living next to their mother country, Hungarians have not been isolated from their own culture. Nevertheless, they suffer from the Romanian government's failure to recognize national minorities. Officially, there are no Hungarians or Germans – only Romanians of Hungarian or German nationality. Over the years, "homogenization"

became the catchword as the government tried to force minorities to assimilate into the Romanian people

In 1919, the Germanic settlers in Transylvania and Banat opted to belong to the new Romanian state, which promised them many rights and freedoms. Including the Germans in Bessarabia, Bukomina and Dobruja, the German minority in Romania grew to around 780,000.

After World War II, many Germans were expelled or fled from Romania. Their departure – and Romania's catastrophic economic situation – have left many settlements in picturesque Transylvania lapsing into decay. Their former inhabitants have left for Germany, hoping to find a better future. The big country estates are falling into disrepair, farms have been abandoned and the churches are locked and boarded up. In the towns of Alba Iulia, Braşov, Cluj-Napoca and Sighişoara, the once-splendid façades of the old merchants' houses are crumbling. Rain

Religious worship (*far left, top*) was suppressed during the period of Communist rule in Romania. But many people continued to celebrate festivals. Most people belong to the Romanian Orthodox Church.

People of German origin (*far left, below*) make up about two per cent of the Romanian population. Other minority groups include Hungarians, Gypsies a Jews. Schools teach Hungarian and German as well as Romanian.

Everyday life (*left*) in Romania contrasts sharply with that in western Europe. Less than one per cent of the population own a car, and only 15 per cent own a television. City dwellers face a housing shortage.

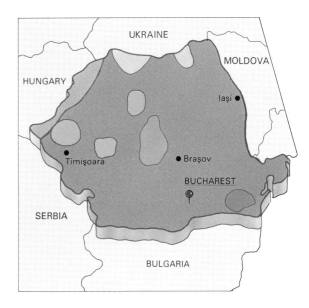

The population of Romania (*above*) includes significant numbers of Hungarians, who live close to the Hungarian border, and Germans who are scattered throughout the northwest of the country.

	Romanian
	Hungarian
	German
	Ukrainian
	Turkish

A fisherman (*left*) propels his boat in Romania's delta region. Among the many fish caught in this region is the sturgeon which produces caviar, a highly prized delicacy in the wealthier countries of the world.

Most rural Romanians (*below*) live in wooden houses. They celebrate weddings, christenings and religious holidays by wearing colourful costumes and dancing to folk music, often provided by Gypsies.

falls through holes in their roofs and gradually reduces them to ruins. Faceless new blocks of flats surround the old hearts of the towns, creating an atmosphere of desolation. There is little to persuade minorities to stay in Romania. Virtually all the 200,000 Germans living there have applied for permission to live in Germany.

Although Hungarian and German schoolchildren are entitled by law to be taught in their own languages, they feel cut off. Romanian is the official language of the country, and the language of everyday life. As a result, many Germans have become isolated and have been forced to abandon their own language.

Ceausescu's "systematization law"

The most outrageous example of the abuse of minority human rights in Romania was the so-called "systematization law". In 1988, Nichólae Ceausescu announced that he was going to destroy over half of Romania's 13,000 villages, in order to create space for gigantic agro-industrial complexes. This policy hit the minorities very hard – especially the Hungarians – and there were fierce protests from abroad, notably from Germany and Hungary. This destructive policy came to an end when Ceausescu himself was removed from power and executed in 1989.

Hungary, a small, landlocked nation of nearly 11 million people, lies at the heart of central Europe. The country's name is a reminder of the time when it belonged to the Bulgarian Onogur empire, north of the Black Sea. In the language of their Slavic neighbours, "Onogur" became "Hungary". Today, native Hungarians make up around 92 per cent of the population and speak a language distantly related to Estonian and Finnish.

Hungarians have few linguistic, cultural or racial links with their neighbours. Romany people (or Gypsies) form the largest ethnic minority within Hungary. There are around 500,000 of them. Other ethnic groups include Germans (two per cent), Slovaks (one per cent) and Southern Slavs, whose number has been swelled by refugees from the former republic of Yugoslavia.

Hungarians refer to themselves as "Magyars". This name comes from the tribe of the *Megyeri*, who were the ancestors of modern Hungarians. Originally they were nomadic horsemen who roamed the plains between the Volga and the Urals. During the 7th century AD they gradually migrated westward, joining up in the course of their journey with various other ethnic groups. Although the country in which they settled was surrounded by Slavs and Germanic peoples, the Magyars retained their own language, which has survived to the present day. The Ottoman Turks ruled much of Hungary from the early 1500s to the late 1600s.

During the late 1800s and early 1900s, Hungary was part of the massive dual empire of Austria-Hungary. Many of the fine buildings of its capital, **Budapest** (*right*), date from this period. No other Hungarian city can match this splendid metropolis on the Danube. One in five Hungarians live in Budapest, which has a population of around two million. The city is not only the political, economic and industrial heart of the country; it is also the spiritual and cultural home for millions of Hungarians around the world.

A divided nation

The Hungarians regard themselves not only as isolated, but also as a divided nation. Under the Treaty of Trianon (1920), which was imposed by the victorious Allies on the defeated Hungarians after World War I, two-thirds of Hungary's territory was given to its neighbours Czechoslovakia, Romania, Austria and Yugoslavia. The borders drawn at that time remain roughly the same today.

Nowadays, more than three million Hungarians live in neighbouring countries, the majority in Romania, where Hungarians numbering almost two million, were denied fundamental human rights under the brutal

Ceausescu regime. This created a constant source of political conflict between the two countries. The situation of ethnic Hungarians in Romania continued to give concern in 1992; while those who lived in the Vojvodina region of Serbia have also suffered, especially as a result of the Yugoslavian civil war.

There are also hundreds of thousands of Hungarians living in Czechoslovakia and Ukraine. The fact that the Hungarian nation is still spread out across several countries continues to cause Hungarians deep regret, as official statements reveal. A further 1.5 million ethnic Hungarians live in the USA and Canada, western Europe, Australia and even Africa. Every year, up to 200,000 tourists of Hungarian origin travel from these countries to visit their mother country.

Although living in the very centre of Europe, Hungarians have always looked towards the traditions and culture of the West. Their gradual withdrawal from the Eastern bloc towards the end of the 1980s set the example for other Communist countries. Hungarians played a courageous part in lifting the Iron Curtain, and will long be remembered for their decision, on 10 September 1989, to allow thousands of East German refugees to cross to the West through Hungary.

A thriving tourist trade

Even when it was part of the Warsaw Pact, the Soviet-dominated military alliance of Eastern European Communist states, Hungary was always a special case. While other Warsaw Pact countries seemed grey, monotonous and joyless places, Hungary developed a thriving tourist trade, attracting over 10 million visitors from both East and West every year. In the eyes of these visitors, Hungary seemed bright, cheerful and pulsating with life, and the Hungarians appeared a spirited and lively people, at home in a wide variety of foreign languages.

Certainly Hungarians enjoy the good life, and are proud of their fine wines and spicy food. They love folk music, and the colourful traditional costumes which they wear on special occasions give their country a romantic appeal.

Although Hungary has few notable tourist attractions, other than Lake Balaton (the largest lake in central Europe) the country was long a popular meeting place for friends and relations from both sides of the Iron Curtain. For visitors from the East it became a shoppers' paradise – providing they could pay in US dollars or another hard currency. Here they could buy all the things which were not available in their own countries. By contrast, Westerners came simply to see the country and to enjoy its hospitality and traditions.

Hungary Today

BEFORE THE COLLAPSE OF COMMUNISM, Hungary was associated with the bloodshed and repression of the 1956 Hungarian uprising and the execution of the reformist premier, Imre Nagy (1896-1958). Yet after the late 1960s, Hungarians enjoyed a level of personal freedom and economic prosperity unique among Communist-run East European countries. Moreover, Hungary's relatively painless transition to democracy after 1989 owed not a little to the contribution of reforming politicians in the Communist Party.

Hungary's gradual movement towards democracy began with the economic reforms introduced by János Kádár in 1968. The policies came to be known as "goulash Communism" reflecting their intriguing combination of different elements – like the Hungarian national dish. Kádár's economic reorganization, particularly the encouragement of private enterprise, soon began to pay dividends. The supply system and the standard of living improved dramatically for many people. Successive governments also tolerated the "grey market", ensuring that many Hungarians were able to earn extra income by taking a second or even a third job, or by starting their own businesses.

These economic reforms were accompanied by a number of "little freedoms". Hungarians were allowed to travel abroad to Western countries, provided that they could obtain the necessary foreign currency. However, for many East Europeans, Western currencies, especially dollars were expensive and difficult to find.

Cultural life, too, was relatively free from

Hungary (*far right*) is one of Europe's land-locked countries. Flat, low-lying plains cover most of the southeast of the country, while low hills and mountains dominate the north and west. The Danube river divides Hungary roughly through the middle.

Budapest's Parliament Building (*right*) stands on the east bank of the Danube river. As the meeting place of Hungary's national Assembly, it witnessed the defeat by election of the Communist regime in the spring of 1990.

FACT BOX

THE COUNTRY
Official name: Republic of Hungary
Capital: Budapest
Land regions: Little Plain (in northwest), Transdanubia (west of Danube), Northern Highlands, Great Plain (east of Danube)
Land area: 35,920 sq mi (93,032 km²)
Climate: Continental and humid with long, hot summers and cold winters. Most rain during summer months (May-July)
Main rivers: Danube, Tisza, Rába, Körös
Highest elevation: Mount Kékes 3,300 ft (1,015m)
Lowest elevation: Near Szeged, 259 ft (79 m) above sea level

THE GOVERNMENT
Form of Government: Parliamentary democracy
Head of State: President
Head of Government: Prime Minister
Administrative areas: 19 counties, 6 cities
Legislature: National Assembly (386 members, elected to 4-year terms). Presidential Council (21 members) between Assembly sessions
Judiciary: Supreme Court, county and metropolitan courts, district and city courts; special courts
Armed forces: About 100,000. Men after age 18 must serve for 18 months

THE PEOPLE
Population (1990): 10,375,000
Language: Magyar (Hungarian). Ethnic minorities speak own language
Religion: Roman Catholic (about 67%), Protestant (25%), Orthodox and Jewish minorities

THE ECONOMY
Currency: Forint
Gross Domestic Product per person (1991): US$3,103
Annual Growth Rate (1985-90): 1.0%
Trade balance in US$ (1988): $606 mill
Goods imported: Machinery, coal, cotton, electric power, oil, fertilizers, iron ore

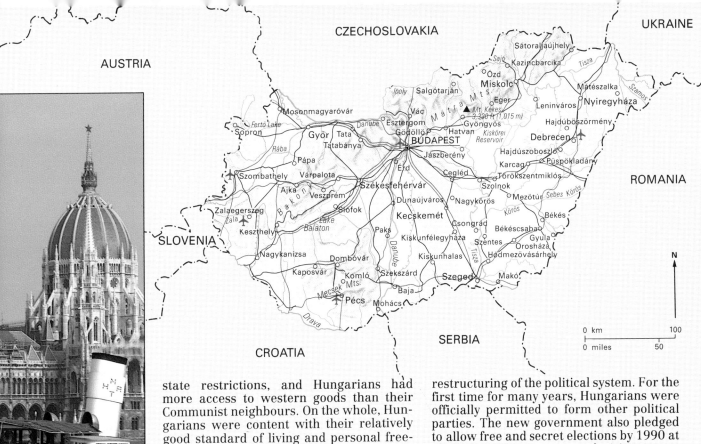

state restrictions, and Hungarians had more access to western goods than their Communist neighbours. On the whole, Hungarians were content with their relatively good standard of living and personal freedoms, yet many social problems remained. But by the 1980s, it became clear that the economic boom had passed its peak.

In May 1988, widespread demonstrations followed Kádár's refusal to make further reforms, and the political leadership of Hungary underwent a radical change. Kádár was forced to stand down as head of the ruling Hungarian Socialist Workers' Party (HSWP). The new leadership embarked upon a programme of much more extensive economic reforms and a complete restructuring of the political system. For the first time for many years, Hungarians were officially permitted to form other political parties. The new government also pledged to allow free and secret elections by 1990 at the latest. This important decision meant that there could be no going back. The whole system and structure of society began to change radically.

One important symbolic move has been the official rehabilitation of Imre Nagy. In 1989, Hungary's Supreme Court declared that his death sentence had been unlawful. Nagy and four of those executed with him were awarded state funerals, and the events of 1956 were at last acknowledged as a popular uprising.

The return of democracy

On October 23, 1989 (the anniversary of the 1956 uprising), a new Republic of Hungary was proclaimed. The new Hungarian constitution is a widely modified and enlarged version of the old one of 1949. It states that Hungary is now a parliamentary democracy, based on a free-market economy.

Hungary's first free elections to the National Assembly were held in the spring of 1990, and resulted in a decisive defeat for the reform Communists.

The surprising victor in these historic elections was the Democratic Forum – a coalition of conservative political groups with new prime minister Jozsef Antall (b. 1932) at its head. The government has made determined efforts to bring Hungary into step with Western economies, including the formation of a stock exchange and moves towards membership of the European Community. But with the loss of traditional markets, an influx of refugees, rising inflation and unemployment, and industrial pollution, the future looks difficult.

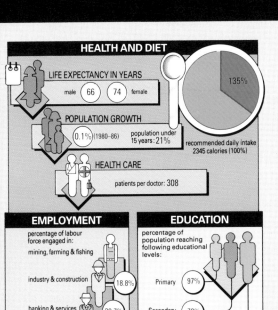

HEALTH AND DIET

LIFE EXPECTANCY IN YEARS
male 66 | 74 female

135%

POPULATION GROWTH
0.1% (1980–86) population under 15 years: 21%

recommended daily intake 2345 calories (100%)

HEALTH CARE
patients per doctor: 308

EMPLOYMENT
percentage of labour force engaged in:

mining, farming & fishing — 18.8%

industry & construction — 39.7%

banking & services — 41.5%

EDUCATION
percentage of population reaching following educational levels:

Primary 97%

Secondary 70%

Further 15.2%

Goods exported: Machinery, alumina, transportation equipment, iron, steel, processed food and beverages, chemical products, livestock
Trading partners: Eastern European countries, Germany, Italy, Austria
Transport: Length of railways (1987): 4,825 mi (7,766 km) Passenger miles (1987): 7,617 mill (12,259 mill km)
Communications: Number of daily newspapers (1986): 29 Circulation (1986): 2,778,000

Nature and Economy

HUNGARY'S HEARTLAND IS ENCLOSED by the Alps to the West, and by the Carpathian Mountains to the north. The Danube River runs through the country from north to south, effectively dividing it into two. To the west of the river lies Transdanubia and further west an area known as the Little Plain. To the east of the river lies the Great Plain, a huge expanse of flat, low-lying land bounded to the north by the Northern Highlands. Most of the Great Plain consists of low hills, wide river valleys and sand dunes. Transdanubia is separated from the Little Plain by the Transdanubian Central Highlands. These consist of several mountain chains, including the Bakony and Vertes ranges. Picturesque ravines plunging between chalk and dolomite cliffs, as well as meandering streams and oak forests, provide a paradise for ramblers. Transdanubia mostly consists of undulating hill country with many streams and rivers. The farmers here are famous for their skill in breeding pigs, geese and chickens. To the south lie the Mecsek Mountains – pleasant wooded hills rising to heights of around 2,300 feet (700 metres).

To the south of the Bakony mountains lies the great "Hungarian Sea", Lake Balaton, which is set amid the rolling hills and low mountains of Transdanubia. Lake Balaton has an area of around 230 square miles (596 square kilometres). Not only is it one of the largest lakes in Europe, it is also one of the least polluted. Because it averages only ten feet (3 metres) in depth, the water is easily warmed by the sun. In the summer it may reach temperatures of around 86°F (30°C). It is a popular tourist resort, pleasantly situated among luxuriant vineyards and orchards.

The numerous thermal springs in and around Budapest indicate the volcanic origin of the mountains east of the Danube. Mount Kékes, in the Mátra Mountains of the Northern Highlands, ranks as Hungary's highest mountain, standing at a height of 3,330 feet (1,015 metres). The Bükk range rises almost to the same height. As these modest elevations suggest, Hungary is not noted for its mountains. Some two-thirds of the country lies less than 650 feet (198 metres) above sea level.

Reclaiming the great plain

The area of Hungary known as the Great Plain bounded to the west by the River Danube, covers almost half the total area of the country. Under Turkish rule, in the 1500s-1600s, the fertile farmland and forest of the Great Plain became a desolate steppeland (the *Puszta*), deserted save for a few thatched huts, cattle herds and wild horses. Today, the Puszta is preserved in a wildlife conservation area near Hortobagy,

Wild horses (*right*) still gallop across Hungary's Great Plain region, although they are now confined to the *Puszta* (steppeland) conservation area near Hortobagy. Farmland covers most of the Great Plain region today.

A country market (*above*) provides rural women not only with a place to sell their poultry, but also acts as a popular meeting place.

Farmworkers (*above*) clear the ground of weeds using long-handled hoes. About 80 per cent of Hungary's cropland is farmed by collectives, but the workers also tend small private plots in their spare time.

Lake Balaton (*right*), so large it is known as the "Hungarian Sea", attracts growing numbers of tourists every year. Its shallow waters warm up very quickly, allowing bathing and water sports throughout the summer months.

The Hungarian landscape (*right*) can be divided into four major land regions. Farming was once the basis of the economy, but industry developed under Communist rule. Hungary exports processed food and machinery.

Green paint distinguishes the gates of the steelworks (*below*) in Ozd, a large industrial town in northern Hungary, close to the border with Czechoslovakia. The factory uses locally mined iron ore and Hungarian coal.

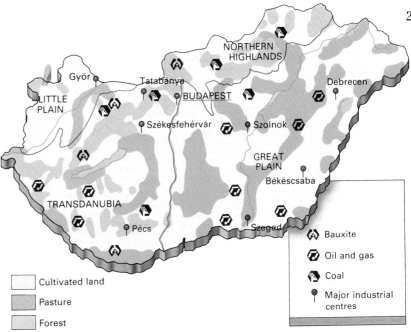

Cultivated land

Pasture

Forest

Bauxite

Oil and gas

Coal

Major industrial centres

and attempts are being made to reclaim the land. Sandy areas have been irrigated to make them suitable for orchards and vineyards. Protected from the wind by tall hedgerows, crops of wheat, sugar beet, sunflowers and melons now flourish on the broad flatlands. Many swamps, which once provided a habitat for waterfowl, have now been drained so that the land can be used to produce corn.

Because Hungary is small, landlocked and varies little in elevation, it experiences few variations in climate. Winters are cold, averaging 29°F (−2°C) in January. The average July temperature is around 70°F (21°C). Rainfall, mainly in May-July, averages 24 inches (60 centimetres) annually.

Agriculture and industrialization
Since the end of World War II, Hungary has undergone rapid and extensive industriali-

zation. Yet agriculture remains an important part of the economy. Farms cover about 75 per cent of the land, and about 15 per cent is forested. The country's most important exports are meat and meat products, fruits, vegetables, sugar beet and grapes. Hungary also produces industrial products such as aluminium, bauxite, steel and electronic goods. It is known as a major producer of transport equipment – especially buses. Hungary's major imports include advanced machinery, vehicles, coal, iron ore, electric power and oil.

In recent years, Hungary has attempted to expand the range of goods it offers on the world market. Efforts have been made to improve the productivity and competitiveness of manufacturing industry through cooperation with the West. These measures are urgently needed, for production figures have fallen steadily since the mid-1980s, both in heavy industry and in key areas of manufacturing industry such as electromechanical, engineering, roller bearings and vehicle manufacture.

Recent economic developments
Since 1989, Hungary has been trying to change to a Western-style market economy. A great deal of encouragement has been given to the private sector in industry. Also, because foreign money needs to be attracted into the country, foreign investors have been offered numerous concessions to set up businesses in Hungary.

In Budapest – Hungary's premier industrial and trading centre – hopes are high for future membership of the European Community. But the new government faces serious problems. Hungary must find a solution for its large foreign debts, old-fashioned factories, declining productivity, rising unemployment and inflation.

In 1991, the Union of Soviet Socialist Republics (USSR), ruled by the Communist Party following the Russian Revolution of 1917, was dissolved. The 15 republics that had formerly made up the USSR became independent states. The city of **Moscow** (*left*), for decades the centre of the Soviet empire, reverted to being the capital of just one republic, the giant Russian Federation. On December 21, 1991, 11 states came together in Alma Ata, capital of Kazakhstan, to form the Commonwealth of Independent States (CIS). The three major powers within the CIS at that time were the Russian Federation, the Ukraine and Byelorussia; the other states were Kazakhstan, Uzbekistan, Azerbaijan, Moldova, Kirghizia, Tajikistan, Turkmenistan and Armenia.

The CIS was not formed as a country with "national" authority over its member states. Nominally, it took over the military and other federal obligations of the former republics that together made up the Soviet Union. The Baltic States – Estonia, Latvia and Lithuania – and Georgia did not join the CIS.

The vast area covered by the CIS created the largest "politically-unified" territory in the world, covering 8,555,060 square miles (22,157,600 square kilometres) – more than the size of Canada and the United States combined. At the formation of the CIS, Russia alone occupied some 77.5 per cent of its territory, stretching from the Baltic Sea to the Pacific Ocean, and claimed about 54 per cent of the total population.

The Alma Ata Declaration that marked the birth of the CIS gave equal status to all member states. However, since Russia is still the largest and most populous of all the states of the former Soviet Union, the reality for the other successor states is a determination to avoid Russian dominance. However, conflicts between members, such as the dispute between Armenia and Azerbaijan over the status of the enclave of Nagorno-Karabakh, threaten the collective stability of the CIS. Another potential focus for conflict is the influence of Islamic fundamentalism in the Central Asian States.

Over the next few years, the successor states of the former Soviet Union must undergo the painful transition from a planned to a free-market economy. The economy of the former Soviet Union depended upon each republic contributing food and materials to a vast, sprawling economy, according to targets set by central planning authorities. The collapse of the Soviet state led many republics to hold back exports for home consumption. In many cases, this has resulted in hardship for ordinary people.

THE FORMER SOVIET UNION ENCOM-
passes a massive area, and extends about
6,000 miles (9,660 kilometres) from the
Baltic Sea in the west to the shores of the
Pacific Ocean in the far east, and about
3,200 miles (5,510 kilometres) from north
to south. Over such a vast expanse the
terrain is naturally extremely varied. The
landscape is most mountainous in the south
and east, falling away to the north and
west, where there are extensive lowlands
and large river systems that flow through
huge marshes. The mountains of the south
include the Caucasus, Pamir, Tien Shan,
Altai, Sayan and Yablonovy systems: the
East Siberian Uplands are mostly barren
peaks and plateaus. The highest point in
the former Soviet Union is in the Pamirs,
and until 1991 was called Communism
Peak: it is 24,590 feet (495 metres) in height.
Major rivers, such as the Volga, Dnepr and
Don, are used for transport and for hydroelectric power generation. Some of the
longest rivers flow northwards through
Siberia into the Arctic Sea: they include the
Ob, Yenisey and Lena. The Volga ranks as
the longest river in Europe, and flows for
2,194 miles (3,531 kilometres) from its
source in the Valdai Hills northwest of
Moscow, emptying into the Caspian Sea.

The overall climate of the former Soviet
Union is greatly influenced by two general
trends. Warmth and sunlight increase progressively from north to south, and drought
and cold in winter increase progressively
from west to east.

Tundra and taiga
Immediately south of the Arctic Ocean
coast, the tundra – the cold, level plain
under which the soil is permanently frozen
– stretches like a band, broadening in the
east due to the severe climate. Even on the
southern edge of this zone, average summer temperatures do not exceed 50°F
(10°C). In the European part of the tundra
zone (west of the Ural Mountains that mark
the division between Europe and Asia), the
average January temperature ranges from
18°F (−8°C) to −4°F (−20°C). In the Siberian
part the temperature ranges from −4°F
(−20°C) to −29°F (−34°C).

The West Siberian Plain, north of the
Altai Mountains, is the largest flat region in
the world. In areas sheltered from the wind,
scrub vegetation struggles to reach waist-
height. Otherwise, lichens and mosses predominate. The few permanent human settlements in the tundra region are sparsely
scattered – mining towns like Vorkuta and
Norilsk, and seaports like Murmansk.

South of the tundra is the taiga, a broad,
forested belt with a more moderate climate.
Average temperatures in summer here
range between 10°C (50°F) in the north, and

20°C (68°F) in the south. However, winters can be extremely harsh; average temperatures in mid-January range from 14°F (−10°C) in the west to a chilly −49°F (−45°C) in the east. The soil of the taiga is generally poor, and agriculture is possible only in certain zones. The main agricultural region of the taiga lies on its southern edge, where soils are slightly richer in nutrients, the average temperature is higher, and the growing season is longer.

Forest and steppe

West of the Urals and in the far east, the taiga adjoins regions of deciduous and mixed forest. In the European part – known as the European Plain – the mixed forest benefits from the influence of relatively humid Atlantic air masses. Average winter temperatures range from 27°F (−3°C) in the west to 10°F (−12°C) in the east, around the central Volga basin. Although this region

The European portion of the former Soviet Union (*left*) is mainly flat or rolling, with numerous rivers and lakes. There are some high mountain ranges in the south. The Urals separate Europe and Asia.

The territory of the former Soviet Union (*below*) runs from the Baltic to the Pacific, and from Arctic tundra to the deserts of Central Asia. The largest portion of this vast expanse is the Russian Federation.

enjoys neither fertile soils nor significant deposits of raw materials, it formed the heartland of the Russian empire from the Middle Ages. It is accordingly the location of both Moscow and St Petersburg (formerly Leningrad), the sites of the largest concentrations of industry.

To the southwest (but still within the European Plain) lies a zone that combines the benefits of the forest with the best features of the semi-desert and desert steppes of Kazakhstan and the Central Asian states to the east. Here, especially in the Ukraine, the humidity of the woodland, a longer summer and better soils have created ideal conditions for agriculture. Wheat and sugar beets are the main crops of this "black earth" zone. Much of the natural vegetation was cleared for intensive farming between the 1930s and 1980s. East of the River Dnepr, which flows through the centre of the Ukraine, the ground is more arid, saline, and liable to soil erosion.

To the east, for thousands of miles, stretch the steppes. Mountain barriers to the south and east make these southern regions subject to a cold, desert climate. In the far south, the sparse and stunted vegetation finally vanishes altogether. Desert areas include the Kara Kum and the Kyzyl Kum, situated in the vast Aral-Caspian Lowland east of the Aral and Caspian Seas.

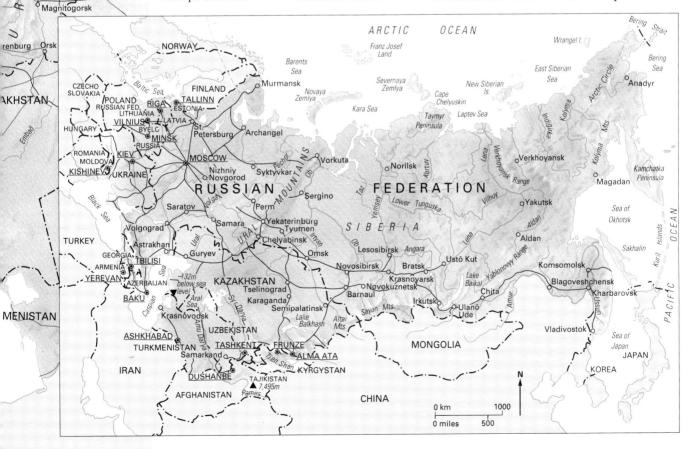

Collapse of the Soviet Union

IN SIX SHORT YEARS, THE MONOLITHIC structure of the Soviet Union was not only dismantled but discredited. Until the mid-1980s, it had been held together by the Communist Party, which had taken power in the Russian Revolution of 1917. The impetus for this historic change came from the General Secretary of the Communist Party of the Soviet Union (CPSU), Mikhail Gorbachev.

Gorbachev's reforms

Upon his appointment in March 1985, Gorbachev assumed power over a state that had often boasted of its overall wealth, massive military strength and the government's popular support. However, he was aware that in fact his country was in a deep political, economic and moral crisis. He saw that there was an urgent need to modernize and overhaul the system he had inherited, to scale down the massive, inefficient administrative structure and halt the corruption within it.

Gorbachev set in motion a programme of limited reform, which he called *perestroika* (restructuring). As a lifelong member of the CPSU himself, he did not intend his reforms to challenge the party's monopoly of power. However, his reforms soon took on a momentum of their own. When he introduced the concept of *glasnost* (openness) – the result was instant and almost unlimited freedom of expression in place of the former strict censorship. Many events that had been previously denied, ignored or misrepresented by the government and security service for years – such as the great purges carried out by Joseph Stalin during

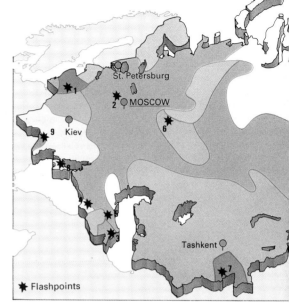

★ Flashpoints

the 1930s – were revealed, and opened to public scrutiny and comment.

Above all, the new policies revealed the poor state of the economy, the relative poverty of national minorities in republics outside Russia, and the total failure of the system of state control of industry and agriculture. The people of the Soviet Union began to realize how poorly supplied with consumer goods they were, in comparison with other countries. It was the CPSU that attracted the fiercest public criticism.

In reaction, the CPSU renounced its monopoly of power. The first steps were taken towards a multi-party political system: partly free elections were held to a new parliament, the Congress of People's

FACT BOX

FORMER SOVIET UNION (to end of 1991)
Official name: Union of Soviet Socialist Republics (until 1991)
Capital: Moscow
Land area: 8,649,500 sq mi (22,402,000 km²)
Land regions: Lowlands in W Russia divided by Ural Mountains from plains, hills and mountains of Siberia; High mountains in S
Climate: Continental, more extreme to E; N-S: Arctic, sub-Arctic, temperate and sub-tropical
Main rivers: Yenisey, Lena, Ob, Amur, Volga
Highest elevation: Communism Peak 24,590 ft (7,495 m)
Lowest Elevation:

Karagiye Depression -433 ft (-132 m)

GOVERNMENT
Form of government: Socialist federative republic
Head of state: President
Head of government: Chairman of the Council of Ministers
Administrative areas: 15 union republics 20 autonomous republics 8 autonomous regions 6 *kraj* 10 autonomous districts
Legislature: Supreme Soviet with 750 members elected for 5-year terms; divided into two chambers (Soviet of the Union, Soviet of the Nationalities)

Judiciary: Supreme Court; Supreme Courts of Union republics; Peoples' Courts; military tribunals
Armed Forces: Total strength:
Army 2,000,000
Navy 485,000
Air Forces 444,000

THE PEOPLE
Population: 287,991,000 (1990)
Language: Russian (official); equal rights for other languages in union republics and autonomous republics
Religion: Christian (Eastern Orthodox), Muslim (mainly Sunni), Judaism, Buddhism

THE ECONOMY
Currency: Rouble

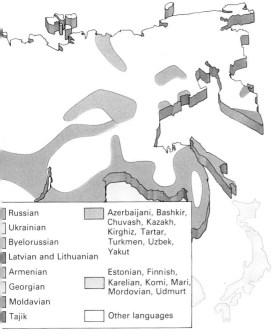

Russian	Azerbaijani, Bashkir, Chuvash, Kazakh, Kirghiz, Tartar, Turkmen, Uzbek, Yakut
Ukrainian	
Byelorussian	
Latvian and Lithuanian	
Armenian	Estonian, Finnish, Karelian, Komi, Mari, Mordovian, Udmurt
Georgian	
Moldavian	
Tajik	Other languages

Deputies. In many republics, nationalist movements sought greater autonomy. Many republics proclaimed themselves independent sovereign states; others, such as the Baltic States of Estonia, Latvia and Lithuania, announced their own independence altogether from the Soviet Union.

The end of the Soviet Union
There was considerable resistance to these changes among the party and state bureaucracy. There was also great alarm among the chiefs of the Red Army, who criticized many of Gorbachev's policies, particularly the withdrawal of Soviet economic and military backing from its former East European satellite states.

The former Soviet Union (*left*) is now divided into 15 independent states, which include more than 90 ethnic and linguistic groups. The demise of Communism has led to conflict in many regions. Some of the most serious flashpoints have been: Lithuania (**1**), where Soviet troops massacred 13 civilians in January 1991; Moscow (**2**), scene of the abortive coup of August 1991. In the Caucasus, area of conflict include the enclave of Nagorno-Karabakh (**3**), focus of war between Armenia and Azerbaijan; Georgia (**4**), where factional violence simmers; and the rebellious Georgian republic of South Ossetia (**5**). Russia's Tatar minority (**6**) have questioned their political status, while the toppling of Tajikistan's government in 1992 (**7**) may herald new upheavals. Russia and Ukraine both claim Crimea (**8**). In Moldova (**9**), Russian nationalists have set up a breakaway state.

Throughout the late 1980s, the economic situation worsened. Ordinary foodstuffs became scarce as republics kept all the food and raw materials they could use for themselves, rather than pass them on.

Gorbachev himself voiced his concern at proceeding too rapidly with political and economic reform. He allied himself with the forces of conservatism in the party and Red Army. A group of leading conservatives then attempted to seize power on August 19 1991. They interned Gorbachev and his family, and declared an emergency government. In Moscow, unprecedented mass demonstrations against the coup took place. The president of the Russian Federation – the former Communist Boris Yeltsin – led public resistance to the coup. On August 21, the coup collapsed.

The reformers' victory gave a tremendous boost to the democratic movement. The Communist Party was immediately declared illegal throughout the Soviet Union; the infamous security service (KGB) was disbanded and its records seized; statues of Lenin and other former Communist leaders were toppled. All the republics expressed a resolve to sever political ties with the former Soviet Union, and formed their own governments. In December 1991, 11 of the former 15 Soviet Union republics – including the Russian Federation, Ukraine and Kazakhstan – formed the Commonwealth of Independent States (CIS). This loose grouping undertook to honour existing international commitments and to maintain joint command over the armed forces of the former Soviet Union. Gorbachev himself left office on 25 December 1991.

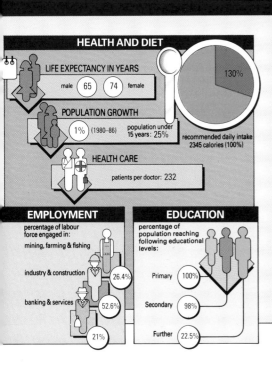

Gross Domestic Product per person: US$5,020 (1989)
Annual Growth Rate -2.0%
Trade balance in US$: $3,330mill (1988)
Goods imported: Machinery, vehicles, cereals, iron, steel, sugar, clothing, chemical products, meat and meat products, shoes, raw textiles, wood, cellulose and paper products, drugs, furniture
Goods exported: Machinery, heavy equipment, oil, natural gas, electricity, ores, metals, coal, coke, plant fibres, fuels, manufactured goods
Trading partners: East European countries,

Germany, Finland, France, Italy, Japan, USA, India, Iraq, Iran, Peoples's Republic of China
Transport: Length of railways: 91,564 mi (147,359 km)
Communications: Number of daily newspapers (1990): 723 Circulation (1990): 133,979,000

Union Republics (1991)
Armenia
Azerbaijan
Byelorussia
Estonia
Georgia
Kazakhstan
Kirgizia
Latvia
Lithuania
Moldova
Russian Federation
Tajikistan
Turkmenistan
Ukraine
Uzbekistan

The Russian Federation

THE RUSSIAN FEDERATION, MORE commonly known as Russia, is the largest country in the world. The name "Russia" was formerly often misapplied to the Soviet Union as a whole. At the end of 1991, when the Soviet Union ceased to exist, "Russia" once more became the name of an independent state. In total, Russia occupies a territory of just under 6.6 million square miles (17 million square kilometres) – almost twice the size of the United States. The European portion stretches from the Baltic Sea and the Black Sea in the west to the steep escarpment of the Ural Mountains. East of the Urals, Russia extends over the vast expanse of Siberia, all the way to the Pacific Ocean. Some of the richest soils in the world are located on the European Plain, the heartland of Russia, in which more than 60 per cent of the population live.

People

The Russian people are Slavic in origin. In around AD 850, Russia was a small European region organized in principalities and subject to raids by surrounding tribes, especially by Norse Vikings. Legend has it that one such tribe, the Rus, were initially invited to rule over a number of feuding factions in the city of Novgorod. The Christian faith arrived in about 980, and was taught in the alphabet devised specially for the Slavs by the missionary St Methodius, who named it after his brother, St Cyril. The Russian language has used the Cyrillic alphabet ever since. Until this century, most Russians adhered to the Russian, or Eastern Orthodox branch of Christianity. However, the collapse of Communism has encouraged a great upsurge in religious belief.

As the Russian state expanded, it absorbed a number of formerly independent states to the north, south and east. Many non-Slavic peoples thus came under Russian rule. Some were governed directly from Moscow, others were allowed a measure of autonomy. The state was unified under Tsar Ivan the Great, and placed under a single administration by his grandson, Ivan the Terrible (ruled 1547-84).

The Communists took over from the Tsars following the revolution of 1917. At that time, most Russians were comparatively poor and uneducated peasant-farmers. By the time the Soviet regime ended in 1991, Russia was only one – but by far the largest – of the 15 republics within the Soviet Union. Russia also contains 16 autonomous republics and regions of varying sizes and populations. Some, including the Tatar Autonomous Republic, have demanded greater local autonomy and even independence.

Language and culture

Today, the vast majority of the 148.5 million inhabitants of Russian Federation are of Russian extraction, and are proud of their culture and heritage. Of around 100 minority groups, the largest are Tatars, Ukrainians, Dagestanis, Bashkirs and Chuvash. Some communities are Turkic or Ugrian in language; others are Asiatic in origin. Russian is the country's official language, although the language of education – which is free and compulsory for all between the ages of 7 and 17 – included some local languages from the 1970s onwards. Russians have always had a strong literary and musical culture. In the 1800s, the country produced many great writers, such as Leo Tolstoy and Fyodor Dostoyevsky.

The present government of Russia is headed by a premier and Council of Delegates responsible to a Supreme Council under an elected president. The president represents the state at international functions and has considerable executive authority. Local administration still relies on the old Soviet bureaucracy, which has been greatly reduced in size. Similarly, the judicial system is now independent of government control. However, most judges held office during Communist times.

The Russian economy has been in a state of crisis since the break-up of the Soviet Union and the abandonment of the system

FACT BOX

Official name: Russian Federation
Capital: Moscow
Land area: 6,592,700 square miles (17,075,000 km²)
Land regions: from W-E: Duropean Plain, Ural Mountains, W Siberian lowland, C Siberian Mountains, E Siberian High Mountains; steppes in S
Climate: From N-S: transition from Arctic through moderate and subtropical zones
Main rivers: Volga, Ob, Yenisey, Angara, Lena

Highest elevation: Belucha 14,783 ft (4,506 m)
Lowest elevation: Sea level
Form of government: Presidential republic
Head of state: President
Population: 148,000,000
Language: Russian (official)
Religion: Russian Orthodox
Currency: Rouble
Gross Domestic Product per capita: n.a.

The city of Yaroslavl, capital of the oblast of the same name, is visible in the distance beyond this riverside church (*left*). Yaroslavl lies northeast of Moscow on the European Plain, and is an important industrial centre. The city's position on the Kotorosi River – a tributary of the Volga, Europe's longest river – also makes it an important focus for river traffic. Russia's great rivers have always provided vital communication arteries in the vast expanses of the Russian plains.

by which the Soviet republics – under central planning and control – all contributed foodstuffs and industrial materials to each other. Many of the goods allocated to Russia under the Soviet system thus now no longer arrive. Individual regions and cities now hoard their produce rather than contribute to the overall welfare of the state.

Of all the successor states of the former Soviet Union, Russia probably has the greatest potential for economic success. Manufacturing industry requires massive investment, both in new machinery, and measures to control pollution. The country has exceptionally rich and diverse deposits of minerals, particularly coal, iron, oil and natural gas. There is also scope for great improvement in the production and transportation of food. Poor roads, transport and storage facilities mean that a large part of the annual harvest goes to waste.

A war veteran (*above*) proudly displays his medals. Russians suffered huge losses in both world wars.

A village (*above left*) near the southern city of Rostov-on-Don reflects the homely lifestyle much valued by the Russian people.

The port of Murmansk (*far left*), above the Arctic Circle on the icy Barents Sea, endures some of Russia's coldest temperatures.

With the demise of Communist rule, Russian children (*left*) in a Moscow kindergarten can look forward to an education largely free of political content. Portraits of the Communist leader Vladimir Lenin, like the one shown in this picture, are uncommon today.

Life in Russia

UNDER COMMUNIST RULE, THE PEOPLE of the Soviet Union had to endure a generally lower standard of living than people in Europe and North America, with shortages of housing, food and basic household goods. Through its control of the economy, education and cultural life, the Communist Party hoped to create a classless society, but only succeeded in stifling individual talent. Following the collapse of the Soviet Union in 1991, Russians enjoyed much greater political freedom. However, the early 1990s have been a time of economic hardship for many citizens. The Russian people have always placed a high value on literature, the arts, sports and pastimes such as chess. But for most people, daily life, family matters and simple survival take up most of their time.

Religion and education

In the early years of Communist rule, the Russian Orthodox Church suffered persecution, and many churches were destroyed. However, traditional religious worship, with its inspiring ritual and beautiful *icons* (painted religious images), survived in the hearts of the people. Religious restrictions were eased in the 1980s. Today, millions of Russians and other Slavs adhere to Orthodox Christianity, including growing numbers of younger people. Muslims make up the next largest religious denomination in the Russian Federation, and the country contains large groups of Buddhists, Jews, Lutherans and Roman Catholics.

Russians have always attached a high value to education, particularly science and technology. Today, the country boasts a highly developed educational system, with about 57 million full-time students. Education is compulsory from age 7-17, and schools are run by the state. A network of special schools, renowned for their high quality, offer technical education or specialized instruction in the arts, foreign languages, mathematics or physics for promising children. More than five million students attend one of the country's 900 institutes of higher education or 70 universities. In the early 1990s, changes to the curriculum emphasized previously-suppressed works of literature, new approaches to Soviet history and business subjects.

Communications and the arts

Although the government formerly exercised strict control, including censorship, of newspapers, radio and television, the late 1980s saw a relaxation of this control. Newspapers and magazines could publish what they chose, and even criticize the government.

The Russian Orthodox Church (*below*) has millions of followers in the Russian Federation. They continued to practice their beliefs in spite of the fact that the Communists tried to discourage religious practice.

A couple (*right*) examine a Leningrad noticeboard advertising homes available for swapping. Housing shortages are a major problem in most Russian cities and many people have to live in cramped conditions or share rooms.

A feast of wild mushrooms and other edible fungi (*above*) covers a stall in Moscow's private market. Russian people often sell food collected from the wild or grown on small private plots near their homes.
A family meal in a Ukrainian farmhouse (*right*) includes a number of local specialities. Every region in Russia has its own distinctive style of cooking based on locally produced ingredients.

Music and the theatre forms a major part of Russian artistic life. The country has produced many of the world's greatest composers. In the 1800s, these included Peter Illich Tchaikovsky (1840-93), composer of *Swan Lake* and *The Nutcracker Suite;* Modest Mussorgsky (1839-81), Mikhail Glinka (1803-57) and Alexander Borodin (1834-87). Under the Communist system, composers such as Dimitri Shostakovich (1906-75) and Sergei Prokofiev (1891-1953) sometimes attracted official disapproval of their musically adventurous works. For many foreigners, ballet represents the pinnacle of Russian artistic life.

The Russian language has always provided a superb means of expression. Before *glasnost*, official Communist policy laid down the law to writers and artists. The official style, known as socialist realism, praised life under socialism. However, in the period immediately following the October Revolution, modernist movements in art flourished, and produced many important artists and film directors. Stalin and his successors enforced socialist realism, with the result that many of Russia's greatest writers suffered persecution. Writers like Boris Pasternak, Alexander Solzehnitsyn and Joseph Brodsky all attracted official condemnation for their criticisms of Soviet life. Often, their works circulated in *samizdat* (self-published) editions.

Food

The Russian people have always been renowned for their hospitality. Visitors always receive a place at the table and a plate piled high with food. Sharing bread and salt represents a gesture of friendship, a social obligation and an honour. In the absence of cafes, clubs and other places where people can meet, the home acts as the social centre for most Soviet citizens. The most impressive part of a meal is the *zakuski*, small dishes of sardines and herrings, gherkins and cabbage, cheese, sausage, various salads with mayonnaise and sour cream, accompanied by black and white bread.

Shortages of products such as onions and fresh tomatoes force Soviet citizens to plan their shopping carefully. Russians look on forests as important sources of food, and many organizations provide buses for their employees to travel to the country to seek the many varieties of mushrooms. Housewives are proud of their jams and preserves, often made of plums stuffed with walnuts, crab apples cooked with their stems or whole apricots with their stones.

Erratic supplies make the Russian a versatile eater; breakfast, for example, may include *kasha* (porridge), eggs, cheese and sausage, herrings and onions or just a glass of yogurt.

Cultural life in Russia embraces art in St Petersburg's famous Hermitage Museum (*above*) or the ballet (*left*). Russian composers such as Peter Tchaikovsky (1840-93) wrote many popular works for the ballet. Today, tickets for performances by leading ballet companies, such as the Kirov in Leningrad or the Bolshoi in Moscow, are often difficult for ordinary citizens to obtain. The country also boasts more than 2,000 museums and art galleries.

MOSCOW, THE CAPITAL CITY OF THE Russian Federation, is one of the largest cities in Europe. Its centre and suburbs are home to more than 8.9 million people. With its surrounding residential areas, the population of the Moscow metropolitan area may number as many as 12 million. Most of these people work within the city, either in the large administrative bureaucracy (now considerably smaller than it was under the former Communist regime), in other service industries, or in the many light and heavy industries that make the city a key economic centre for the state. Transport to, from, and within the city is thus of great importance. Eleven railways meet at Moscow's nine major stations; 13 major highways converge on the city; there are four airports (one of which is for international traffic); and the Moscow Canal provides a much-used link with the Volga River. For Muscovites, the main means of transport is the Metro (inaugurated in 1935), which carries five million passengers daily, and the numerous tram and bus lines.

History
On a site inhabited from Neolithic times, the present city of Moscow began in 1156 as a wooden fortified citadel (*kreml*) on the hill between the rivers Moskva and Neglinnaya. The settlement grew rapidly, and by 1400 had become the capital of the powerful principality of Muscovy, which continued to expand and incorporate adjacent principalities such as Novgorod and Kiev. In 1480, after Grand Duke Ivan III (the Great) unified the territory and subdued the Tatars (Mongols), he gave himself the additional title "Tsar of all the Russias". It was from around this time over the following century that the city's system of radial and ring roads was marked out. The radial roads went out to the different suburbs, each of which had its own layout and major economic activity. The ring roads followed early lines of fortifications. The innermost ring road enclosed the old trading quarter of the Kremlin, its surrounding stone walls built in the late 1400s and encircling Kremlin Square. From 1490 to the 1700s, no fewer than four cathedrals and another church were built in this square, for Moscow had been the centre of the Russian Orthodox (Christian) Church since 1326. It was on Kremlin Square that the Grand Palace of the tsars was built during the 1800s. After 1918, the palace became the location of the Supreme Soviet of the USSR.

The inner ring road also encloses Red Square, just outside the Kremlin wall. Until 1991 the square was the site of Soviet military parades on May Day. Red Square holds the Lenin mausoleum, where the former leader's body lies in state for public

The wall of the Kremlin, Moscow's ancient fortress, bounds Red Square (*top*) at the city's heart. Once the scene of military parades, Red Square now belongs to Moscow's increasing number of tourists.

Shoppers throng GUM (*above*), Moscow's famous department store. Situated on Red Square, this shopping complex displays goods from all over Russia: from caviar to clothing, from wood carvings to canned fish.

inspection. In Russian, the word "red" also means "beautiful". Red Square remains impressive today, particularly the magnificent cathedral of St Basil the Blessed, constructed in 1554-60, with the famous onion-shaped domes on the top of its nine chapels.

Around Red Square, and within Moscow's inner ring road, there used to be the suburb of *Kitay Gorod* (Fortress City), originally the residence of the merchants who traded with the aristocracy and court of the Kremlin. The walls of this district were demolished during the 1930s, but the modern Boulevard ring road follows the line of the wall.

Moscow lost its primacy in 1712, when Peter the Great moved his court and administrative offices to the newly-founded city of St Petersburg. In 1918, St Petersburg was too insecure for the Bolshevik (Communist) leaders of the Russian Revolution, who again made Moscow their capital. The city expanded rapidly, and underwent considerable industrial growth during the 1930s, when steel, machinery and vehicle assembly plants were set up. After World War II, the growth of industries such as textile, furniture and paper manufacture, chemical synthesis and food processing, and more recently, electronics production, caused new high-rise suburbs to sprout around the outskirts in order to accommodate the workers. An outer ring highway was constructed, some 68 miles (110 kilometres) in length.

Life in Moscow

One of Moscow's greatest problems is a shortage of housing. Many families live in very cramped conditions in small apartments, and young married couples must sometimes wait many years to obtain an apartment of their own. Wealthier residents maintain well-appointed wooden houses (*dachas*) in the forests outside the city, to which they can escape to at weekends.

To Western eyes, Moscow can seem drab and old-fashioned. Stores and shops are dull and mostly poorly stocked. For ordinary citizens, queuing for hours is part of daily life. Russia's economic crisis means that even basic goods are often in short supply or else unavailable. Shops for foreigners (or those with foreign currency) offer a wider choice, but at high prices.

Yet Moscow has at all times been the cultural capital of the Russian people, the seat of its most prestigious institutions of learning. Within the city – of which many residents are fiercely proud – are more than 120 museums and galleries, 35 well-attended concert halls and theatres (including the Bolshoi Ballet and the Moscow Arts Theatre) and many cinemas.

Graceful street lanterns tower above the crowded Arbat (*left*), a Moscow street long famous as the haunt of writers and artists.

Moscow (*right*), capital of the huge Russian Federation, spreads in rings outward from its historic heart on the Moscow River. The city was founded in 1147 by Prince Yuri Dolgoruki.

Multi-coloured tulips are offered for sale by a Moscow street vendor (*below*). Private enterprise began to flourish in the Moscow under the more liberal regime of the late 1980s.

Ukraine

THE REPUBLIC OF UKRAINE IS A LARGE country situated in Eastern Europe. With an area of 233,089 square miles (603,700 square kilometres), Ukraine ranks as the second largest European country (after the Russian Federation). To the north lies Byelorussia; to the northeast and east the Russian Federation; to the south are the Sea of Azov and the Black Sea; to the southwest are Moldova, Romania and Hungary; and to the west lie Czechoslovakia and Poland. The country also ranks as the third largest member of the Commonwealth of Independent States (CIS), the loose association of the successor states of the former Soviet Union. Ukraine is second only to the Russian Federation in terms of population and in agricultural and industrial output. The capital, Kiev, lies on the Dnepr River.

The country's terrain is largely flat or rolling, although the Carpathian Mountains rise in the far southwest and smaller ranges dissect the Crimean Peninsula (disputed between Ukraine and the Russian Federation). Northern and northwestern Ukraine has large expanses of mixed coniferous and deciduous (leaf-shedding) forest. Here the lowlands surrounding the Dnepr and Donets rivers boast excellent arable land, although there are also sizeable areas of marshland. Slightly farther south, the plains are rich in an unusually fertile black soil called *chernozem*, which is ideally suited for raising crops. Farther south and east lie the major industrial complexes of Dnepropetrovsk, Krivoy Rog, Kharkov and Donetsk. In the far south the lowlands are much drier. This is a region of steppe (grassy plains) almost completely lacking in tree cover.

History

The Ukrainians, also known as "Little Russians" or Ruthenians, are an eastern Slavic people. Their ancestors first arrived in the region during the AD 500-600s. Their settlement at Kiev became the focus of a culture now known as Kievan-Rus. This was the original nucleus of what was eventually to be the Russian empire. Kiev grew into a wealthy and powerful principality, and extended its influence to west and north. It was captured and destroyed by the Mongols in 1237-41. A century later, Ukraine became part of the Lithuanian state, and subject thus to Polish influence. It was as a border territory of Poland that Ukraine got its name: *u-kraj-na*, which means "on the border". To oppose foreign rule, a resistance movement made up of renegade serfs (known as *kozaks*, or Cossacks) grew up. This met with little success, but invited the Russian tsar to step in. By 1793, almost all of Ukraine was officially annexed by Russia.

In 1917, after the overthrow of Tsar Nicholas II, Ukrainian nationalists declared the country independent. But after the Bolsheviks (Communists) seized power, Ukraine became a highly valued Soviet Socialist Republic within the Soviet Union. Under Joseph Stalin, any form of Ukrainian nationalism was rigorously suppressed. A famine – possibly caused deliberately – in the wake of the forced collectivization of the agricultural system claimed the lives of millions of Ukrainian citizens during the 1930s. During World War II, occupation by German forces led to massive death and destruction.

Ukrainian nationalism re-appeared during the late 1980s. In 1990, the republic's government again declared independence. The Ukrainian language – which is closely allied to Russian – was decreed to be the sole official language.

FACT BOX

Official name: Republic of Ukraine
Capital: Kiev
Area: 233,090 sq mi (603,700 km²)
Land areas: Mainly flat; mountainous only in E (Carpathians) and S (Crimea); deciduous forests and bogs in NW; steppes in S
Climate: moderate continental; sub-tropical in Crimea
Highest elevation: Goverla 6,761 ft (2,061 m)
Lowest elevation: Sea level
Form of government: Presidential republic
Head of state: President of Parliament
Population: 51,800,000 (1990)

Languages: Ukrainian (official), Russian
Religion: Mainly Russian Orthodox
Currency: Grivna
Gross Domestic Product per capita: n.a.

This pleasant square (*top right*) in the Ukrainian capital, Kiev, reflects the city's European outlook. Kiev is located on the Dnepr River. The city has extensive parks, and numerous broad boulevards lined with cafes and shops.

Queues for basic foodstuffs (*right*) are a familiar feature of daily life for most Ukrainians, despite the republic's great agricultural production. Ukraine today faces the challenge of setting up a free-market economy.

People

After about 200 years of Russian domination, only 73 per cent of Ukraine's population are of Ukrainian extraction. A further 21 per cent are Russian. The Russian minority live almost exclusively in the larger industrial cities of the southeast. There are also small minorities of Byelorussians, Romanians, Poles, Bulgarians and Hungarians. In religion, most Ukrainians are (Russian) Orthodox Christians, Eastern Catholics (a Church affiliated to Roman Catholicism) or atheists. There is a small Jewish community.

The present government of the Ukraine is headed by a premier and Council of Delegates responsible to a Supreme Council under a president. The president represents the state at international functions. The state retains one of the three seats at the United Nations allocated in 1945 to the Soviet Union.

The economy

The economy of Ukraine suffered serious decline during the early 1990s, but is well placed to recover rapidly. The fertile chernozem soils at the centre of the country have the potential to produce vast quantities of cereal crops and sugar beets if the agricultural industry can be modernized. Ukraine also possesses substantial deposits of minerals – notably coal, iron ore, oil and natural gas, and manganese. The state is highly industrialized, with an emphasis on heavy industry.

The Black Sea port of Odessa (*above left, middle*) is one of Ukraine's largest cities.

The wheatfields of Ukraine (*left*) are among the world's most fertile farmlands.

Large factories, like this locomotive plant in Dnepropetrovsk (above) are the basis of the Ukrainian economy. The republic was relatively privileged under the Soviet system, and so its infrastructure is well developed.

Byelorussia

THE REPUBLIC OF BYELORUSSIA – ALSO known as Belorussia, Belarus or "White Russia" – is a landlocked state located in eastern Europe. To the north are Lithuania and Latvia; to the east is the Russian Federation; to the south the Ukraine; and to the west Poland. Byelorussia covers a total area of only 80,155 square miles (207,600 square kilometres) – roughly five-sixths the size of the United Kingdom. Its capital is Minsk, located in the centre of the country. This important industrial centre is home to about 16 per cent of Byelorussia's total population of 10,260,000 people.

The terrain is mostly flat, and there are large areas of birch and pine forest. The only upland areas consist of ridges that represent glacial moraines deposited at the end of the last Ice Age. The soil is generally not of a quality suitable for cultivation, but is excellent for pasture and for the growth of the forest and scrub, which covers up to a quarter of the republic's land area. The forests are interspersed with large peat bogs and numerous lakes.

History

Human beings lived in the region from before Neolithic times, and Byelorussia was settled by Slavs between the AD 500s-800s. The small Slav principalities soon fell under the control of the Kievan state. However,

FACT BOX

Official name: Republic of Byelorussia
Capital: Minsk
Land area: 80,155 sq mi (207,600 km2)
Land area: 80,155 sq mi (207,600 km²) Byelorussian Ridge; extensive deciduous forests
Climate: Moderate, with mild winters and warm summers
Highest elevation: Dzerinskaya 1,135 ft (346 m)
Form of government: Presidential republic
Head of government: President of Parliament
Population: 10,260,000 (1990)

Language: Byelorussian (official), Russian
Religion: Mainly Russian Orthodox
Currency: rouble
Gross National Product per capita: 2,578 roubles (1988)

Kiev fell to the Mongols in 1236-41, and many of the Byelorussian towns were destroyed by the invaders. A century later, the area passed into Lithuanian hands. After the union of the Lithuanian and Polish ruling houses in the 1500s, it was Poland which exerted the strongest cultural influence over the inhabitants, helping to spread Roman Catholicism. The partitioning of Poland in the 1700s caused Byelorussia to become part of the Russian Empire. During the 1800s, a repressive campaign of "Russification" prompted the first stirring of Byelorussian nationalism. This was aimed against both Russian and Polish cultural dominance. In 1918, after heavy fighting between German and Russian forces during World War I had caused devastation throughout the region, the people proclaimed the establishment of the Byelorussian Democratic Republic. But in 1919, Byelorussia became a Soviet Socialist Republic within the Soviet Union.

During World War II, about 25 per cent of the entire population died as German and Russian forces again battled for supremacy across the territory, and again caused massive destruction. At the end of the war, the country regained some of the land it had previously ceded to Poland, and was granted one of the three seats at the United Nations then allocated to the Soviet Union.

Events in Russia during the later 1980s led once again to the emergence of Byelorussian nationalism. The republic declared its independence in 1990. In 1991, Byelorussia was instrumental in the formation of the Commonwealth of Independent States (CIS), the loose grouping of many of the states of the former Soviet Union.

People

Of the population, some 80 per cent are of Byelorussian extraction. They speak the country's official language, Byelorussian (which is closely allied to Russian). The largest minority are Russians, who make up around 12 per cent of the population. The Russian minority live mostly in the industrial cities. There are also small communities of Poles and Ukrainians. Most Byelorussians adhere to the Russian Orthodox or Roman Catholic faith, or are atheists. The are a small number of Jews; although in 1939 Jews made up 40 per cent of the population of Minsk.

The present government of Byelorussia is headed by a premier and Council of Delegates responsible to a Supreme Council under a president. The president represents the state at international functions.

Today, the Byelorussian economy faces serious decline. Apart from its forests, the country has few natural resources. Extensive pastureland is used for rearing livestock for meat and dairy products, and peat from the bogs is used as fuel, even for industry. There is some market gardening around Minsk. Timber products, including furniture, paper and matches, are the most economically significant exports. There are also small reserves of coal, oil and salt. The Soviet system introduced a number of industrial enterprises in the towns.

The bustling station square in Minsk (*above*) is the hub of the Byelorussian capital. The city is one of the oldest in Eastern Europe, and is a major cultural and economic centre.

The rolling, forested Byelorussian landscape (*left*) reveals its magic in subtle ways. The country has no major highland areas, but its many lakes and wetlands are a haven for wildlife. Byelorussia's extensive forests are one of the country's major natural resources.

For farmers (*above*), the relatively barren soils of Byelorussia make livestock rearing the most profitable activity.

Folk dancing (*right*) carries on the traditional customs of the Byelorussians.

Moldova

THE REPUBLIC OF MOLDOVA (ALSO known as Moldavia) lies in the extreme southwest of the former Soviet Union, on the border with Romania. The Prut River forms Moldova's western border. The tiny country occupies a total area of 13,011 square miles (33,700 square kilometres), and embraces the region once known as Bessarabia. The name "Moldova" refers to the former Principality of Moldavia, of which Bessarabia formed the eastern sector.

In the north of the country lies the treeless but extremely fertile Beltsy Steppe. Central Moldova is an area of forested hills, some of which reach as high as 1,312 feet (400 metres). The southern part of the country is a region of dry, flat steppe (grassy plain). Moldova's long, hot summers and mild winters allow a long growing season, and the country ranks as a major producer of tobacco, wine and fruit. The capital, Kishinev, lies in the central part of the country.

Moldova has a population of roughly 4,400,000, some 64 per cent of whom are Romanian (native Moldovan), with Ukrainians and Russians making up 14 per cent and 13 per cent of the total. Gagauz folk, who speak a Turkic language, make up about 4 per cent of the population. The Moldovan language is a dialect of Romanian,

FACT BOX

Official name: Republic of Moldova
Capital: Kishinev
Land area: 13,011 sq mi (33,700 km²)
Land regions: Fertile steppe in N; forested hills in C; dry steppe in S
Climate: Moderate continental, with warm summers
Highest elevation: Kodra 1,407 ft (429 m)
Lowest elevation: Around sea level

Form of government: Presidential republic
Head of state: President
Population: 4,400,000 (1990)
Language: Moldavian (official), Russian
Religion: Mainly Russian Orthodox
Currency: rouble
Gross Domestic Product: n.a.

Horsemen in traditional garb (*right*) toast the health of newly-weds, outside a village in southwest Moldova. For special occasions such as this, Moldovans favour traditional costume: embroidered shirts hanging just over the trousers and white embroidered waistcoats. The sheepskin caps of the horsemen are, by tradition, part of Romanian folk costume. The majority of Moldovans are ethnic Romanians.

and is written using the Roman alphabet. Since 1991, it has been the country's official language.

The economy of Moldova is based mainly on intensive agriculture. The main crops include wine, fruit, tobacco, wheat and sunflowers. Industry is not well developed, and is mainly restricted to the production of foodstuffs, building materials, textiles, chemicals and some consumer goods. There are no significant mineral reserves.

History

For much of its history, the Principality of Moldavia was ruled by Hungary. From the 1300s, the whole of Bessarabia came under Turkish rule. In 1812, following the war between Turkey and Russia, control of Bessarabia was transferred to Russia. In 1918, Bessarabia came under the control of Romania. However, the secret supplementary protocol to the 1939 Hitler-Stalin Pact placed Bessarabia in the Soviet sphere of interest. In 1940, Romania was forced to cede control of the region to the Soviet Union. The southern part was annexed to the Ukraine. The main part became the Moldavian Soviet Socialist Republic. Its territory came to include the tiny Moldavian Autonomous Soviet Socialist Republic (founded in 1924), a narrow strip of land along the eastern bank of the Dnestr River. During World War II, Romania regained control of the territory, until driven out by the Red Army. In the 1947 Paris Peace Treaty, Romania formally recognized the Soviet annexation.

As in the other non-Russian republics of the Soviet Union, the Soviet leadership deported many thousands of native Moldovans to other parts of the federation. Many Russians and Ukrainians settled in Moldova, and Russians generally occupied the most responsible positions in government and industry. State policy denied Moldova's close ethnic and linguistic ties with

Romania, and decreed that the Moldovan language be written in the Cyrillic instead of the Roman alphabet. Private contacts between Moldovans and Romanians became almost impossible to maintain, although Romania was itself Communist-ruled. The Romanian dictator, Nicolae Ceaucescu, frequently raised the question of the Soviet annexation of Moldova.

The path to independence

Nationalist sentiment began to emerge in Moldova during the late 1980s, encouraged by the reform policies of Soviet leader Mikhail Gorbachev. In 1989, the Roman alphabet was re-introduced. In the summer of 1990, Moldova declared its independence. After the collapse of the Soviet Union in 1991, the republic was slow to join the Commonwealth of Independent States (CIS), the loose grouping of many of the states of the former Soviet Union, but was one of the first Soviet successor states to be recognised by the international community.

With independence, the relationship between Moldova's Romanian majority and the various ethnic minorities has become an explosive issue. In 1989, the Russian-speaking minority on the east bank of the Dnestr declared an independent republic known as "Trans-Dnestria". Violent clashes broke out between Russians and the Moldovan authorities. Russians appealed for help from neighbouring republics and from the former Red Army. In the south, the Gagauz set up their own republic, known as "Gagauzia". The Moldovan government has refused to recognize these two republics. The most important question facing the country is reunion with Romania. Cultural and economic links between the two countries have increased greatly since Moldovan independence and the end of Communist rule in both countries. Most Moldovans want to reunite with Romania, but the country's ethnic minorities vehemently oppose it.

Modern high-rise apartment blocks (*above*) define the skyline of Kishinev, capital of Moldova. The city is situated on the right bank of the Byk River, in a fertile wine- and fruit-growing region. Kishinev is Moldova's main industrial centre.

The apple harvest (*left*) on a large fruit farm reflects the agricultural focus of the Moldovan economy. Under the former Soviet regime, the country was a major exporter of fruit and wine.

Georgia

THE REPUBLIC OF GEORGIA LIES IN THE Caucasus Mountains, at the southeastern edge of the European Plain. It covers an area of some 26,911 square miles (69,700 square kilometres). It is bordered to the north by the Russian Federation, to the west by the Black Sea, to the south by Turkey and Armenia, and to the east by Azerbaijan. The Greater Caucasus Mountains, a range of jagged peaks cloaked by dense forests, extends across northern Georgia. Its highest peak, Mount Elbrus, rises to a height of 18,511 feet (5,642 metres). To the south runs the Lesser Caucasus range. Between these mountain chains lie the warm valleys of the Kura and Rion rivers.

People

Georgia has a population of some 5,500,000 persons. About 69 per cent of its people are Georgians. They trace their descent from a number of tribes who have lived in the region for millenia. The population also includes small minorities of Armenians (about nine per cent), Russians (seven per cent), Azerbaijanis (five per cent), Ossetians (three per cent), Abkhazians (two per cent), and a number of Adzharians. The Georgian, Abkhazian and Adzharian peoples speak Caucasian languages; the Armenians, Russians and Ossetians speak Indo-European languages; the Azerbaijanis speak a Turkic

tongue. Most Georgians are Christians, and belong to the Georgian Orthodox Church. The Azeri minority and some Ossetians are Muslims.

The Soviet government recognized the national identities of the Abkhazian, Adjarian and Ossetian peoples in 1921-22, when it established three independent administrative units within Georgia: the Abkhazian Autonomous Soviet Socialist Republic; the Adzharian Autonomous Soviet Socialist Republic; and the South Ossetian Autonomous Region. Today the future of the Abkhazian and Ossetian regions is uncertain. Both are violently opposed to the central government in Tbilisi, the Georgian capital.

Georgia's economy is based on its rich mineral deposits, which include manganese, coal and copper. Agriculture is also of great importance to the country, which was by far the largest producer of tea in the former USSR, and still grows vast quantities of wine and table grapes, citrus fruits, sugar beets, tobacco and cereals. Georgia's manufacturing industries, powered by large resources of hydroelectricity, include food processing, textiles, engineering and the production of iron and steel.

History

Georgia has been a distinctive state since ancient times, when the region came under to Persian, Greek and Roman influences. Christianity was introduced around the AD 300s, probably from Armenia. "Modern" Georgian nationhood may be said to have emerged with the development of a written language and literature.

Although some areas were held by Armenia between the 600s-1100s, progress towards independent nationhood continued under native Georgian rulers from around the 800s. In the 1100s-1200s Georgia was a large state, and extended from the Black Sea to the Caspian Sea. Its flourishing culture was largely destroyed by Mongol invaders in the 1300s-1400s. Russia claimed the eastern part of the region for its own in 1810-11, and by 1878 had secured all of what is now Georgia.

In May 1918, following the Russian Revolution of 1917, Georgia declared itself an independent republic, and in 1919 a Menshevik (moderate socialist) government took power following free elections. The Bolshevik (Comunist) government of Soviet Russia recognized Georgia's independence in May 1920, but soon took steps to end it. In February 1921, Georgian Bolsheviks rose against their government and called for Soviet aid. The Red Army marched in and Georgia became a Soviet Socialist Republic.

Georgian nationalism remained strong throughout the years of Communist rule. In the late 1980s, the republic was in the

FACT BOX

Official name: Republic of Georgia
Capital: Tbilisi
Land area: 26,911 sq mi (69,700 km²)
Land regions: High mountains in N and S, lowlands in W and river valleys between Caucasus ranges
Climate: Moderate; sub-tropical in W
Highst elevation: Schara 16,496 ft (5,028 m)
Lowest elevation: Sea level
Government: Presidential republic
Head of government: President

Population: 5,500,000 (1990)
Language: Georgian (official), Russian
Religion: Mainly Georgian Orthodox
Currency: rouble
Gross Domestic Product per capita: n.a.

forefront of the general move towards re-assertion of national identities in the Soviet Union. Support for independence grew after the Red Army brutally crushed mobs in Tbilisi in April 1989. Georgia's first free elections took place late in 1990, and put into power the Round Table-Free Georgia independence movement. In March 1991, nearly 90 per cent of the population voted for the restoration of the independent Social Democratic Republic of 1918.

Georgia was one of the few successor states of the Soviet Union not to join the Commonwealth of Independent States (CIS). This isolation, which must threaten its future, is largely due to the eccentric, nationalistic policies advocated by President Zviad Gamsakhurdia, elected in May 1991. The president's policies alienated many Georgians. Gamsakhurdia was violently toppled from power in early 1992.

The Narikala fortress overlooks Tbilisi (*to left*), capital of Georgia. In 1992, the city was the scene of violent disturbances, as President Zviad Gamsakhurdia was ousted.

During Georgia's struggle for independence, funeral ceremonies (*below*) often became the occasion of political demonstrations among minorities.

The Caucasus Mountains (*far left*) divide Georgia from its neighbours. In the background rises Mount Kazbek.

Tasting the new wine (*left*) is a pleasant duty for these wine-producers in the region of Kakhetia. As well as wine grapes, Georgian farms yield bountiful crops of citrus fruit and tea.

Armenia

THE TINY REPUBLIC OF ARMENIA covers a total area of only 11,506 square miles (29,800 square kilometres). It is bordered to the north by Georgia, to the east by Azerbaijan, and on the south and west by Iran and Turkey. The Nakhichevan Autonomous Republic, an Azerbaijani territory, is an enclave within Armenian territory.

This mountainous country occupies a highland called the Armenian Plateau, extending from the Caucasus Mountains in the northeast to beyond the Turkish border. Deep valleys lie between its mountain ranges; some are well-watered and have fertile soil. Others are filled by lakes such as Lake Sevan, in the east. Armenia lies in a region subject to violent earthquakes. The last major tremor, in December 1988, destroyed many communities and killed some 25,000 people.

The great majority (around 93 per cent) of Armenia's population of some 3,300,000 persons is Armenian. They trace their ancestry to tribes who entered the region in the 600s BC. Minority groups include Russians (1.5 per cent) and Kurds (1.7 per cent). Armenians also live in Georgia, and there are important Armenian communities abroad, notably in the USA and France. Around one-third of all Armenia's people live in the capital city, Yerevan, and overall

FACT BOX

Official name: Republic of Armenia
Capital: Yerevan
Land area: 11,506 sq mi (29,800 km²)
Land regions: In N rugged mountain range of Low Caucasus; to S Armenian Highland, divided by several valleys
Climate: Continental, with hot summers and cold winters
Highest elevation: Aragac 13,415 ft (4,090 m)
Lowest elevation: In Armenian Highland
Government: Presidential republic
Head of state: President
Population (1991): 3,376,000

Language: Armenian (official), Russian
Religion: Mainly Armenian Apostolic
Currency: Rouble
GDP per person: n.a.

some two-thirds are city dwellers. Most Armenians are Christians belonging to the Armenian Apostolic Church. The official language, Armenian, is an Indo-European tongue with its own, ancient, written form.

Armenia has valuable deposits of copper, lead, zinc, aluminium and molybdenum; marble, granite and other building materials are dug in large quantities. Manufacturing industries include chemicals (mainly fertilizers and synthetic rubber), food processing, mechanical engineering and electrical goods. In the mountains agriculture centres mainly on livestock farming (cattle and sheep); cereals, wine grapes and other fruits, sugar-beet and cotton are the major crops grown in the river valleys.

Armenia is an ancient nation, established as a semi-independent province of the Persian Empire by the 600s BC, at about the time that the ancestors of the modern Armenians moved into the Armenian Plateau. Although nominally under Persian and then Greek rule, ancient Armenia preserved a high degree of independence. It was much larger than the modern state. Under King Tigran II (ruled 95-55 BC), it extended from the Caspian Sea to the Mediterranean.

Christianity came to Armenia, the first nation to adopt it as the state religion, in the early 300s and the Armenian alphabet was

developed about one hundred years later. From around the 600s the Byzantine (Eastern Roman) Empire, Arabs and Turks all struggled for possession of Armenia. Independent kingdoms were established in various parts of the ancient state, but the last fell to Mameluke (Egyptian Arab) invaders in 1375. Western Armenia formed part of the Ottoman Turkish Empire from the early 1500s; eastern Armenia was under Persian rule from 1639 until it was taken by Russia in 1828.

Under Muslim Turkish rule the Christian Armenians were often savagely persecuted. Tens of thousands died in a genocidal campaign waged by Turks and Kurds in 1894-96. Even worse atrocities were committed in 1915-16 when Turkey, fearing that Armenians might rise in support of Russia, its enemy in World War I, began mass deportations from Turkish Armenia to desert

areas in modern Syria. Some Armenians sought refuge in Russian Armenia; of the rest, some 1,000,000 are thought to have been murdered.

In 1918, after the Russian Revolution, Russian Armenia declared itself an independent republic. Early in 1920 an independent Greater Armenia, made up of both Turkish and Russian Armenia, won international recognition. This was short lived. Soviet Russia used a Communist rising on the border with Azerbaijan as an excuse to send in the Red Army. Eastern Armenia was soon proclaimed a Soviet republic; western Armenia returned to Turkish rule. In 1922 Armenia was forced to unite with Azerbaijan and Georgia in the Transcaucasian Soviet Federal Socialist Republic, but in 1936 all three states became constituent republics of the USSR.

Since 1988 Armenia has been in conflict with Azerbaijan over Nagorno-Karabakh, a district in Azerbaijan where Armenian Christians are in the majority. With the disintegration of the USSR in the early 1990s, Armenia regained its independence, which was approved by some 95 per cent of its electorate in September 1991. Its future is shadowed by the dispute over Nagorno-Karabakh, where savage fighting raged in 1992.

Lenin Square (*left*) in Yerevan contains the Armenian capital's parliament buildings. Fountains, wide streets, and buildings constructed from the attractive local pink tufa stone characterize the city.

An ancient chapel (*below*) stands on the bank of Lake Sevan, surrounded by high mountain ranges. The lake, Armenia's central physical feature, lies nearly 6,500 ft (2,000m) above sea level.

The village of Spitak (*left*) was completely destroyed by the massive earthquake which shook Armenia in December 1988. Survivors of the quake are still living in temporary accommodation three years after the disaster, which killed 25,000 people and left many more homeless.

A trader (*left*) at an open-air livestock market near Yerevan evaluates a potential purchase. The Armenians are an ancient people with a distinguished culture. In the 20th century they have suffered severely, including a genocidal onslaught by the Turks during World War II.

Azerbaijan

THE REPUBLIC OF AZERBAIJAN, WITH AN area of 33,400 square miles (86,600 square kilometres), ranks as the largest of the three Transcaucasian republics of the former Soviet Union. It includes the Nakhichevan Autonomous Republic (an enclave along the Iranian-Turkish border, separated from Azerbaijan by Armenian territory) and the disputed Autonomous Oblast (independent region) of Nagorno-Karabakh. To the north and west, where it borders on Georgia and Armenia, the terrain of Azerbaijan is shaped by the southern ranges of the Caucasus Mountains, which slope down towards the Caspian Sea on its eastern border. Iran lies on the country's southern border.

The broad valley of the Kura River crosses central Azerbaijan. With its major tributary, the Araks River, the Kura flows through a wide, marshy plain to a delta on the Caspian Sea. North of the delta lies the oil-rich Apsheron peninsula, site of Azerbaijan's capital city, Baku.

Azerbaijan has a population of 7,029,000, of whom around 82 per cent are Azerbaijanis. About eight per cent are Armenians and eight per cent Russians. There are also small minorities of Ukrainians, Tatars, Jew, Talysh, Georgians, Kurds and Turks. Most Azerbaijanis, also known as Azeris, are Shia Muslims, although a substantial minority adhere to the Sunni branch of Islam. They speak a Turkic language: under Soviet rule it was written in Russian-style Cyrillic letters. In 1991, the government decided to change to the Roman alphabet.

The republic's economy depends mainly on its oil resources. There are extensive oilfields on the mainland and in the Caspian Sea and huge refineries at Baku. However, the oil industry requires considerable new investment to modernize equipment and production methods. Azerbaijan also has important deposits of iron, aluminium and copper ores, zinc, cobalt and lead. Its major industries are petrochemicals, iron and steel, mechanical engineering, textiles and footwear. Although drought is a frequent occurrence over much of the country, large irrigation schemes have made possible the successful cultivation of cereals, cotton, grapes, other fruits and vegetables, tobacco and rubber.

Oil fields near Baku (*below*) provide a major source of income for the newly independent republic of Azerbaijan. The petroleum is refined at Baku.

Baku (*right*), capital of Azerbaijan, situated on the Caspian Sea, displays a mixture of the old and the new, with minarets and mosques in the foreground.

FACT BOX

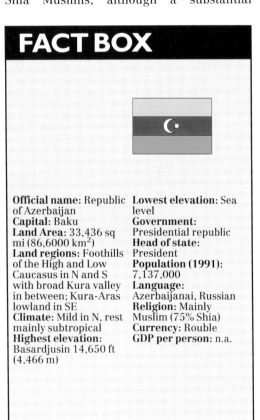

Official name: Republic of Azerbaijan
Capital: Baku
Land Area: 33,436 sq mi (86,6000 km²)
Land regions: Foothills of the High and Low Caucasus in N and S with broad Kura valley in between; Kura-Aras lowland in SE
Climate: Mild in N, rest mainly subtropical
Highest elevation: Basardjusin 14,650 ft (4,466 m)
Lowest elevation: Sea level
Government: Presidential republic
Head of state: President
Population (1991): 7,137,000
Language: Azerbaijanai, Russian
Religion: Mainly Muslim (75% Shia)
Currency: Rouble
GDP per person: n.a.

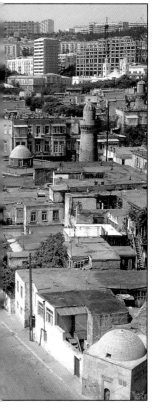

Origins of the state

From ancient times until the early Middle Ages, Azerbaijan was dominated by the Persian empire. During the 700s, Arab conquerors brought Islam to the region. Azerbaijan subsequently split into several small states, ruled variously by the Persians, Mongols and Ottoman Turks. Russia moved into the area from the 1700s onward. In 1829, after war with Persia, Russia took northern Azerbaijan as part of its empire. Southern Azerbaijan stayed under Persian control, and remains part of modern Iran, consisting of the provinces of East and West Azerbaijan.

In 1918, after the Russian Revolution, Azerbaijan proclaimed its independence under the leadership of the Islamic Mussavat (Nationalist) Party. However, Communists in Baku rose against the regime and called for Soviet aid. The Red Army intervened and the Azerbaijani Soviet Socialist Republic was swiftly established. In 1922-36 it formed part of the Transcaucasian Soviet Federal Socialist Republic with Armenia and Georgia.

The Nagorno-Karabakh dispute

The disintegration of the USSR in the later 1980s, and its final collapse in 1991, brought independence to Azerbaijan. The country became a member of the Commonwealth of Independent States (CIS), the loose association of 11 former Soviet republics, and sought to develop closer relations with its Muslim neighbours, Turkey and Iran. In June 1992, elections saw the instalment of Albufaz Elchibey as leader.

The rewakening of nationalism in Transcaucasia has also brought conflict that owes much to ethnic and religious differences between the Muslim Turkish Azeris and the Christian Armenians. In the late 1980s, conflict arose over the status of the enclave of Nagorno-Karabakh. Soviet authority established this part of southern Azerbaijan as an independent region in 1923. It has an area of 1,700 square miles (4,400 square kilometres) and a population of some 170,000 persons, of whom more than 75 per cent are Armenian Christians.

Trouble began in 1988, when Armenian leaders in Nagorno-Karabakh demanded that the region should leave Azerbaijan and become part of Armenia. The leaders of both Azerbaijan and the USSR refused the request. Fighting between Armenians and Azerbaijanis began in Nagorno-Karabakh, while in Baku and other cities the Armenian minorities suffered attacks. The increasingly bloody civil war in Nagorno-Karabakh threatened to become an open war between Azerbaijan and Armenia. In June 1992, Armenian forces wrested the enclave from Azerbaijan, but the conflict was far from over.

Armed Armenian women (*top*) in the Azeri enclave of Nagorno-Karabakh reflect the tense situation in a territory where 75% of the population are Christian Armenians, surrounded by a hostile Azeri population. Fighting began in 1988.

Muslims pray in a grove (*above*). The great majority of Azeris are Shi'ite Muslims, like the Iranians; but their lifestyle tends to be more secular, a result of many years of Communist control, when organized religion was actively discouraged.

Central Asian States

IN 1990-91, THE FIVE CENTRAL ASIAN republics of the former Soviet Union became independent states. Uzbekistan, Kyrgyzstan, Tajikistan and Turkmenistan form what was the southern boundary of the Soviet Union, bordered on the south and east by Iran, Afghanistan and China. North of them lies the huge republic of Kazakhstan, extending from the Volga River and Caspian Sea in the west to the Chinese frontier in the east, and bordered on the north by Siberia (part of the Russian Federation). Kazakhstan covers a total area of 1,049,155 square miles (2,717,300 square kilometres), and ranks as the second largest successor state of the former Soviet Union.

Much of the southern Central Asian region is desert. Along its southern and eastern edges lie the Pamir and Tien Shan Mountains. These mighty peaks are partly covered by glaciers. Their western slopes receive just enough rainfall to allow small-scale cultivation. Rivers fed by the glaciers flow westward to the deserts, where some feed oasis regions. Since ancient times, the central steppes of Kazakhstan have been inhabited by nomadic herdsmen. Cattle and sheep are still raised there, but irrigation schemes have seen large areas of northern Kazakhstan given over to cereals, while cotton is extensively grown in the south.

People

Most of the peoples of the Central Asian republics, notably the Kazakhs, Uzbeks, Kirghiz and Turkmen, are Turkic-speaking, but the Tajiks speak an Indo-European language which resembles the Farsi language of Iran. In the late 1930s, the Soviet government decreed that Central Asian languages should be written, like Russian, in the Cyrillic script (devised in the AD 800s by Greek missionaries). The newly independent states hope soon to reintroduce the Roman alphabet.

Most of the people of the Central Asian states are Sunni Muslims, but under Soviet rule large numbers of Russians were settled in Central Asia. In Kazakhstan, Russians make up 41 per cent of the population; in Kyrgyzstan, some 25 per cent.

With the exception of some areas of Kazakhstan (which was the centre for the Soviet space programme and the site of its major nuclear testing grounds) the region is economically underdeveloped. Cotton ranks as a major crop, and Uzbekistan is among the world's leading producers. Agricultural development depends on large irrigation schemes. However, the demand for water has led to the increasing depletion of lakes and rivers, notably the Aral Sea (shared between Kazakhstan and Uzbekistan) and the Issyk-Kul Lake in Kyrgyzstan. The area around the Aral Sea has suffered severe environmental damage, both from chemical fertilizers and pesticides used in cotton production, and from the build-up of salt in the soil left by irrigation.

Kazakhstan is particularly rich in petroleum and gemstones, and throughout the region there are valuable deposits of coal, copper, tin, mercury, chromium, iron ore, lead, nickel and zinc.

Russian rule

The former Soviet Central Asia was once known as Turkestan. The western part included areas ruled by Persia from the 600s BC until the AD 600s. Eastern Turkestan was ruled either by China or by nomadic conquerors. Western Turkestan came under Muslim control from the AD 700s, and was generally Turkic-speaking by the 1200s. Independent khanates (Muslim states) established around oasis cities such as Bukhara, Samarkand and Tashkent were overthrown from the 1700s by Russian invaders. By the late 1800s, the Russian empire extended over all Western Turkestan, which until 1917 was divided into the Governor-Generalship of Turkestan, and the semi-independent Khanate of Khiva and Emirate of Bukhara.

Muslim Turkestani nationalist movements opposed Russian domination, and after the Revolution of 1917 waged a long

FACT BOX

Kazakhstan
Capital: Alma Ata
Land area: 1,049,155 sq mi (2,717,300 km²)
Population (1991): 16,793,000

Kyrgyzstan
Capital: Bishkek (Frunze, 1926-91)
Land area: 76,640 sq mi (198,500 km²)
Population (1991): 4,291,000

Tajikistan
Capital: Dushanbe
Land area: 55,250 sq mi (143,100 km²)
Population (1991): 5,358,000

Turkmenistan
Capital: Ashkhabad
Land area: 188,455 sq mi (488,100 km²)
Population (1991): 3,622,000

Uzbekistan
Capital: Tashkent
Land area: 172,741 sq mi (447,400 km²)
Population (1991): 20,708,000

The Pamir Mountains (*left*), which attain heights of some 20,000ft (6,0960m), are located mainly in Tajikistan in Central Asia. Called the "Roof of the World", they include the tallest peaks of the former Soviet Union.

Women attend a bazaar (*below*) in Tashkent, the fourth largest city in the former Soviet Union. Turkish-Mongolian Uzbeks dominated the Turkestan region of Central Asia until their overthrow by Russia in the 19th century.

Dominated by a ruined mosque, Bukhara's market (*left*) combines Asian and European influences. The city lies in Uzbekistan. Muslim Uzbeks make up the third largest nationality group of the former Soviet Union.

A veteran of Soviet battles (*above*) poses before a Buddhist shrine, typifying the contrasting cultures of Central Asia.

struggle with the Red Army, but by 1922 the Soviets had secured control over Central Asia. Between 1920 and 1936, the region was divided into the present five republics. During this period, boundaries were often arbitarily changed, as the Soviet government split up areas long unified by cultural and economic factors. The redistribution of territories was done on a supposedly nationalistic basis. It ensured that people native to the region could hold senior administrative posts, but that real power would always be firmly placed in the hands of the Soviet central government far away in Moscow.

Problems of independence

With the collapse of the USSR, the Central Asian republics achieved independence. This has brought new problems. Soviet rule firmly discouraged Islamic traditions, but with its end ancient mosques and Islamic schools were swiftly reopened and new ones established. Islamic political parties calling for religious reforms were opposed by others seeking democratic reforms along others seeking democratic reforms along Western lines. In Tashkent, a "Turkestani Party" called for "reunification" of Turkestan. Ethnic conflict has also arisen, notably between Uzbeks and Kirghiz, and between Uzbeks and Tadjiks.

Acknowledgments

Contributors
Dr Heinz-Jürgen Axt
Thomas Baden
Professor Dr Günter C Behrmann
Ursula Blombach-Schäfer
Dr Patrick Brauns
Dr Heinz Joachim Fischer
Wolf-E Gudemann
Antonia Hansmeier
Irena Hendrichs
Dr Michael Jacobs
Peter Jason
Dr Jan Kaestner
Professor Dr Adolf Karger
Ute Kleinelümern
Hans Dieter Kley
Kurt Klinger
Werner Ludewig
Gisela Maler-Sieber
Hans-Georg Michel
Professor Dr Franz-Dieter Miotke
Amanda O'Neill
Richard O'Neill
Professor Dr Alfred Pletsch
Jens Reuter
Karl Römer
Peter Schäfer
Peter Schröder
Monika Unger
Inge Weissgerber
Lena Young

Translation:
Robert Aylett, Elizabeth Doyle and Mark Woolfe
in association with First Edition Translations
Ltd, Cambridge

Editorial assistance:
Christian Adams
Thomas Baden
Arthur Butterfield
Mike Darton
Sue Dyson
Sabine Günther
Lucy Johnson
Ute Kleinelümern
Keith Lye
Richard O'Neill
Linda Sonntag
Madeleine St John
Peter Schäfer
Nicholas Tanburn

Index:
Indexing Specialists, Hove, East Sussex,
BN3 2DJ, UK

Maps:
Kartographisches Institut Bertelsmann,
Gütersloh
Euromap Ltd, Pangbourne, Berkshire

Layouts:
Hans Rossdeutscher, Malcolm Smythe

Diagram visuals: Eugene Fleury, Jean Jottrand,
Ted McCausland

Illustrations: John Davies, Bill Donahoe,
John Francis, Michael Gillah, R Lewis,
Tom McArthur, Michael Saunders, Leslie D
Smith, Ed Stuart

Photographic acknowledgments:
Abbreviations
b bottom; **c** centre; **l** left; **r** right; **t** top;

Apa Photo Agency/*APA*; Bridgeman Art
Library/*BAL*; Britain on View/*BOV*; Deutsche
Presse-Agentur GmbH/*DPA*; Frank Spooner/*FS*;
Gamma Frank Spooner/*GFS*; Hulton Picture
Library/*HPL*; Hutchison Library/*HL*; Jürgens Ost
und Europa Foto/*JEP*; Northern Ireland Tourist
Board/*NITB*; Paul G Pet/*PCP*; Spectrum Colour
Library/*SCL*; Survival Anglia/*SA*; Susan
Griggs/*SG*; The Image Bank/*TIB*; Zefa/*Z*

12-13 R Gaillarde/*GFS*; **13** HPL; **14** CNES; **14-15**
Gutekunst/*GFS*; **16-17** Sam Zarember/*TIB*; **20t**
Damm/*Z*; **20b** Damm/*Z*; **21t** D Woog/*Z*; **21b**
Helbing/*Z*; **22** Adam/*Z*; **22-3t** Streichan/*Z*; **22-3b**
Starfoto/*Z*; **24-5t** Damm/*Z*; **24-5b** K Lehnartz/*Z*;
25 Bildarchiv Preussicher Kulturbesitz; **26**
Michael Pasdzior/*TIB*; **26-7** Horst Munzig/*SG*;
27t T Schneider/*Z*; **27bl** N Bahnsen/*Z*; **27br** *JEP*;
28-9 Bavaria Verlag/*SCL*; **29t** M Thonig/*Z*; **29b**
R Friedrich; **30-1** V Phillips/*Z*; **32-3** Michael St
Maur Sheil/*SG*; **34-5** Monique Jacot/*SG*; **35t**
Ruth L Aebi/Gstaad Aelpler/*APA*; **35tr** Michael
Kuh/*TIB*; **35b** Horst Munzig/*SG*; **36-7t** B
Benjamin/*Z*; **36-7b** Linthom/*Z*; **37t** Giegel/*SNTO*;
37b Horst Munzig/*SG*; **38-9** K Kerth/*Z*; **39t**
Adam Woolfitt/*SG*; **39b** Chip Hires/*GFS*; **40-1**
Scholz/*Z*; **43** Damm/*Z*; **44** Adam Woolfitt/*SG*; **44-
5** Damm/*Z*; **45** Adam Woolfitt/*SG*; **46** Pohn/*DPA*;
46-7 Aberham/IFA-Bilderteam GmbH; **47t**
Koch/IFA-Bilderteam GmbH; **47rc** Neumeister;
47b Markowitsch/Osterr.
Fremdenverkehrswerbung; **48** Herbert
Kogler/*SA*; **49** Hans Verkroost;**50-1** HL; **52-3**
JEP; **54** Liba Taylor/*HL*; **54-5t** *JEP*; **54-5b** *Z*; **55**
Liba Taylor/*HL*; **56, 56-7t, 56-7b** *JEP*; **57** Liba
Taylor/*HL*; **58-9** Wolfgang Meier/Bavaria
Bildagentur; **61** *JEP*; **62-3t, 62-3b** *JEP*; **63tr,
63b** J Morek/*JEP*; **64** Julian Nieman/*SG*; **65t,
65c** *JEP*; **65b** B & U International Pictures; **66**
Dr Franz-Dieter Miotke; **66-7t** J Behnke/*Z*; **66-
7b** Sam Hall/*JEP*; **67bc** Robert Francis/*HL*; **67br**
Horst Munzig/*SG*; **68-9** B & U International
Pictures; **70-1** Kotoh/*Z*; **73** G Sirena/*Z*; **74**
Michael St Maur Sheil/*SG*; **74-5t** Kotoh/*Z*; **74-5b**
Mosler/*Z*; **75t** Bernard Gerard/*HL*; **75b** Michael
St Maur Sheil/*SG*; **76-7** PCP; **79** PCP; **80t** PCP; **80**
Mohn/*Z*; **80-1** PCP; **81tr** PCP; **81b** Mosler/*Z*; **82**
PCP; **82-3t** D H Teuffen/*Z*; **82-3b** Colin
Molyneux/*TIB*; **84-5** PCP; **86** PCP; **87** PCP; **88**
John Kegan/*SG*; **88-9, 89l, 89r** PCP; **90-1t, 90-
1b, 91c, 91b, 91r** PCP; **93** W Saller/*Z*; **94t** PCP;
94b T Brettmann/*Z*; **94-5t** *Z*; **94-5b** PCP; **96-7t**
Vladimir Birgus/*HL*; **96-7b** *Z*; **97c** Vladimir
Birgus/*HL*; **97b** Chip Hires/*GFS*; **98** Alvis
Upitis/*TIB*; **98-9t** *JEP*; **98-9b** Steven Burr
Williams/*TIB*; **99** *JEP*; **100, 100-1t, 100-1b** *JEP*;
102 *JEP*; **103tl** Lars Einarsson/Kalmar Museum;
103r *JEP*; **104-5** Brian Boyd/*BOV*; **106** O
Henson/*BOV*; **108** BOV; **108-9t** BOV; **108-9b**
BOV; **109** Channel Tunnel Group Ltd; **110-11**
Colin Molyneux; **111t** Camera Press; **111bl** *BOV*;
111br *BOV*; **112, 112-13t** *Z*; **112-13b** Barry
Hicks/*BOV*; **113tl, 113tr** Adam Woolfitt/*SG*; **113b**
BOV; **114** Michael St Maur Sheil/*SG*; **114-15** T
Wood/Stockphotos/*TIB*; **115t** Julian Nieman/*SG*;
115bl Adam Woolfitt/*SG*; **115bc** Peter and
Georgina Bowater/*TIB*; **115br** Bernard
Gerard/*HL*; **116-17, 117t** NITB; **117c**
Bradley/*GFS*; **117b** Short Bros plc; **118-19** Adam
Woolfitt/*SG*; **120** Brian Lynch/Bord Failte; **122,
122-3t** Adam Woolfitt/*SG*; **122-3b** Athlone
Jerunladen/*APA*; **123** G P Reichelt/*APA*; **124-5**
Shuji Kotoh/*Z*; **127** PB/Rex Features; **128,
128-9t** Adam Woolfitt/*SG*; **128-9b** Rijksmuseum,
Amsterdam; **129t** Van Phillips/*APA*; **129b** *TIB*;
130-1t Streichan/*Z*; **130-1b** Adam Woolfitt/*SG*;
131t Van Phillips/*APA*; **131b** PCP; **132** Guus
Dubbelman/*GFS*; **134-5** E Streichan/*Z*; **136**
Photo News/*GFS*; **136-7** Charles Friend/*SG*;
138-9 *Z*; **139t** Agence Belga; **139bl** PCP; **139br**
Weinberg Clark/*TIB*; **140** John Heseltine/*SG*;
140-1 John Heseltine/*SG*; **141t** HL; **141b** Charles
W Friend/*SG*; **142-3t** D & J Heaton/*APA*; **142-3b**
Bazin Scorcelletti/*GFS*; **143t** Patrick
Dougherty/Stockphotos/*TIB*; **143b** Bazin
Scorcelletti/*GFS*; **145** A Davies/*Z*; **146-7** Ian
Yeomans/*SG*; **150-1t** K Kerth/*Z*; **150-1b**
Knight/*APA*; **151** Bordis/*Z*; **152-3t**
Billon/Colorsport; **152-3b** Marvin Newman/*TIB*;
153t Adam Woolfitt/*SG*; **153bl** Colin
Molyneux/*TIB*; **153br** Joyce/*APA*; **154** B & U
International Pictures; **154-5t** Christine
Pemberton/B & U International Pictures; **154-5b**
Z; **155** Tim Motion/*Z*; **156** Adam Woolfitt/*SG*;
156-7t PCP; **156-7b** E Winczewski/*GFS*; **157t**
Bill Wassman/*APA*; **157b** PCP; **158-9** HL; **160** De

Nombel/Colorsport; **160-1** B & U International
Pictures; **161** APA; **162-3** Tor Eigeland/*SG*; **164-
5** Rossenbach/*Z*; **168-9t** Rob Cousins/*SG*; **168-9b**
Jean Krugler/*APA*; **169t** Robert Frerck/*SG*; **169b**
APA; **170-1t** Ben Nakayama/*APA*; **170-1b** Bill
Wassman/*APA*; **171** Adam Woolfitt/*SG*; **172**
Damm/*Z*; **172-3t** Damm/*Z*; **172-3b** Robert
Frerck/*SG*; **174** HL; **174-5t** SCL; **175bl** Louis
Castaneda/*TIB*; **175br** Tor Eigeland/*SG*; **176**
PCP; **176-7t** K Kerth/*Z*; **176-7b** Dr Mueller/*Z*;
177 PCP; **178** Nathan Benn/*SG*; **178-9t, 178-9b,
179** Robert Frerck/*SG*; **180-1** Robert Frerck/*SG*;
183 Charles Friend/*SG*; **184** Robert Frerck/*SG*;
184-5t K Kerth/*Z*; **184-5b** Jean Krugler/*APA*;
185 Anthony Howarth/*SG*; **186** Reflejo/*SG*;
186-7 B & U International Pictures; **187t** Ian
Yeomans/*SG*; **187bl** Bill Wassman/*APA*; **187br**
J Redditt/*HL*; **188-9** PCP; **192** Starfoto/*Z*; **192-3t**
Studio Benser/*Z*; **192-3b** PCP; **194t** Adam
Woolfitt/*SG*; **194b** Gert von Bassewitz/*SG*; **194-5**
John G Ross/*SG*; **195t** Adam Woolfitt/*SG*; **195b**
Santi Viselli/*TIB*; **196** SCL; **196-7t** Francesco
Venturi/KEA/*SG*; **196-7b** Ted Spiegel/*SG*; **198c**
Galleria degli Uffizi/*BAL*; **198bl** Sta Maria della
Victoria/*BAL*; **198-9** Galleria della Accademia,
Venice; **199** Vatican Art Galleries/*BAL*; **200,
200-1t** John Heseltine/*SG*; **201t** John Egan/*HL*;
201b Studio Bemser/*Z*; **202l** Francolon/Hires/
Magnum/*GFS*; **202t** Adam Woolfitt/*SG*; **203t** B &
U International Pictures; **203b** Ted Spiegel/*SG*;
204-5 SCL; **205** SCL; **206** Adam Woolfitt/*SG*;
207l B & U International Pictures; **207r** Heinz
Stucke/*FS*; **208-9** D & J Heaton/*APA*; **210** D & J
Heaton/*APA*; **212** David Beatty/*SG*; **212-13t** Rick
Strand/*APA*; **213bl** B & U International Pictures;
213br Michael St Maur Sheil/*SG*; **214** Michael St
Maur Sheil/*SG*; **214-15** G P Reichelt/*APA*; **215l**
David Beatty/*SG*; **215r** PCP; **216** Pierette
Collomb/*HL*; **216-17t** PCP; **216-17b** Key Color/*Z*;
218 PCP; **218-19** PCP; **219** *Z*; **220-1** *Z*; **221t** B &
U International Pictures; **221b** D & J
Heaton/*APA*; **223** SCL; **224-5** D & J Heaton/*APA*;
224-5br/*GFS*; **228t, 228b** Klammet; **228-9**
Boutin/*Z*; **229** Bilderberg; **230** Rossenbach/*Z*;
230-1 Ziegler/Transglobe; **231** Everts/IFA-
Bilderteam GmbH; **232** Helga Lade/Postl; **232-3t**
Klammet; **232-3b** Löbl-Schreyer; **233**
Fiedler/IFA-Bilderteam GmbH; **234-5**
Neumeister; **235l** GFS; **235r** Damm/*Z*; **236**
European Press/*DPA*; **236-7** Eugen/*Z*; **237**
Moldvay/STERN-Syndication; **238**
Janicek/Transglobe; **238-9t** Kranawetter/Bruce
Coleman; **238-9b** Camera Press/*DPA*; **239**
Schneiders/Kinkelin; **240, 240-1, 241tr** *JEP*;
241b Adam Woolfitt/*SG*; **242-3** *JEP*; **244,
244-5t, 244-5b** *JEP*; **244-5b, 245t** Adam
Woolfitt/*SG*; **245b** Charles W Friend/*SG*; **247**
Adam Woolfitt/*SG*; **248t** Adam Woolfitt/*SG*; **248b**
JEP; **248-9t** Charles Weckler/*TIB*; **248-9b, 249**
Adam Woolfitt/*SG*; **250-1** TOM/*Z*; **252-3** Dr H
Kramarz/*Z*; **254t** Horst Munzig/*SG*; **254b** HL;
254-5t *JEP*; **254-5b** *JEP*; **255** HL; **256-7** Mecky
Fögeling; **262-3t** Steenmans/*Z*; **262-3b**
Honkanem/*Z*; **263tl, 263tr** *JEP*; **263b** John
Bryson/*TIB*; **264t** *JEP*; **264bl** B Meyer/*HL*; **264**
John Bryson/*TIB*; **264-5** Robert Francis/*HL*;
265c Heinz Stucke/*FS*; **265b** Novosti/*GFS*; **266**
Leslie Woodhead/*HL*; **266-7t** *JEP*; **266-7b** Nik
Wheeler/*SG*; **267** Victoria Juleva/*HL*; **268-9t**
TASS/*DPA*; **268-9bl** Weihs/*DPA*; **269c** Sunak/*Z*;
269br Havlicek/*Z*; **270** AFI/IFA-Bilderteam
GmbH; **270-1** *JEP*; **271bl** Malanca/Sipa Press;
271br *JEP*; **272** Novosti; **272-3, 273** TASS/*DPA*;
274-5t, 274-5b Steenmans/*Z*; **275t**
Pinkhassov/Magnum/Focus; **275b** TASS/*DPA*;
276-7t Koene/Transglobe; **276-7b**
Armineh/SIPA Press; **277t** Backhaus/*DPA*; **277b**
DPA; **278-9t** AGE; **278-9b** Jildirium/SIPA Press;
279t Johannes/Transglobe; **279b**
Abbas/Magnum/Focus; **280-1t** Mike
Andrews/*SG*; **280-1b** Dr H Kramarz/*Z*; **280t** HL;
280b Alexis Duclos/*GFS*

Index

Page numbers in *italic*
refer to the illustrations
and captions